Alan Ayckbourn

GRINNING AT THE EDGE

For Penny

Alan Ayckbourn

GRINNING AT THE EDGE

A biography by

Paul Allen

Methuen

Methuen

10 9 8 7 6 5 4 3 2 1

First published in Great Britain by
Methuen Publishing Limited
215 Vauxhall Bridge Road
London SW1V 1EJ

Copyright © Paul Allen, 2001

The author has asserted his moral rights.

Methuen Publishing Limited Reg. No.3543167

A CIP catalogue record for this book
is available from the British Library

ISBN 0 413 77136 9

Designed by Bryony Newhouse
Typeset by Deltatype Ltd, Birkenhead, Wirral
Printed and bound in Great Britain by
Cox and Wyman Ltd, Reading, Berkshire

Contents

Acknowledgements

Much is said about the problems of writing a biography, especially of a living person. Can you be objective? Can you do justice to a life that continues, develops and changes after your last full stop? The answer to both questions is obviously 'No', but then all historical accounts (and their first draft, journalistic accounts) are provisional; even the most accurate is only definitive until more facts are known and different perspectives assume importance. At least with the biography of a living person you know where you stand. And the central fact of this biography is that I have had a thoroughly enjoyable time with it. I like and admire my subject and I have been able to spend many hours hearing him talk about life, the theatre and the cosmos.

He is, therefore, my principal source. Much of his life has been lived in the semi-public but unrecorded arena of the rehearsal room and his own subject matter is what goes on between people. I owe a huge amount, therefore, not only to him but to the people who have worked and lived with him, in some cases stretching back more than 40 years, on the producing and administrative sides of theatres in Scarborough, Stoke-on-Trent and London. If this book has a particular virtue it is that much of it is first-hand: I have been interviewing Alan Ayckbourn himself, on and off, for about 20 years, have seen the work, met his colleagues, even taken part in a formal appraisal of 'his' theatre. The theatre people who are quoted in this book all willingly gave time and hospitality and views, out of a sense in many cases that they owed it to Ayckbourn, in others that they just like talking about him. Are their stories personal and subjective? Yes, often. That makes them useful and interesting. My thanks to them. Jen Coldwell has heroically transcribed hundreds of hours of their taped interviews.

Staff of the Stephen Joseph Theatre, paid and voluntary, have always made it a welcoming place to visit as a critic and that warmth and efficient help have been extended to me in this capacity too. I have also had help, with material other than straight interviews, from Margaret Boden, Peter Cheeseman – who, I hope, will produce his own account of theatre in Stoke – and from Mary Parker, Sarah Hughes, Keith McFarlane, Amanda Saunders, Caroline Smith, Alan Strachan, Jeannie Swales, Bob Watson, Ian Watson and Stephen Wood. I want also to give credit to all the photographers, many unknown, whose work enlivens these pages. I have made strenuous efforts to contact copyright holders before publication. If notified, I undertake to rectify errors or omissions at the earliest opportunity.

Alan Ayckbourn's plays are published by Faber and Faber and Samuel French and I am grateful for permission to quote from them.

Above all Heather Stoney has let me into her home, pointed me to the fine archive she maintains in the attic and kept me fed and watered while researching more times than I could begin to count.

I have had regular help and support from Methuen, from the moment Michael Earley commissioned the book to David Salmo's tactful and constructive editing.

And finally, my thanks to the late John Hodgson, the former principal of Bretton Hall, University of Leeds, who was commissioned by Methuen to write a biography of Alan Ayckbourn before me but died before he started writing. His family and partner, Donald Howarth, generously made his research available to me, particularly the taped interviews John conducted with Alan Ayckbourn's mother. She made a great deal up – she was a writer of romantic fiction – but her memories were often a crucial springboard for the discovery of other information.

So, yes, there are problems with biography; but they are enriching ones.

Preface

Pittsburgh, 2001. America's fourth production in four years of *By Jeeves*, a musical inspired by the stories of P. G. Wodehouse about an irresponsible English upper-class twit, Bertie Wooster, and the 'gentleman's gentleman' whose calm ingenuity gets his master out of every scrape. The audience has stood and cheered, and at the reception afterwards autograph hunters approach the group that includes the two actors who play the leading roles. The actors sign, in high good humour, and one of the fans, a woman, says: 'We've already got Lord Webber' – the composer Andrew Lloyd Webber – 'we've got *everyone* now.' The actors burst out laughing and the third man in the group grins wryly as the autograph hunters move away without bothering him. He directed the show. He wrote it. He is probably the most successful-in-his-own-lifetime playwright there has ever been.

London, 1973. With five plays running concurrently in the West End, British theatre's commercial heartland, Alan Ayckbourn has achieved what nobody else has, before or since. Soon he also has four plays running concurrently on Broadway; New York renames a street Ayckbourn Alley to mark this, also unique, record.

No revolution is conducted single-handed but the statistics (36 new plays in London in as many years, some 60 overall; as many revivals, roughly, as Shakespeare) only hint at the transformation of British theatre led by Alan Ayckbourn. I simplify, but where once we had comedies in which hero and heroine lived (together) happily ever after, or tragedies in which one or both of them died, now we can expect to be spun in seconds from a roar of laughter to pitying tears or calm resignation. What is at stake is not life or death necessarily, or even love (though this may ignite the story), but mental health, sanity, hope or despair; the possibility of happiness and the probability of messing it up. In an age of relative material well-being our ability to make each other and ourselves wretched is a major issue facing advanced society. In this area, where politicians seem irrelevant or uninterested, Ayckbourn is a political writer. Nobody who has seen much of his work will think an anxious woman or a clowning man merely a figure of fun again. He has also experimented with time, with chance, with scale and with the perception of reality; in almost every play he does something he has never done before.

To some people, a lifetime's productivity suggests a workaholic. True, there is a compulsion to put down on paper the ideas that keep bubbling up out of his psyche and then – more importantly – to try them out on the stage floor. True, he and his wife, Heather Stoney, went 18 months without a holiday of any kind between the autumn of 1998 and the spring of 2000. But the nature of his relationship with the theatre is much more complex; it turns on the idea of 'play'. It is not a pun to make a connection between what is enacted before an audience and what the young of all species (and adult humans) do for recreation; the word, derived from Old English, is the same, and has associations with dancing and lightness of heart. Both are ways of rehearsing life at its best and worst without real danger. When things go wrong in his life and work, Ayckbourn will describe them with wan understatement as 'not much fun'. When they go well, as they generally do, he is plainly having the time of his life and sharing it with everyone else. 'I'm lucky enough,' he says, 'to go to work to do what I enjoy doing most.' Playing, making plays.

West London, *circa* 1943. Four-year-old cousins are about to present a play in a suburban garden, a rudimentary curtain held up between them. One child drops his corner of the sheet whereupon the other flies into a rage and has to be hauled off, kicking and raining blows, while the adults alternately remonstrate with him and snigger. The boy is already at least half-separated from his father.

The creative artist (and many a genius in other fields) has something of the self-absorption of a child. Ayckbourn is diffident in person, rarely making sustained eye contact in conversation, and he has few close friends. In public he will speak when called upon to do so, though in private he is tremendous company, a devastating mimic and natural story-teller. When fans or journalists meet the tall man smiling affably at the edge of gatherings they generally ask where his characters come from, those ordinary people behaving monstrously. Invariably he says they all come from inside him. This is true as far as it goes, but how – and when – did they get in? What other 'edge' has he faced with his ambiguous grin?

Chapter 1

Intimate relations

---

1 : Lolly

At the end of February 1999 Alan Ayckbourn's mother died. For her funeral at a Scarborough crematorium on 3 March he wrote the following address:

To someone . . .

who gave me gin as a baby to help me sleep at night . . .

who decided that, during the air raids, we should sleep in the front hall, she with her feet up the stairs, me curled up under the letter box . . .

who in 1943 introduced me to my nice American Uncle Al whom I was never to see again . . .

who, when we were evacuated to Weston-super-Mare, picked up a sailor who spent the afternoon throwing the ball down the beach for me to fetch in the hope of getting in at least one decent snog . . .

who once introduced me to a strange man in a beret on top of a bus in the Strand as a previous husband . . .

who used to sit every day at the kitchen table typing away on her Underwood portable and bought me a smaller machine when I was six so that I could do the same . . .

who made me a birthday cake when I was seven, short-sightedly using salt instead of sugar . . .

who once threw my father's framed photograph at me in a fury and told me all men were bastards . . .

who took me regularly to London to have lunch at the Women's Press Club, thus putting me off women for 11 years . . .

who arrived at a school sports day in a hat so outrageous that I totally ignored her all day . . .

who, taking the vet's advice, put two ailing new-born puppies in the oven, and forgot about them . . .

who once wet her knickers on the bus and made me walk close behind her from the bus stop all the way home . . .

who smoked like a chimney and, with her discarded cigarette-ends, set fire to and entirely gutted our kitchen and, on another occasion, caused the family car to self-destruct in a pub car park . . .

who wrote to me when I was at boarding-school to break the news that she was getting married again . . .

who once, during lunch, hit my stepfather over the head with a serving spoon full of mashed potato . . .

who insisted I accompany her on a driving lesson and drove the entire journey with the clutch and foot-brake pedals confused . . .

who, one night, fell through my front door so drunk that I had to carry her to bed . . .

who had more names than The Jackal, including: Irene Maud Worley, Rene M. Worley, Mrs Neville Whatever-her-first-husband's-name-was, Mrs Horace Ayckbourn, Mrs Cecil Pye, Boo or Auntie Boo, Mary Irene James, Mary James, Ruby, Lolly, Lollygran or Loll, to name but a few . . .

who gave me far more complexes, hang-ups, phobias, prejudices, inspirations and self-insights than any writer has a right to expect from a parent . . .

to her, many thanks, much love and farewell.

There is a kind of telescoped autobiography in that address and at least one intimate echo of Ayckbourn's plays; so *that's* where the unseen bed-bound mother in *The Norman Conquests* got her reputation for picking up men on the sands at Weston. It is also written in the classic English style: real feeling, albeit mixed, is hitched to the pulling power of revealing stories, told with the sparest of detail. Above all, it bears the author's unmistakable signature: a ruthless frankness (those puppies, those wet knickers) has teamed up with a despairing, affectionate compassion and a reflex comic response. This rackety, bohemian, riveting, infuriating woman, who died six weeks before his sixtieth birthday, played a huge part in making her only child into the man he became, not least in giving him a ringside seat at an unhappy marriage.

That raffish-sounding nickname was the most prosaic thing about her, coined by Alan and his stepbrother Christopher Pye when they were unwell and she brought lollipops back from the shops. She was Lolly to them both until the day she died. It solved the difficulty either boy might have had in calling her 'Mummy' by this time. Irene Maud Worley was her baptismal name. She disliked Irene, so Rene M. Worley was for her earliest literary efforts, including her novels. Mary James was the very successful writer of short stories for women's magazines and it remained her 'public name' until she died. She was Boo to her sisters (or just possibly half-sisters). Ruby was a nickname her son gave her in his childhood, for reasons now lost. And as for her married names, one was correct, one wrong and one half-way.

When Lolly was in a nursing home, in her last months, it wasn't her son who visited regularly. Seriously squeamish, he passes out at the sight of blood. He will quickly divert or fall silent in conversations about illness or death. A month or two before his mother died he told me: 'I don't think in the last few years we were remotely close.' But then he picked up a knife from the table in front of him and added in an unusually vehement voice: 'Her arms have wasted away to *this* thick, and her legs, and you wonder how anybody can live in this condition. Some days her breathing's so shallow, you wonder if she's still alive. And then the next day she's up and a sort of anger keeps her going.' He seemed to have surprised himself by being moved at her tenacious hold on life, reflecting a long and hungry appetite for it. But she wouldn't necessarily have welcomed him or even recognised him if he had visited her more often. Instead, his wives would go: Christine, to whom he had been married for almost 40 years, and with whom he had remained friends even though they had spent more than 30 of those years apart, and Heather, his partner for the last 30 years and his wife since 1997. It was Heather who at the funeral actually spoke the address Alan had written.

Is Lolly in the plays? More than anyone else, apart from the author himself, but never as a simple copy. Apart from the lusty off-stage old woman in *The Norman Conquests* (written in 1972 when Lolly herself was only 66, far from bedridden and, she said, still sexually active) the most profitable character to mine for her is Susan, the tragic heroine of *Woman in Mind*, a middle-aged vicar's wife having a breakdown because her husband has no conception of the needs and frustrations after their son has left home.

But it is in the yawning gaps between intimate people that many of Ayckbourn's plays exist, and perhaps Lolly – who in 1975 gave an interview to the *Scarborough Evening News* saying she didn't much like children, who managed to avoid having them with her other sexual partners, who even said that she considered an abortion when she became pregnant with Alan – gave him as a start in life that sense of a relationship in which the two parties are at once passionately close and divided by a chasm. Half-scathing about her, half-proud, he has also inherited her taste for a good story rather than a literally accurate one, though in his case this means anecdotes are polished, edited, improved rather than wholly invented.

Lolly's story begins with the reinvention of her own parentage. Her birth certificate, a copy dating from 1948 in time for her marriage to Alan's stepfather Cecil Pye, shows that she was born in Basildon, Essex on 12 March 1906, to Joseph William Worley and Lillian Worley, née Morgan. Her father was a Shakespearean actor, good enough to be a member of the company led by Sir Ben Greet (a founder of the Old Vic and a pioneer of Shakespeare for schools), and her mother began as a male impersonator in music-hall but later 'went legit'. A further six daughters and a solitary son were born to them. Lolly told friends that one of her young sisters eventually married an Australian, an older man who wasn't much liked by the family. In revenge he once asked Lolly if she had ever wondered why she had straight fair hair when that of her siblings was dark and curly, and why her nose was a different shape from theirs. Maybe she had a different father? She had not, she said, believed a word of this but had gone to tell her father who had shocked her by confirming the story. He had added that her mother's brothers had offered him money to marry Lillian when she was already pregnant but that he had not needed the bribe. He loved her and wanted to marry her anyway. Furthermore, he loved Lolly as much as her sisters and her brother, who were his children. Lolly told John Hodgson, among others, that her parents hadn't married until after she was born. The fact that she was born in Essex and her parents' home address was in Birmingham seemed to add credibility to the story – as if they had gone away to have the baby somewhere they were unknown. Lolly even speculated on the identity of her 'real' father, proposing a member of the Scudamore theatrical family. In the 1890s Daisy (later known as Margaret) Scudamore left home at the age of 15 to join the show-business side of the family in London and was disowned by her Portsmouth shipwright father. She later became the mother of the actor Michael Redgrave. Her granddaughter Vanessa Redgrave tells the story in more detail in her autobiography (Hutchinson, 1991), which Lolly read. It is splendidly romantic and dramatic. Lolly – who was very tall – thought she might be related to Vanessa, conjuring up the entertaining possibility that our most politically engaged actors might be distant cousins of our least politically engaged playwright. Unfortunately F. A. Scudamore, the best-known member of the family, died too early to have fathered Lolly. Joseph Worley and Lillian Morgan married towards the end of 1905, less than six months before Lolly was born, so at least she could claim to have been conceived out of wedlock. This may be why the marriage took place in the relative obscurity (for a couple from Birmingham) of County Durham, though an equally simple explanation is that Worley was on tour at the time. Lolly added a neat circumstantial touch by saying she got on better with Worley because he was not her real father, and was therefore less distressed at her subsequent escapades. Conversely she described her mother as grudging and not very affectionate, and Lillian may always have thought of her first-born as the reason she had to get married in a hurry: sex outside marriage plays rather a large part in this story. But Ayckbourn remembers Granny Worley as 'a jolly old soul'. Whoever Lolly's father was – and Ayckbourn himself favours the grandfather he actually knew as a rather 'dry old stick' – the future playwright had two grandparents who worked in the theatre, but it is more significant that he had a writer for a mother.

Lolly was precocious. She first met and was attracted to Horace Ayckbourn when she was 13 and she sold her first story to the *Co-op Journal* in Manchester at about the same age. Her parents quite reasonably put a stop to the relationship with Horace, a 22-year-old survivor of the First World War, with the added glamour of being one of a number of professional musicians who were regular visitors to the family home. Her writing at the time inclined to the 'slice of life' narrative and one of her first stories was about a visit to the dentist, a subject which combines the prospect of pain with rough comic potential and demands accuracy of observation. Not a bad preoccupation to pass on.

At 17 she left home for a bed-sitting-room in Bloomsbury (secretly checked out by her father) and got a job running the competition page on *Little Folks* magazine. She sent her own first novel, *Off the Pavement*, to Michael Joseph. Not yet a publisher, Joseph, a literary agent and author (of books on writing for profit and of a play) was to become one of the most important men in her life, though her own account (to John Hodgson) of a lifelong relationship is regarded by some of the people who knew her best as more of Lolly's 'romancing'. Certainly her description of their first meeting would make a good scene, but that doesn't make it untrue.

Lolly's story was that Joseph couldn't tell which sex she was from her novel (which he liked) or her covering letter, so he invited her to his favourite restaurant, the Criterion. 'It was usually Lyons' Corner House, so I was impressed,' she said. Lacking a 'grown-up' hat, she decided to dye her old school straw hat green (or, in another telling of the story, blue) and Joseph afterwards said that his most vivid memory of the occasion was of a green (or blue) stain on her neck when the dye ran. Nine years older than she was, he astonished her by asking first if she would marry him and then, when she refused, if she would live with him. Stimulated by the little wine he had given her she promised to stay friends. She thought he was a wonderful man. Lolly's stories are very short on dates and there is no indication when Joseph became her first lover. In 1926 his own first marriage (which has another significance in this story) was dissolved and he married his second wife, Edna. Lolly said she herself wouldn't marry him because he was Jewish and marrying out of the faith would have cost him too much. Four years later she accepted Neville Whatever-his-name-was, a young man with a monocle who said he was in the film business. Her parents were living in Reigate, Surrey, and on a spring Saturday in 1930 she went to church there and became Mrs Neville Monroe, but not without trying to telephone Michael Joseph first. His secretary told her he was on the golf course, but she believed he was in his office, too upset to speak to her. Not a strictly religious Jew, Joseph might indeed have been in his office on the Sabbath.

Lolly and Neville were horribly poor, and when they went to see the Ballets Russes (who first visited Britain in 1933) at the old Alhambra Theatre they sat in the 'gods' and borrowed a programme from the man sitting next to them. Lolly was delighted to see that Horace Ayckbourn was in the orchestra. Neville made no objection to her idea that they should go round to the stage door afterwards and see him. He was optimistic that Horace would provide them with free tickets in future – and he did.

2 : Horace

Alan's mother teases the biographer with mystery deliberately added to an already complicated life-story: a maze of stories. His father's mystery is one of the things left out. Although Horace had lived a public life as a violinist, becoming deputy leader of the London Symphony Orchestra, even the news of his death was kept from Alan for a time. He was given nothing to remember his father by and eventually he became thoroughly confused about when Horace had actually died.

Ayckbourn was always an uncommon name and it has become more so. Eight Ayckbourn births were registered in London in the five years 1871–5; only four, including Alan's father, in the five years that ended the century. Now, you scour the registers for them almost in vain. In Victorian England they were mostly to be found in Southwark, though Horace

Mervyn's birth was registered in St Pancras in 1897. The name's very English sound probably means 'oak by a stream'. The existence of mid-nineteenth-century Ayckbourns makes another of Lolly's stories improbable; she used to say that the family's real name was Eichbaum ('oak tree') but had been changed from the German when war broke out; she claimed Alan had German-speaking cousins. Not only are they rare, Ayckbourns resolutely refuse to seek each other out, some because they fear Alan would think they were after something, Alan because he does at least half-think so.

He never knew his Ayckbourn grandfather, but believes that in the 'great tradition of Ayckbourn husbands' he left his wife and went to Australia where he disappeared, possibly murdered while panning for gold. Lolly added more detail, saying Horace's father had also been a violinist. He had met Horace's mother when he put up at a farm on a walking holiday and ran off with the farmer's daughter. There were two sons, Horace and Philip, who had both continued to do well after the father absconded. Horace was winning medals at the Guildhall and Philip was, Lolly thought, an analytical chemist, when their mother told them she was going to stay with an old friend and they were not to pursue her: she could barely read and write, she said, let alone keep up with them. They did try to trace her but without success. Lolly thought the family had lived in Norfolk and years later Alan got a letter from a very old schoolmaster there: was Horace, he wondered, the Ayckbourn who had been his pupil there? It was certainly to Norfolk that Horace later retired and his widow, Alan's stepmother, still lives there. They are not in touch.

These figures stepping from the shadows, outlined with a few broad brush-strokes, are curiously like characters emerging from the wings into the brightly lit arena of the stage, vivid and physically present but rooted in absences and obscurities. Ayckbourn is content to leave his forebears thus.

Not long after his initial encounter with the teenage Lolly and her family Horace married someone else, Dorothy Horne. A son, Peter, was born in Kingston in 1923. Lolly knew of this – she mentioned it in conversation with John Hodgson – but neither she nor Horace ever mentioned it to Alan.

After they made contact again back-stage at the Alhambra Lolly was determined to have Horace. She had already decided that Neville, who was mildly suspicious at all the references to HA in her diary, was feckless. Lolly could barely earn enough to keep them both. They had lived on bread and dripping washed down with cocoa and she believed she had suffered from malnutrition. To save electricity she would read the proofs of her work by lying on her back in bed and trying to see by the flickering light of the gas fire, or go on to the Embankment and read by the light of the street-lamps. 'No wonder I've got no eyesight,' she said towards the end of her life when she did indeed go blind. She said she had also caught Neville going through her father's pockets, and that when her father missed £10 he banned his son-in-law from the parental house. She had been given a five-novel contract on the strength of *Off the Pavement* and when she completed her last, *October Week-End*, she gave Neville half her advance payment and told him they were going their separate ways. He made no great fuss and Lolly thought he eventually went off to the film industry in America, though he makes one more brief appearance in this story. She went back to her parents who were, she said, very nasty about it, as were her sisters except for the youngest, ten-year-old Peggy, who put her arms round her in the greenhouse one day and told her everything would be all right.

Lolly and Horace quickly made up for lost time. Much of his work was with opera or ballet companies, sometimes abroad. In Rome, Lolly stumbled in on a rehearsal, and in Paris, she got hopelessly lost and just waited for a passing musician to return her to the hall they were playing in. At home in Britain, Horace liked to drive overnight to whichever city the orchestra was booked to appear in; most bookings were for a week. In his sports car, with him singing extracts from Debussy's *Pelléas et Mélisande*, they would be on the road for ten hours at a time, travelling to Edinburgh or Glasgow or the industrial towns of the north of England. Sometimes the schedule would include a sound-check in the morning and a rehearsal in the afternoon. Lolly and Horace would begin the lunch break with sex. On other occasions the rehearsals were in the morning and the whole afternoon was free . . . Lolly told Horace she didn't want a child, reasoning that if she couldn't travel with him 'he'd be sleeping with the harpist'. To John Hodgson she said that they had got married mainly because it was difficult to find lodgings if they didn't have the same surname. Landladies in Cardiff had been particularly hard to convince they should be allowed to sleep together. Horace was contracted for the summer season at Glyndebourne in Sussex, famous for opera performances with a long interval so that the audience can picnic in the grounds. He and Lolly took a cottage in the nearby village of Glynde, and it was here, Lolly believed, that Alan was conceived. The marriage, she said, had taken place at Marylebone Register Office and after some sandwiches together, Horace had gone to work and she to tell her mother and father.

It was Alan's stepfather, the late Cecil Pye, who revealed in 1991 that Lolly had had to get divorced from Neville, not Horace, to marry him; this is confirmed by the registers. On the whole she invented things to make her seem less respectable, more exciting. So why would she lie about this? Presumably because there was a child involved and, by the respectable 1940s and 1950s, she was no longer a Hampstead bohemian but married to a country bank manager and sending the said child to public school. We rarely hear the word 'illegitimate' now, and 'bastard' has largely lost its specific meaning, but the social and moral climate changed out of all recognition in the half-century between Alan's conception and his discovery of the truth. He never showed his mother Cecil Pye's letter nor did he discuss the detailed contents with her. He thought it 'rather romantic' that his parents had never married.

Lolly panicked at her pregnancy. She broke the news to Horace when he was in a foul temper after snapping a string at a chamber concert. He brightened at once, and when she raised the question of having an abortion he wouldn't hear of it. Abortions were illegal, and if performed by criminal and unqualified abortionists in filthy premises they were acutely dangerous too. In the event, after being angry at the unborn Alan because he kept her from gadding about the country with Horace, Lolly described the months when she was expecting him as the most peaceful time in her life. For once she was neither falling in love nor falling out of it. Her hair started to curl for the first time, and typically she wanted it straight again after having been jealous of her sisters for so long. She told Michael Joseph she was pregnant and he asked her if the child could be his, but she pointed out that he had been away in America for a year; he had been badly hurt when she told him how much in love she was with Horace.

Lolly believed Alan's love of music was encouraged by the amount of live performance she attended while she was carrying him, though her own taste was ridiculed by Horace: she loved Ravel's *Bolero*. The couple lived in London, at first in a bed-sitting-room plus kitchen over a laundry in Haverstock Hill. She wrote in the kitchen while he practised in the other room: she enjoyed 'the background music'. When they moved to Regent's Park Mews, where you could hear the animals in London Zoo, Horace told her it was like making love in the jungle. If the imminence of war figured in the lovers' thoughts Lolly didn't say so.

When Alan was born in a Hampstead nursing home on 12 April 1939, Horace was playing in the pit orchestra at the Lyceum in London and had plans to play bridge afterwards. Lolly said this was code for flirting with other women. She didn't mind very much 'because he hadn't had much fun with me for the past nine months'. The stage-doorkeeper at the Lyceum refused to interrupt that night's performance to tell Horace he had a new son.

Alan's earliest specific memory is of sitting under the dining-table at some sort of gathering when a 'very pretty woman' bent down and offered him a drink. The other adults told her not to be silly but she pointed out that the drink was only cold tea, the customary theatrical substitute for beer, whisky or brandy. War was declared in September, five months after he was born, but unlike many London children he was never dispatched to an unknown destination, to be cared for by strangers. Lolly took him to Weston-super-Mare, scene of her tryst with a sailor, Grange-over-Sands and, he thinks, Leeds, and she herself recalled going to a village in Worcestershire, which she found nice enough but quiet, too quiet; moreover, Luftwaffe pilots after raiding Birmingham used to jettison unused bombs on the countryside. Worried about how Horace was passing his time between concerts and a little composing, especially when she couldn't get through to him on the telephone, Lolly decided to return.

The only child, now, in Regent's Park Mews, Alan was fussed over accordingly. Many bombs fell on NW1, allegedly because there was an ammunition dump in the Penguin Pool at the zoo. The flat had a garden and there was a gap in the hedge just big enough for Alan to get through. He would return with bunches of flowers for his mother. The neighbours included Elsie and Doris Waters, sisters who did a music-hall double act, and the Yorkshire-born comedian Syd Howard. Entertainers were busier than ever during the war, in demand to boost morale. According to Lolly, nobody minded Alan plundering the park's flower-beds. He was a polite child, rewarded by his grandfather Worley with a biscuit for a 'good morning'. Lolly claimed his less sympathetic grandmother was inclined to regard him as precocious – not then a term of approval – but Alan recalls visiting his grandparents in their first-floor flat near Clapham Junction and says she mashed up sardines for sandwiches, got food in her straggly grey hair and had a tendency to set herself alight while cooking. He believes their financial fortunes went up and down dramatically and that when they died his Uncle Ted – the only male in the Worley brood – carried their cheap furniture away on his back by night and dumped it in neighbours' gardens. Lolly resumed her writing, but was more interested in selling short stories than novels. At Michael Joseph's suggestion, she adopted a new name – Mary James – and submitted stories to the *Daily Express* and the 'wireless', BBC Radio, as well as the women's magazines.

Horace was 42 when Alan was born, Lolly 33. Alan has no real memory of the three of them living together but isn't sure whether his mother kicked his father out after one affair too many – 'He was at the front of the strings section. He just had to turn round and there was another curvaceous second violinist and off he went' – or his father met a woman who wouldn't settle for a fling. When he became involved with another violinist, a young woman called Daphne Collis, Lolly had a telephone call from Daphne's mother asking her to intervene; she didn't take it very seriously.

It may be that she had continued to see Michael Joseph while living with Horace. Late in life Lolly told Scarborough friends that she had left the infant Alan sleeping alone in Regent's Park while she went off to a night-club – and then had to pick her way back in the black-out during the blitz. She also told John Hodgson that she was able to walk from Regent's Park over Primrose Hill to Michael Joseph's place in St John's Wood while Alan slept alone – and be back by morning. This doesn't square with a remark elsewhere that she never went to Michael Joseph's home.

The 'marriage' to Horace broke up in stages. At first Lolly and Alan moved to a borrowed flat in Ealing, in West London. Alan remembers being in his mother's lap while she sat in a bomb shelter, in a deck chair. Aware that the deck chair was starting to collapse, he thought he 'mustn't wake Mummy'; she, for her part, kept completely still, thinking Alan was asleep. He remembers the air-raid sirens clearly, and being woken by the sound one night to see his mother on her knees at the foot of the bed, the only occasion he saw her do anything remotely religious. Lolly told John Hodgson the only time she remembered Alan being frightened was when he caught *her* looking frightened. In 1944 London was the target of V1 bombs, or doodle-bugs; when the rocket's engine cut out, you knew the explosion was imminent. Characteristic of all Ayckbourn's stories is a kind of sound-effects tape running behind them. 'It was like a sort of two-stroke motorbike engine really – dub dub dub dub dub – and after it stopped, occasionally BOOMPH.'

Taken to the circus as a small boy, Alan was terrified by the grotesque make-up of a clown, and bit him. He has been wary of audience participation ever since. At a funfair, he clutched his father's knees and screamed with terror on one ride, but his parents assumed he was squealing with delight. On another occasion, supposed to be playing with a boy of his own age in an adjacent flat, he was brought home red-faced and sullen. The other boy's father said: 'We don't like liars in our house and when Alan persisted in a lie, Simon punched him.' Alan had insisted that a favourite children's book – called *Nicky Takes a Holiday* – was written by his mother, and it was. Lolly also created the character of the Little Princess at around this time, inspired by the future Queen Elizabeth II but made much more cheeky and capable of an extended series of adventures.

It was towards the end of the war that Alan launched his ferocious attack on the cousin who dropped the curtain just as they were about to present a play in the garden. His first experience of the theatre was a show by the Crazy Gang, his father's choice, a mixture of the sentimental and the filthy which passed over his head. Alan was not taken to his father's concerts even when they were close to home. In fact, he told Ian Watson (*Conversations with Ayckbourn*, Faber, 1981) that his father actually loathed music 'like a lot of professional musicians'. Part of the interest in this is that Ayckbourn would later say something very similar about his own mentor in relation to the theatre, and plenty of people have wondered out loud how far the same thing applies to Alan who is not the world's greatest theatregoer. Horace Ayckbourn was bored by Beethoven ('Doesn't know how to end', he would complain after playing the Fifth Symphony) but he did admire the great virtuoso performers, Kreisler and Rubinstein, for example, and lighter musicians such as the singer Al Bowlly; Alan himself was to spend his first money on classical records and only came to popular music in its most theatrical form (the extravagant rock concert) with the approach of middle age.

Towards the end of the war mother and son moved to Staines in Middlesex, where he remembers a street party, presumably for the outbreak of peace. He thinks his parents must have separated completely soon after the war ended because he and his mother moved much further away, to Sussex. They took a rented cottage called Dunelm in Wisborough Green, near Billingshurst. It was attached to a farm, and became the setting for a profoundly formative period.

3 : Mother and Son: Almost an Idyll

It would last two years at most. But while his mother typed away furiously on the kitchen table and he pounded the smaller typewriter she had bought him, two important images were united: that of a woman being the breadwinner and that of writing being a perfectly rational way of winning that bread. The little boy had what would nowadays be called a role model. And above all it meant that he interpreted the adult world through a woman's experience. It is the single most important explanation for his sympathetic but far from idealised writing of parts for women.

It was a precarious life. Lolly was successful in her field but the living to be made from writing if you didn't have a blockbuster success was, then as now, unpredictable. The magazine market offered the quickest rewards. Lolly contrived to find some freedom of expression, but the conventions of the publications she was writing for, mainly *Woman*, *Woman's Own* and *Home Notes*, were firmly fixed. In some instances she would be sent pictures of characters (often American in origin) and she would write round these. Usually she was not allowed to let her heroine fall in love with a married man. When it was permitted, she was forbidden a happy ending. Lolly set about such restrictions with a wry expertise. She had allowed her career as a novelist to fade and reckoned she needed to sell three or four stories a month to make ends meet. The prospects of long-term security were poor and she had a hungry son to look after. He was growing to be tall, like her.

Moreover, war had been dangerous but exciting, and Lolly thrived on excitement. Post-war Britain was an exhausted nation with an exhausted economy, short of food and short of fun. Moral and social rules – relaxed for six years – were reintroduced with relief. Horace was now engrossed with Daphne but would turn up irregularly with money, invariably in some splendid open-topped roadster and wearing a pilot-style flying cap, which impressed his small son and disrupted her small life in roughly equal measure. The armchair psychologist always at a biographer's elbow points out that in Alan's later life there would be a need for an influential father figure and that his children's plays would often involve an absence of fathers. *Mr A's Amazing Maze Plays* has one who was wearing a flying cap when last seen and who returns just in time to prevent the mother remarrying.

His first school was a convent, not because of anyone's religious allegiance but because convents were thought to offer a better education and more discipline. Besides it was just across the road. Alan found it 'a horrendous experience'. Never having seen nuns close up before he thought them frankly scary. A handful of small boys was outnumbered by about 150 girls at the school, mostly older and – in Alan's memory – using the boys as doll substitutes on which they could practise bossy motherhood. He thought he had to get out.

The cottage he and Lolly lived in was not itself very attractive, being in plain red brick, but it sat in the middle of quite a large garden which was connected to the farm by a little bridge. Across this came the milk, still warm, straight from the cow: unthinkably unhygienic by today's standards, but they survived. There were gooseberry and blackcurrant bushes in the garden and water was either drawn from a well or collected from rainfall. Less attractively, a sort of open trough led to a septic tank and there is a nasty memory of raw sewage being pumped out. The cottage had a dark kitchen-cum-living-room, a couple of bedrooms and a lean-to extension. 'It wasn't very big but it was a jolly nice place to be brought up and I could run round the garden barefoot.' There were occasional trips to London to meet publishers and Lolly's magazine colleagues – the ones who were to put Alan off women for so long – and on one of them came the encounter with the man in the beret on a bus in the Strand. He addressed Lolly by a name that Alan didn't recognise, so that the little boy thought he was an impostor, claiming an acquaintance he didn't have. After several minutes' conversation they got off and Alan asked who it was, getting the airy reply that it was the man she used to be married to, Neville. He had no idea until then that she had been married before.

Neither the idyllic cottage nor the daunting nuns and bossy girls lasted for long. Told one evening that he couldn't listen to *Dick Barton – Special Agent* on the radio if he hadn't done his homework, he went to his room and defaced his books. Lolly decided he needed discipline and masculine company. He left the virtually all-female convent for an all-male preparatory ('prep') school, Wisborough Lodge. He became a boarder by the age of seven even though the school was within walking distance of his home. When he and his friends passed the cottage on school walks the little boys would formally doff their caps to his mother. Initially he went home at weekends but this soon changed to boarding for the whole term.

Having enjoyed what seemed like his mother's undivided attention, he was now plunged into the strange micro-society of the single-sex boarding-school in which corporal punishment was taken for granted and shows of tenderness or emotion were discouraged. What effects did that have? Men of a certain age may assert that a good beating never did them any harm, but the harm it did them lies in their readiness to subject other small boys to a good beating: it is a commonplace that the abused are likely to abuse, or condone abuse, in their turn. The secret of survival, it seemed, was never to admit to being hurt. And if you were unhappy at a school to which your parent or parents had made sacrifices to send you, weren't you some sort of failure and ungrateful with it? So it became better to bury the pain somewhere even you couldn't find it. More objectively, the war had left schools short of quality staff. The food was often disgusting as these small private institutions tried to operate profitably in a country still suffering from shortages. Alan recalls a meal at which a rabbit's head appeared on his plate. Dormitories were large and unheated. Lavatories were often out of doors (and the times to use them rigidly rota-ed). Sport was compulsory, whatever the weather. These conditions were endured by many children not at boarding-school, naturally, but they usually had mothers around to comfort them.

The good thing about it, as George Orwell discovered, was that if you survived boarding-school, in later life you could handle yourself socially, whatever the environment. You could certainly run the Empire, or face up to powerful industrialists, volatile film stars or even West Indian fast bowlers, if you had learned to live with the odd drunk or sadistic emotional cripple wielding a cane (and paid for the privilege by your parents). But this quaint world also attracted men who weren't habitually drunk or inherently sadistic but had almost saintly vocations, teaching small boys everything from Latin grammar to the arcane subtleties of spin bowling and fundamental moral decency; this last might come with or without the underpinning of religion, which was more or less ubiquitous but only in the tactfully unobtrusive form encouraged by the Church of England. In fact, after a few years at prep school most of us would have been happy to accept God as a thoughtful bowler of leg breaks and googlies, who could distinguish between the gerund and the gerundive and would reprimand 'beastliness' – but not go on about it. Furthermore, boarding-school offered the solitary child constantly available company: a chance to play. Though not with females. Very unhappy at first, wetting the bed and waking up miserably in the night, often ill, hating football, Alan survived. He now regards his prep school, like the cottage, as something of an idyll. He has reason to believe he got very good teaching there.

Intimate Exchanges (1982) with its eight possible variations, all of which start with an alcoholic headmaster and his anxious, perplexed and initially self-blaming wife, is the only on-stage clue to his prep school experiences. Ayckbourn recalls his own headmaster: 'He wasn't averse to the odd tipple. He and his wife had endless rows which you could hear ringing through the house at night.' Part of his affection for this school, he thinks with hindsight, derived from the knowledge that it was doomed:

> It became apparent, even to the pupils, that it wasn't actually surviving. By the last couple of terms they were keeping it open for about six of us who

had to sit our Common Entrance exams. We were like family by then. Most of the place was just closed up. The gymnasium had become pigsties. They'd turned it into a farm and I used to spend days and weeks with a scythe just clearing hedges and ditches, acres of brambles and stinging nettles. Very cheap labour . . . I loved doing it. I think they ploughed up the cricket pitch.

Years later he drove back with Heather Stoney, to look at the dormitory that was turned into a bungalow: 'Curious and, yes, sad.'

In *Intimate Exchanges* the school is called Bilbury Lodge. Toby Teasdale (the headmaster) is by now only passingly concerned with the fact that boys are supposed to be educated there. It is June and cricket is mentioned a lot. And emotion is indeed there to be suppressed. When he comes across his wife's skivvy, Sylvie, swearing and crying her eyes out at the recalcitrance of the gardener who is supposed to be her boyfriend, he says:

Fancy crying over Hepplewick. Doesn't leave you much emotional reserve when something really important happens to you. I mean, how the hell's she going to behave when she gets a flat tyre on her bike?

The suppression of emotion is widely agreed to be psychologically disastrous, but it would give the adult Ayckbourn not only something to write about but a way of writing it. No dramatist catches better the English gift for putting feelings into code. There is an anecdote about his diverting a conversation from somebody's cancer to a missing button on his coat, as if that were more important: not absence of feeling, but its near-opposite, a fear of direct emotion. Half a century on he leaves the pastoral side of running a theatre company to colleagues, protecting himself from the pain of others. It is different with animals. When Cleo, the family spaniel, made distressed noises under the dining-room table, it was Alan who bent down and extricated the bone stuck in her mouth.

The importance of cricket in *Intimate Exchanges* is no coincidence. When Alan as a small boy was struck on the head by a cricket ball, bowled full toss, it seemed for a moment as if all sports were to be as miserable as football. But, still dizzy, he got up and decided that if he was to stop the ball hitting him he would have to whack it first. He stopped trying to be a technically correct batsman and set about using his good eye and quick reactions to clout the ball round the field. He also discovered wicket-keeping which, besides demanding similar skills, places you always at the centre of the action and even allows you to 'direct' it a little. He added another role by volunteering to be the First XI's official scorer, which meant he travelled to the away matches.

4 : Cuckoo in the Nest

Soon after he became a boarder at Wisborough Lodge he was made to realise that his place in his mother's life was more limited than he had thought. She told him – by letter – that she was getting married. Lolly told John Hodgson that she had thought Alan should have a man around at home as well as at school, because she had no idea how to bring up a child. The choice had been between the bank manager and a GP. The doctor had been very sympathetic when he called at the cottage and found her struggling alone in the cold. Alan's 'funny illnesses' – often glandular – meant a doctor would have been useful, but 'he was a sweet, gentle man' to whom marriage would have been disastrous. Besides, she had an overdraft.

Cecil Pye was Lolly's bank manager. Alan was nine when the ceremony took place in Horsham in the early summer of 1948, in his absence. Then chief clerk at the Billingshurst branch of Barclays Bank, Cecil was soon promoted manager and it is as 'the bank manager' that Alan refers to him. Lolly's name went down in the register as 'Ayckbourn or Worley'. When the couple returned from honeymoon in Ireland, Alan politely shook his stepfather's hand and listened carefully to see if his mother had already picked up an Irish accent. The family, which now included Cecil's son by a former marriage, Christopher, was moving into a bungalow Cecil was having built which they would name Delgany ('thorny place') after the village where they had spent their honeymoon.

Both Alan and Christopher take the view that the couple were incompatible from the start. Lolly said later that Horace tried to stop the marriage, which would have strengthened her resolve. She wasn't used to being on her own or good at it; she wanted security for herself and Alan. In the event, for much of their married life Lolly was in a higher tax bracket than Cecil, and was able to pay for Alan's education herself.

And what was in it for Cecil? A bank manager in those days had a more social role to play in a rural community. A wife who could also be a hostess was an acknowledged asset. His son Chris needed a mother. Besides, Chris says, 'He was always a sucker for a pretty face.' Lolly in her early forties was more than pretty. That would be part of the problem.

Chris says: 'My father was a countryman, perhaps a little Victorian, and aware that he had to keep up a good reputation. Alan's mother was probably a little bohemian, coming from a background of writing and music. No one was particularly at fault.' After taking his mother's part for the next 40 years, Alan now agrees. He believes Lolly used to taunt Cecil with the idea that life had been much more fun with artists and musicians than it was with a bank manager. Cecil reasonably pointed out that she'd chosen to marry a bank manager and it was irrational to expect him now to take up the violin.

Possibly the meanest thing Lolly did to Cecil was to make him take her back to Glyndebourne, where she had not only enjoyed Mozart operas but had a torrid time sexually with Horace. The tickets were bank perks, there was no picnic in the grounds in the interval, and Cecil 'didn't have an ounce of music in his soul'. What a terrible time he must have had. She may also have been visiting Michael Joseph on her trips to London. Lolly said later that she was in bed with Joseph when the news came through that his second wife, Edna, had died of cancer. That was in 1949, within a year of the marriage to Cecil. Joseph had reacted by saying: 'I suppose, my love, I really should ask you to marry me.' And she had responded: 'Good God! What a terrible idea.' A year later he married Anthea Hodson, whose father was a judge, privy councillor and war hero, but Lolly claimed her relationship with him continued more or less until his death in 1958. It is hard not to feel sympathy for Cecil.

The incident both Alan and Chris quote as an example of their parents' confrontations is the dinner-table assault referred to at Lolly's funeral. How it began is now lost in the mists of domestic vituperation but Chris says it was to do with criticism of the food – Lolly was always a haphazard cook. The two boys suddenly saw that Cecil was rubbing her face with a dishcloth and she responded with the serving spoon full of mashed potato descending conclusively on his head. Alan recalls thinking, as he watched the potato slowly slipping down Cecil's brow, that this was very funny but that if he were to laugh it would make the situation even worse. Chris told me: 'I'm laughing now as I'm remembering it, but at the time I just thought it was embarrassing. I wanted to tell them to behave themselves.' It is an indelible memory, connecting farce with anger.

Alan is pretty sure Cecil used to hit Lolly, but concedes he didn't see much real evidence of it. Chris doubts it; he is three and a half years younger and may have been told less, true or false. Lolly certainly later claimed he did, and this was the specific charge – inferred from the word 'bullying' in an article in a national newspaper – that finally led Cecil and his last wife, Brenda, to join Chris in writing to Alan in 1991 to reveal that his parents had never been married. They also threatened to go public if Alan continued to quote only Lolly's side of the years of marital discord. She, in turn, was fond of a drink, to an extent that wouldn't have raised eyebrows in her own circle in London but which in the managerial middle class in rural Sussex would have seemed embarrassing.

But the misery wasn't unrelenting. Chris remembers Lolly being wonderfully entertaining, the life and soul of the party, when things were going well. And both he and Alan remember a camping holiday near Pitlochry in Scotland when Alan tried very hard to play golf with his stepfather. Lolly hadn't gone with them, and one day Alan (who used to refer to Cecil as Cappy because his initials were C. A. P.) said to Chris: 'Cappy's not such a bad bloke, is he?'

For the first five years or so the boys got on pretty well. Alan was not only older, he was tall for his age. Christopher and his father were of stockier build. So Chris, in his own words, 'followed Alan around like a little dog'. When they went to the pictures together, scrounging money off Lolly so they could see both programmes at the local cinema each week, Alan would walk the mile each way while Chris scampered behind, trying to keep up. Afterwards they would re-enact some of the films. Alan led the way into scrapes. When they were recovering from whooping cough, they went on to Chailey Common, near where they were then living in a cottage in a wood. The common was War Department property and had been used for wartime training. It was midwinter and a water-filled crater had an inviting layer of ice on top. They got half-way across . . . On a beach in Scotland after seeing a prisoner-of-war film they set to digging a tunnel. Or rather, Chris was deputed to do the tunnelling because he was smaller; when he got far enough in for only his feet to be showing the tunnel duly collapsed . . . Chris thought his big brother was wonderful.

Alan was already preoccupied with drama, both in its formal and informal sense. When he was asked by Lolly what he wanted to do for a treat he decided a French revue sounded interesting. It turned out to be a nude show, which was legal then only if the women didn't move once all their clothes were off. The music included Ravel's *Bolero*, he remembers, Lolly's despised favourite. Was she being game, or naughty, or just rather naive in agreeing to take him to this? Probably naughty.

He appeared in a school play about which he remembers only that he played a Sea Scout, got a laugh by pulling a face and thought: 'This is the life.' He was already writing, selling a poem called 'The Moon' to a children's magazine, always typing and submitting work himself, and – according to Lolly – trying to hide it if it was sent back, rejected. He wrote his first play at Wisborough Lodge, an adaptation of the comic novels by Anthony Buckeridge, himself a master at a Sussex prep school. These very funny stories featured two schoolboys called Jennings and Darbishire, their assorted friends and a number of masters, one of whom was explosively bad-tempered and always threatening terrible deeds which, like King Lear, he could never quite specify. Alan had tailored the part of the dreamy clergyman's son Darbishire for himself but then fell ill and missed this early chance of acclaim from his peers. Encouraging messages, however, were shouted through the sick-room window. It took him nearly a year to throw off the illness. A craze for conjuring petered out at school but flourished at home – with Chris forced to wear a turban as the magician's assistant. There were model theatres to be constructed, puppet shows to be performed and more plays to be written. Chris contentedly played all the walk-on parts while Alan starred. They also had a table, meant for table-tennis, on which they constructed an entire landscape for epic adventures involving towns and model cars, lead soldiers, matchstick guns and – from Alan, who very early on was the proud possessor of a reel-to-reel tape recorder – full sound-effects plus running commentary. Taking a holiday cottage at West Wittering, by the sea near Chichester, they discovered a huge snooker table. Having no idea how to play the game, the boys made the different coloured balls into invented characters who rolled around and cannoned into each other. In these productions, surely, are not only evidence of a rather solitary boy constructing his own private world of the imagination but the embryonic antecedents of his great theatrical 'events' – *The Norman Conquests* in which three plays happen simultaneously and cover one disastrous family weekend, the four variations of *Sisterly Feelings* which turn on the toss of a coin, the eight versions of *Intimate Exchanges*, the two-part *Revengers' Comedies*, and *House* and *Garden*, the double play in which a single company performed simultaneously in two auditoria (Scarborough 1999 and the National Theatre 2000).

Alan and Christopher are chalk and cheese, physically and mentally. But initially rows were more likely to be about them than between them, specifically about how they were treated differently by the parents. Even this owed more to their different temperaments than to any real favouritism. In the 1950s children took the 11-plus public exam and were sent either to the grammar schools, which took the cream of the state education system's pupils, or to the secondary moderns, which took the rest. Alternatively the parents sent them to fee-paying private ('public') schools. Alan won a scholarship to a leading public school, Haileybury, whereas Chris, practical rather than academic, failed the 11-plus and was sent to a private school called, just to confuse matters, Shoreham Grammar School. It was at this stage, coinciding with Chris's adolescence, that they started to grow apart in a whole range of ways. Chris became an Elvis Presley fan. Alan was still keen on classical music and jazz. Christopher started to go to local youth clubs and chase girls. Alan was still in his room conjuring up stories, or just conjuring. And as the parents drew further apart, each boy took his own parent's side and so they grew apart too. Perhaps the most disruptive thing was that Lolly, deploying considerable sarcasm, would point out that she had the cleverer son, and she'd take Alan off to Brighton to hear a concert and meet the musicians, or to see a play. (When she announced to a bar that he had got a scholarship to Haileybury he walked out in angry embarrassment.) When it became clear that Alan's intention to go into the theatre professionally was serious, Christopher – who was headed for market gardening – adopted his father's view that this wasn't work for a grown-up.

Meanwhile Horace Ayckbourn had taken early retirement from the orchestra and sold his Stradivarius violin to buy a cottage in Tacolneston, deep in the country south-west of Norwich; with his new wife Daphne he was breeding St Bernard dogs. It is typical of the Ayckbourn life (and of comic fiction) that rather than ordinary dogs they should have chosen a breed big enough to carry a brandy cask through Alpine snowdrifts. Horace and Daphne had two prize bitches, Hermione and Tina, who were kept apart because a fight between two St Bernards in a half-timbered cottage is likely, literally, to bring the house down. If Hermione was in the sitting-room, Tina was in the kitchen; if you wanted to take a tray of food and drink from one to the other, you had to go out of the back door and re-enter through the front door. There were more dogs in kennels in the garden.

Alan would travel up on a coach to visit his father for a week or so in the school holidays, enjoying his first real opportunity to get to know him. Alan says: 'The bond was quite strong. We shared the same sense of humour, which made wife number two get quite stroppy. So it became a bit strained occasionally. She and I got on all right but he and I used to get on terribly well. And he used to invent board games, a bit like Reg in *The*

Norman Conquests. There would be a lot of dice rolling and she – very like Sarah, Reg's wife, that Penelope Keith played – would say: "Put this stupid game down."' Ingenuity in the pursuit of play for its own sake, as well as the related love of fast cars and his engagement with music, are Alan's gifts from his father.

Alan was also impressed at the time by Daphne's insistence on formality at the dinner table – she used to dress for dinner in 1950s rural Norfolk. He befriended or was befriended by the big dogs, and could sometimes be seen trying to persuade two of them, Romulus and Remus, to walk a bit further than half a mile (0.8 km), indeed to walk anywhere at all. This, plainly, was more fun than the now poisonous atmosphere in Sussex, which compounded the normal difficulties of growing up.

Alan now describes his childhood as lonely but not particularly miserable. It is as if the principal impact of his mother's remarriage was that she became Mrs Pye, a name he found immensely risible with its suggestion of Happy Families. He still sent love to the 'Pies' when writing from Haileybury. Lolly only used the name when functioning as the Bank Manager's Wife, accepting tributes of pheasant and the like from Cecil's rural clientele. But he had long since got over the feeling of sickness at heart at the beginning of each new term. He missed school in the holidays more than he missed home in term time, bored without school's intensive social life, especially drama (although he sometimes got neighbours to watch or take part in plays he wrote). For both boys, school had begun to feel more like family than home did. By the time he reached puberty he had been at close quarters to the failed relationship between Horace and Lolly, the faltering one between Horace and Daphne and the explosively painful one between Lolly and Cecil. A number of Alan's oldest friends and most trusted colleagues, especially the women, see in him today a boy looking for care, reassurance, approval and love as well as relishing all kinds of games and other playfulness. Although he commands total authority, the words 'big kid' crop up regularly. It is an exaggeration to describe even the Scarborough theatre company nowadays as a family; there isn't the wholly unconditional love and support that children can expect from parents and in any case its members including Alan have real families of their own. But it is more like a family than any other place of work I can think of, with actors showing long-term commitment, and production and administration staff staying on devotedly for years. It is Alan's view that in the end it is the parents who suffer most from sending their children away to school; they cut themselves off from future filial responses. When Lolly had written to him at Wisborough Lodge to say she was getting married to Cecil, he wrote back: 'Dear Mummy, I hope you'll have a very happy marriage. Love, Alan.' The wretched thing about the letter is that its intention is to say something nice.

5 : A Teenager Defends Himself

Its full title was Haileybury and Imperial Service College, its aim to train boys to be governors of what remained of the British Empire. New boys, called New Governors, soon realised that they were bottom of a large heap of 500 Governors. How many real governors would there ever be room for?

Alan went there in 1952, writing home to Lolly:

> Life here is very strange but I expect I shall soon get used to it. We had a trial rugger game. Everyone is friendly apart from a few 'bad hats'. There's a fellow who claims to be the head of our common room who is in a junior form to me about the same size who is bossing us around. We have a *cold* bath every morning, quaint school for tradition. We have visited the Grubber and they sell Cream-Soda. *The Galloping Major* is on tonight. I can't write any more until later. Love till I write again.
>
> Alan
>
> SPS Send some stamps for my letters.

Some salient preoccupations – food and drink, that evening's film, the resentment of bossiness – are recognisable 50 years later, but this is chiefly the letter of a boy who finds he is small again while remaining sharp enough for the aside: 'Quaint school for tradition.' That cold bath is a reminder of just how much of the spirit of *Tom Brown's Schooldays* survived into the 1950s and beyond. It was designed to lick the new boys into shape, but what shape? At one point 104 boys were ill with influenza. Public schools expected boys to conduct themselves like junior men while obeying rules and orders without question. Apart from religion, of which more in a moment, the classic expression of this was the Combined Cadet Force, the elementary military training which was compulsory after a couple of terms. Lolly kept a batch of 25 letters which are not dated with any precision but cover his first and second academic years, the period either side of his fourteenth birthday (including the Queen's Coronation in the summer of 1953, which seems to have generated no interest whatsoever). They reveal him as sometimes scathing about the CCF, giggling at boy soldiers turning in all directions on the parade ground and wandering around firing blanks at each other on the annual field day: did he expect live ammunition? But he was also pleased to be complimented on his turn-out by a visiting major-general and proud to have wormed his way through some long, wet grass to within 5 yards (4.5 m) of 'sentries' on an exercise.

He read voraciously. Dennis Wheatley's *The Devil Rides Out* was gleefully described as 'chinespilling' (*sic*). *The Robe* by Lloyd C. Douglas was 'religious in a funny kind of way but I enjoyed it'. There were regular film shows. He preferred Noël Coward's *Blithe Spirit* to Anna Neagle in *The Lady With the Lamp* and enjoyed comedian Will Hay and *The Card* with Alec Guinness. The language of public schools in the 1940s and 1950s was pretty close to that of the cinema and popular fiction of the time, partly no doubt because actors were as likely to be trained in 'charm' as in acting and fictional heroes were usually the products of public school and Oxbridge or a fashionable Guards regiment. Most things in the letters could be covered with 'a damn bore' or 'damn good'. A rather dazzling list of masters' nicknames matches this tone: Killer Cook, Tank (Bugger) Bentley, Pussy Williams, Hiker T (Thompson), Piggy Abbott, Porkey Yarney, Babs Spencer and Bogus Manning. That 'Bogus' would, you feel, make it impossible to command any respect at all. The master in charge of his class, or 'form beak', was Moses Keay who was 'quite a nice chap', and his housemaster, Laz Newbold, was credited with laying on a good Sunday tea. The house system in public schools dictated whom you lived with, whom you played games for and where you did your 'prep' and spent any indoor leisure time. The housemaster took responsibility for everything from looking after your pocket money to your moral welfare. Houses at Haileybury were named after historians and Alan was in Trevelyan. Generally, people were 'jolly decent'.

Few friends were named, though there was reciprocal hospitality – 'a grubber tea' – for a boy called Cooper, and one tantalising reference: 'I have made friends with a chap who lives in Ealing called Crichton. His father is something to do with the film business.' Charles Crichton was the director of *The Lavender Hill Mob* (1951) and other Ealing comedies. His son David was the first person to tell Alan how boring it was being round film studios or having to behave at home because John Mills was coming to dinner.

His ever-present hunger was partly assuaged by parcels from the family cleaner, Flo, and his permanent penury by the occasional sub from his

Uncle Ted. There was talk of a food parcel from Australia too and the possibility of 'Aycky's' parcel arriving by kangaroo became a running gag in the house. The letters of a boy thrown into a new and potentially intimidating environment, they are designed to show him managing, fitting in, not letting anybody down. He had the priceless asset (in a boys' school) of being reasonably good at games. At rugby his height and strength got him into the unglamorous second row of the scrum. He also took up boxing and was commended for it in an end-of-term report. His height helped but the letters don't mention that he had his nose broken in the ring. The story only came out when he revisited Haileybury in 1988 to open a theatre named after him; it had been built in the old gym.

But cricket remained 'the only game'. Alan 'fagged' – acted as a personal servant – for Holden, the school wicket-keeper, whose newly whitened pads crunched horribly under Alan's feet one morning as he made Holden's bed. Luckily Holden decided to take the younger boy under his wing. Cricket is the ideal sport for someone who is a bit different from his peers. Other than at the top level it may require practice but rarely real training. And it is a team game for individuals.

Alan *was* different. Other boys were not writing home encouraging their mothers ('my working gal') in their work. Some other boys might have been producing poems and pieces for the school magazine but not writing *Calamity at the Chez Goulier* – 'pretty crackers but all right to entertain our seniors' – in which he was playing a woman so needed to have some clothes sent; nor, I imagine, submitting articles to the publisher Collins. It was when the latter rejected him that he suddenly revealed another side to his experience of school. At first he made a joke of it, saying the limit of 600 words wouldn't have been long enough for 'one of my explosive opening paragraphs'. But then he wrote again, only two days later. 'Dear Mummy' (no pet names this time):

> I've not been feeling so good lately and I shall go up to the san later on this afternoon. I am not sure what is wrong with me but I nearly passed out in the grubber of all places. I believe that the old man is going to give me a sex talk in a few minutes. I bet he can't tell me much that I don't know already! I am looking forward very much to seeing you at the Coronation and to tell you the truth I feel rather homesick. Still I expect I'll get over that after a bit I hope so in any case. I haven't ridden my bike for quite a long time as I haven't felt up to it really. In fact to sum up this miserable letter – I'm damned unhappy. My love and best wishes to you all,
>
> Alan

He was 14. The misery may have been partly physiological in origin – he used to have 'a sort of health lapse' at some point in every term – and this is the only letter in this mood. But equally it could have been the other way round, the health lapse provoked by the misery. And one other curious piece of evidence supports the idea that he was more often miserable than he let on. For years he has told family and friends that when he was 13 Lolly came to the school to tell him his father had died in grim circumstances. In fact this happened four years later when he was already working in the theatre. Might the discrepancy be due to his lumping a number of wretched memories together?

What he had to say in that letter about sex education is the usual bravado. The truth was that 'I'd make sly tentative trysts with girls from next door, but we didn't really know what to do with them except sort of stand there. The streetwise butcher boy would have made his way through most of the girls in the village and I was still wondering whether to ask her out.' It may be that the butcher boy's alleged experience is the product of an envious imagination, but Alan and his friends were easy prey: one boy 'knew for a fact' that women were unable to lift their arms above their heads owing to the formation of their breasts; you couldn't count javelin-throwers because they'd had operations. None of the others could remember a mother or sister actually raising her arms that high, so they made an expedition to the village shop, where a young woman worked, and asked for something off a high shelf. She got a step-ladder and climbed up so that she didn't have to reach above her head. The authoritative boy had his credibility confirmed. Ayckbourn says: 'Going back to the school now and seeing it with girls fully integrated you see what a civilising factor that has brought. Doors on the lavatories – there never were any, to prevent "unnatural practices". Heating has arrived in some of the dormitories, I believe, and all sorts of nice things happen instead of just the annual dance versus Queenswood (girls' school) when they were bussed in and allowed to wear make-up and perfume for one day. You could smell the bus about a mile away.' Even then he thought it unfair that the girls were made to stand in line while the boys were allowed to take their pick.

The sex talk from 'Laz' Newbold didn't help much. Ayckbourn mimics a dry, reedy voice: 'You may have noticed, between your legs, a finger of flesh. Well, it's useful for two or three different reasons.' Two or three? Newbold stared into the fireplace. Nobody does the comedy of sexual embarrassment better than the English public schoolboy.

Academically he started well. No longer always top, as he had been at Wisborough Lodge, he was finishing in the top five in a much bigger pool. But after the success of his first term he was promoted still further, so that he was competing with boys a year or 18 months older than he was. Not only was the competition harder, he found the masters somehow fiercer too. At first he was frustrated and rather disoriented 'but then came the philosophy: Oh well! Bugger it. And I stopped trying.' His school reports tell the story rather more gradually and he got a respectable six 'O' levels in 1954 and then two 'A' levels – he chose English and History, because they seemed the nearest thing to creative writing. What changed was something in the tone of the comments in his reports, particularly for English at which he generally did well. In spite of his weakness in grammar and a tendency to be erratic, his English master was almost excited: 'Much promise'. But from Easter 1955 onwards 'JBWT' concedes that he can be quite methodical but finds him 'lacking in inspiration'. This is picked up by his housemaster, although next term the latter is applauding his efforts with the magazine and house plays. Reading complaints that his work was unplanned, that his knowledge of set texts wasn't thorough, that he tended towards unsupported generalisations, I thought I caught just a whiff of adult males 'taking down a peg or two' a bright adolescent with the priceless, infuriating ability to make his peers laugh. But there is another side to this. Alan remembers reducing one of his more vulnerable masters to tears by repeatedly asking 'Why?' after everything the master said.

Education in the liberal humanities does not immediately create liberal or humane young males. Ayckbourn tells a story now that illustrates a casual cruelty taken for granted by the people involved, including (we must assume) the adults in charge. A fair-haired boy with a pink face and watery blue eyes was easily identified as ripe for bullying because he spent the compulsory sport sessions sitting on the touchline, making daisy chains. Other boys would punch him casually as they went past. But he turned out to be rather heroic in his way: 'He was just superb. People used to go and kick him, and he'd cry. He had this sort of permanently swollen face from crying. But he was not going to get up and play. He was a Galileo, we could punch him, but he would continue to make daisy chains, torture him how we may.' Ayckbourn doesn't dissociate himself in retrospect from the bullying pack.

Homosexuality at single-sex boarding-schools was for most boys a badly frustrated dress rehearsal for the days when girls would be miraculously available to them. Alan himself, tall and angular, was left alone, but when he first arrived at Haileybury he shared a desk with a boy who wasn't.

> He was a very blond, beautiful child. One of those boys of 13 who have beautiful red lips and big blue eyes and long eyelashes. He looked a bit like Doris Day and he became an object of great interest. I couldn't quite work out why. He would take advantage of this and food parcels and gifts would arrive. And because I was his friend I got drawn in and given notes to pass on to him. I was the plain friend really. But I did get a lot of perks. He'd say: 'I can't eat any more of these, would you like some?' There were rumours of photographs of him circulating the senior studies.

Ayckbourn developed his own strategy for avoiding the *ad hoc* beating up that characterises communities of locked-up males: 'I think I was known as Smiley. I just used to smile at everyone all the time so nobody punched me. I didn't mind the suggestion that I may have been slightly half-witted as long as I was left alone.' Grinning at the edge.

Meanwhile the interest in theatre was being refined and hardened. In his admirable book *Alan Ayckbourn* (Methuen Modern Dramatists, 1983) Michael Billington writes of the 'iron philistinism of the English public school . . . as a positive incentive to those with dramatic or literary leanings to form their own defensive clique'. It is a complex philistinism which replicates that of the country at large: the British actually go to the theatre rather more than anybody else (they also generally enjoy dressing up for anything from law-courts to rag weeks). But they object to subsidising the theatre or otherwise taking seriously the people working in it professionally. Haileybury, like many other schools, had house plays and school plays as well as various visiting cultural performances. Ayckbourn wrote house plays – often not much more than a sketch – and he was producing sub-Betjeman comic poems about women in tea-shops which rhymed and scanned and were intelligible enough to win poetry competitions. He wrote most of his own house's magazine, often under pseudonyms and invariably at the fifty-ninth minute of the eleventh hour before the deadline. If Haileybury had a defensive clique for arty types it was the Senior Literary Debating Society, whose members wore their hair as long as they could get away with and rebelliously loosened their ties a bit.

But Ayckbourn was never the school aesthete or dissident. A key lesson in 'team playing' that boys placed under authority will learn, if they don't want to be singled out as serious mavericks, is loyalty to each other and their own rough justice. One unfortunate boy, a natural victim in any case because he was fat, was found guilty of eating somebody else's food. He was made to remove all his clothes and run round the quadrangle naked after dark. He had almost completed the circuit when he ran slap into a prefect. By then of course all the other boys had disappeared, leaving a neat pile of clothes. The unfortunate Billy Bunter figure, by now suspected of seriously deviant behaviour, was given a 'prefect beating', caned not by masters but by three or four older boys.

The worst beating, at least in the attention drawn to it, was from the headmaster. In between came the housemaster beating, and Alan was on the end of a few of these, getting caned for something he hadn't quite managed to do: typically, he had overslept and missed a midnight boozing session planned for the end of term, but was the boy found belatedly out of bed when a dropped cigar box woke not only Laz Newbold but his wife and daughter too.

Another loyalty he developed was to God. It is no coincidence that confirmation classes, in the Church of England anyway, arrive at around the same time as the onset of puberty. The theory is that you are now of sufficiently mature and independent mind to take up for yourself the promises others made on your behalf at baptism. It also means you have been thinking about God and sin a fair amount just when your hormones start signalling various otherwise barely containable imperatives. God and a cold bath work in close alliance here. A series of Lenten talks was initially welcomed as a way of getting out of prep. Confirmation classes followed and then a memorable occasion when a monk came to preach in Chapel (where attendance was compulsory). 'He was a terribly muscular and aggressive Christian with knots in the rope which was his belt. And for a time we all wanted to be monks and tied knots in our dressing-gown cords. But we really didn't appreciate the idea of poverty and chastity. Let alone obedience.' Like most boys, Alan wanted a powerful car, a busty blonde to go in it, and nobody to tell him where to go with them. He now believes that art moved in to fill the place left by his waning commitment to God, though he retains a conviction that it is desirable to retain a faith in something which is 'bigger than yourself, preferably not another human being', and values spirituality while confessing to embarrassment and self-parody when he tries to explain what this might be. He supports his parish church's social action committee and admires the genuine selflessness of people, like his daughter-in-law Telma, who engage in work with the disaffected youth of the town.

His closest schoolfriend – the only one with whom a relationship lasted even a little beyond Haileybury – did stay faithful. And when Alan announced that he wasn't going to the voluntary chapel services any more, only the compulsory ones, Arthur Hugh Mead begged him not to give up. The service at issue was Holy Communion; because you could only receive the bread and wine after you were confirmed it had, especially in the strictly hierarchical world of the public school, an element of privilege about it. Also, growing boys almost fainting with early morning hunger were ripe for the exalted, mystical experience which the piety accompanying confirmation encourages them to look for. But it also deprived Alan of precious sleeping time. When he told Arthur Hugh that communion didn't mean anything to him any more he woke up one Sunday morning to find his friend kneeling at the foot of his bed, praying for him. The friendship survived, helped perhaps by an incident when they were walking to compulsory chapel one day. 'Careful,' said Alan, 'the path is very, very slippery.' Arthur Hugh replied: 'Ayckbourn, if I slip it will be the will of G-o-o-o-o-o-o-o——' And down he went. Nice to think that God likes a bit of slapstick. Arthur Hugh went on to be Professor of Theology at Cambridge and godfather to one of Alan's boys: 'He kept sending him Bibles.'

But Arthur Hugh Mead's response to being picked on by a bully at the age of 13 inspired Ayckbourn's admiration. Mead got the boy hooked on a board game he had invented – a war game. 'One day I said to Arthur in the dorm: "Arthur, I've been watching you play this game now for about a month. No one can ever win, can they?" And he said: "Don't ever say anything!" I promised not to, and he admitted it was impossible. I thought, that's how you survive.' The mature Ayckbourn has a profound dislike of bullying and jacks-in-office. He rarely confronts either directly, but when a public school fails to teach you discipline it usually does teach you how to get round it.

6 : Launched by Shakespeare

By far the most important thing that happened to Ayckbourn at Haileybury was that he got involved in the school Shakespearean production, not because he loved Shakespeare (who was to bring him one of the bigger disappointments of his professional life) but because it fed his now-overwhelming ambition to be in theatre as an actor. The Haileybury Shakespeare production was run by a master called Edgar Matthews, one of those teachers who always seem to feature somewhere in the stories of successful people. He taught French but had a passion for drama in general and Shakespeare in particular. He organised schoolboy productions which toured abroad, mostly to European countries, every year except the war years from 1930 to 1957.

You were not allowed to audition for this until you were 15. The year that Ayckbourn first applied, the play was to be *Romeo and Juliet*, with a boy Juliet, and the plan was to take it to Holland. He got the smallish part of Peter, the servant in the Capulet household who trails round after the Nurse. It is – surprise, surprise – a largely comic role, and we can assume he played it pretty effectively because it was mentioned in a school report and because of the extent to which Matthews backed him in the future.

The Dutch tour involved stupendous under-age drinking and enormous warmth from the families on whom the boys were billeted; a decade after the end of the war they still thought of the British as their liberators. Ayckbourn enjoyed every minute and promptly signed up for the following year. He earned no great kudos in the school that he remembers: 'Half the guys were in it for a nice free skive. And then there was the serious half of us who also cared about the art. We wanted to get that right, to do a good show. Mind you, we still managed to get legless.'

The production for 1955 was to be more ambitious still. The play was *Macbeth* and it would tour the United States and Canada. Alan didn't want to play the Porter, the character entrusted with such light relief as is to be had in *Macbeth*, but the hero. Matthews, with a more realistic assessment of his range at this age, gave him the tyrant's nemesis, Macduff. The tours were budgeted to break even but parents were asked to cover their sons' expenses in advance. When ticket revenue started coming in the poorest parents would be reimbursed first. There was additional excitement this year because girls were brought in for the first time and they all crossed the Atlantic on the *Queen Elizabeth*, travelled around by Greyhound bus and returned on the *Queen Mary*.

This clinched Ayckbourn's ambition to work in professional theatre. Until then he had still been toying with journalism as a likely career, though it was journalism in the sense of contributing to magazines, as his mother did, rather than being a reporter. Having made up his mind he applied to Edgar Matthews for help. At this period Matthews' daughter Imogen was working as 'secretary, personal assistant and general dogs-body' for the flamboyant, egotistical actor-manager Donald Wolfit (por-trayed simply as 'Sir' in Ronald Harwood's play and film, *The Dresser*). From a Nottinghamshire working-class background, Wolfit was one of the greatest actors of his generation, but his declamatory style in the classics and his habit of surrounding himself with inferior colleagues meant that he was never as fashionable as his famous contemporaries – Laurence Olivier, Ralph Richardson and John Gielgud. 'Olivier is a tour de force,' ran the old and very adaptable joke, 'Wolfit is forced to tour.' But Matthews' letter of recommendation to his daughter's employer brought a response that Ayckbourn still possesses: 'Certainly I will see the boy you mention – would it be possible for him to come with me to Edinburgh to walk on? This would mean rehearsing in London for two weeks ... and being three weeks in E/bro. I could manage £3-0-0 a week expenses there.' The letter is dated exactly one week before rehearsals began on 6 August 1956 but it shouldn't be assumed from this that Wolfit was desperate. It has always been possible to find actors at the last minute and if you're paying them expenses only you want *them* to be desperate.

Ayckbourn's last contribution to Haileybury was in an end-of-term variety bill. Most school plays were classics, or semi-classics such as the literary 'plays of ideas' of George Bernard Shaw, or would-be classic contemporary plays, including somewhat daunting verse dramas. This was different. You could choose to do a musical or comic turn. It was short of material on this occasion and Ayckbourn decided to put in the first act of the Whitehall farce *Reluctant Heroes*, with himself playing the part enjoyed in the West End by the most popular farceur of the day, Brian Rix (now Lord Rix). He persuaded the schoolboy actor who had played Macbeth in America to be his comic foil as the sergeant-major in this comedy about National Servicemen.

At that stage it was just about the funniest play I'd ever read. The evening up till then had been rather turgid and this was just sensationally successful. People were standing and cheering and I just thought 'I've just got to wait here and say this line and I know it'll happen. This is just giddy-making.' I remember thinking how glad I was that on Monday I was starting serious theatre. I'd felt what it was like to have an audience in the palm of my hand – for 25 minutes at most. Although it was to be redirected, that was quite an influential moment in my life.

Was his career mapped out at this point? Not in the least. He had actually moved away from writing to performance and he had no idea of what he would be doing when the three weeks in Edinburgh were up.

He still consumed films indiscriminately each week, specifically (and perhaps improbably) *A Matter of Life and Death*. Made in 1946 (by Michael Powell and Emeric Pressburger) it features David Niven as an RAF bomber pilot who bales out of a blazing aircraft without a parachute. He has been reciting poetry to a radio operator he has never met, and miraculously is washed up alive on a beach near her station. The rest of the film is a battle for the pilot's right to stay on earth, which is in colour, rather than go to the next world, a soul-less black and white Elysium filling up rapidly with war dead. A caption at the start of the film says the action takes place in the Niven character's head while he undergoes brain surgery for his headaches and hallucinations; the film touches on neurology and psychology somewhat inexactly. But it connects in two powerful ways with the adult playwright: it has two narrative frames – a story happening simultaneously in two different worlds – and it deals with that overlapping area between mental health, the life of the imagination and some sort of subdued spiritual dimension occupied by so many of Ayckbourn's heroes and heroines.

The other precious memory of boyhood is *The Goon Show*, a cult radio programme written largely by the anarchic surrealist genius Spike Milligan and performed – after Michael Bentine's departure from its small team – by Milligan with Peter Sellers and Harry Secombe. The latter played the hero (Ned Seagoon) in a series of wild episodes parodying popular adventure stories. Like many of a generation that grew up with radio as a more popular medium than the infant television, Ayckbourn can quote in detail the plot-lines, individual jokes and above all caricatured voices which the Goons gave to history.

But Spike Milligan and Peter Sellers were more personal heroes than direct comic influences. There was (and is) a powerful tension between Milligan's natural anarchy and his need for creative discipline, his loathing for authority and the need for order to get a radio programme made. Ayckbourn's own temperament responds to this. Only one attempt was made to give him any authority at Haileybury. He was put in charge of allocating chores and duties among fellow juniors. He used it, he told his mother, as a way of getting out of doing too much himself. His housemaster found him 'rather disappointing' in the post.

So in 1956 at the age of 17, he consciously took his future into his own hands for the first and almost the last time. Resisting the usual pressure to try to get into university, including the offer by Barclays, his stepfather's employers, of an extension of his scholarship, he left Haileybury with his two 'A' levels and a promise of work, on meagre expenses only, in Britain's most precarious profession. In his background: a family who probably spoke their minds too much and a school where the natural thing was not to speak your mind at all. He had learned to smoke. What else? 'If public school had taught me anything it was just generally to shoulder your way to the front when you wanted to,' he says now. And was the child father to the man to any great degree in his case? 'Oh yes, I think so. I begin to see now more of what I was then and why I'm like I am now. The relationships with people, which are quite hard to establish. I don't have vast numbers of friends. That's probably all from a quite lonely childhood. Even now, I think I'm happiest when I'm sitting down with a play and the whole world is under one's control.'

He left school without regret. He was leaving home as well. And so – to save herself from destruction – was Lolly.

The Shakespearean tours meant he had missed substantial parts of the previous two long summer holidays but when he did go home the deteriorating relationship between his mother and stepfather was obvious. Lolly had stopped writing, and he thought she was 'going under'. She was having electro-convulsive therapy, still a relatively new treatment for depression, not much understood and terrifying for her squeamish son. His perception at the time was that she had married an ogre and must leave him. Subsequent developments in therapy would probably have led to a different analysis but the same conclusion. Cecil was no more an ogre than Lolly was an immoral bitch; the destructiveness was mutual, but the solution was still for her to leave. So the boy's first really adult act was to find her a flat and a job – secretarial work for another writer. There was someone else to offer practical aid to Alan – the sister who had been Lolly's sole comforter when she left Neville – and he duly went to live with his Aunt Peggy in a flat near Sloane Square in London. Peggy was supposed to keep him on the straight and narrow – he wasn't that adult – but she mixed with a hard-drinking Australian crowd and gave him a very good time. *Look Back in Anger* had opened at the Royal Court Theatre in

Sloane Square, reportedly ushering in a revolution in British drama. He didn't see it.

Chapter 2

Enter an actor

---

1 : A Star Is Not Born

Donald Wolfit was still a year away from his knighthood in 1956 but he was quite intimidating enough for a nervous schoolboy. When he rang to confirm the engagement, Alan – who loathes the telephone to this day – couldn't take in what the most resonant bass in the British theatre was saying. The YWCA on Tottenham Court Road in Central London was the first of the many rehearsal rooms in which his life is measured out. Wolfit had had a major success with Fritz Hochwalder's play *The Strong Are Lonely*, which much later (1986) would be filmed as *The Mission*. Wolfit played the Father Provincial of a mission in Paraguay whose attempts to serve the indigenous population aroused the anger of the Spanish colonial powers and his Jesuit superiors in Rome. At the end of an ecclesiastical trial scene the Father Provincial submits to authority, but is then killed when his own supporters refuse to do likewise. A play of ideas, and Wolfit had had to show some determination to get it into the West End. Now he planned to extend the success by taking a company (including his future biographer, Ronald Harwood) to Edinburgh to appear on the Festival 'fringe' in Lauriston Hall, the Jesuits' own hall in the city.

The cast was all male, disappointingly, and seemed very elderly to Alan. He made friends with a young man fresh out of the London Academy of Music and Dramatic Art (LAMDA) called Andreas who he thinks was a Greek Cypriot, cast because of his olive skin; everyone else playing South American Indians had to try to match it. After two weeks' rehearsal (when Alan wasn't even paid expenses) the company took the night train north. He was one of two acting assistant stage managers – 'acting' in the sense of going on stage, not of being temporary: *everybody* was temporary. He was to travel third class but the stage manager offered him his bed in first class 'for an hour or two' while he himself had a meeting, intending to take the bed over when it finished. But Alan can sleep for Britain. He was unwakeable. So it was as the freshest of the party that the 17-year-old ASM watched Lauriston Hall being transformed into a theatre by a bleary-eyed stage manager and his team under the direction of a dinner-jacketed stage director. The dinner jacket, he was told, was to 'show he's the governor, he doesn't dirty his hands'.

Having found a back door into theatre Alan decided the smartest thing was to watch, learn and be ready to step into a breach if a crisis developed, which it usually did. As well as a couple of small acting parts, he was the call-boy and was to make some of the props, including the big map that Wolfit used to tear from a wall with a kind of lion's roar. It was made of two bits of canvas with jagged edges that were stuck together with paper so that the rip followed the same, interestingly zig-zag line every night. However, if the ASM arrives very late, as Alan once did, and glues it together minutes before the curtain goes up, so it doesn't get the chance to dry, it will part with the rude sound of (at best) a deflating balloon and leave the star with a bit of soggy canvas in each hand. Alan also had the job of making sure Wolfit's supplies of alcohol – Guinness and gin – were maintained. Wolfit tried to make sure there was no drink in evidence when the Edinburgh Jesuit Superior was visiting, but Ronald Harwood records Father James Christie SJ entering, sniffing the air and saying: 'Ah, Guinness.' When Alan failed to supply water to mix with his gin, Wolfit topped it up from the church's holy water.

One of Alan's 'acting' roles was to be part of the Spanish army, eight men lined up in three-cornered hats, wigs, pigtails and breeches. They had to carry muskets too. Alan believes he got the job because he'd been in the school cadet force and could stand on parade for 40 or 50 minutes, unflinching; his predecessor had passed out right in the middle of Wolfit's big speech, upstaging him with a vengeance. But at the costume call Wolfit, inspecting his troops like the major-general at Haileybury, got to Alan, growled and said: 'You're one of those unfortunate people who look funny in a hat.' Ayckbourn said: 'Sorry about that.' He was told to take the hat off. And then, so that everybody would look the same, all the hats were ordered off, to the accompaniment of a little whimpering noise from the designer in which the words 'historical' and 'accuracy' could just be distinguished. Ayckbourn was impressed: Wolfit could have just got rid of the unfortunate no-good-at-wearing-hats actor but instead he cut the hats. And Ayckbourn didn't pass out, although the five-kilowatt lamps blazed down like the sun in the Sahara desert.

You have a close-up view unavailable to anyone else from the bottom rung of the theatrical ladder. At the end of Act II the Father Provincial, his life in ruins, kneels centre stage and starts quietly reciting the Lord's Prayer until his voice falters and he begins to cry. He is left in a pool of light as the curtains slowly close. Not a dry eye in the house. One night the curtain jammed while the speech was in progress. The Spanish army (Alan and colleagues) looked up to see a stagehand crawling along the bar behind the makeshift proscenium arch towards the curtain motor, right above where Wolfit was kneeling. The man was hidden from the audience by the arch itself, and it was only when he dropped a spanner that Wolfit saw him. He stopped the show completely and ordered the unfortunate electrician down, more spanners clattering to the stage as he crawled back, while the stage army stifled its laughter. Wolfit, always paranoid about being upstaged, was furious. Ayckbourn the writer learned thoroughly what it takes in the way of mechanics to provide a platform for the art, and Ayckbourn the director has the smoothest, speediest and most pain-free technical rehearsals in the business.

Wolfit was a generous man if you gave him the chance to display his greatness of spirit. When Alan and Andreas told him they wanted to be actors too, he agreed to audition them. Andreas unwisely did two speeches from roles in which Wolfit regarded himself as definitive, Shakespeare's *Othello* and Marlowe's *Tamburlaine*. He growled that Andreas had given complete misreadings of the roles. Alan did something – he can't remember what – very intense, after which Wolfit told him he was 'full of tricks'. This may have been true but was a bit rich coming from the most mannered of the great actors on the British stage. He recommended drama school – specifically Webber-Douglas, on whose board he sat. Even if he'd wanted to go back to education Alan couldn't have afforded it. However, he had an appetite for learning and he discovered how easy it then was during his free mornings to slip into a theatre and watch dress rehearsals of companies like the Piccolo Theatre of Milan or Hamburg State Opera, who were playing in the official festival. His love affair with theatre came on apace.

But after three weeks, Alan was back in London with no job and no prospects. He followed up the one other contact Haileybury had given him. Robert Flemyng was an old boy of the school (and as a classical actor something of a boy of the old school as well) and he invited Alan to tea in Hove, where he lived. He had few contacts, he said, but they did include Melville Gilham who ran the Connaught Theatre in Worthing and who agreed to take Alan, sight unseen, as a theatre student. This was another unpaid job and he had to be prepared to do anything, in return for which of course he might well learn everything. Lolly, looking years younger in spite of her new employer's tendency to throw books at her, owned a holiday caravan which she now sold to finance Alan in Worthing. He went to live with 'three spinster ladies who treated me like a missing son'. One of them worked in the box office of a local cinema, so he got in free there. He was acting again, this time in weekly rep: a permanent company performing one play at night, rehearsing next week's during the day and – in their own time – reading through the one they would be doing the week after. The student ASM could also expect to make props, paint the set, fetch the tea and feed the theatre cat. And after going through drama school this is where serious actors got their practical training, building up their range through playing substantial parts rather than, as now, getting 'a cough and a spit' in a long-running television series and launching a career that way.

In the company in Worthing were Daniel Massey, Roland Curram, Ian Holm, Richard Pascoe and Elizabeth Spriggs, all names the National Theatre and the RSC (and film and TV companies) would later be pleased to get. Alan soon found himself acting in Emlyn Williams's play *The Corn Is Green* about an evangelistic woman teacher who persuades a rural community that education is worth having even if it means delaying paid work on the farm or in a colliery. It had been filmed in 1945 with Bette Davis giving the teacher plenty of emotional fire-power, but was based on Williams's own life in North Wales. So there was Alan, 'one of the Welsh boyos on a bench, singing', with Spriggs as the teacher. He loved it. And a couple of weeks and a couple of shows later came the moment cherished in showbiz fiction.

Alan was in the scene dock late on a Monday night, painting away, when word came through that the actor playing the juvenile lead in an American play called *It's a Wise Child* had simply run away after the first performance. So Alan was handed a script and told to go home and learn it for Tuesday. He wouldn't get a rehearsal with the rest of the company because they were already rehearsing the next week's play. But he would get a session with the director. The spinster ladies prepared a pile of sandwiches, and he learned the long part overnight. On Tuesday they ran it through once and then did it. 'It was a bit hairy, but I got through.' Peter Byrne (later famous alongside Jack Warner in television's *Dixon of Dock Green*) had learned not only his own part but the whole play, as was his custom. When Alan forgot something he would say: 'I think I can guess what you're going to tell me . . .' and add the necessary information. Elizabeth Spriggs gave Alan a huge hug, the rest of the cast offered congratulations and then the manager, Kenneth Ewing, said: 'Well done, well done, well done.' And when Alan thanked him, added: 'You'll be pleased to know we've got a proper actor to do tomorrow night, but can you do the matinee?' No star was pinned on his dressing-room door; he slunk back to the scene dock.

There was a further setback when it came to the Christmas pantomime, *Cinderella*, with the neighbours from his infancy, the sisters double act of Elsie and Doris Waters (Jack Warner was their brother). Alan was given the key task of working one of the two 'limes', the lights which were trained on the two central performers and followed them round the stage. The technique was to put your face against the side of the lamp so that you could aim it straight and keep it steady. The lamps crackled and sparked and by the time you arrived in the bar after the show half your face was black with soot, leading to a number of tasteless jokes about half-breeds. Alan's partner on the other 'lime' was an Irishman who suddenly asked Alan one night to widen the focus of his light to cover both the stars on his own. He was doing his best to oblige when suddenly a tiny spot of limelight picked out a nubile dancer from the chorus, a luminous fairy in the gloom. 'She's coming out with me tonight,' said the Irishman. 'These little dollies – they'll do anything for light.' Alan got fired from the 'limes' and demoted to stage crew. One of his jobs here was to hold up a wobbly bit of set when – with Prince Charming about to do his rounds with the glass slipper – the Ugly Sisters thrust Cinderella into a rickety cupboard. The first time he did it, Susan Beaumont (playing Cinders) catapulted through the cupboard door and said: 'Hello. Are you new?' She instructed him to bring some playing-cards the next night because she was stuck in the cupboard for a long time. All was fine until the night the audience got particularly vehement in shouting at the comedian Ted Rogers (playing Buttons): 'She's in the *cupboard*!' So he opened it, and there was Cinderella playing cards with an unknown man who was holding the set up with one hand and dealing with the other.

The next mistake couldn't be blamed on panto-hardened campaigners exploiting a 17-year-old's naivety and might have had tragic consequences. The pantomime had a major transformation scene for Prince Charming's Ball. A front-cloth was lowered and the stage crew had to run in fast and put in place a staircase which Alan then had to secure by two pins that attached it to a fixed rostrum behind it. He was standing in the wings enjoying the scene – the guests being announced and then descending the staircase to fanfares and applause – with his hands characteristically in his pockets, when he realised the two pins were there too. There was nothing to keep the staircase in place. 'It could have slid away from the rostrum at any minute and probably killed a dozen actors. I watched as each guest was announced and stepped on to it and it was just moving by a few millimetres each time. I was thinking: "Please don't anybody bounce down. Please just walk down." And we got through. It didn't collapse. And I ran on to change the set again and I just palmed the pins because I didn't want anybody to see me *not* taking them out.'

But he was strong, a good man to have on crew, capable of putting up a whole set on his own. And he was learning a lot, fast. It was the lack of ambition he sensed in some of the Worthing company (a young colleague said she was in theatre to meet and marry the singer Dickie Valentine) that made him decide he should move on.

Cary Ellison of the actors' directory *Spotlight*, a family friend (so families have their uses), arranged for him to have lunch with Hazel Vincent Wallace, the formidable woman who ran the rep at Leatherhead. She was just losing an ASM, as luck would so often have it for Alan, and so he did the second half of the season there. Because she liked the look of him, he did more acting too: Percy in Terence Rattigan's *Flare Path* and Jimmy Curry in *The Rainmaker* by N. Richard Nash. Over 40 years later Hazel Vincent Wallace – still campaigning for the Thorndike Theatre with no great support from the funding bodies – remembered Alan in *The Rainmaker*, for 'a very dark, deep, good voice', and as an ASM who was efficient and good to work with. She thought he would be 'all right' in the theatre although she had no idea of the direction his talent would take.

And this is where Lolly came to break the news that his father had died. She gave John Hodgson a very full account of the episode, but placed it when she and Alan were still living with Cecil. Since they left eight months or so before Horace died we must assume that it describes a process longer drawn out than her racy narrative suggests. She said that Daphne Ayckbourn had asked to meet her in Brighton and told her that Horace had 'shown his true nature', which was not something to be fond of; so Daphne had left him. Horace also telephoned to say that Daphne had left him and Lolly recalled Alan's saying that this was a cry for help. Cecil warned her that if she went to Horace she should 'take her brat with her' and never come back, and accused her of still being in love with Horace. She didn't deny it but she didn't go. When she next telephoned Daphne at her new address in London she was told Daphne had left for Norfolk because her husband had died. There was, unsurprisingly, no love lost between Lolly and Daphne.

Alan's grim version of events is much shorter (and we have seen that he shifted it to a time four years earlier in his life) but it includes the story that Horace and Daphne had had a huge row, Daphne had left, Horace had had a heart attack and only been found when someone called to find out why the dogs were howling. The news had been kept from him and nothing of his father's had been passed on to him. Lolly confirmed the last point, saying that everything had been sold before she had a chance to do anything about it. Daphne Ayckbourn would be able to throw more light on the circumstances surrounding Horace's death, but she chose not to comment.

We know from Horace's death certificate that he actually died in hospital – Wicklewood, near Norwich – in March 1957, and that the cause of death was cancer. This does not of course rule out the possibility of a heart attack.

Lolly went down to Leatherhead to tell Alan (she said her going was Cecil's idea, which is surprising, as she had left him eight months previously, but not impossible). When she arrived, Alan was preparing one of his first big acting roles. They met for coffee in the pub where she was staying the night and when she broke the news he simply said: 'Really?' Shortly afterwards he left to walk back to his digs. She thought it hadn't meant anything to him. Looking back on this over 40 years later Alan had no great difficulty accepting that it had happened when he was in Leatherhead rather than when he was at school. He remembers being very depressed and the rest of the stage management team asking why he was being so horrible to them. Almost certainly he told nobody else of his loss; Hazel Vincent Wallace was unaware of it. When something awful happens, he says now, he appears at first – even to himself – not to have been affected. Literally years later it hits him. He has also described this reaction as 'spreading the emotion out over several years'. This was one of the occasions that prompted Lolly to describe her son as never wanting to show emotion, shy, secretive and unknowable.

But – perhaps as much as 15 years later – Alan told her he had been conscious of his father's presence walking beside him in Scarborough. She said she was glad because she had been shocked at his reaction at the time. And he replied: '*I* was shocked. That was all I could say.' His father's company (and perhaps interest) had always been erratic, apparently withdrawn as rapidly and intensely as it was given. Now the chance to get to know him properly had been taken away for ever.

Long after the event, Daphne did try to get in touch with Alan and, having no address to write to, left messages at the theatre in Scarborough. By that time, he had no interest in making contact.

Hazel Vincent Wallace was a demanding boss, committed to raising production values, and the pressure on the young jack-of-all-trades intensified accordingly. The company performed over 40 plays a year in Leatherhead and then ran a summer season by the sea. The turnaround between plays was so tight that once, during the final performance of one production, as soon as the window-curtains were closed in the set in the third act, he set to work to paint a new back wall for the next one. Unfortunately some actor in improvisatory mood decided to open them again and instead of the night sky over Surrey the on-stage characters – and the audience – suddenly saw a man up a ladder painting the landscape.

Ayckbourn stuck to his lifelong policy of standing around and smiling a lot, to ward off the malice of any actors who might think he was after their jobs. In the (mostly) comradely environment of the company he learned how to use make-up, not to turn away from the audience, elementary stagecraft. He was beginning to take responsibility for the theatre's sound-effects and, in his spare time, to play more constructively with his beloved tape recorder. With a friend he experimented on a drama set on the London Underground, crudely recorded and edited but allowing them to learn how microphones worked and how what you hear can help tell a story. On Sundays off they would go to the Royal Festival Hall and explore the music repertoire.

And he was coming into close contact with women of his own age who seemed vastly more experienced than the young man who had been at a single-sex boarding-school until a few months before. Some of them were 'game for a snog in the props room', but he had a lot of ground to make up on that village butcher boy of his imagination.

2 : Stephen

'Where's Scarborough?' he wanted to know. Leatherhead's stage manager, Rodney Wood, was going to Scarborough as general manager and during the final production at Leatherhead he had asked if anyone was looking for a job for the summer. It was as stage manager (missing out the middle rung, deputy stage manager, completely). Alan's second question was: 'What the hell's theatre-in-the-round?' He was directed to the Mahatma Gandhi Hall in Fitzroy Square, close to the heart of London University and home to the British Drama League, where on Sunday evenings in the winter the Theatre-in-the-Round Company was producing plays. In January of the previous year two of the best-known drama critics of the day had been to see what was going on. Kenneth Tynan was writing nominally about job prospects for actors and therefore about the state of British theatre in general:

A less tightly organised [than Joan Littlewood's Theatre Workshop] guerrilla outfit has lately been formed by Stephen Joseph for the purpose of popularising the technique of stagecraft known as theatre-in-the-round. Inadequate actors and a bold but bad choice of plays have thus far hampered his efforts; at one production I saw there seemed to be twice as many false moustaches as members of the company.

One admits that theatre-in-the-round costs very little, in that it cuts scenery down to a bare minimum and needs only an auditorium with an open space in the centre and chairs set around it. But its aesthetic advantages are extremely dubious. The argument that it produces a 'three-dimensional effect' is particularly specious.

Tynan argued that a well-designed production in a conventional theatre with the stage tucked away inside and behind a proscenium arch has a three-dimensional effect anyway. This heretical article, cut from a South African newspaper but written by the dazzling, youthful and influential critic of the *Observer*, is in the archive assembled by Peter Cheeseman for the New Vic Theatre (also in-the-round) in Newcastle under Lyme. It is certainly the case that Stephen Joseph's recruitment and casting policies were eccentric – he once cast an actor because he identified some Bach correctly – and Tynan may have seen some bad acting. That is not, however, what struck Bernard Levin, writing in *Truth* magazine:

As an absorbing evening's theatre it succeeded handsomely. The most extraordinary thing about this experiment was its lack of extraordinariness. Two minutes after it had begun, one could hardly recall having been in an ordinary theatre.

There was, wrote Levin, no upstaging, no 'masking' – blocking the audience's view – of one actor by another, and performers were acting to each other instead of speaking sideways to a distant audience. But he thought there might be some other 'tyrannies' in the conversations of people still not quite facing each other either as they spoke, reaching over their interlocutors' shoulders towards the audience. He was pretty impressed with the actors he saw, and thought the staging worked well for the short Pirandello plays he had watched, but wondered how it would be for Terence Rattigan, British theatre's most popular living writer, or Shakespeare, the French classics or Restoration plays.

The arguments go on to this day, and the idea that there is a single right way to stage all plays can now be recognised as itself tyrannical. A well-designed theatre-in-the-round is, however, egalitarian: every member of the audience has an equal view. It is relatively cheap to stage and puts all the attention on the actors and above all the text of the play itself. It also, crucially, puts actors and audiences in the same room. Stephen Joseph had encountered it in American universities and returned with a missionary zeal to implant it in British theatre.

What Ayckbourn saw at the Mahatma Gandhi Hall was Sartre's *Huis Clos*, usually translated as *In Camera* or *No Way Out*: a short, intensely claustrophobic play for three people, each of whom is passionately attracted to one of the other two but not to the one who is attracted to him or her. Gradually they discover that this is what hell is: 'other people'. British productions of Sartre's play were often so concerned with getting the triangular symmetry right (Sartre had written to a brief to provide three equal parts) that they omitted to explore the lust driving the characters. This production 'was quite an explicit, sexual version', Ayckbourn remembers. There were only four rows of seats and he was in the third, but the proximity galvanised him. His attitude to theatre deepened with the realisation that as well as being fun to do it could also be at least as visceral to watch as his beloved films.

An excited young man joined the train to Yorkshire. He knew he was to play a substantial part, the son of the house in J. B. Priestley's *An Inspector Calls*, and to take responsibility for the whole of the tiny company's stage management. His first discovery was that the theatre's tape deck had been ingeniously modified. Reel-to-reel recorders had no 'pause' buttons then, but someone had screwed a little metal lever, with a prong on it, to the capstan winding the tape. If he pulled the lever back, the tape stopped; when he let it go, it started again precisely where he wanted, playing the music (gunfire, car engine, jungle cicadas) exactly on cue. Hearing that this was an invention of the absent Stephen Joseph, he instinctively warmed to the man. A little later, doing the lighting on another show, he was trying to operate the series of primitive individual dimmers to achieve a smooth black-out at the end of one scene before bringing up a different set of lights for the next. Sparks were flying and the odd jolting shock was coming through, when he became aware of a big man behind him. Alan rather hoped the man wouldn't interfere and make him miss a cue. Eventually the man said: 'There's a better way to do that.'

ALAN: Sorry?

THE MAN: There's a better way to do that. What you need is a piece of wood.

ALAN (*sotto voce*):   Who the hell are you?

MAN: You get a piece of wood like this . . .

ALAN: Excuse me, there's a show going on.

MAN: . . . and you lay it across all the dimmers and bring them down together like this.

ALAN: You've blacked out the stage.

MAN: Oh Jesus!

And he ran out. Alan could hear the actors, soldiering on in the pitch dark, and then Clive Goodwin, the director, arrived: 'What the bloody hell are you doing? You've blacked out the big scene.'

ALAN: Well this big man came in with a piece of wood and . . . you're not going to believe this . . .

CLIVE: Oh, is Stephen here?

ALAN: That was Stephen Joseph?

CLIVE: Do you think anyone else would do that?

And so, finally, he met the most influential man in his life, the son of the very man his mother claimed as her longest-lasting lover. Stephen was to become Alan's surrogate father, within a few months of the death of his real one.

Like many a great artist, Stephen Joseph was a practical dreamer, a visionary who completely understood how the things he was visionary about actually worked. Alan characterised him early on as 'half genius, half madman'. He was the son of Michael Joseph and his first wife, the actress Hermione Gingold, the kind of star for whom the word 'sophisti-cated' might have been coined, flourishing initially in the heyday of revue. By this time she had been in the business for half a century, having made her debut at 11 with Sir Herbert Tree in something called *Pinkie and the Fairies*. In Alan's second summer in Scarborough she would be making the film *Gigi*.

Stephen was tall, well over 6 feet (1.8 m), and striking to look at; dark, with chest hair which pushed its way out of his shirt even when it was buttoned at the collar. In Scarborough in the 1950s he wore a leather suit – there is a picture to prove it in the theatre that now bears his name. And in a dinner suit, according to Alan, he 'didn't half frighten the Mayor'. The actress Elizabeth Bell (then a Scarborough schoolgirl, soon to head off to drama school in London) remembers him habitually dressed in paint-stained overalls, hammer in hand, like some sort of socialist realist poster: a Hero of Yorkshire Theatre. And the actor Stanley Page, going to meet him in a ramshackle flat in Chelsea about the possibility of working in Scarborough, was greeted by a giant in T-shirt and jeans with bare feet.

It was Page, an Australian, who learned the story of Stephen's wartime service. As a gunner in a destroyer in the Mediterranean, Stephen worked out that if his gun on the forward tower fired at a certain angle it would blow the front off the ship, which he duly reported to the captain. The latter wasn't having an Ordinary Seaman telling the Royal Navy it didn't know how to design its ships but Stephen's fellow gunners agreed. So when, in battle, the captain ordered precisely the firing he'd been advised against, Stephen refused to obey. The captain came down to him with a drawn revolver, threatening to shoot him as a mutineer. An Australian lieutenant threw himself across the deck, knocked the gun out of the captain's hands and added that he also thought Stephen was right. The navy vindicated Stephen, sweetening things as best it could by recommending him and the captain for exactly the same decoration, the DSC. Even in wartime, Stephen could have gone into the navy at a much higher level than Ordinary Seaman if he chose. This story may have been enhanced for dramatic effect. Would the captain have left the bridge? Was Stephen, by this time at least, not a gunnery officer rather than an Ordinary Seaman?

He was unquestionably a maverick, and his devotion to theatre-in-the-round led him into an opposition to the proscenium arch which probably expressed itself more fiercely than he really meant. When Laurence Olivier and Vivien Leigh led a demonstration against the demolition of the St James's Theatre in London he carried a placard in the opposite direction, urging that it be replaced with a lucrative office block which would provide funds for a more sensible theatre in the basement.

There has been some speculation about Stephen's sexuality. I had understood him to be homosexual and when I suggested this to Alan he said: 'Yes, I suppose he was, wasn't he?' as if nobody had been crass enough to mention it before. But Stanley Page was clearly surprised at the idea and Margaret Boden added that 'the gay fraternity liked to claim him' but without justification. There was a persistent story that he had once lived with a woman but had 'found the whole thing very badly arranged physically'. Nobody I have spoken to remembers Stephen allowing any woman to get very close to him, and theatre was one of the few places where it was relatively safe to be a homosexual in the 1950s, given that it was still illegal and could get you a bad beating. But Ian Watson, who was employed by Stephen after being his student, has always thought of him as asexual. Not everyone whose sex life is quiet is repressing something, and it seems likely that Stephen was essentially a shy man (part of the bond with Alan) despite his occasionally flamboyant appearance, and one of those people – including many fine teachers – who are more comfortable in the company of his own gender without there being much in the way of sexual dimension. His vocation really was his passion; he would do anything from driving lorries to working in children's television to pay for it, and would tackle every job in it, even acting (very badly) and writing (worse) if he was needed.

For Alan, Stephen was 'just the bloke you'd sort of follow, really'. Alan is too matter-of-fact, too *English* somehow, for such a word as 'disciple' to seem quite appropriate. And he has achieved more than his master. But Stephen defined Alan, or gave him the room to define himself. Stephen knew everything, had an opinion on everything and wanted everything. To be with him anywhere was to have an informal guide book always open at the right page. He had a passion to which Alan (who has never really had an ambition beyond the next project) readily hooked himself. That passion, for theatre-in-the-round and new writing, made a small town on the 'bracing' coast of North Yorkshire synonymous with both, and famous around the world because of it. But this was achieved through the staying power of his protégé, not his own more volatile force of personality.

Why Scarborough? The repertory movement throughout Britain grew up more as a result of individual enthusiasms than sensible bureaucratic planning. The relevant individual in this case, however, was himself a bureaucrat, the County Education Officer of the old North Riding of Yorkshire. John Wood heard Stephen speak at an adult education college and urged him to stop talking about theatre-in-the-round and do something. With the help of W. H. Smettem, Scarborough's soon-to-retire director of libraries, museums and art gallery, he found the Concert Room above the town's central library in Vernon Road.

When Stephen was asked 'Why Scarborough?' by the *Yorkshire Evening News*, he replied: 'I honestly don't know. Except that the town attracts a cross-section of the public during the summer months and I personally like the place.'

There is much to like. Scarborough has as beautiful a location as any large seaside resort in Britain, a high and rocky headland with a ruined castle on top, a picturesque but working harbour below and huge sweeping bays to the north and south. The holiday industry is not what it was in 1955 and the impressive railway station is out of all proportion to the two- and three-coach trains that ply the routes from York and Hull. But it is still impossible to arrive there from the old industrial cities of west and south Yorkshire without getting into holiday mood. This of course colours the experience of going to the theatre. The Grand Hotel, modelled on a French château and dominating the sands of the South Bay, was the largest hotel in Europe when it was built in the middle of the nineteenth century. On the curving main street from the station to the harbour there are a few gypsy fortune-tellers left and the (now closed) doors of the largest seaside postcard shop in the world, a temple to the kiss-me-quick jollity of women who are either enormous battle-axes or mouth-watering beauties, and men who are either seriously oppressed runts or slick-haired rat-up-a-drainpipe opportunists. Maybe this Donald McGill vision colours the experience of going to the theatre too.

But Scarborough has a longer, more genteel pedigree too. Mineral deposits in the water helped create an eighteenth-century spa fit to rival Bath, according to Daniel Defoe. Sheridan set *The Rivals* in the latter, but as Ayckbourn later discovered to his delight, he also wrote *A Trip to Scarborough*. Some of the town's best building is Georgian or Regency, and for 100 years it was a resort for the relatively well-to-do. Anne Brontë set part of *Agnes Grey* there and is buried in the churchyard (1849). But Scarborough was ancient even before it was a spa. The headland was occupied and fortified in the Iron Age and then by the Romans. It was named by Icelandic Vikings, put to the torch by other Norsemen and laid waste again by William the Conqueror's Norman French. Newborough, the name of the upper part of that main street, was 'new' in the twelfth century. The three or four parallel streets rising with the contours above it towards the castle were, even then, the Old Town. And Scarborough Fair, subject of the old song further popularised by Simon and Garfunkel, ran from the Feast of the Assumption through to Michaelmas, six weeks every August and September: Scarborough has always had a 'season'.

Even the Victorian holiday-maker, looking at the Scarborough skyline, would have seen not just hotels but churches – and windmills: this is the market town for a vast agricultural hinterland. After the Second World War (when the hotels and the great Spa building itself were occupied by the military) the town had more than 3,000 homeless people. A major programme of building housing estates (using prisoners-of-war as labourers) and developing new roads began. Inevitably much of the town's well-loved architecture was lost. Many Scarborians believe they lost the soubriquet 'Queen of the Yorkshire Coast' at this time, although throughout the nineteenth century there had been demolition and redevelopment of similar kinds. The post-war local authority was determined not only to house its own people but to modernise the resort so that it would appeal to new markets. Even then, fewer holiday-makers were coming for the whole of their annual fortnight in the summer. In future day-trippers and the conference trade would become key factors in the town's bid to sustain its economy. While some resorts declined to little more than retirement villages, Scarborough's ancient status as a market town would reassert itself.

This is now the town of McCains, the frozen chips and pizza manufacturers, of the new Scarborough campus of Hull University, as well as colleges of further education, of its own newspaper and radio station, of night-clubs, hypermarkets and branches of department stores. The fishing fleet is a shadow of what it once was, but locally landed haddock is still on the menus. And the tourist industry was estimated in 1997 to be worth £2.6 million annually to the borough, which includes Filey and Whitby. The theatre is thought to make a significant contribution to this, and there is no other town with a producing theatre within 45 minutes' fast driving.

The permanent population of the town itself, according to the 1951 census, was just under 44,000 (it is now under 40,000). The summer population was much bigger and there was a mass of live entertainment available. Forty-five years after Stephen Joseph's inaugural season, Margaret Boden was still able to list the competition. She and her late husband Ken, both heavily involved in the amateur theatre movement in the town, had been recommended to Stephen by William Smettem as likely helpers; Stephen had wisely and almost uniquely in the professional theatre decided to make friends with the local amateurs rather than snub them. Margaret – among many other things – looked after the box office. In the summer of 1955 the York rep company was doing *Beside the Seaside* at Scarborough Opera House; there was a variety bill at the Spa, with celebrity classical concerts on Sundays and marionette shows for children; *Oklahoma!* was at the Open Air Theatre with an amateur chorus of 150; the comedian Leslie Crowther was going down well in *The Fol-de-Rols* at the Floral Hall; Dickie Henderson was at the Grand Hall. A revival of music-hall was being tried in a new venue, the Vernon. Reg Varney was in *Showtime* at the Arcadia. The holiday camps had not only very big variety houses but also smaller theatres, with 400–500 seats, where three or four plays were performed in a week so that people on short holidays could see the entire repertoire. The audience for popular theatre, comedies and thrillers with familiar titles, was still strong.

Something very different was about to happen in the little room above the Library. Stephen Joseph announced four brand-new plays for the summer season of 1955, listed in the *Scarborough Evening News* of 12 July: *Circle of Love* by Eleanor Glaser; *Apprentice Pillar* by Ruth Dixon; *Dragons Are Dangerous* by David Campton; and *Turn Right at the Crossroads* by Jurneman Winch. And seats, of which 248 were available, cost 5 shillings (25p) each.

Stephen had met the writers in London, on courses he ran at the Central School of Speech and Drama or the British Drama League. Eleanor Glaser was 'a Midlands housewife', according to the local paper, who dictated her play into a tape recorder while doing the ironing. She was also a qualified teacher who specialised in work with backward and maladjusted boys and her play dealt with an acute family crisis precipitated by a woman's love for her son, so possessive that her husband had been shut out of the relationship and was seeking comfort elsewhere. On the first night Hermione Gingold was in the audience and was quoted as saying that the view of the South Bay from her hotel was 'just like the Mediterranean'. The reviews were mostly good and the experience of being a member of an in-the-round audience was compared with eavesdropping at an intense domestic drama. However, Norman Shrapnel in the *Manchester Guardian* pointed out that this could be embarrassing as well as exhilarating and that the trouble with plumbing the depths might be that you also sounded the shallows only too well.

Of those first four writers only David Campton went on to make a substantial reputation and, at 77 in 2001, is still particularly popular with the amateur companies for whom he has tended to specialise in recent years, particularly with one-act plays for women. He recalls that the summer of 1955 was one of the hottest for years, which almost led to disaster. Stephen had prepared a graph showing how much they needed to take at the box office. Dipping below an ominous black line meant: 'We close in a week.' He needed about 100 customers a night to break even and on 28 July the *Scarborough Evening News* reported that the best house so far had been 75, the worst 'about 15'. Had it been wise to open with all new plays? But on the opening night of *Dragons Are Dangerous*, it rained. The audience reached the magic 100 and the following Tuesday the house was actually full. National newspapers announced the reprieve. At the end of the season there was a net loss of £800, which included the cost of preparing the building itself. Apart from favourably wet weather it seems likely that *Dragons Are Dangerous* – billed as a 'light-hearted comedy' – had the strongest comic element in it. It is a modern reinterpretation of the story of St George, and its hero takes in a delinquent female who burgles his next-door neighbour.

The most ringing endorsement of the staging came in a paper called the *Socialist Leader*, where a writer attending a summer school of the Independent Labour Party in Scarborough compared its excitement as well as its layout to that of a boxing ring and pointed out that it offered an intimacy to rival films and the new popular medium, television. Not all the natives were as happy. One letter-writer complained about a lack of publicity (someone always does) and another argued that going to a play where there was no scenery was like going to a restaurant, being presented with raw vegetables and being told to imagine the cooking.

Only the Edinburgh Festival Fringe or some London pub theatres give any idea what it was like to be crammed into the tiny Library. The Concert Room itself was 40 feet by 50 feet (12 × 15.2 m); once the seating was in place this left an acting area of 14 feet by 18 feet (4.2 by 5.5 m) the size of a decent-sized living-room. For comparison, the Lyttelton Theatre – the conventional auditorium of the National Theatre in London – is 45 feet across (13.7 m) at the proscenium. Two adjoining rooms were made available, one just big enough to be divided by a few screens into male and female dressing-rooms, office, wardrobe, stage management and Green Room; the other provided exhibition space and 'refreshments' – a tea urn and orange squash. There was one cold tap and to use the lavatory actors had to take their turn with the audience, so to maintain any kind of distance and mystique you really couldn't 'go' after the audience started to arrive. The donkey work of getting this ready each season fell to the amateur helpers, led by Ken and Margaret Boden. In addition to them, Stephen had the devoted services of Mrs Veronica Pemberton-Billing, universally known as PB, who had been married to an MP of mixed reputation and left as a widow in genteel poverty. Going for a job as a housekeeper, never having cooked in her life before, she'd been employed by Stephen in the crumbling old vicarage he'd bought in Longwestgate in the Old Town. Utterly devoted to him, she was instructed to cook for the whole company one day – 'Have lunch ready at one, PB' – and, having a dim memory that if you put some meat and some fat in an oven in a roasting tin it would be edible eventually, she got away with it once and then spent the summer learning to cook. Eventually she maintained a constant supply of cakes for the company and became its catering manager.

Stephen's first Scarborough summer season was endorsed the following

January by Councillor N. Walsh, former mayor and now chairman of the Libraries Committee of Scarborough Borough Council as 'a very deserving cultural activity', and a second season went ahead and then a third, the one Alan joined in 1957. It would be wrong to suggest it made much impact, with its 100-strong audiences, on the town as a whole, however. At the Open Air Theatre (sometimes referred to as Merrie England after the operetta which had opened it in 1932), there were 8,000 people a night for *Oklahoma!* staged by amateurs with considerable professional input. Attitudes formed then towards the experiment in producing professional theatre and creating new work may still inform the ambivalence with which some Scarborians regard Ayckbourn's work. The Open Air Theatre, sadly, is now unused and deteriorating.

In July 1957 the *Scarborough Mercury* published a picture of the new company. Among an otherwise sunny bunch of smiling actors in open-necked shirts there is one intense young man in jacket, collar and tie who is quite unseduced by the camera. What was Alan like at 18, still with less than a year's experience of professional theatre? Physically he was tall and thin. The eyes were deep-set and intense, the hair full and wavy and the cheekbones prominent. He has an unfamiliar, ascetic look and seems, from the formality of his clothes, to have been very self-conscious. And although he was learning fast, he also knew how little he knew.

In his first acting job in Scarborough, Eric in *An Inspector Calls*, he merits routinely favourable mentions in the press but according to Margaret Boden he rushed off without attending the first-night party and was thought to be wandering on the sands. Speaking with hindsight 40 years on Mrs Boden describes him then as 'like a lot of geniuses, rather frightened. But such fun.' He was discovering how much power there was under the bonnet – of theatre itself and of his own talent – but he was also uncertain exactly where talent ended and sheer temper began. Not yet out of his teens, he could be alternately tongue-tied and ferociously articulate. He was not comfortable with his own ability to devastate others with words; the flip side of the fun.

He had a second acting job in that four-play season, winning his first nod of approval from the *Manchester Guardian* in a play by Catherine Prynne called *The Ornamental Hermit*. He played 'a young country-bred poet of engaging dishevelment'. The fourth production was also new, *Honey in the Stone* by Ruth Dixon (author of *Apprentice Pillar* two years before). His own verdict at the end of the season was enthusiastic: 'I was really captivated by this outfit, mainly because it gave me such freedom.

You weren't the ASM, you were everything you wanted to be: actor, lighting, scenic designer – we all chipped in.' He was beginning to do what he has done ever since, which is to express himself most freely through work and in a working, not domestic or social, environment.

Physically it was hard and the hours were long, but at least Stephen Joseph kept stage sets to a minimum. There is a coat-hanger in the Ayckbourn cloakroom to this day which belonged to Stephen and represents the symbolic inheritance of theatre-in-the-round. The same on both sides, it swings round easily, and is simple, functional and yet elegant. It can hold all the visual resources an actor really needs in addition to his or her own body. This still embodies Alan's principles, although he will take pleasure in – and challenge designers to provide – some ingenious settings too. The seating was arranged on rostra so that the audience was raised slightly above the action, an essential feature of staging in the round. It means spectators can look over one actor to another, who will not therefore be 'masked'. The acting area itself was covered with whatever Stephen could use in his own house when it was finished with; for a long time there were some black and white squares which for some plays were laid out like a chessboard and for others would have all the white ones round the edge and the black ones in the middle, or vice versa; less of a design statement than a renunciation of design. At least it prevented the treacherous polished parquet of the Library floor from turning every drama into a farce. On this 'stage' there would be at most a chair or two and a large box, conceivably a small flight of steps if the box was to be mounted (to represent a Shakespearean castle, for instance). When everybody got bored with the box, Stephen just said: 'Paint it!' But with each show running a week initially and then being brought back more or less frequently through the two-month summer season (according to how many tickets it sold) there was no laborious set-changing.

Back at the house on Longwestgate, PB would flutter round when Stephen arrived with the entire company and staff (about 15 people) without warning and demanded supper. Alan recalls: 'There'd be a bit of rustling of pans, when a lot of women would have dotted him one, and she'd come up with a passable meal. We'd sit around in our chauvinistic way and talk about Art, the Future of Theatre, How to Build a Better Rostrum, and she'd occasionally ask if anyone was going to help her and we might carry a few pots out. She was relegated to the kitchen. But she just thought this was all wonderful and it was a very exciting time.' The only way you could really upset PB was to criticise Stephen.

Ayckbourn recalls an extraordinary achievement with *The Glass Men-agerie*, the gently tragic chamber piece in which Tennessee Williams puts on stage his callow younger self, his fading Southern belle of a mother, and the slightly disabled sister Laura that the mother is desperate to marry off. Stephen was always urging that theatre should be taken out into the community and he arranged a deal with the manager of Wallace's holiday camp (motto: Wally Days and Jolly Days) to show the play there in a ballroom 'the size of Earls Court', the worst possible environment for such a delicate piece. But at the end, after Laura had limped off, having lost her 'gentleman caller', as Alan and his colleagues were stacking the chairs a man approached and said how good the show had been. As they thanked him he added: 'And, me and the lads, we've just had a whip-round for the lass wi' the crippled foot.' They'd collected about £5, a week's wages for some people in 1957, and to their shame the company went and drank it away. Alan, who lit the show with the eight lamps at his disposal and added a snatch of jazz soundtrack, says: 'I don't think we could ever tell him because we were too ashamed of nicking the fiver – but that would have really thrilled Stephen because that is exactly what he wanted. Never for a minute did it occur to them that we might have an actor who was pretending. I mean where the play finished or started must have been confused in their minds. Did they think we just put in all those lines about her foot because we happened to have an actress who had to wear a leg brace?'

The emotional intensity of *The Glass Menagerie* is presumably what persuaded the holiday-maker of the truth of the performance and it is a testimony to the surprising effectiveness of Stephen's bizarre approach to directing. Many actors have described his disconcerting habit of reading a newspaper or even going out to the lavatory while they worked – and then coming back and giving them notes. When they complained that he hadn't seen what they had done he would simply retort that he knew how they acted anyway. And the notes were usually helpful. The director Clare Venables, now running the education department of the Royal Shake-speare Company, was a star student of his at Manchester University in the 1960s. She recalls that all his directing consisted of asking you questions. Stephen believed that in the round, if you had equally matched and above all unselfish actors, a scene with two or three people in it could more or less be allowed to take its own course. The job was less to direct productions than to train actors. Theatre, he argued, should be a passionate love affair between the actors and the audience. Everything else was incidental except the script. The director simply had to create an atmosphere in which the actor could create. He wasn't a great believer in improvising, unlike some advocates of the supremacy of the actor, though he did use it as a training exercise. Alan believes Stephen knew more about directing and play-writing than anyone else he has met but that he couldn't write himself and as a director he wasn't strong enough to sort out any problems. He adds something strongly reminiscent of his assessment of his father's dismissive attitude to much classical music: 'I think he felt rather cornered. Like a lot of people in theatre he didn't really like it very much.' Certainly he got bored quickly. He was a great cutter of plays, sometimes seeming to tear pages out almost at random because he didn't believe there was anything that didn't need cutting.

Alan was slow to acquire social graces. There was a party for all the theatre companies in town at which he was encouraged by a 'gnarled old stage manager' to drink vodka and cider, a lethal mixture. There was a particularly beautiful young ASM with the York Theatre Royal Company, sitting on a settee and wearing a low-cut dress, surrounded by personable young men. Alan remembers getting more and more resentful that she wasn't mixing with the other stage managers, while his older colleague goaded him with the taunt that he wouldn't be able to get near a woman who was so obviously destined for higher things. Eventually he went over to her, clutching a bottle of wine, and invited her to have a drink with him. She barely turned her head before politely declining. He insisted. She refused. He tried again, to no avail. So he poured the wine down her cleavage. Time stood still, as they say, before all hell broke loose. He woke up next morning, naked, on top of his own bed and rather badly bruised.

Some 40 years later he was at a London reception when he was introduced to Dame Diana Rigg. 'Ah! Alan Ayckbourn from Scarborough,' she said. 'No I won't have a drink, thank you.'

3 : A Term at Oxford

There was no winter employment in theatre in Scarborough then, and while Stephen Joseph drove lorries round London for breweries and coal merchants to raise money for his cause before coming home, having a bath and setting out to give a seminar on new writing somewhere, his actors sought jobs elsewhere. Among the professionals who had been to see the Scarborough company was the Greek director Minos Volanakis

who, with Frank Hauser, was running the resident company at Oxford
Playhouse. Minos said to Alan (in Alan's Greek-accented version) after the
show one night: 'I seen you twice. In one you are so good. So good. In the
other, so fucking awful. I think you must be very interesting.' He
responded in the way he still does to embarrassing encounters in the
theatre bar before, during or after the show: 'Thank you very much' (it has
a variety of intonations, including one for polite bewilderment). Minos
said: 'I think you should read for us.' So Alan went for an audition with
the two men. He was asked to read the part of a woman while Frank
Hauser read the part of a man who is seducing her. According to actors
who have read with him, when the auditioning boot has been on the
other foot, Alan reads women rather well. Frank was saying: 'Oh, no, no,
you're more frightened of me' and then: 'That's wonderful! We must use
you', so he left the flat with a promise. He was then given a 'recall', an
invitation to a second audition. This turned out to be with Minos on his
own and involved a serious, literally hands-on, examination of his
breathing. He found himself mentioning a non-existent girlfriend rather a
lot. But he got the job and played Willy Nilly Postman in Dylan Thomas's
Under Milk Wood, again as an acting ASM. There was a 'nice set of girls'
around too.

Then one night he was at dinner with Minos and Frank and the
dialogue went something like this:

FRANK: Wasn't he good tonight?

ALAN: Thank you very much.

MINOS: He was fucking awful, terrible, the worst thing on stage.

ALAN: Thank you. Can I have some more potatoes?

MINOS: I'm going to give you a part, Baby Boy, In *Mademoiselle Jaire*.
It's a most interesting play, much more interesting than what you are
doing.

ALAN: Oh, thank you very much.

FRANK: Well, I'm looking forward to seeing this!

Alan thought he had got his first starring role in the Belgian playwright
de Ghelderode's 1934 play on the New Testament story of Jairus's
daughter, raised from the dead by Jesus. The part turned out to be Second
Coffin Bearer in a 'terrible play' which featured Joss Ackland in a big red
wig as Christ. Alan's scene involved helping to carry a coffin downstairs
into a bedroom where a young woman sits on the bed. When the bearers
ask where the body is, the woman replies: 'I am.' Alan thought this was

quite funny – they had had no instructions or notes about the play from Minos who just said: 'Come on. Do it' – and decided to try out the 'double take' he had been practising, which is admittedly one of the crudest ways of getting a laugh in the theatre but an essential part of the comic actor's repertoire. So, they rehearsed. 'Where's the body?' 'I am.' Alan did his double take and heard a dreadful scream from Minos: 'I don't want to see such terrible things in a production of mine. You are a disgusting animal! Get off! Get off! Disgusting!' Alan duly left the stage and on the advice of the stage manager went off to busy himself quietly making props. This is what he continued to do throughout the rehearsal period, with the First Coffin Bearer complaining – but only privately – that he was now bumping the coffin downstairs on his own. They agreed among themselves that if nothing had been said by the final dress rehearsal Alan should go on when it came to the first night, which he did. 'Where's the body?' 'I am.' And before he could stop himself Alan did the double take and the audience erupted with laughter, for the first and last time that evening. After the performance was over Alan could hear Minos working his way up, telling everyone else they were wonderful, until he got to Alan in the top dressing-room: 'Very clever, Mr Smarty. But don't think it will always work.' Alan never worked with him personally again. And of course Alan today wouldn't permit an actor to do a sudden double take in an otherwise laughter-free play, should he be directing one.

The names of Frank Hauser and the Meadow Players are highly respected today but he remembers his time with them more for the anecdotes than the work. Mai Zetterling – later a film director but then an actress in the company – was also the epitome of what Swedish blondes were meant to look like. She was aware that she had more or less pole-axed Alan and called him into her dressing-room to unhook her dress while she pulled off the Elastoplast she used to keep her breasts in the position later achieved by Wonderbra. After ten years in boys' boarding-schools, no wonder the young ASM's hands shook.

But Frank Hauser was an excellent director for him to be observing at close quarters. Whereas Volanakis directed from a seat in the stalls, occasionally shouting things like 'act with your spine', Hauser was forever bounding up on to the stage with the actors. Alan eventually played a number of featured roles in Oxford, if not large ones, including an appearance in *Henry IV* by a playwright exerting a strong influence at the periphery of British theatre at the time, Pirandello. The Meadow Players season ended in the early summer but he was invited back for the following autumn, suggesting that his work had been more seriously useful than the anecdotes suggest. He also had an offer from Hazel Vincent Wallace in Leatherhead, but he was about to make one of the few conscious choices in his young life.

4 : A Guerrilla in the Revolution

Some of Ayckbourn's leading characters are rather passive figures, though they can create havoc by never saying 'no' to people who do seem to know what they want; they rarely strike out for themselves. Apart from writing, which generally takes place in an empty room or in the writer's head, this is a reflection of his own life up to the age of 19 and much of it since, though there must be some level at which he seeks out the people, mostly men, who push him gently in the right direction or protect him from disaster. He is a great believer in chance, as some of his plays also demonstrate, and has never been troubled by specific personal ambition or a career plan. Now, however, he made a conscious choice, rejecting the established companies in Oxford and Leatherhead and throwing in his lot with Stephen Joseph and the room over a library in Scarborough. This had little to do with Stephen's ideology and everything to do with his inspirational qualities.

The 1958 summer season was a typical, extraordinary Stephen Joseph mixture of programming, and the most influential of Alan's short working life. It included one of Frederick Knott's two lucrative thrillers, *Dial M for Murder*, with Alan as a whistling policeman, Dennis Cannan's *Captain Carvallo* (Alan as Private Gross), Pirandello's haunting short play *The Man With a Flower in His Mouth* (the supporting role of the valet) and a rarely performed French play, *Martine*, by Jean-Jacques Bernard. According to Desmond Pratt in the *Yorkshire Post*, Alan was 'forthright, matter-of-fact' as a stolid, unimaginative farmer whose unhappy young wife escapes briefly into the arms of a more sophisticated lover. As a valet pretending to be a Count in Marivaux's comedy of sexual manners, *The Game of Love and Chance*, he was further praised: 'A constant joy. There is an immensely happy abandon about his two-faced double-voiced impostor.' Acting more and more – and causing a few young hearts to flutter in Scarborough according to the then teenage schoolgirl Elizabeth Bell – he also appeared in Kataev's *Squaring the Circle* and David Campton's new play, *Ring of Roses*, of which more anon. This was the summer the company stopped playing the National Anthem before performances, causing a huge postbag of complaints to the local press and leading to the resignation of the treasurer of the Scarborough Theatre Guild, Maurice Plows, who – as luck would have it – was a bank manager. He would return much later to have his say in the theatre's affairs as a borough councillor and he is the inspiration of the pedantic councillor on the committee formed to celebrate the 'Pendon Twelve' in *Ten Times Table*. Alan had by now opened his own bank account, with Lloyds. When they asked him why he hadn't stayed with Barclays, given his Barclays scholarship to Haileybury, he told them: 'Because I don't want my stepfather looking at my account.'

He lived with two other male members of the company in a tiny house. One was married, and when his wife came up to visit, the sitting-room became out of bounds to the other two. Alan shared the bedroom, and when his room-mate started picking up Scarborough women Alan would be confined to the kitchen for the night, which he considered seriously unfair as he was paying the same rent as they were. Eventually he too found a girlfriend and went round to her house. The Scarborough company was still tiny. Although he placed enormous emphasis on new writing Stephen Joseph never had a resident writer as such because he couldn't afford anybody to do only one job. So David Campton, who was writing more than anybody else before Alan got started, had to play the small part of an innkeeper in J. B. Priestley's 'time' play, *I Have Been Here Before*. From that point on he was also an actor. And when Rodney Wood, who as well as directing some of the plays was the company's general manager, got another job outside theatre, Campton took on the job of general manager too and did it rather successfully, income equalling expenditure for the first time ever at the end of the season. Alan, who is never politically correct and values the fact as one of his creative resources, describes Stephen as 'being Jewish, very clever with his pennies', which seems not to have been any more true of Stephen than it is of Jews in general. As to casting, according to David Campton, Stephen chose actors partly on the basis of whether they laughed at his jokes or not (not a bad test of temperament as long as no one is faking it) and partly on the recommendation of friends. Otherwise he seems to have taken the view that anybody could do more or less anything in the theatre if they wanted to badly enough. He almost bore this out himself, being a good enough carpenter, on top of everything else, to make a perfectly good, properly jointed new step for the stage half an hour before the show was due to begin. So although Alan is probably unique in being capable of doing every job in the theatre (except perhaps front-of-house, Margaret Boden points out) he was growing up in a climate in which everyone was expected to try. Joan Macalpine, who joined the company because she wanted to be a playwright, was actually taken on because her application said she could drive a lorry. It's said that she signed her letter only with her initial, not her first name, and that because Stephen was too shy to look at anyone who came to see him, but stared at his blotter instead, he had appointed her before he knew she was a woman. She did drive the company lorry but with Alan alongside her to pull the heavy handbrake on, standing up and using both hands.

The extraordinary repertoire of plays that Stephen Joseph produced is also a key part of this climate. Some of it seems idiosyncratic now, to say the least. He became very frosty when Alan poured scorn on a largely forgotten play called *Victoria Regina* by Laurence Housman (in which Alan was said to be surprisingly lifelike as Prince Albert). Stephen said it was one of his favourite plays. Overall the repertoire is rather more ambitious than Ayckbourn would think appropriate to programmes for Scarborough now.

But the standard repertoire of theatre in the post-war period is relevant. Three major playwrights – Harold Pinter, John Osborne and Alan Ayckbourn – had all been acting before they made their writing debuts at the end of the 1950s. A fourth, Arnold Wesker, had done a variety of jobs, from furniture-maker to pastry-cook, but also acted as an amateur. None of them had been to university. In analyses of the revolution perceived to take place in the British theatre in the 1950s these four are rarely grouped together, for Ayckbourn, ten years younger than Osborne, didn't achieve prominence until fully a decade later, by which time other writers such as Joe Orton and Tom Stoppard were also on the scene. It has also been argued that the real revolution came less with Osborne's *Look Back in Anger* at the Royal Court theatre in 1956 than with Samuel Beckett's *Waiting for Godot*, directed by the youthful Peter Hall at the Arts Theatre in 1955 (it had already been seen in Paris, in French, in 1953). It divided its own cast, never mind the audience, confronting it at a sensitive time with the idea that God was dead and humanity was on its own.

The truth of all this rather depends on which revolution you are looking for, and on how you view the theatre of the post-war period before the middle 1950s. Peter Brook (*Threads of Time*, Methuen, 1998) has pointed out that there was a hunger for charm and for simply enjoyable experiences among audiences who had lived through the war and only recently discovered its full horrors. One of his own earliest successes was with the French playwright Jean Anouilh's *Ring Round the Moon*, which offered Paul Scofield an almost Ayckbournian double part as twin brothers, one of whom was likeable but a bit dull, the other sharply intelligent and less pleasant. But many of the plays on offer were far from the unambitious lightweights we are sometimes invited to believe. T. S. Eliot and Christopher Fry were writing thoughtful, psychological and spiritual verse dramas. Terence Rattigan's comedies dealt seriously with matters of class, morality and personal relationships. In *An Inspector Calls*, first produced in 1945 but set half a century before, J. B. Priestley targeted the old British hypocrisies and abuse of wealth and privilege; his rage matched the national mood, and the Conservative wartime Prime Minister Winston Churchill was swept from office the same year. Just into his sixties by 1956, Priestley could reasonably be categorised as an angry old man. Osborne's play, seen with hindsight, was no more political or angry than this. In form *Look Back in Anger* was a conventionally shaped three-act play. In content it now seems – like *Romeo and Juliet* or Noël Coward's *Private Lives* – to be a heartfelt drama about people who cannot live together but cannot live without each other either. But whereas Priestley's enemies were a northern bourgeois family to whom London theatre audiences had no difficulty in feeling superior, Osborne's lower-middle-class anti-hero sneered brilliantly at a nice old gentleman. Beckett's perceived nihilism (hotly disputed by Peter Brook and others) was more subversive, and more magnetically written, than his Absurdist predecessors. But 1956 was also the year of the Hungarian uprising against the Russians, the Suez adventure of Britain, France and Israel – and, for some of us, the discovery of rock 'n' roll. Allied to growing fears that nuclear weapons might bring about mass destruction, these events combined to create a revolutionary *mood*. It was in this context that the publicist of George Devine's English Stage Company at the Royal Court (where *Look Back in Anger* was premièred) coined the phrase Angry Young Man to cover a whole range of disparate artists, some of whom – the genuinely angry Joan Littlewood at Theatre Workshop, for instance – were neither men nor especially young. John Osborne in particular was rarely out of the newspapers, protesting in Trafalgar Square or firing off a 'Damn you, England' tirade for the middlebrow newspapers. All this was more written about in the London media than actually experienced in theatres. Most people did their theatregoing in regional towns or on Shaftesbury Avenue; despite Kenneth Tynan's announcement in the *Observer* that he couldn't love anyone who didn't want to see *Look Back in Anger* it wasn't a popular success. The destructive incomprehension which greeted Harold Pinter's arrival was even more obvious. It's my contention, therefore, that the revolution was actually achieved in the 1960s and that while it reflected social and political change what was most visible and audible about it was the fierce new energy and 'edge' it brought to the theatre.

With the partial democratisation of the education system through the 1944 Education Act and the partial democratisation of society through the war itself, new actors were coming into the theatre. John Osborne's Jimmy Porter, with his coruscating invective and thin-skinned alertness to public and private hurt, provided a lightning conductor for the energy of a whole series of actors, starting with Kenneth Haigh. It is no accident that Osborne's next major play, *The Entertainer*, appealed to the canny veteran Laurence Olivier himself as a vehicle. We cannot separate this new energy in the theatre, which didn't need charm or 'niceness', from the policy of building spanking new (and subsidised) civic theatres enabled by the Local Government Act 1948. Repertory theatres generally were moving from week-long to fortnightly or three-weekly runs of plays, trying to invest them with higher standards requiring longer rehearsal periods which argued a new seriousness of intention. There was a sardonic new realism in the novel (Kingsley Amis's *Lucky Jim* was published in 1954), the films of Lindsay Anderson and television drama, all taking up writers with 'provincial' accents and finding a like-minded audience.

The 'revolutionary' plays took a decade or so to reach most regional audiences but Stephen Joseph (the 'guerrilla' of Kenneth Tynan's phrase) was one of the first to present both the Beckett and the Osborne play. He also offered the Scarborough public Giraudoux (French new-minting of Greek myth in *Apollo of Bellac*) and Strindberg (*Easter* as well as the more common *Miss Julie*, or *Miss Julia* as Stephen preferred it to be titled). And he would be one of the first to take up – and give work to – Harold Pinter. But he also sought to give Scarborough books-balancing light relief like *Bell, Book and Candle* (John van Druten's American comedy about reasonably benevolent contemporary witchcraft) and described his task as attracting visitors whose holidays had been spoiled by the rain.

How sensitive was Ayckbourn to this revolutionary mood? What sort of a guerrilla? No political labels have been attached to him convincingly at any time, and he resisted Stephen's preoccupation with doomsday issues such as the bomb and over-population. He was aware that 'something pretty horrible' was going on in Hungary in the year he began to work in the theatre, and thoroughly baffled by Suez, having studied history in a climate where the British were portrayed as always in the right. Directly influenced (dramaturgically but not politically) by Pinter, he would become the most formally inventive of that gang of four, and he belongs absolutely to the revolution because he changed for ever the theatre's currency in relation to female characters. Rather before popular feminism and other movements made the case that the personal *was* political he had started to dramatise it. He also showed us almost from the start that comedy and tragedy, so far from being separate genres, were as organically connected as Siamese twins. But the crucial quality of these actor-playwrights, it seems to me, is an understanding of the need to grip an audience on a line-by-line basis for two hours. All of them knew first-hand what it felt like for an audience's attention to slide away. All understood, in a way less viscerally important to playwrights who take a more intellectual and 'willed' route to the craft, that the actor's energy has to engage the audience. Anger is wonderfully energising. So is the alliance of comedy and pain. And so is masterly experiment with the way a story is told.

Bertolt Brecht's company, the Berliner Ensemble, had also visited London a few years previously and influenced many writers including Osborne and another of Stephen Joseph's protégés, Robert Bolt. But Ayckbourn has still never seen a Brecht play; the German doesn't figure, directly anyway, in the practical education he was having while other writers were at university.

Chapter 3

Birth of a writer

1 : I Could Do Better . . .

Ayckbourn always says that while he was playing Nicky, the young warlock in *Bell, Book and Candle*, he complained to Stephen Joseph about the roles he was getting and was told that if he wanted a better part he should write a play with one in. Stephen would stage it, if it was any good. A pleasing story, but *Bell, Book and Candle* was actually on at the same time as Alan's first play for the company, *The Square Cat*. On 17 June 1959, the *Yorkshire Post* reviewed the John van Druten play: 'Alan Ayckbourn has improved in technique since he was last here . . . gives an amusing interpretation.' And the same day's *Yorkshire Evening Post* announces *The Square Cat* by Alan Ayckbourn and Christine Roland.

David Campton told me that a year earlier, 1958, Alan was in his play *Ring of Roses* (later *Roses Round the Door*) when the complaint was made to Stephen and the challenge thrown down. Campton bears no grudge. The play had been written at Stephen's request; he'd asked for something Hermione Gingold could star in to make them all a lot of money. 'It was very thin,' says Campton now. Presumably Ayckbourn shaped the story so as not to hurt a friend and colleague and that is how he now remembers it. John van Druten, though London-born of Dutch extraction, was in America, rich and able to look after himself. It was Dutch Week in Scarborough during the run of *Bell, Book and Candle* and one night Alan came on-stage with a tulip in his button-hole adding the ad lib: 'Just popped along to the bulb fields', which got a laugh from the audience and a bemused look from Dona Martyn as his sister, the lovely witch. He was getting bored and needed things to go wrong to make them interesting. It was a sign, he now recognises, that he should move on. Off-stage, there had already been a major development.

Six weeks before the notice in *Bell, Book and Candle* (only amusing, eh?) the *Yorkshire Post* had announced his marriage to Christine Roland, another member of the acting company, at Chelsea Old Church. He was

20 and she a little older. Lolly's story was that she told him that he was much too young to get married but that he said he was going to do it anyway and stalked off, only to return huffily when the priest who was to marry them pointed out that he was too young to be married without parental permission. Alan dismisses this story: 'There couldn't be any question of us not getting married. We had to.'

Christine – now known to her friends as Christina – had joined the previous year with several seasons of rep and children's theatre already behind her. She had met Alan at a pre-rehearsal cast party, noticing a pale and thin young man who said little but who made her laugh when he did speak. They were playing opposite each other and consequently spent a great deal of time together. After the 1958 season was over, Christine wrote:

> He rented a tiny flat and we enjoyed a happy and snowy Christmas, including an out-of-work actor who arrived on the doorstep with no money and nowhere to stay and who later appeared as 'HB' in *The Honeymoon*, a play Alan wrote shortly after our marriage the following year.

The Honeymoon seems to have sunk without trace and Alan thinks it may never have got further than a reading anyway. Alan and Christine remain good friends and it is a considerable tribute to the two of them that their hasty marriage didn't completely wreck their lives and those of their sons. Alan describes his immaturity at the time by saying that switching almost overnight from a boys' boarding-school to a theatre company made him 'like a boy let loose in a sweet shop. You just tend to grab the biggest jar and run, don't you? Never stop to consider there might be other jars on the shelf. This'll do! I'll marry this one!' He told the *Daily Mail* in 1991 that he fell in love with all the young women he worked with, but with one of them more than the rest.

In fact he had already been engaged to a stage management colleague; she had been in a half-hearted relationship with another man who had left the company with the time-honoured instruction to Alan to 'look after her'. Alan did so to such effect that when the man returned he and she were engaged, though when Alan met her parents her father begged him not to marry her. As it turned out, she broke the engagement off after a few months.

Theatre mythology, which Alan thinks is probably true, has it that he passed the ring on to Christine the very next day. They were on the autumn tour after the Scarborough season when whoever was handling publicity in Leicester suggested that an engagement in the company would get a few column inches in the local press. As he and Christine seemed friendly, why not announce theirs? They could always get disengaged later. Facetious reminiscences – he told another interviewer that he had married the second woman he had met 'to see what they were like' – reveal a much later perception of this early marriage as something that needs to be explained. By today's standards he, along with his generation, was desperately inexperienced; after boarding-school had come good-natured girls, game for a snog in the props cupboard, and the teasing proximity of Mai Zetterling's breasts. However well they were brought up, teenage men and women floundered when they were whisked from the dry land of celibacy to the deep waters of a sexuality they were expected to portray and eagerly longed to indulge. Additionally, the very fact that Alan had never had the emotional security of a happy family atmosphere or the sustained love and undivided attention of a woman made him more anxious to achieve it for himself. He snatched at his opportunity when it came. In other words, being close to an unhappy marriage was a reason for, not against, following the same path. His half-brother Chris also got married at 19 (that marriage failed too). In any case marriage was what you did in the 1950s; although most people had much longer engagements, in those pre-contraceptive days there were fewer socially acceptable intermediate stages – from one-night stands via shared holidays to living together – with which to test a developing relationship. There were no such stages once the woman was pregnant.

The fact that they wrote *The Square Cat* together is often overlooked although Alan makes no secret of Christine's help. The pseudonym (Roland Allen) under which it was produced is a combination of both their names. Christine's parents lived in Bray, in Berkshire, and Christine told the local press there (who liked to give Ayckbourn an extra 'e' on the end, setting an example since followed by many) that they had written the play in a fortnight and that they hoped to have another ready for Christmas, not to mention a series of six half-hour scripts for television.

Alan had been writing all his short life, at both schools and at home in Sussex, but much of what he had written had been essentially revue material, good enough to make friends and family laugh but not possessing the musculature of a full-length play. He had shown Stephen Joseph some juvenile attempts to write like Pirandello and – a more lasting influence – Ionesco. 'Yes,' Stephen had said, 'that's a Pirandello play all right.' He had also done his share of what he calls 'Damn you, Mother' writing – the most widespread expression of Angry Young Man literature of which one of the best examples (ironically, as the new wave was beginning to wash him away) had been Noël Coward's early play *The Vortex* (1924). Alan's mother had suggested an agent to him – Joan Ling – who was bombarded with these early scripts and who implored him to write less. No one is more conscious than Ayckbourn, as he tries to advance the cause of young writers, that he completed a good many plays, probably eight, that never saw the light of day at all. 'Now,' he remarks, 'it is a matter of three strikes and you're out.'

The Square Cat was exactly the right vehicle for Alan in emerging publicly from his middle-class shell: a rock 'n' roll idol. The play would not only meet the need to glory in his virtuosity but explore it. Michael Billington and others have pointed out that *The Square Cat* contains seeds of Alan's later preoccupations as a writer: the unpredictability of characters who are nevertheless psychologically recognisable and a sympathetic view of the plight of an unfulfilled woman locked in a marriage that has gone stale; it also – in the action if not the language – suggests that the satisfying of women may be a rather more demanding proposition than is always acknowledged, and that life can turn sour for men too. Alice, a 42-year-old mother-of-two, fantasises about a young pop guitarist and singer, Jerry Wattis; less probably, she makes an assignation with him in the house of an absent relative. She only wants to dance with him. He, presumably, hopes for the worst. Their plans go awry when her husband turns up, angry and jealous, and so does her son (rather stupid) and her daughter (very pretty). But the rock star has turned out to be a Jekyll-and-Hyde figure: alternately a rather timid youth in spectacles and suit whose real name is Arthur Brummage, and the rampant lust-on-legs of rock legend when he slings his instrument around his neck. The shy self duly falls in love with the daughter, and the embittered husband reveals that he too was once a romantic dreamer. Untypically it all ends happily but the sadly comic central situation takes on a farcical quality when the leading actor has to play both sides of the hero more or less simultaneously and is made to change from one to the other before our very eyes. In the Library, that meant within a few feet of the audience.

Stephen Joseph offered some dramaturgical advice – useful on structure, completely useless on additional gags – and directed the play himself, not minding that none of his suggestions for new lines was incorporated. As Jerry Wattis/Arthur Brummage, Alan won immediate applause for his bout of rock 'n' roll. This didn't really add up to much. The intention was to learn five chords in two weeks from a teacher called Donny but they seem to have stuck at two. They picked a song for which this would be enough and when it came to the opening night Alan was too nervous to get out even the title words of the song, 'I Gave My Love a Cherry'. He struck precisely one chord and nodded at the stage manager on the lighting desk to put him out of his misery with a swift blackout. On other nights he played both chords and sometimes managed a whole line of the song.

The tradition is that there is little merit in his youthful plays, and he has tried to collect all the scripts so that they don't get unauthorised productions and damage his reputation. But this 'cool comedy in three acts' (actually played without an interval) was rather successful. It was brought back later in the season at the expense of David Campton's *Frankenstein* (whose monster provided a part with very few words to learn for Stephen Joseph himself). Campton – a man of distinctly Pickwickian appearance even then – played the husband in *The Square Cat*. The company also included Dona Martyn as Alice, Faynia Jeffery (who as Faynia Williams was to become a distinguished and original director) as the daughter Susan, and William Elmhirst as the son. The latter belonged to the immensely wealthy and liberal Yorkshire family who endowed Dartington Hall in Devon. Alan was next to him in the dressing-room when a £5-note appeared on the floor between them. Alan knew it wasn't his – he rarely even saw a fiver – but Elmhirst swore blind it wasn't his either and made Alan take it; an informal and tactful piece of private patronage of the artist. Christine's input into that first play, Alan says, was substantial. Most of the actual lines were his but she particularly helped to shape the plot and her acting experience was valuable in timing, structure, pace and practical matters like the length of time it takes an actor to do a costume change and get back on stage. That December their first son, Steven, was born and named (with a spelling change) after Stephen Joseph. The latter continued to put everybody to use, and Christine was now assigned to wardrobe duties but she was too shy ever to take a man's inside leg measurement and some 'very wooden performances' were caused by tight trousers that made it impossible for an actor to move. In *Ten Times Table* there is a character called Philippa, too shy to speak loud enough for anyone to hear, who trails round everyone involved in the local pageant with a needle and thread, conducting running repairs to their costumes. It is an indication of the way Alan's psyche offers the raw material back to him when he needs it that he wrote this part for the excellent comedienne Diane Bull and has no memory of its being inspired by Christine. Her active interest in theatre probably and understandably began to evaporate at this time.

Although the degree to which Alan's perception of his mother's and his stepfather's marriage influenced his portrayal of unhappy relationships is well documented, Christine's parents also contributed to Alice and her husband, Sidney. Charles and Elaine Roland had had Christine relatively late and she was a much-loved only child. Her father in particular was very shocked at the speed of the marriage and the fact that she was pregnant. Their relationship with Alan soon settled down but he always got on better with Elaine than Charles because although she was in terrible pain from arthritis she was 'incredibly jolly'. She was also quite a religious woman, though, and plainly sometimes thought Alan irresponsible. He recalls telling her a joke she didn't really approve of. She responded: 'I wish I could laugh at that, Alan', a line which he gleefully stored away for later use. Charles was of working-class origins and had substantially educated himself from books, with the result that he often didn't know how to pronounce the words he understood and dared not use them in conversation. He also had a gift for painting but had 'sensibly' devoted his working life to insurance. Alan believes this led to an unspoken resentment on his part, and an unspoken guilt on the part of his wife and daughter, permeating the household. He identifies as a further source of tension a feeling that the lively Elaine had, as a young woman, had the pick of the more exciting young men around but had decided to marry the safe one, and this had led to her feeling a little smothered by the marriage. The grim irony is that when Charles got to 60 and was able to retire and take up painting again, his eyesight started to fail. The 'probably selfish' lesson Alan took from that was not to give up what he enjoyed doing when suggestions were made that now that he had a wife and family he should get a proper job. Charles and Elaine fed the despairing view of marriage that emerges in the plays.

The Square Cat is set in a country house near London. Ayckbourn's fictional Pendon, which slides around the country and from village to town and back again, according to each play's demands, was originally located in Berkshire or Buckinghamshire; in other words close to Bray. And the name suggests both 'written about' and 'hemmed in'. But it would be wrong to make the Roland household sound unhappier than it was and Alan's mother-in-law steadfastly typed out his early plays on an old office Underwood so that they could be sent off to Windsor Rep nearby. Many years later Windsor's shrewdly populist director, John Counsell, purveyor of comedy to the middle classes since 1938, would ask why Alan hadn't submitted plays to him since he had local connections. Alan pointed out that he had probably sent in about 20. Although Charles and Elaine fussed over their grandchildren, and this brought out Alan's irresponsible streak, their home – a kind of large, prefabricated building left over from the war, rather like a Nissen hut but with a good garden – was a great resource for the young family otherwise confined to the poverty and near-squalor of actors' digs. They were as supportive as they could be. When Alan and Christine eventually went their separate ways Elaine remarked amicably enough that however bad things had occasionally been, the relationships had also been productive.

Looking back at *The Square Cat* now, Alan says:

> It was funny and it was what was needed here [Scarborough]. It wasn't that I sat down and consciously thought about it this way but that I do tend instinctively to respond to a market. Due to the encouragement of Stephen I've always had audiences if not uppermost then at least prominent in my mind. I would never dream of writing a play unless I considered what the audience might or might not enjoy at some stage. I might then decide to baffle them or push it a bit beyond them but I would always have them in the frame. It sounds like something everybody would do but I think there are writers who don't, for better or worse, consider the audience at all; they are much more concerned with what's happening at their end.

Ayckbourn and his young family were as close to starving in the days when he started writing professionally as anyone actually in work can be, but the idea that he wrote primarily to make money is absurd. He wrote and still writes to engage with people, something he finds as artistically profitable as it is socially difficult. He earned £47 as his first royalty payment – the figure is etched in his memory – equivalent to four weeks' wages as an actor at the highest rate he would ever achieve in the Stephen Joseph companies. He thought it rather handsome at the time, but he would have had to write 13 plays a year at that rate to earn the same meagre annual income as an actor in full-time employment. In all, around 2,000 people saw his writing debut and no critic signalled the arrival of a great new writing talent though they acknowledged the effectiveness of his performance.

2 : National Service: Stalled before Take-off

Conscription, introduced in wartime, remained in force in Britain until the early 1960s. Alan should have been called up for National Service when he was 18 but had managed to dodge it effectively for two years by always being on the move. But in 1959, aged 20, he was tracked down to Scarborough and an official was sent to make sure he attended a kind of assessment exam.

He was handed a paper with a series of multiple choice questions. Thinking he was being pretty clever he decided to tick all the most obviously wrong answers, though one of them turned out to be right, which was a bit of a shock. The young man sitting at the next desk, who really wanted to be accepted, copied all his answers in spite of Alan's best efforts to discourage him. Instructed to indicate which of the forces he wanted to join, he ticked the Royal Air Force, giving as his reason that RAF personnel wore shoes whereas army and navy uniforms included boots. He sat back, confident that nobody would want him.

The RAF recruiting officer found Alan's paper – 1 out of 100 – unusually interesting in view of the fact that he also knew Alan had two 'A' levels: 'I'm sure Haileybury wouldn't be very proud of you.' The officer was inspired by this to try to tempt Alan (with the possibility of flying Vampire fighters) into signing on for more than the standard two years, and making the RAF at least a temporary career. If he went in as a National Serviceman he would have to settle for something boring like medical orderly or radar operative. Alan thought radar operative sounded pretty good because it meant working mostly in bunkers, less risky in the event of the nuclear attack which had become such a vivid fear at the end of the 1950s. As he fainted at the sight of blood, he said, he wouldn't be a very useful medical orderly anyway.

For a while he heard nothing. National Service was known to be on the way out, and he hoped they had either forgotten about him or were simply not going to bother with this awkward customer. Roland Allen duly completed the play promised for Christmas, *Love After All*. Then in January 1960 he got a letter telling him to report to RAF Cardington in Bedfordshire and he knew he would be away for at least eight weeks' basic training. He and Christine and the month-old baby were staying at Stephen Joseph's London flat and he toyed with the idea of trying to break his foot in the mechanism of the lift but didn't have the nerve. He said his goodbyes and was delivered by a lorry to what seemed to be the middle of nowhere. New arrivals were herded into a classroom where he took a seat at the back. When their names were called they had to say how long they had signed up for. Amid the varying answers – 4 years, 7 years, 15 years – came his: 'As short as possible, sir.' He got his laugh. He had turned up a day early with the regular servicemen who were making the armed forces a career. The conscripts weren't due for another 24 hours. He offered to go away, but having got him the RAF was not ready to let him escape. He spent the evening with a bunch of regulars who were enjoying themselves enormously with the story of a wife's revenge on a hated drill sergeant, a womaniser who also beat her up. When he had gone away on a three-week course she had stayed on in the barracks and shared her unhappiness with what seemed like every man in the hut. So this was the real world! When they found out he was in the theatre they all gave their addresses to him and he never wrote to any of them.

Eventually a corporal put him on his own in a Nissen hut with 60 beds and an unlit stove and told him to get some kip. He picked a bed about ten down from the doorway, to avoid any draughts, put on his new RAF blue pyjamas and got in. As usual he quickly fell asleep but soon afterwards woke up, freezing; he stripped the blankets from six other beds and piled them on his own. The next time he woke it was to the sound of bugles and men stamping on the parade ground. It was half past eight and he now spotted a large notice in the hut reading ALL MEN WILL BE ON THE PARADE GROUND AT 6.30. Another gave inch-precise instructions on how bedding was to be folded. With half a dozen beds to rebuild to military specifications he saw the corporal at the door and started apologising for not hearing any bugles at any time. But the corporal was another in the long line of men and women who have been seized by an unexpected outbreak of kindliness at the sight of Alan. It had worked even in Alan's sleep: he had looked so peaceful, said the corporal, that looking in on him before dawn he had decided to leave him. He sent him across to the NAAFI (forces' canteen) for breakfast at his leisure, sent him back there again when the arrival of his fellow conscripts was delayed, kept him apart from a batch of 'high-spirited' Glaswegians, and once he was completely awash with NAAFI tea introduced him to his fellow conscripts of whom only one – an art student – shared his desire to get out as fast as possible. The others were looking forward to an adventure.

Alan was put in charge of the hut and he was just congratulating himself on being spotted as officer material when it was made clear exactly what was expected of him. His main responsibility was making sure there was enough coal for the stove, and for every bucket he ordered he was to order one extra, which went straight to the corporal who presumably sold it on the black market. Army pay was terrible but many men came out better off than they went in and once again Alan's brush with responsibility was mildly corrupt.

Eventually the time came for his medical examination. They took some blood from his earlobe and he fainted as promised. He had also fainted on the parade ground when the buckle of his braces dug into his chest; he thought it was a rib sticking out. Next he was to join one of four queues for the doctors conducting personal medicals: a lottery. Alan saw a man with two perforated eardrums and a host of other ailments passed fit for service and his heart sank, knowing that he had nothing wrong with him except a slight knee injury he was hoping to play up. He joined a queue at random and met a well-spoken young doctor with the sort of assistant then labelled an 'oik' by the officer classes.

DOCTOR: Strip orf. Stand on the glass mat. Got anything to report?

ALAN: Very peculiar knee, sir.

DOCTOR: Oh yes? (*Pause*) Oh. I see you write.

ALAN: Well yes, I do a bit of writing. I've written a couple of plays.

DOCTOR: I'm writing. I'm writing my memoirs.

ALAN: Oh right. (*Thinks*: He's writing his memoirs at 23?)

DOCTOR: Have you got a good agent? Anyone you think I could send it to?

ALAN: Well, you could send it to my agent. (*Thinks*: See where sending it to Peggy Ramsay will get you.)

DOCTOR: Thanks very much. D'you really want to do this?

ALAN: No.

DOCTOR: Tell me about the knee again.

ALAN: Well, it's –

DOCTOR: Well, I haven't examined it, but I can tell you from here I don't like the look of it.

ALAN: Really?

DOCTOR: No, no, not at all. Could you walk to that wall, unaided?

ALAN: I'll have a go for you, sir, but –

DOCTOR: I don't think you could.

ALAN: I think I might sort of fall down round about that chair.

DOCTOR: I've got some bad news for you. I'm afraid we can't take you. Because what'll happen is, you'll be marching around on the first day, and that knee's going to give way and we're going to be paying you a pension for the rest of your life. I can't allow the RAF into that sort of financial obligation.

ALAN: Oh, damn.

DOCTOR: I'm sorry. Absolutely not.

OIK: Nobody ever did anything like that for me.

DOCTOR: Because you're an oik, Wilkins, and what possible use are you out in the real world? You're better off in here. Well, thank you, I'll expect my cheque in the morning.

ALAN: Thank you very much, sir.

(*Exit, limping heavily.*)

If this scene had appeared in *The Goon Show*, Peter Sellers would have played the doctor, Harry Secombe the innocent hero and Spike Milligan the unfortunate oik.

The next day he found a glum regimental sergeant-major sitting in his hut. Looking at the discharge form, he said: 'Well, good fucking riddance. We don't want you in the fucking National Service – it's a professional organisation.' When Alan got to the gates he just started running. Someone called out that there was a bus to the station every 20 minutes but he wasn't risking that. He ran all the way, clutching his precious piece of paper. He caught the train and got home to Bray where Christine and the baby had taken refuge. Three weeks later he got a letter inviting him, after his long and successful service, to join the RAF Club.

The episode has become a terrific set-piece anecdote, complete with accents and soundtrack. It has been shaped, edited and polished. There is some small variation in the detail between the 1981 version told to Ian Watson and the 1999 version I was given, and Peggy Ramsay didn't in fact become his agent until much later. With some writers such stories would go more or less wholesale into their work.

As soon as he got home he telephoned Stephen Joseph, who said: 'I've just lost a stage manager. He walked out. Do you want to rejoin? We're in Newcastle. Can you be here by two o'clock because we've got to light tonight's show and I'd love you to do it because you know what I'm like on ladders, old chum.' Unfortunately he failed to specify Newcastle under Lyme. Alan set off for Newcastle upon Tyne. By the time he got to the one in the Potteries it was six o'clock and he was four hours late. He opened the doors of the municipal hall, ran upstairs to the room in which the theatre was set up, saw Stephen standing there and opened his mouth: 'If you're asking how the lighting went,' said Stephen, 'I fell off the ladder. I not only fell off the ladder, I broke my arm. I not only broke my arm, I broke the ladder. I also landed on the general office which was behind the rostra.' He had smashed the typewriter and dented the cash box.

3 : Back to Basics

The Square Cat had been playing successfully with another actor in the role written for Alan, Barry Boys. It and *Love After All* had been included in the group of plays taken on tour. The theatre's archive shows *Love After All* as directed by Stephen Joseph but Alan says it was actually given to Clifford Williams, later a distinguished director at the RSC who achieved his greatest fame with Kenneth Tynan's revue celebrating permissiveness, *Oh, Calcutta!* His production of Strindberg's *Miss Julie* was famous in Scarborough for the graphic way in which he pointed out to the cast that it was all about sex.

Love After All was, according to Ayckbourn himself, pinched from *The Barber of Seville*, but has been translated into 'a farce set in gay Edwardian days when love, folly and disguise cause a tangle of personal relationships', to quote the publicity. The miserly Scrimes (David Campton again) is trying to marry off his daughter (Dona Martyn) to a rich heir rather than the man of her choice, described on the cast list as 'Jim Jones, a hero', the part Alan had also written for himself. It involved a series of disguises as Jim attempted to sneak himself into the house as a string of different men and, once, a woman: another part for an actor to show off in. An anonymous critic in the *Scarborough Evening News* thought it technically better than *The Square Cat*, if not as funny. The *Guardian* found it 'lacking in wit'. But when Alan himself eventually appeared in the revival, 'leaping from disguise to disguise' he scored 'a tremendous character acting hit', according to the *Evening News*. His tall, thin woman with horn-rimmed glasses and the longest string of false pearls in the history of cross-dressing was 'alarmingly convincing', according to Christine Ayckbourn. David Campton says of *Love After All* and *The Square Cat*: 'They were both good nights out. Audiences fell about, we didn't always know what at, which is the mark of good comedy.' The revival had a new director whom Stephen sacked after two shows because he'd already spent the whole season's budget. Alan also points out darkly that the newcomer had decided to change quite a lot of the play, including bringing it up to date and altering the rather jokey names: 'I don't think it actually gained very much as a result of that.'

In that winter of 1959–60, when he had his brief affair with the RAF, the Scarborough company appeared in Hemel Hempstead, Southampton, London (Fitzroy Square again) and at Dartington in addition to Newcastle under Lyme. The repertoire was astonishing: the two plays by Alan; three by David Campton (*The Gift of Fire*, which was the Frankenstein story renamed so that audiences wouldn't think of it as something which ought to be in the cinema, *The Lunatic View* and *Memento Mori*); Sartre's *Huis Clos/In Camera*; *Alas Poor Fred* which introduced the writing of James Saunders; *Wuthering Heights* (adapted by Jurneman Winch); and a double bill of *Miss Julie* and *Viennese Interlude*, a one-act play about Strindberg by one of the original Angry Young Men, Colin Wilson. The company performed in towns where there was no history of producing theatre so for many members of the audience the whole experience was new. Small amounts of money had started to become available from the Arts Council of Great Britain, as it then was. Stephen also, during a winter break, imported Racine's *Phèdre* to Scarborough with a rather grand company headed by Margaret Rawlings: a reminder that his own enthusiasm was for theatre that engaged with the audience but was by no means simply populist.

Stephen would encourage his authors in the direction of certain issues, which is why David Campton's writing suddenly became preoccupied with the Bomb, whereas his real strengths later turned out to be in the field of personally dramatic stories. David took notice of Stephen's suggestions. Alan went his own way. Stephen next tried to engineer a collaboration between the two, and gave them an extraordinary brief. But before it happened there was to be another significant meeting of talents, a further testimony to Stephen's extraordinarily catholic vision of what theatre could be.

He invited Harold Pinter, smouldering from the critical reaction to his early plays, to direct *The Birthday Party*, rehearsing in London and then performing in Birmingham and Leicester. It would be nice to report that his fellow writers immediately recognised Pinter's powerful theatrical genius but Ayckbourn says: 'It was absolute gobbledegook to me.' And David Campton: 'It might as well have been a Japanese Noh play for all the sense it made to me.' Pinter had to cast from the existing Scarborough company and he met them in a pub in Brewer Street in Soho. Alan was cast as Stanley, the victim who is taken away by the enigmatic gangsters, Goldberg and McCann. As they started to rehearse, Alan recalls:

One got, first of all, extremely suspicious of him, because we thought he was a complete charlatan, and then as we began to proceed there was a passion behind his eyes ... in his eyes anyway his play had been completely misdirected before and the fact that it had got a severe roasting merely justified his self-belief, which seemed quite strong. So we were swept along by him. When we opened in Birmingham he proved gobsmackingly right. I think by that time we were convinced, although we didn't know what the audience would make of it.

In the course of rehearsals Ayckbourn had asked Pinter about Stanley's background: parents, upbringing, education, etc. The reply he got was: 'Mind your own bloody business. Just say the lines.' That at least is how Alan remembers it, with enormous glee. Recalling it in 1999 Harold Pinter said: 'I can't believe I actually did say that but it's too good a story to deny.' His wife, Lady Antonia Fraser, remarked: 'It sounds rather like you, Harold.' If actors ask Alan now about their characters' history he will usually invent something on the spot if it seems likely to help, but essentially he shares Pinter's view that the job is to get on with the play you've got, that the useful material is all in there somewhere, waiting to be brought out.

In 1962, Pinter came to Scarborough for a production of *The Caretaker*. Alan remained determined to learn what he could from the older writer and invited him to the pub during rehearsals. As they sat drinking, a stranger came in and told them an agonised story about his temper finally snapping with his bullying mother-in-law. He had hidden his pay packet from her and she was looking for it up a chimney when the man had seized her legs and jammed her further up. Harold gave him the measured advice to go and fetch her down before she inhaled soot and he found himself on a murder charge, which he accepted gratefully. After he left Alan said: 'What an extraordinary man!' A pause, and then Harold's bass chimed in: 'Was he?'

Pinter and Ayckbourn grew up in utterly different worlds. In the East End of London even after the war there were fascists on the streets. If you were Jewish, simply to exchange a greeting with these thugs could earn you a beating. One result was near-monosyllabic dialogue which gave nothing away. Family life in rural Sussex had quite different problems. But both playwrights start as realists, observing the world in which they live, and then turning up the heat on their characters. Ayckbourn invites us to see the comedy in the personal politics, Pinter the menace. Ayckbourn creates infinite variation in narrative form, Pinter refines it. But each deals with brutality observed but not necessarily explained. Each is pretty determined to have the words spoken as they are written for the very good reason that rhythms and sense and style have an organic relationship with content, and have been crafted with care and purpose. And one of Ayckbourn's exercises with fledgling writers, if a scene lacks edge, is to suggest that in a duologue between two characters it is worth seeing what happens if you take one character's lines away completely, so that the other character's words are greeted with the blank wall of silence. It is surprising how often the result sounds like Harold Pinter.

They got on well as individuals and Pinter, discovering that Ayckbourn was a writer, offered 'to get me in with Radio 3'. BBC Radio drama at that time and for a generation afterwards was the great patron of writers who were badly handled by the theatre. Nothing came of it because, Alan says, 'I wasn't really Radio 3 material.' It was still the Third Programme then and more culturally elitist than it is now. Harold also chuckled merrily when, at the end of the season, Ayckbourn and his magic tape recorder were involved in the first, and probably best, of 'two thousand million take-offs of Harold Pinter's dialogue'. Sadly, it doesn't survive.

Pinter and Ayckbourn are not especially close today. But each of these diffident, vulnerable and privately generous men is in his element as a writer-director surrounded by actors, creating the kind of safe environment that makes work hardly feels like work at all. There is genuine mutual respect. But let us not overdo this: Alan is as likely to join a political grouping as he is to fly to Pluto – which he would prefer, curious about the gadgetry, as long as he knew what the food was going to be like.

Ayckbourn happily accepts the influence of Pinter, and regards just doing *The Birthday Party* as a turning point in his own career. Pinter was in turn influenced by Beckett, while Ayckbourn once actually dropped off to sleep during his own performance in *Waiting for Godot*. But in one respect Beckett changed the expectations of theatre audiences to Ayckbourn's ultimate benefit. There is no 'closure' for the two tramps at the end of the play; their situation (and ours) will just continue. Ayckbourn would have difficulty ending his plays in his turn, but that became a virtue, part of what he has to say about life; it goes on regardless.

Paying tribute to Ayckbourn on his sixtieth birthday Pinter said that at first he thought it a mistake that Alan was going to concentrate on writing rather than acting: 'He was born to play Hamlet. About three thousand plays later,' said Pinter, 'I must conclude that he made the right decision. What he has given to the theatre is immeasurable.'

Ayckbourn never did play Hamlet though he was an effective Claudius. When he returned to duties in Scarborough his roles included Heathcliff in a revival of *Wuthering Heights*; it brought him what seems to have been his first ever really bad review, and he was hurt: 'Said I was unattractive and spindly and not at all our critic's idea of Heathcliff, who should be good-looking and dashing.' Alan telephoned the editor and demanded a confrontation with the anonymous critic. The review, he said, was a personal attack on him physically and he wanted to take it up with him. He threatened to take it further if this opportunity was denied, though he wasn't at all certain where he would take it. The critic wouldn't be available until late afternoon, or more precisely until after school came out. The regular critic had been double-booked and had handed the tickets on to a schoolgirl friend. Alan says he has never taken much notice of critics since: 'After that, pinch of salt time.' This didn't stop him remembering, 40 years later, exactly what the *Guardian* had said about *Love After All* but it confirmed his feeling that he was tiring of performance and he went off to write his third play for the company.

Why Stephen Joseph thought it would be a good idea for Ayckbourn and Campton to collaborate nobody knows. The second part of his idea seemed even barmier, even to the devoted Ayckbourn. 'Stephen just said: "Um . . . will you be putting any ballet into your play?" And I said "WHAT!" and he said: "Ballet." Well, I pointed out that I didn't write ballet but Stephen just said I should.' Stephen had met a choreographer – Gerard Bagley, who was directing the British Dance Drama Company – and liked his work. Realising that there would never be the funds to pay for them to work together properly, he proposed that the dancers should rehearse in Birmingham, where they were based, while the actors rehearsed in Scarborough. They first met at the dress rehearsal. The collaboration between playwrights never came to anything but David Campton did get as far as a basic synopsis taken from Mary Norton's classic for children, *The Borrowers*, in which the tiny people living under a house's floorboards equip themselves with items 'borrowed' from the humans. Ayckbourn asked: 'Well, how do you write a ballet anyway?' and when told to supply a story-line for a choreographer to work from, came up with a reasonably ingenious idea: the actors in *Dad's Tale* would be the occupants of a house from which items were inclined to disappear without explanation, and the scenes in which items were spirited away would be danced without words. Martin tells the story of a family Christmas in his childhood when hopes of a decent dinner were slight until the neighbours' provisions were delivered to them by mistake. The author dismisses a sentimental alternative to Martin's version in which the family claims the food was taken straight back to the rightful owners, who shared it. The play ends with Dad (Stanley Page in his first Ayckbourn role) casting doubt on the Tinies' existence. 'Emily,' he says to Martin's aunt, 'if you saw little people, I'm a budgerigar.' And on come the Tinies to grab hold of Dad's arms and flap them up and down as he flies off into the dark.

Stephen had scheduled the play for his new winter slot, aiming it at an audience of children, but hadn't investigated whether there was such an audience or how to reach it. *Dad's Tale* opened in the few days between the schools breaking up and Christmas Day. The big pantomimes had already negotiated all the potential party bookings with schools and big employers long since. There was, Alan says, an audience of four, which included Stephen and PB. Alan's own attempt to play seven different parts in a range of moustaches did lead a woman in the sparse audience one night to shout: 'Oh no! Not him again.' He took comfort in the presence of some pretty dancers.

But he was beginning to feel disenchanted in spite of an acting success in the other play of that winter season, Peter Shaffer's *Five Finger Exercise*. He played a German tutor and an accent or a disguise always helped him. But Desmond Pratt's review in the *Yorkshire Post*, apart from indicating that Pratt himself has also begun to 'adopt' Alan, suggests a much deeper performance:

> I remember this young actor from the very first days of Theatre in the Round. He has matured into a most sensitive performer with a gentle, humorous understanding of this part. He has attained the stillness of grief remembered and ever present, and a withdrawn and quiet pride. Above all this is a musical role spoken with great beauty and tenderness. This is a performance to remember.

Not bad for a 21-year-old. Desmond Pratt was a truly extraordinary critic, as anyone who reviewed with him, let alone anyone who was reviewed by him, will testify. His status as the most important critic in Yorkshire – indeed the only serious critic in some parts of the three Ridings – meant that he could get away with arriving late and leaving early; and sometimes he did. He checked that the actual performance had taken place and then filed copy written beforehand about the play itself, based on close scrutiny of the script, a memory of other productions and a very fair idea of what the actors you saw on a regular basis were going to be like. For anyone in the theatre who believed he or she was doing something really special just this once, such a procedure could be heart-breaking. Yet there were plenty of other times when the critic of

'Yorkshire's national newspaper' would reveal himself to be anyone's equal as a perceptive and original critic catching the quality of a performance with a skill that was hard to match, whether he was praising it or identifying a cardinal problem. His support for Alan as an actor and playwright came early, when it was most useful, and Alan is grateful for it, whatever his general thoughts about critics.

But there was another side to his performance in *Five Finger Exercise*. The German tutor is suspected of leading his student into homosexuality. Stanley Page, who played the boy's father, recalls: 'My character was desperately worried, and Alan and I had this interview scene. I had to sit him down, stare into his eyes and say, "Tell me the truth." And *every* time, I don't know what happened, it just seemed funny. Alan wouldn't laugh – he would just smile, or twinkle. I would laugh outright, which used to get me into appalling trouble. He was a difficult chap to act with seriously.' Alan's gift for keeping a straight face was an important part of his ability to make other actors 'corpse'. But he could somehow get Desmond Pratt to talk about 'stillness of grief remembered' while all this was going on, not necessarily in the first-night performance of course but certainly in rehearsals and certainly on later nights when he started to get bored with a play.

And he still had his temper. Stanley Page was almost ten years older but had arrived from Australia with a certain sense of trepidation about the sophisticated mother country. He was as vulnerable as any pre-Barry Humphries Australian to suggestions of intellectual or cultural inadequacy. Alan once terminated an argument with him with the blistering remark: 'The trouble with you, Page, is you're half-ignorant and half-Australian.' He loved Alan – still does – and was very badly wounded.

That winter Alan also wrote a double bill of one-act plays for some Scarborough amateurs, *Follow the Lover* and *Double Hitch*. He appeared in *Follow the Lover* himself, and *Double Hitch* featured Ken Boden and was directed by Margaret Boden: a farce, it featured two couples arriving on honeymoon at the same cottage, and the man from one couple going off with the wife from the other. Christine Ayckbourn has described his writing process early in his career:

> It did not come easily. As the deadline loomed ever nearer he would manifest certain physical symptoms (as in the onset of influenza or childbirth) becoming broody and withdrawn. No use expecting an answer to even the most vital question. Vague and abstracted, he would pour salt over the cornflakes, throw away the toothbrush or don the odd red and the

odd yellow sock. Then would come the playing of music (loud), cigarettes, coffee, pacing round the room, the sharpening of pencils and other avoidance tactics, until finally, around midnight, when all was quiet, he would settle and after a few desultory doodles in the margin, he was away.

On throughout the night the writing would flow, from pencil to pad with very few crossings-out or alterations, percolator bubbling on the stove, cigarettes to hand, until dawn, when he would collapse into bed for a long, deep sleep.

I would type the finished play on a small, portable, weather-beaten Brother typewriter which had a will of its own so one could never predict the results. Exclamation marks would appear in inappropriate places and the ribbon would change from black to red and back again – and as for all those carbon copies . . .

It is a cliché that writers need deadlines to generate adrenalin that in turn produces their creative energy. I think there is another aspect to the eleventh-hour sessions fuelled by stimulants: writers want to delay handing over their material (for possible criticism or even rejection) as long as possible, and preferably until it is too late for it to be rejected. Adrenalin is generated less by laziness than by fear.

In the warm afterglow of *The Square Cat* – which they had written and then delightedly read together – the couple had assumed that fame and fortune were, in Christine's phrase, 'only a whisker away'. The pseudonym Roland Allen had been maintained, even though everyone had known – even the newspapers – from the first night of *The Square Cat* onwards that the plays were written by the young actor. Stephen Joseph argued that it wasn't right, somehow, to have the same name credited as writer and actor. This didn't seem to apply to David Campton, perhaps because he had been identified as a writer before he started to fill in as an actor too. But fame and fortune hadn't arrived, and the mistiming and curious provenance of *Dad's Tale* meant that Alan's audiences had actually grown smaller. It was absurd to expect real success at the age of 21, but the two and a half years he had spent with Stephen Joseph were more than a tenth of his young life, the only part of it he had seriously chosen. As he entered 1961 he wasn't using his own name for his plays. He wasn't yet directing them. He wasn't finding as much fun and fulfilment in acting. His workload was phenomenal, and Lolly claimed that Stephen Joseph complained that he wasn't always able to learn his parts properly. Lolly, not perhaps entirely without malice, suggested that he wasn't getting enough sleep because of the amount he also did at home, and attributed the eventual failure of his first marriage partly to this. Money, for a man with a wife and son and another child on the way, was incredibly tight. The highest salary he would ever earn as a company member in the theatre was £800 a year, and that was the maximum wage in Stoke when he was associate director. Most of the time he earned about £9–£12 a week. Lolly sometimes helped out, once joining them for the summer to work as a waitress in Debenham's department store – 'the waitress from hell', he imagines – and sharing her tips with them at the end of the day. At other times she would slip a fiver in the post when she had sold a story. But it was hard making ends meet. Stanley Page says that for the first four years he knew him Alan invariably wore a blue pullover with a hole in it that he had bought from a jumble sale. He also formed the impression that in spite of all the japes in rehearsal Alan was in many ways more mature than he was, that he had had more experience of life, including the things – marriage, relationships – that his plays would be about, and that there was 'a sense of, not bitterness, but sadness about it. As if life wasn't what it should be, even then.'

4 : And then a Director . . .

Since 1970, despite his worldwide reputation as a writer, Alan Ayckbourn has been a director who spends about 10 per cent of his year writing plays. The first step towards this role came in 1961 and it happened with the apparent casualness common to Alan's career and Stephen's planning. But Stephen's belief in letting talented people have their heads paid off at once when he invited 'Ayckers' to direct Patrick Hamilton's classic psychological thriller, *Gaslight*. The play itself is pertinent. It has a clever technical effect: the lights in the house in which it is set have to flicker and fail. And although it takes the form of a police detective investigation its theme is that of a bullying husband trying to persuade his psychologically fragile wife that she is going mad. A review said Alan found 'snatches of humour' in it; I bet he did. He also recognised the play's reality. That season also included his three roles, including the lifelike Prince Albert, in *Victoria Regina*, and another of his alarming female impersonations, a cook in one of David Campton's short plays grouped together under the title *Four Minute Warning*.

This was one of two batches of plays about the threat of nuclear destruction that Stephen had prevailed upon Campton to write. Stephen then suggested an 'issue' for Alan: he should 'do something about over-population'. I don't imagine he really held Alan personally responsible for this, though in the summer of 1961 Philip Ayckbourn was born – like his elder brother, in a hospital across the Thames from Bray. The result was *Standing Room Only*, which premièred in July and was the first play billed as 'by Alan Ayckbourn'. Stephen wanted the play to be set on Venus after overcrowding on earth had become so severe that people had moved planets. Years later, in a children's play, Alan would set a story in space. But in 1961 'some commercial gene in me' led him to set it on Shaftesbury Avenue, the heartland of the West End theatre, at a point in the future (1997) when traffic has come to a permanent standstill in London. The action takes place on and around a double-decker bus which hasn't moved for 20 years. Its tyres have rotted and the central characters are living on the lower deck. We also see a battered car behind – specifically a 'Vice-Consul' – in which a second-rate violinist practises painfully from time to time. When it begins, we find Pa (the bus driver) with his electric razor plugged into a Keep Left sign. He has taken the name of his bus's theoretical destination, Hammersmith, for himself. One daughter, Cora, is the conductor and assorted travellers have turned into house guests.

The threat of complete government control over people's personal lives, including their right to breed, seems to have been Ayckbourn's major concern about the future, rather than over-population. In *Standing Room Only* women have to take an Advanced Maternity and Housewife's Exam before they can give birth. Pa's second daughter is illegally pregnant and her fiancé a pompous stuffed shirt from the City unable to do much more than lobby for a state-apportioned room on the forty-fourth floor of a tower block that gets the sun between 11.20 and 12.25. The arrival of a State Illegitimate Child posing as a bus inspector provides the catalyst for the plot.

The play opened in Scarborough to a particularly enthusiastic review from *The Stage*. In fact the paper's local correspondent had been unable to attend but it was then regarded as acceptable for the theatre to send in its own review. Joan Macalpine, lorry driver and would-be playwright whose adaptation of *David Copperfield* Alan was to direct later the same season, was also acting manager and had the job of supplying the review. She included the inspired line: 'Will no one drive this bus to Shaftesbury Avenue?' The impresario Peter Bridge read it in his office in the West End and shot up to Scarborough; he liked the play enough to take out an option on it but not quite enough to transfer it as it stood. Fame and fortune did seem to be around the corner again, but tantalisingly out of reach. Bridge needed a star, and a number of famous actors looked over the script. Sid James, who supplied a cackling, lust-driven persona for a score of *Carry On* films as well as providing a foil for the great Tony Hancock, was interested in playing Pa; but, he told Alan, there weren't enough 'rudes' – dirty jokes, swear-words, *doubles entendres* – in it. There was even talk of the bulky Hattie Jacques as one of the young daughters, talk of half the *Carry On* team. Alan rewrote and rewrote, adding characters and at one point drafting in a fleet of helicopters to evacuate the jammed traffic. Different directors were lined up for it, and they would invite Alan to their homes and tell him exactly what the play needed. But there was no way of giving *Standing Room Only* one or two star parts and reducing the rest to supporting roles, the formula demanded by the West End until Ayckbourn's own plays changed expectations over the next decade. It still reads as a very actable comedy, celebrating the animal ingenuity and reproductive drive of humanity, but lacks the devastatingly sharp-edged relationships of Ayckbourn's later work. Biographically it is important because it shows him both learning things about the West End, some of which leave him justifiably suspicious to this day, and as a 22-year-old father-of-two clearly affirming his own contempt for a society that seeks to control everything without even being able to get the buses running, which seems not without relevance four decades later. It ends with quite the opposite conclusion to the one Stephen Joseph had wanted: more babies, not fewer. Natural dissident that he was, he was beginning to find his own voice. In the meantime, Peter Bridge had put him in touch with a literary agent, the formidable and eccentric Margaret (Peggy) Ramsay. Her importance to twentieth-century theatre has been made clear in John Lahr's biography of Joe Orton, *Prick Up Your Ears* (Vanessa Redgrave played her in the film); in Colin Chambers's biography, *Peggy*; in Simon Callow's extraordinary memoir, *Love Is Where It Falls*; and most recently in Alan Plater's dramatic portrait, *Peggy for You*. Alan is never quite sure why she took him on (and ungratefully started trying at once to renegotiate his contract with poor Peter Bridge, with a letter that reduced the latter instantly to tears) because her other writers were much more obviously avant-garde. When she came to see a later version of *Standing Room Only* she failed to recognise Alan, peering at him out of her trailing scarves with apparent disbelief. And Callow recalls that her first remark to him was: 'Do you think Alan Ayckbourn will ever write a really good play?' He was, however, her most lucrative talent. She never really influenced Alan's writing in spite of regular dissections of the plays and lavish unwanted advice.

5 : Another Round

Peter Cheeseman was Portsmouth-born, thought of Newcastle upon Tyne as home and had been to ten different schools as his father, a civil servant working for the Air Ministry, had been moved around the country. At Sheffield University he had been thrown out of the honours school because he spent too much time on student theatre but he gained a general degree and a teaching diploma. He spent three years teaching in the RAF, relishing the task of trying to instil a love of Shakespeare in senior NCOs, hard flight sergeants who wanted to get on in the world beyond the armed forces. By the time he was offered a job by Stephen Joseph he had already worked at Derby Playhouse and fallen out with the theatre board there over the need to make actors rehearse as hard when they moved up from weekly to fortnightly rep. He had a vision of the theatre in which actors would stay in the same place and become as rooted in the community as miners, steelworkers, railwaymen and potters, contributing in the broadest sense to the regional economy and body politic. He had gone to the house in Longwestgate in Scarborough, where he was 'overwhelmed by Stephen's quality' and invited to help set up a permanent theatre in the Potteries.

For all Stephen's gifts, he was not a settler. If anything, he would actively turn his back on the final phase in his campaigns. For a number of years he worked for a theatre to be built in Croydon and Alan was with him when a council officer rang through to say they had at last got the go-ahead. Stephen refused even to take the call. Others had to mount the final charge. The town of Newcastle under Lyme had supported his winter visits for many years and now there was a proposal to spend £99,000 to build a permanent theatre-in-the-round. Stephen wanted a manager to help him do it, and Peter Cheeseman's job in Derby had been that of manager with the added right to direct one production in every four. Newcastle's plan fell through and Stephen, white with anger when he was told by the town clerk, wanted nothing further to do with the town. Cheeseman argued that they should find a temporary home and build from there, and Stephen – although he said that no one would really take theatre-in-the-round seriously until it had a new building – grudgingly let Peter try.

What became the Vic – the Victoria Theatre in Hartshill, Stoke-on-Trent – was a club about to lose its licence after alienating the police and local residents (a combination of late-night noise and a woman discovered wearing nothing but a snake). As the strippers moved out, the actors moved in. When the Arts Council had backed the development, its drama director (Jo Hodgkinson) had said to Cheeseman, mindful of Stephen Joseph's mercurial nature: 'Make it stick.' And that is precisely what he did. He argued that Stephen's policy of picking up each year in a town after an absence of so many months meant that much of the work was frittered away: 'How do you get people to come to the theatre? Theatre to me only made sense when there was a sort of relationship with the audience, a relationship between the theatre company and the region.' The Scarborough company moved to Stoke with Stephen as a largely absentee managing director who was taking up a job in Manchester University's Drama Department. Alan was to be associate director, acting and writing as well, so that the burden of directing most productions fell immediately on Peter, who dearly wanted to direct though his job title remained manager. These distinctions turned out to be painfully important. It is also said by David Campton that Jo Hodgkinson's original hope and intention had been that Stephen should run the company in a more hands-on way, but if this is what the Arts Council wanted it never put it on the record.

There was one complete newcomer to the company: Caroline Smith, now a fine and sensitive director, especially of new plays, arrived as acting ASM. Elizabeth Bell, who had been to drama school and taken Steven Joseph up on an invitation to get in touch, had joined the company in Scarborough in the summer; so had Heather Stoney, now Lady Ayckbourn but then still some years away from her relationship with Alan. They had met when she arrived at the Library Theatre to do a play by William Norfolk called *The Birds and the Well-wishers*. Alan was on a long bench outside the auditorium bouncing a little brown baby on his knee. She thought him remote at first but felt accepted when, in almost the last week of the season, he greeted her with 'Hello, Stoney'. When they travelled to Stoke they met by chance on Crewe station and arrived at the new theatre together, causing Caroline Smith to assume they were a couple.

Although the city of Stoke was and is much bigger than Scarborough it has never felt much like an urban metropolis. To tease the gullible let them loose in Stoke with instructions to find the city centre. It was the perfect place for Peter Cheeseman to test his theories about the relationship between a theatre and a community, and the company set about installing some rostra in the old strip club, painting the auditorium black and putting in some seats. As a place to live with very little money, however, it seemed pretty grim. Alan and Christine put their elder son, Steven, to sleep in the bath for want of space in one flat – and then both woke in a simultaneous panic in case a tap was dripping and he had drowned. He hadn't. Later they woke up one morning to find building workers coming in – the landlord had sold it over their heads and it was about to be gutted. Their next house was so cold they only lived in the downstairs rooms. Their diet was mostly baked beans.

That first season, they took no significant risks with new writing but nor did they play safe. It began with a revival of *The Birds and the Well-wishers*, in which Alan's 'triumph' was praised in the *Guardian*:

> Angular and open-mouthed in an army shirt and light blue draped suit, his performance at Mrs Trigger's party is almost painfully hilarious.

His voice was 'like balsa wood'. He looked 'like a bedspring'. It seems as though Alan really didn't like William Norfolk's play very much and was overacting furiously to make it tolerable for himself as well as more broadly comic for the audience. He put on a flat, comic cockney intonation which Elizabeth Bell then imitated, reducing the central love story to near-farce. Heather was commended for her 'well-chiselled nosiness'. That was followed by a George Bernard Shaw double bill, *The Caretaker* by Harold Pinter, and then *Usher*, David Campton's adaptation of Edgar Allan Poe's horror novel *The Fall of the House of Usher*. The company had been joined by another actor with an interest in writing, David Halliwell. Alan played the hero, Roderick Usher, Elizabeth Bell was his sister Madeline and Halliwell a louche manservant. The power of theatre-in-the-round was demonstrated in one performance when Madeline's hand suddenly appeared, pushing up the lid of the coffin in which she supposedly lay dead. One member of the audience vomited and half the rest trooped out, nauseated by the stench.

After a revival of *The Rainmaker*, the opening programme ended at Christmas with a children's play from Alan called *Christmas v Mastermind*. It was probably his worst disaster ever, even including the original *Jeeves*. Stanley Page played a grumpy Father Christmas whose principal gnome

(David Halliwell) leads a strike in the toy factory just before the present-giving season. Alan himself played the manipulative master criminal, the Crimson Gollywog, with Elizabeth Bell as his secretary and Heather Stoney as Father Christmas's secretary. The company had also recruited yet another actor who was a playwright-in-waiting, Peter King. As with *Dad's Tale* in Scarborough two years before, the idea of doing a children's play at Christmas was not inherently bad, but it was unsupported by any further planning. Marketing would not be invented, as far as theatre was concerned, for another two decades. Publicity was still something managers did in their spare time, maybe. The Vic had no heating and the few people who turned up either shivered throughout or were so thickly wrapped against the cold that even if they had clapped the cast wouldn't have heard them. Heather injured her eye putting nail varnish remover on a contact lens. David Halliwell spoke the line 'I stand before you, a fully elected democratic representative' at one performance as 'fully erected' and brought the house down for the only time (38 years later Alan gave the line to a womanising would-be MP in *House* at the National Theatre). Caroline Smith played Policewoman Trout, a detective who had to wear a small Christmas tree as a disguise for much of the evening. Alan was so demoralised that with one brief exception he didn't write for children again for over 20 years, although he then turned out to be one of the most successful children's writers we have.

For the first (and last) time the première of one of Alan's plays was directed by Peter Cheeseman. A doughty and stubborn campaigner for the regional producing theatre in general as well as his own kind of drama rooted in local communities, Cheeseman has often acknowledged Alan's box office appeal as a second source of subsidy after the Arts Council. The two men are now friendly and have enormous respect for each other's achievements. But in 1962 and 1963, when they were supposed to be close colleagues in the founding company in Stoke, they were divided in their fundamentally different personalities and their often diametrically opposed philosophies of theatre. Alan perceives the period as character-ised by spectacular arguments; Peter wryly comments that the problem with Alan was that you could never have a decent row with him. Certainly Alan baited Peter, ganging up with Caroline Smith to steal the second-hand safe, Peter's pride and joy, purchased for £7 10s (£7.50). Stanley Page remembers Peter saying to Alan: 'If you were half as nasty as you make out you are, nobody would speak to you at all.' But the disagreements were also professional. Alan played the part of Sir Thomas More in Robert Bolt's great hit, *A Man for All Seasons*, and won a terrific review from 'C.V.R.' in the *Evening Sentinel* for 'a most powerful performance'. The critic continued:

> Here was the dignity of humility, the massive inner strength of faith and the firm resolve of a character bred of rare metal.

There was also praise for Heather Stoney acting 'most sensitively' as his daughter Meg and Elizabeth Bell as his wife in what was evidently a fine production by Peter. But there is a scene with Meg in which More has an impressive speech about the limits to which his conscience will let him accede to the wishes of King Henry VIII. It takes place by the Thames, and Peter Cheeseman was enormously pleased with the lighting effect conjuring up the river running through the acting area. Unfortunately it meant there was no light elsewhere. Alan, aware that audibility in theatre is mysteriously connected to visibility, to Peter's fury stepped into the 'river' to deliver the important speech. There were other differences of approach to the physical business of staging a play. Stephen's penchant for using a simple box as a rudimentary set for almost anything had been refined by Peter into a commitment to as bare a stage as possible so that all the attention was placed on the actors. This is, of course, one of the underlying principles of theatre-in-the-round but to Alan it seems unnecessarily self-denying, and likely to be boringly repetitive. When he came to direct *The Caretaker*, therefore, he took great pleasure in filling the acting area with all manner of clutter and junk. And Peter took great pleasure in the act of the theatre cleaners who assumed it was rubbish and cleared it away.

They have gone their separate ways since the mid-1960s. Peter has sometimes been regarded as a purist bordering on the puritanical, Alan as an essentially frivolous boulevardier playing with the mechanisms of story-telling. In fact each man finds his own theatrical way to tell the truth about the world he lives in. Alan once summed up the difference between them by saying that he thought Peter believed that for an actor to play a brain surgeon, he should steep himself in research about brain surgery: knowing as much as it was possible to find out about brain surgery would enable the actor to 'be' a brain surgeon for the necessary two hours or so. He, Alan, on the other hand believed that if the play was well enough written the actor would find the character in it and in himself. Peter wasn't altogether convinced by this description of his own approach but his documentary plays at Stoke – a form he pioneered in the theatre – do place great emphasis on literal authenticity. The first of these pieces, *The Jolly Potters*, dealt with the most famous local industry and, in its original version in 1964, did have some of the music-hall elements popularised by Joan Littlewood with Theatre Workshop at the Theatre Royal, Stratford, in East London. But gradually Peter insisted more firmly that the dialogue of the documentaries had to consist of words already spoken by the real characters his actors were to portray and that the music should be authentic too. These plays, scripted by his then wife, Joyce Holliday, made a unique contribution to British theatre; at their best – *The Knotty* about workers on the local railway line and their families, *The Fight for Shelton Bar* which campaigned to keep a local steelworks alive – they had an immediacy and an exhilaration that were entirely their own. But Alan's insistence that all his characters come from inside himself leads logically to the idea that all the words do too. Sometimes journalists have asked why, since Scarborough and Stoke were 'sister theatres', he didn't also do local documentaries. He usually says something about coach-building and chip-freezing (Scarborough's main manufacturers) not having the working-class glamour of miners, steelworkers or railwaymen, but the truth is he simply isn't that kind of dramatic artist. He doesn't consciously research anything at all. Ever. Indeed, if pressed, he will argue that for his kind of theatre it is best to write about things that everybody already knows.

With the failure of *Christmas v Mastermind* at the box office, the fledgling Stoke company was in dire trouble. The whole season had gone poorly. Peter Cheeseman called a meeting – Peter does his work through meetings; Alan does his by avoiding them at all costs – and announced that some members would have to leave and the rest to take a pay cut, but that there was no question of the theatre closing. At this point he achieved exactly what Jo Hodgkinson at the Arts Council had urged: he 'made it stick'. It was at a cost, with married members of the company coming down to £9 a week, the rest to £6. The workload for the tiny company that remained became almost ridiculously heavy. Caroline Smith, originally employed as an acting ASM, found she was the entire technical staff: 'We certainly had no carpenters, no wardrobe staff, no designers, nobody at all. I wasn't experienced enough to run the whole technical side, and it was then that Alan was the absolute saviour of that theatre. He understood how lights were wired up. He understood sound, obviously, because he was a sound maniac. Between us, for two or three months, we were the only technicians.'

They were also appearing on stage. In Anouilh's *The Rehearsal*, which set the Vic's house record for attendances, Alan played the Count, Heather the Countess and Caroline the young ingénue. Just before the first performance she was still painting the floorcloth and found she couldn't get the Prussian Blue off her hands. Distraught, she begged Alan not to greet her in the play, as rehearsed, by turning her hand palm upwards to kiss it. Of course he did though, making it unbearably worse by murmuring: 'Hello . . . typhoid, I fear!' They would work all-nighters on Saturday, Sunday and Monday between the end of one production and the opening of the next on Tuesday. When Peter – always bright in the mornings with the energy of true conviction – made another demand, Caroline in particular would snap back at him. He fired her five times, but always took her back. Eventually, they ganged up and talked him into going off to London and hiring another ASM. He found one, but the first time the newcomer was called on to set up a new show, he climbed up to the lighting rig high above the acting area – and threatened to jump. The next morning he disappeared, leaving a note on his pillow saying the job was too much, so Peter was sent off to London again.

It is in this climate that Alan seems to have given a thoroughly rotten time to the author of *The Birds and the Well-wishers*, William Norfolk. The fourth production into the 1963 season, Stoke's second, was another Norfolk play, *An Awkward Number*. Stanley Page recalls:

> Peter was directing, and he was saying things to the effect that it was 'the new Strindberg' but Alan loathed it. And when Alan doesn't like something he can be amazingly cutting and very witty. The rest of us of course were in stitches and Peter was gritting his teeth and pushing on, and the author was sitting there in front of us. On the first day he was in the front row, on the next he was about half-way back; third day, he was on the back row and on the fourth day he's written a note saying he couldn't stand any more and was going. We never saw him again.

Alan's technique was to say of line after line: 'You know, I don't think I actually need to say this. I can act it better by just being there and looking.' Eventually the part was whittled down to nothing. It sounds cruel and it was. Alan would never let another writer suffer like that today and describes himself then as 'the kind of actor I would hate to work with'. But under near-impossible conditions he was fighting for his own life as an artist without the benefit of the presence of the father figure, Stephen Joseph. He was appearing in *Waiting for Godot* while he rehearsed *An Awkward Number*; and then rehearsing (as director) his new version of *Standing Room Only* – now with one more character in it than in the Scarborough version – while appearing in *An Awkward Number* at night. With no days off – precious few hours off, in fact – and living on his diet of baked beans with two small boys at home, plainly his sense of solidarity sometimes gave way to that rage or savage comedy that had been there from early childhood. It must have been a somewhat bitter irony for William Norfolk that *The Stage* commented:

> the fifth member in the unhappy collection of people brought together in a hotel is played with satisfying assurance by Alan Ayckbourn, one of the most talented members of the company.

Caroline Smith recalls good houses for *Standing Room Only* and a happy company doing it. Peter Bridge still couldn't put together a West End production, however, and while he held the rights to the play nobody else could do it either. Fame and fortune were as elusive as ever. Alan is genuinely disinterested in both as such, though he enjoys what they make possible. But theatre is an industry and an art form that is psychologically and creatively dependent on at least the possibility of there being an audience.

The 1963 season in Stoke was in two halves, included some 16 productions in all, and was to bring him tantalisingly, almost heart-breakingly, close to triumph at the ripe old age of 24. He followed *Standing Room Only* with his personal success in *A Man for All Seasons*, then directed Strindberg's *Miss Julie* before appearing with Heather Stoney in Caroline Smith's first production as a director, William Gibson's New York comedy *Two for the See-saw*. Positively reviewed for both acting and the cinematic quality of the production, this show would eventually prompt his farewell to acting. In the second half of the year Peter Cheeseman directed a Pinter double bill, *The Collection* and *The Dumb Waiter*. (Stanley Page approvingly recalls his insisting the plays were like poems by T. S. Eliot 'and if you're doing a poem by T. S. Eliot you don't alter a word'. He believes there was still a letter from Harold Pinter drawing attention to the difference between a comma and a semi-colon.) Cheeseman also found time to organise a series of four public sessions – two at the Vic, two at Keele University – with leading playwrights: J. B. Priestley, Arnold Wesker, Robert Bolt and Pinter himself. When it came to Pinter's turn the audience sat in anticipatory silence for what seemed like ages, beginning to get restive, only to hear Pinter inform them that he really hadn't got anything much to say about his plays. The event's chairman then said he would talk about them instead and when he argued that Pinter was the Noël Coward of the 1960s it satisfactorily provoked Pinter into a rather cross reply after which he never looked back. And in the course of the event he told the audience there was a young actor among them of whom they were going to hear a great deal more: 'His name is Alan Ayckbourn.' Alan, sitting next to Stanley Page, squirmed with embarrassed pleasure.

Chapter 4

His own man

1 : *Mr Whatnot*

And then, in November 1963, came the first of Alan's plays with which he
is sufficiently happy to allow it to be produced today, the first to be
produced in the commercial theatre, and the first he wrote to show
himself off as a director rather than as an actor. It was, however, written
very much for the Stoke company and for the particular talents of the late
Peter King. The future writer and radio drama producer had an enormous
gift for mime. Alan also detected what he typically describes as a
specifically Welsh dark and rapacious lust in him. Peter King was a
thoroughly instinctive actor rather than an educated one, though he was
to educate himself later, and he was a natural focus for Alan's arguments
with Peter Cheeseman about whether or not an actor should have an
intellectual understanding of politics if he was to play a Prime Minister.
But with absolutely nothing to say there was little intellectually for Peter
King to master in *Mr Whatnot*. Alan has acknowledged the influence of the
French film director René Clair in writing this, but was also paying
homage to childhood heroes in Buster Keaton and Harold Lloyd (he is not
a Charlie Chaplin fan) in creating a central role for a deadpan character
who is mute. A piano-tuner goes to a big mansion on the wedding-day of
the daughter of the house, Amanda Slingsby-Craddock. The family never
takes any real notice of him, never even learning his real name (Mint, as it
happens) and the upshot of the play is that although Amanda's marriage
to the vapid Cecil goes ahead it is Whatnot with whom she ends up in
bed.

Initially Alan wanted the rest of the cast to be wordless too, or more
specifically to distort the aristocratic braying dialogue he had written for
them into wordless sounds, but he changed his mind when he discovered
how funny the dialogue was in performance. And then there was the
soundtrack. As Mint makes his progress through the house and garden, as
doors open and close, dogs bark and the thud of ball on racket-strings is

heard from the tennis court, there are recorded sound-effects running right through the play, something like 150 of them. Naturally Alan made the sound tape himself. In the middle of the night neighbours complained they heard a dog barking in the theatre, repeatedly, as if in some distress. The policeman who investigated found Alan barking into a microphone, alone in the control room. When the show opened Alan was free to run the sound tape himself. Caroline Smith, who played two roles, also had to sprint up to the control room to do the lighting changes. In addition to cashing in on Peter King's mime skills and the other actors' particular qualities Alan had put the whole frantic Stoke ethos into the play. *Mr Whatnot* makes a kind of icon of the near-manic activity that made it possible, just, to get two plays on stage each week.

Mr Whatnot was a turning point, the first play Ayckbourn identifies as one that could have been written only by him. It is beautifully constructed on its own quirkily logical terms, it is a devastating account of a family – apparently such a strong unit but as completely unable to defend itself against the depredations of a foxy outsider as a coop of well-bred chickens – and it is as preoccupied with how the story is told as with what that story is. The organic link between the 'how' and the 'what' of dramatic story-telling, sometimes overlooked in the hot pursuit of 'content', is of critical significance to the artist. But it is not what people became accustomed to label, not quite accurately, as an 'Ayckbourn play', meaning one that is concerned with the personal relationships of the middle classes.

Mint, working-class if he is anything, is a voiceless person in the society in which he finds himself. Alan has said: 'He has nothing to say' but it seems to me he chooses not to speak, just as a piano-tuner sometimes chooses not actually to play the piano. If he were totally submissive, the society wedding would have gone ahead with absolute normality. The fact that he is fuelled by lust (and that, at some level, lust is also what the bride wants rather than the hearts-and-flowers sentiments of her drippy fiancé) may indicate the sexual havoc these upper-class males fear the working class may set in motion. To describe this brilliantly conceived farce as a political or class-war play would stretch credibility, but it enjoys Alan's natural mix of anarchism (in the sense of the subversion of authority) with the phenomenal discipline required to produce it effectively.

There is some evidence that around this time Alan himself had made up a lot of lost ground on the butcher boy he had envied as having had 'every girl in the village'.

Although his marriage to Christine didn't break up straight away (and there has never been any criticism, to my knowledge, of or by her) there is no doubt he felt trapped by the institution itself. In interviews over the years he has described it as 'rotten' and argued that it is irresponsible to allow young people to make public promises of a kind they cannot reasonably expect to keep. Well, some people do keep their promises and some take to the institution happily and permanently. He has re-entered it himself without anyone loading a shotgun and he cheerfully gives his blessing to couples who tie the knot at his own theatre. But as a description of what had happened to him, his analysis cannot be faulted. He had married at 20 when he and Christine were both still growing, and they grew into different people. Although Christine had continued for a time to work on costumes (certainly up to *Standing Room Only* in both Scarborough in 1961 and later in Stoke) she had become more and more absorbed in her two sons than in the theatre. Alan did involve himself in what is now called parenting and childcare – to a fault, Lolly suggested, certainly as much as was common at the time – but work, which was also play, came first.

He interested his sons in the theatre early on, and Philip Ayckbourn can remember being taken to see *Mr Whatnot* even though he was only 3 when it had its London run. Both sons also have memories of not merely happy but exciting times with Alan whom they have always called by his first name rather than 'Daddy' and who felt more like a big brother than a father. He was still only 24 in 1963. At Bray, he had stripped down a pram so that both boys could climb aboard to be pushed at breakneck speed round the garden, alarming the grandparents and making Chris wonder if she had three kids on her hands just when she needed the support of a grown-up. Although the family continued to live together for a few more years, and Christine has never ceased attending Alan's first nights, reliable testimony from Stoke says that he was already seeking consolation elsewhere by this time. Lolly wasn't always a great help. Alan said much later: 'She was always a man's woman, not the sort to be counted on to take the wife's part if her son had a ding-dong with the au pair, much more likely to have said she'd have left the wife years ago.' In later life Lolly would spice up dinner parties by wagging her head at some unfortunate woman down the table and saying, irrespective of the truth: 'He's had her, you know.'

In any case the Stoke company was shortly to break up. As it happened, Heather Stoney was one of the first to decide that enough was enough and she should give herself a chance of working elsewhere; one of her longest-running jobs would be in the radio 'soap', *Waggoners Walk*. Peter Bridge had committed himself to producing *Mr Whatnot* in London and Alan decided to leave the company in April 1964 to work on it. But I believe he would have left in any case because his theatrical instincts and experience were so different from Peter Cheeseman's and neither of them was really at ease deferring to the other. Peter was in any case only a few years older than he, and his was an authority – unlike Stephen Joseph's – that Alan felt inclined to rebel against. A letter from Peter Cheeseman to Peggy Ramsay (dated a month after the eventual London opening) says he had found out Alan was leaving only when 'his wife told my wife'. This should not be taken as evidence that Alan and Peter were not speaking; Alan will always go through a third party, if he possibly can, to avoid a confrontation over a difficult subject. After 18 months of phenomenal strain, everybody wanted a break, and Peter needed to recruit a company that felt the same way as he did about permanence. Alan wrote to Peter from Cardiff, where he was playing four parts in *The Doctor and the Devils* for the director Warren Jenkins, and from the vantage point of a playwright with a show about to open in London said he would like to come back to Stoke 'when I am free' but might be a bit more selective about what he did. In the Cardiff production he had met an actor who would play pivotal roles in some of his greatest future successes, Christopher Godwin: two tall, thin, cadaverous young men who occupied opposite ends of the bar in the Angel Hotel nursing halves of bitter and perfecting their *Goon Show* impressions. At the end of their time in Wales the men had swapped their threadbare jumpers like rugby players bonding at the final whistle of a well-contested match.

Alan had had enough of acting. The crunch came when Caroline Smith's production of *Two for the See-saw* was revived for a short tour, opening in Rotherham. They didn't know the theatre and there was no dress rehearsal. That Monday night they reached the point where Alan's disillusioned New York lawyer – looking rather like an elongated Frank Sinatra with his hat perched on the back of his head – had been invited home by Heather's Jewish 30-something dancer. She went off-stage to fix some food while he chatted away in the living-room. When Heather failed to reappear at the appointed time, Alan gamely ad-libbed but got more and more distracted replies from off-stage until he decided to ask if she 'needed any help back there'. Yes, she jolly well did. The props – plates, stage food, cutlery and so on – hadn't been unpacked when they arrived at the theatre and she was struggling to find them for herself. Alan decided there and then that the rewards of acting were not enough to compensate for that kind of hassle. The young ASM on the production was apologetic. Had there been a bit of a problem? He would sort it out. In the meantime he thought they had both been brilliant. It was a privilege to be working with them. His name was Bill Kenwright, subsequently the busiest commercial producer in Britain.

How good an actor had Ayckbourn been? According to Stanley Page, he was at his best with a German accent or some other disguise, very powerful when menacing, even in the enigmatic Beckett. Chris Godwin agrees: 'He was a very idiosyncratic actor. Give him a hump, a limp, and he was tremendous. Very Grand Guignol.' Sometimes it is an insecure actor who grabs at a 'crutch' for his characterisation. But both Peter Cheeseman and Caroline Smith described him to me as a very good actor indeed, though Peter once told Stanley Page that Alan's range was limited – that he wasn't in fact an actor for all seasons.

Heather Stoney, who has seen more of his acting at close quarters than most, told me: 'He had burning eyes, so you could get very concentrated when you were working with him. He had a fair amount of humour in his work and he could be quite passionate on stage. But I always thought his movement was pretty terrible. I always remember the sensation of him moving his arm and his leg at the same time. I think overall he probably wasn't the world's best actor, but he was probably as good as a lot of us in that company.' The problem with movement was never addressed because he had no training. Alan acknowledges this, and points out that he had the good sense to keep still whenever he could. This is sometimes an enormous relief in the theatre when everyone else is rushing about, especially in theatre-in-the-round where some movement has to be encouraged in order to give the whole audience a sight of each character's face. A great quality in itself, it is singled out in some of his best reviews and by Stephen Joseph's own reference to Alan ('tremendous power in complete stillness') in his book, *Theatre in the Round* (Barrie & Rockliff, 1967). Stillness allows the audience to add its own emotion to anything you are doing. Heather believes that if he had taken an early opportunity to act on television, this stillness and powerful gaze would have made him very successful in the medium, and might also have solved his principal problem as an actor: boredom. Almost from the start, he got bored with even the good work after a few performances: 'Absolutely, gobsmackingly bored,' is how Caroline Smith puts it, 'and then he started messing about and doing terrible things to corpse us rigid.' As for what he regarded as bad work, he did not possess the tolerance (or the ability to fool himself) to make it endurable. Because there were so many productions in so short a time he never had to endure a really long run, and having played 50 or so parts he swiftly became one of the country's most experienced in-the-round actors, which inevitably informs his work as a writer and director.

Could he have earned his living as an actor if he had had to? Almost certainly, but it might have driven him to distraction.

Peter Bridge's first, delighted response to *Mr Whatnot* (which other producers had also travelled to Stoke to see) was to take the production and cast as they stood into London. The tiny Arts Theatre near Leicester Square was not in-the-round but nor was it a large barn in which the play would be lost, and he thought he might be able to fill it without star names. But as time went on his confidence evaporated. There was a need in the first instance to find a director. Alan asked for Clifford Williams, with whom he had got on well in Scarborough. Williams looked at the play and liked it but by then he was busy with the RSC. He suggested his fellow-Welshman, Warren Jenkins, who had employed Alan in Cardiff (Alan half-suspected a Celtic conspiracy of some kind). Peter King was to repeat his role as Mint, but all the rest of the cast were new, headed by Ronnie Barker as Lord Slingsby-Craddock and Judy Campbell as his wife (replacing Heather Stoney); Ronnie Stevens was cast as Cecil, the hapless fiancé originally played by Bernard Gallagher, Diane Clare took over from Elizabeth Bell as Amanda, Marie Lohr played one of Caroline Smith's parts and Judy Cornwell took the other. The company also included Peter Stephens and Christopher Godwin.

But the play had been written to celebrate the skills and lunatic commitment of young and inexperienced actors rather than the subtleties of more practised (not to say old) ones. There was something sadly pointless about the aged Marie Lohr injuring her knee badly as she chased about the stage miming a wildly energetic tennis match. There had been no designer at Stoke, and the point about the sound-effect of a creaking door is that you don't actually need the door. Peter Bridge brought in Peter Rice to provide the country house and garden, cramming it on to the tiny Arts stage. Julian Chagrin was imported to supervise the mime. Lighting and sound specialists – Robert Bryan and David Collison – were also drafted in. And incidental music (by the composer of *Mr Cinders*, Vivian Ellis) was added: charming, melodious English tunes from the great country-house era, whereas Alan would have preferred some 'spiky French music by Ibert or Poulenc' to point up the brittle absurdity of what was going on. The result was to be, in Christine Ayckbourn's words, 'camp and flowery': qualities to which Alan has never aspired, even in his waistcoats.

In that letter from Cardiff, Alan told Peter Cheeseman he had been 'playing the precocious young author and upset things by altering the script to my satisfaction and not theirs, rejecting their ideas owing to the style which always sounds convincing, I feel'. If that sounds like a man riding for a fall, he was. People had been telling him how much money he was going to make, that the only problem would be how to invest it, that he shouldn't buy too many cars, although he was aware that he hadn't been able to pay for the typing paper yet. The opening night was a disaster.

The press was more or less uniformly bad and Alan felt he was under personal attack precisely because this was the first play that was unmistakably his own. 'It felt like getting 25 poison pen letters at once, saying why didn't I go back where I came from.' What is always galling, when you have reason to believe the audience in a regional industrial city without the habit of theatregoing may be harder to please than that used to the often effete fare of the metropolis, is a London critic writing: 'They may put up with this sort of thing in Stoke-on-Trent, but . . .' Much of the country-house dialogue was effectively a parody of the things actors had to say when they were in the West End at its worst, and then in regional theatres when West End successes percolated through to them. Alan had had to speak it himself.

Alan was running a high temperature by the first night, aware at some level that things had gone horribly wrong. His first response was to dive beneath the bedclothes, according to Christine, and not re-surface. Peter Cheeseman, loyal and ready to come out fighting, harangued Peter Bridge for 'buggering [Alan] up'. He said it had worked in Stoke because Alan had followed his own judgement and had his own way and that is, not unnaturally, the consensus of the people who were involved in the original production.

Peggy Ramsay, the agent who had only just taken him on as a client, was in her office with Alfred Bradley, who wanted to talk about his own writing, when her telephone rang. Would she, her secretary wanted to know, speak to this distraught dramatist? She would, and as he cried down the telephone she told him not to give up, not to let them get him down, to go away and start again. Alfred Bradley, perhaps aware that he was only going to get any of Peggy's attention if he found a way of getting rid of Alan, told her to tell him to apply for a job that had been advertised in the previous week's *New Statesman*, that of BBC radio drama producer in Leeds, where Bradley himself was senior producer and deeply revered discoverer of writers. He was also an extraordinarily joyous and life-enhancing man whom only the BBC would have used to full advantage and only the BBC would have eventually frustrated and let down. At this point he was in his prime and of course he knew both Alan's writing and that he was exactly the man to be a good radio drama producer.

Alan is not a natural *New Statesman* reader but he found an old copy, applied for the job and got a reference from Peter Cheeseman: it said he had been paid £800 a year when he left Stoke, top of the salary scale at the time, and that he had 'a particular gift for dealing with actors and actresses which inspires them to give of their best in a calm and kindly atmosphere'.

In October he was interviewed – given a 'board' in BBC parlance – and wrote to Peter saying he thought he'd 'ballsed it up'. But the BBC had more sense than to be put off by somebody 'doing a bad board' in those days and in any case Alfred Bradley would have taken a lot of stopping if he had made up his mind. Alan got the job just before Christmas and wrote to Cheeseman to say so, recommending in passing a colour picture of Marianne Faithfull in *Radio Times*. A handwritten note from Christine referring to Peter's own last letter says: 'Whenever Alan's depressed he takes your letter in a corner and reads it and comes out big-headed and objectionable.' Cheeseman, who had been mercilessly teased and often opposed by Alan in the company at Stoke, hasn't always received universal praise for his work or his handling of colleagues, but he comes pretty well out of this.

And one thing vindicates his faith: Alan had already written another play, aimed for Stoke: 'basically a comedy,' he wrote, 'but I've loaded it a bit more than usual this time and once again have tried to use the round in a new and different way. I think it will upset Joseph anyway. It's breaking most of the rules.' His readiness to get back to work is the mark of a real writer but either the play in question sank without trace or he is being disingenuous, because his next première would have a markedly different relationship with 'the rules' and Stephen Joseph would have played one last instrumental part in his life.

2 : The Young Man from the BBC:
Relatively Speaking

The BBC in Leeds operated out of a former neo-classical Quaker meeting-house using equipment that was almost as benignly antique. Alan's experience of radio, apart from listening to it which may be the best qualification, was that the playwright Alan Plater had had a couple of scripts performed (on a Stoke double bill) which had started life as radio plays. Alan had directed them with enjoyment, because radio and theatre-in-the-round have intimacy and naturalistic speaking in common. Alfred Bradley's success in finding new writers had backfired in the sense that he was now inundated with perfectly good scripts that he himself had neither the time nor resources to produce. Accordingly BBC North Region, which was based in Leeds (Manchester was then North-West, and separate; the North-East, based in Newcastle, had not yet been invented), found some money to create a two-year post to tackle the backlog. After they left Stoke, Alan and the family had been living at Christine's parents' old home, The Retreat in Bray, and he had effectively hidden there after the failure of *Mr Whatnot*, drawing the dole for long weeks while the BBC made up its mind about him. When he finally got the job he was thrown in at the deep end. He watched Alfred produce a couple of things and then went over to observe a Manchester producer – Trevor Hill – at work. He walked into the studio, introduced himself, and was promptly handed a tape and asked to cut ten minutes out of it. Which he did.

When, after a month or so, the time came for him to do his own first production, Alfred promised that he would be there, saying nothing but keeping an eye on things; that Alan would have experienced studio managers over from Manchester who could practically produce the programmes on their own; and that the actors would be amenable and experienced radio performers, led by the late Henry Livings, himself a playwright and a very funny actor.

A radio drama studio is divided into different areas for different acoustics, and the cubicle – separated from the studio proper by soundproof glass – is where the producer and the studio managers are seated. One studio manager sits at the 'panel' opening and closing microphones, balancing the sound, getting the acoustic right. Another operates the tape machines and plays in sound-effects of birdsong or car horns. And a third dashes into the studio from time to time to create the 'spot effects' – the sound of a door slamming (using real doors in a specially built structure), tea-cups (also real), or the sheets of a bed (old tape, crumpled together). The actors stand by their microphones, scripts in hand, sometimes turning elegantly away from the mikes to suggest they are at a slight distance. And the whole thing goes like clockwork and a short play is completed, from first read-through to final 'take', in a couple of days.

A week before they were due in the studio, Alfred cried off, with heartfelt apologies. His father was very ill. On the day itself, one studio manager cried off with terrible flu. Alan asked the tapes SM if she could operate the panel. She was a trainee, and she was training on a much more recent panel than the antiquated one in use in Leeds, but with an author (nearly always present in radio drama, unlike other media) and six actors turning up imminently, she agreed to have a go. When a substitute did arrive he turned out not to have worked a panel for years. He had become an administrator.

Alan knew he would be all right with the read-through of the script, so he set about that while the trainee tapes SM sat down at the panel and tried to work out how to operate it. But the play took less than half an hour to read and by the end she still hadn't found out which fader opened which microphone. Alan allocated actors to different spots in the studio and asked them to talk among themselves while he went back into the cubicle and they tried to identify the microphones. Eventually they got one right and the volume came up on an actress saying: 'Poor love, he doesn't know what he's doing, does he?' Sounds inadvertently amplified from a recording studio would come into their own in *Making Tracks* (1981). Somehow they muddled through. The play was recorded in sequence from start to finish, with all the retakes in, and Alan took his big spool of tape off to an 'editing channel' where a bald man called Curly with a deep-seated hatred of drama was waiting for him with reels that had nothing to hold the tapes on to them. Alan thought this a bit risky but Curly, speaking very slowly as if enunciating a difficult litany to a child, started to speak: 'I've been. Working. Thirty years. On open reels. And they have never – Atchoo! Don't anybody move!' There was tape all over the floor. Did Alan have a copy, Curly wanted to know. No copy. So this was the only version? Yes, and it was now wrapped round their knees and on the floor. 'Don't anybody move!' And everyone froze as if they were surrounded by nitro-glycerine while Curly found the end and painstakingly wound the tape back on to the open reels.

It was broadcast and there was no response whatsoever until a senior manager rang up some time later about something else and said: 'By the way, heard your programme on Sunday. Who did the sound? Had a bit of a problem, did you? Yes, sounded like it.' It took a year to send him on a production course, by which time he had made about 50 programmes at a rate of one a week and was really quite experienced in drama, features, talks, poetry. So, along with another young producer called Alan Yentob, he sent the Staff Training Unit up – rotten.

All the trainees were sent out to record an interview with someone who had never been interviewed before, equipped with the heavy Uher reel-to-reel tape recorders which were standard at the time. They were instructed in the need for a clean start – no ums and ers – and relevant questions, and for finding somewhere with a good acoustic and not too much extraneous noise. They were even told a story about a recording made with interviewer and interviewee huddled under a coat because they were in such a noisy room. The interviews were to be done after work one day and played back the next morning completely unedited. Alan put it off, partly because he didn't want to do it and partly because he was by now seeing a lot of Heather Stoney and the fortnight in London was a golden opportunity to spend time together with meals subsidised by the BBC allowance. In the restaurant that evening he suddenly remembered he had to do the interview and persuaded Heather he should interview her, playing the role of An Actress, and he would deliberately do everything wrong because if the BBC didn't know by now that he could actually produce programmes, it never would.

The tape started with 'Ha, hum. One, two, three, four, testing' – the usual stuff. The interviewer got the name wrong and the interviewee had to correct it. Then Alan announced that he was just going to close the window, acoustically. And the conversation proceeded:

ALAN: I wonder if you'd mind if we just –

HEATHER (*getting rather sexy*): Ooh, no, not at all –

ALAN: I think the sound is a little bright in here. I'm just going to put this coat over us –

(*Suggestive rustling noises*)

ALAN (*muffled*): How does someone as attractive as you find time to do interviews?

HEATHER: Well, I always find time to –

ALAN: I'm just going to switch the machine off –

And so, the listener imagines, to bed. It all seemed a jolly wheeze the night before with a couple of drinks inside him. The next morning as they handed in their tapes it seemed less of a good idea and Alan wondered if he could accidentally contrive to lean with his elbow on the tape machine when his tape was put on, and damage it beyond repair. He got more nervous as other trainees' tapes were played and an earnest conversation with a Kentish pig farmer was followed by the memories of a flower-seller. His tape was the last one. As it started the high-powered BBC panel all began making furious notes but by the end they were laughing. Producers on subsequent courses have been played the tape as a glorious example of what not to do.

As a radio producer Alan was energetic and conscientious if sometimes naive, casting Yorkshire plays with Lancashire-accented actors, for example, not realising that the difference mattered. He had difficulties, too, with scripts written phonetically in Geordie dialect and often seeming to deal with leek-growing. But the glorious Northern 'rep' of radio actors usually saved his bacon. Alfred Bradley insisted that every writer who submitted a script should get some sort of individual reply, so mountains of plays were read, or at least skimmed, even if they were transparently rubbish from page one. As a writer who had been given the opportunity to learn his craft over a sustained period he saw the force of Alfred's argument. He now believes that having to write reports in preparation for the gentle rejection practised by BBC North indirectly helped him formulate his own precepts and thus affected his own writing. Occasionally he found himself having to do plays that he actively disliked, because they had been commissioned by someone else who was no longer available to produce them. And he was able to learn from this too – the golden rule not to take your resistance to the play out on the actors who can really perform only if everyone seems to believe in the project: 'Sometimes, after walking in breezily and saying you were going to make it good, you actually did.' Because plays were done in such a short time it made him into a much more concise director, giving broad, clear notes and only 'going in close' if things got desperate because long note sessions at the end of a day's rehearsal were impossible. On the other hand, many radio actors would hang on in the evening for the promise of an extra pint or two in the BBC Club or the Fenton – the pub across the road – and do something experimental with poems and monologues which could later be sold to the network. The North Region was far enough from London in those days, and BBC management itself less paranoid about knowing what everything would sound like before it was commissioned, for a creative producer to be allowed much more freedom. Some programmes were broadcast only in the North Region itself until 1967 when radio was restructured into Radios 1, 2, 3, 4 and local radio.

Alan's biggest embarrassment was when he received a story in the post from Lolly which he didn't think right for radio. He was able to tell her he wasn't responsible for *Morning Story* and sent it on to somebody else for gentle rejection.

It is sometimes said that Alan was bored stiff working for the BBC. It is true that radio didn't engage him quite so excitedly as the theatre, which made it possible to lure him to Scarborough in his summer holidays, but he committed himself to it, did it well and certainly engaged with the people he worked with. He earned a reputation for being able to construct a clear and vivid sound picture and, although initially he was working on the backlog of work by writers commissioned by Alfred (who included Stan Barstow, Keith Waterhouse, Willis Hall) he was also very proud of his productions of the early plays of Don Haworth. The confidence he gained, I suspect, played an important part in changing the prickly young rebel into the responsible leader he eventually became. But Alan never actually wrote for radio himself. There was always something more pressing.

No other theatres wanted to produce *Mr Whatnot*. They forgot it had been hugely successful in Stoke and Peggy Ramsay explained her failure to 'sell' it by saying that 'often bad plays seem dazzlingly good in the round'. After its failure in London Alan had tried various other kinds of writing – a monologue for Tommy Cooper, for instance, which didn't work because he faithfully put down Tommy Cooper's habit of saying everything twice. As a result when Tommy Cooper read it aloud he said everything four times: 'Good evening, good evening, good evening, good evening. There are too many good evenings here.' More successful, in due course, was his secret collaboration with Ronnie Barker. The latter had developed, out of Lord Slingsby-Craddock in *Mr Whatnot*, a character called Lord Rustless whom he made the basis of a series of short individual comic plays under the series title *Futtock's End*. Alan supplied much of the material, but because it was for ITV (for whom he was prohibited from working by his BBC contract) he could never take the writer's credit. A problem arose when the series won a writer's award so they invented a reclusive genius who wouldn't turn up to public ceremonies.

Stephen Joseph got him back into the theatre, renewing contact a few months after Alan started at the BBC. Stephen had seen *Mr Whatnot* and liked it, recognising that Ayckbourn had mastered the principles of writing for theatre-in-the-round and the art of suggesting a whole structure from the merest suggestion of its existence. This was when he added the famous advice that if Alan was going to break all the rules in future it might be good to write a play which kept them first, so that he knew what they were. He offered the one thing a playwright needs more than any other, the prospect of a production, for the summer of 1965. Alan found a little gap in his BBC diary and stayed up several nights in the cottage in Collingham, North Yorkshire, where the family was living, writing a play he had told Stephen would be called *Meet My Mother*. There was a cat in the cottage next door; finding someone else up and about in the middle of the night, she pressed herself against the window until Alan let her in. She then sat on his lap, purring contentedly, while he wrote on the note pad that he balanced on her back. She was called Pamela, one of a number of cats with whom he has been more physically demonstrative in public than with the humans he loves. Andrew Lloyd Webber gave him a champagne-coloured beauty called Bollinger (Bolly for short) who was allowed to curl up on his neck while he wrote. The latest incumbent is Charlie Brown.

Bearing Stephen's advice in mind, Ayckbourn deliberately took a step back from the experimental narrative of *Mr Whatnot* and set out to write a well-made play. He now thinks that if he had not done this – if he had carried on trying to dazzle with new departures – he would have eventually run into a brick wall and stopped writing. But at the time he thought the new play he had written was really rather 'easy and glib. In fact I was rather ashamed of it.' He sent it off to Stephen without much faith and, true to Stephen's style, heard nothing back.

This was a bit worrying because he had left the play until the last minute, finishing it in May, and it was supposed to go straight into rehearsal in June under Stephen's direction. On BBC business in Manchester one day he was walking down Oxford Road when he bumped into Stephen who, he thought, should have been at rehearsals in Scarborough but who still held his job in the Drama Department of the university nearby. A sardonic memory of Stephen's penchant for directing rehearsals without actually being in the same room as the actors came to mind. It is not easy to envisage the conversation which followed between two men unwilling to meet each other's eyes, but Alan asked how it was going and Stephen asked how was what going and Alan said the play Stephen was directing, of Alan's, and Stephen said pretty well. He had, he added, cut a bit, but it was jolly good. Was he sure, Alan asked. Yes, repeated Stephen, it was jolly good and Alan should come and see the first night.

There were some surprises when he did, on 8 July 1965. The title had been changed, to *Meet My Father*, but it fitted the play just as well and since Alan had supplied the original title well before he had supplied the play he felt no great need to complain. Stephen had indeed cut it, 'rather a lot of important bits, because he didn't seem to mind where it was cut as long as it was cut. When he did this you would point out that there were some important bits of information missing, but he'd just say: "Don't worry, people. They'll follow it" and they generally did. It was very good, and Peter Bridge came up with the director Nigel Patrick and they declared it was great. It needed a new title and a new first scene but it was great. So we thought up a new name.' And so *Relatively Speaking* was born. Less than a year after the traumatic failure of *Mr Whatnot*, the first play not designed to show him off as an actor or a director was his first hit.

But if Margaret Boden is right it did have him in it, as a character. Greg is a young man passionately in love with Ginny, in whose bed-sitting-room we find them in that problematic opening scene. Although they only met a month ago, he wants to marry her. She says she has to go down to the country, alone, to break the news gently to her parents before she can accept. In fact she has to confront her married lover while his wife is at church, stop him from sending barrow-loads of flowers and chocolates, and get back some compromising letters. Greg impulsively decides to follow her and, after a mix-up over taxis and trains, arrives first at The Willows, Lower Pendon, Bucks.

Greg is socially and physically clumsy. He treads on something sharp, causes the entire contents of a drawer to tip out and above all fails to say who he is when he meets Philip and Sheila (who is not at church at all). For much of the play Philip believes Greg wants to marry not Ginny but Sheila, and has come asking him to divorce her. To Sheila, who denies that Ginny is any daughter of hers, he responds with a speech haranguing her for puritanical rejection of her own kith and kin. It is a comedy of mistaken identity and its plotting therefore observes some of the rules of farce rather than the high comedy of accurate social and psychological observation. But the characters are real, if comically drawn. The young man in whom Margaret Boden recognised the author is alternately tongue-tied and effusive; and he is less comprehensible when he is running off at the mouth than when he holds his peace:

> I get nervous at meeting new people. Not just you. Everybody. Even bus conductors. You know there's some mornings, I get on a bus and, I don't know if you feel the same, but I'm sitting there, and there he is, the conductor, working his way down the bus towards me, and I think to myself, this morning I'm not going to be able to speak to this bloke. Not a word. He's going to say: 'Where to, mate?' And I'm going to open my mouth and go huuuhhh . . . open my mouth and nothing comes out. So when I feel like this, I have to practise, you see. I sit there, saying it over and over to myself . . . fourpenny one . . . one morning I was doing this, I was rehearsing this, even rehearsing the 'Good morning' I was going to say to my landlady . . . and I got on the bus and asked for ten cigarettes. I couldn't speak for the rest of the day after that.

This small aria of bewilderment comes from a young man who finds himself attracted and attractive to women but is always a step or two behind them when it comes to an intuitive understanding of what is going on. Before we get carried away in identifying Greg completely with

Alan, however, it is worth remembering that by this time Ayckbourn wasn't an innocent young lover hoping to get married but – like Philip – a married man engaged in another serious relationship.

It took almost two years for *Relatively Speaking* to reach London. Peter Bridge's original plan (with a cast to include Alec McCowen and Lynn Redgrave) fell through. Nigel Patrick asked for changes, believing that the West End audience, even in the middle 1960s, wasn't ready for an opening scene that suggested people might have had sex in the afternoon. Ayckbourn agreed to move the scene to the morning, but initially resisted other changes on the grounds that to give way on a word or two was to start down a road that might end with taking out a whole character. He had rewritten *Standing Room Only* until it had lost all its buoyancy. He had seen *Mr Whatnot* misdirected to disaster (a line added at Peter Bridge's suggestion would be singled out by Bamber Gascoigne in the *Observer* as an example of poor dialogue). He had had to swallow the humiliation of an amateur company in Hampshire saying they didn't think his revised version of *Standing Room Only* was right for them (they would be more at home with Greek tragedy) even as he was reworking the opening scene of *Relatively Speaking*. He approached the West End without confidence although he knew Nigel Patrick would direct the play well and that his new cast could hardly be bettered as a London attraction.

Michael Hordern (Philip) had been persuaded to read the play by his wife, who had seen – and loved – *Mr Whatnot*. Celia Johnson (Sheila) was simply a national treasure, one of the most popular actresses in London with whose resistance to temptation in the film of Noël Coward's *Brief Encounter* half the nation had sighed; a *grande dame* of theatre, she was known to invite theatrical colleagues to dinner but those who weren't fellow actors might find themselves eating with the cook in the kitchen – and nobody minded, because she was so gracious. Jennifer Hilary was Ginny, and Greg (Alan's old colleague Peter King in Scarborough) was played by a rising young television star, Richard Briers.

Not much was seen of Alan in rehearsals. Richard Briers remembers him appearing for the read-through and then disappearing back to provincial Leeds with his mackintosh and only suitcase. Briers is a great admirer of Ayckbourn's work and his commitment to the theatre and to Scarborough. He believes that being cast in *Relatively Speaking* was one of two turning points in his own career (the other was being recruited by Kenneth Branagh for his theatre and film company) and he regrets never having been directed by Ayckbourn. But it is worth noting, since this is supposed to be the well-made play that kept the rules, that he found that opening scene in the bed-sitter full of planted jokes and difficult to act. Nigel Patrick told him he would have to make it work or the audience would leave before the 'real stars' came on, so he invested his considerable adrenalin into bringing it off and getting to the point where the play took off, the meeting between Greg and Sheila.

The play had a short tour before opening in London. In Scotland a reviewer enjoyed the play but said that it fizzled out at the end. Working in Peter Bridge's office in London was a young American, Tom Erhardt, who told his boss the play should end as it started 'with the slippers'. In Scene 1, Greg's suspicions are aroused by the presence of a pair of man's slippers under Ginny's bed. We assume they are Philip's but – following a telephone call from Tom – Alan now made it clear at the end that they weren't his at all: Ginny has further secrets which the hapless Greg may or may not discover. Ayckbourn has often had difficulty ending plays precisely because life (and especially marriage) is open-ended, not climactic. Erhardt later went to work for Peggy Ramsay and is now not only Alan's literary agent but one of a small circle, a dozen people at most, of reasonably close friends.

The London first night – 29 March 1967 – seemed to go well but Alan waited cautiously for the reviews. The first was from Fergus Cashin in the *Daily Sketch*. 'He said it was dreadful, one of the worst plays he had ever seen, and I thought: "Oh fuck, here we go again." But it turned out to be the only bad review we received. Even the critics who didn't like it, liked it. Nobody was cruel or destructive.' Tom Erhardt was particularly proud of a line which went up outside the theatre: 'Fun to the last drop'. But there was also an object lesson in the way even a good press can backfire. One critic wrote something to the effect that here, at last, was 'a dramatist for real people'. Playgoers who had enjoyed other writers' work were naturally miffed at the notion that they weren't real people and somehow got the impression that Alan had made the claim himself. He had never spoken to the critic. But in theatre there is usually someone who likes even your worst disasters and there is always someone who hates your greatest triumph. Sure enough, after the first batch of reviews a small reaction set in. John Russell Taylor was not a lone voice when he wrote in *Plays and Players* that Greg was forced to behave in a false way because of the demands of the narrative.

Ayckbourn's own view of the play at the moment of completion – 'easy and glib' – is to some extent borne out by this. The play has the possible plotting of farce and the seriously probable characterisation of high social comedy, and hovers between the two. That didn't stop it from being hugely enjoyable for audiences, nor does it now; a revival toured successfully in 2000. Even that first scene reads very well. It is, incidentally, one of the very few places in an Ayckbourn play where one character says 'I love you' to another and isn't made to suffer for it. Whatever problems some critics had with it, the play was endorsed by one unimpeachable authority. A telegram arrived at the BBC in Leeds which Alan assumed to be a practical joke, especially when it turned out there was 14 shillings (70p) to pay for the delivery. It read: Dear Alan Ayckbourn All my congratulations on a beautifully constructed and very funny play I enjoyed every moment of it = Noël Coward. Coward – actor, playwright, composer, singer – was habitually referred to as The Master. His generosity to the young playwright was therefore magisterial. Soon Ayckbourn would be regularly compared with Coward, a journalistic habit which does little justice to two very different creative personalities but which derives from The Master's huge range of success, the only benchmark by which Alan's future successes could be measured.

On that night in early spring Ayckbourn took his biggest single career leap forward, at least financially. Although he was earning £38 a week at the BBC, more than double his wage in Stoke, he had actually got into debt just before hitting the jackpot. He thinks he owed about a month's salary to the bank, whose manager was giving him a difficult time (this was the first great period of economic stringency under the Wilson government). But from the beginning of the pre-London tour, money suddenly started to come in. The BBC in Leeds is close to the university and most of the accounts at the local branch of Alan's bank belonged to students and were consequently very small. Alan's account went up towards the black line, as he puts it, and just went on going up so that his account was soon one of the largest. It took him as much by surprise as the bank manager, and how sweet it was to have a respectful bank manager at last.

3 : A Battle Avoided

The Ayckbourn family had moved from Collingham to more rented accommodation in Tadcaster, a brewing town on the A64 from Leeds to York and Scarborough. Although Alan and Heather Stoney were seeing each other whenever possible, Alan hadn't left Christine and the boys, and Heather didn't expect him to: their relationship had developed gradually, without any dramatic moment of falling in love and only after he had worked his way round to her; and, to be even-handed about it, she had worked her way round to him. It was Chris's choice that their first family home in Leeds itself should be a flat in Seacroft where, says Alan, the boys came back from school with accents he couldn't understand and even the school reports were badly spelled. Seacroft is a big development on the eastern edge of the city, just inside the ring road. Like many before him and since, he decided that his basic belief in equality of educational opportunity notwithstanding, he was going to have Steven and Philip educated privately, and they went as day-boys to a local prep school, Moorlands. He is now glad that they experienced enough of the other side of education to retain a sense of perspective when they eventually went to Bryanston public school in Dorset (and Steven and Philip share that view to a varying extent). Alan still believes in fundamental fairness through equality of opportunity, but also that it is unforgivable to deny children a good education if it is within their reach. As soon as they could afford it they moved beyond the ring road to Adel, in the more affluent north of the city. In this leafy community with a village atmosphere Alan bought his first house.

Steven Ayckbourn recently took his Brazilian-born wife Telma to see the council estate in Seacroft where they had lived. Their old home looked as though it had been condemned because heavy bars had been welded across the entrance to the flats and it reminded him of blocks seen in Communist countries. He thought he and Philip had been 'pretty wretched' at the council school because they didn't fit in – an obviously middle-class family in a working-class environment. Philip remembers his little bike being stolen – by a close friend. Chris took him round to the friend's house and there it was, hanging up in a cupboard. The bike was returned but the theft was accepted as normal. In later life – and later plays – Alan would express a fear of and horror at the most deprived and lawless urban estates, often projected into the future for further exaggeration. This has its roots in Seacroft. But neither boy was victimised because of their father's comparatively posh job and burgeoning success. Before they left, the family was posed by a *Radio Times* photographer, sitting in harmony on the settee and pretending to read scripts. Steven was only seven when *Relatively Speaking* opened in London, Philip almost two years younger. Alan had learned to drive in his first car, folding his lanky frame into a Mini. Philip remembers them not being allowed to get in it when Alan passed his driving test, but being made to walk while Alan drove triumphantly alongside them.

Work on the London production and the job in Leeds had – perhaps
conveniently – kept him out of an immensely unhappy development that
had been taking place in his twin theatrical homes, Scarborough and
Stoke. In January 1967 the *Evening Sentinel* in Stoke had announced:
'SHAKE-UP SHOCKS CITY'S THEATRE-IN-ROUND: FIVE QUIT BOARD.' The story had
been going on unreported for some time before that and represented a
struggle for power and principle between Peter Cheeseman and Stephen
Joseph. Alan says Stephen had asked him to go to Stoke to replace Peter
long before but that 'one of the things I have always been rather proud of'
is that he had refused. Stephen had become seriously ill with cancer, and
Peter Cheeseman now maintains that it was as a result of the illness that
Stephen was acting irrationally in trying to get rid of him. This
explanation would be congenial enough to leave both men with
reputations intact. And Elizabeth Bell thinks Stephen took on the fight 'to
keep himself alive – to give himself a project'. Contemporary accounts in
the press certainly suggest that a straightforward personality clash was an
important ingredient, although the battle was presented as being about
whether a theatre should be run by people who were on the spot and in
the community, or by the faraway company that the visionary Stephen
had set up to promulgate the gospel of theatre-in-the-round. Stephen, of
course, wasn't against local accountability (he had worked with the local
authority in Newcastle under Lyme for years before Peter had been
involved, but he had pulled out when plans for a new theatre fell through)
and he offered to set up a new board with local members. He was, for
whatever reason, against Peter assuming total control of the Stoke
company's affairs. After four years these had grown to the point where
Stephen argued the need for a separation of the jobs of management and
artistic direction, and said that increased income – including Arts Council
and local authority grants totalling £20,000 – made a staffing increase
possible and desirable. He was quoted as saying that Peter was offered the
job of artistic director with complete artistic control but as part of a team
of management, that he had done everything he could to persuade Peter
to accept this, but that as soon as Stephen had fallen ill Peter had told
other directors he would resign instantly unless he was elected to the
board of directors. Peter, on the other hand, argued that Stephen's
proposal for a three-strong executive was designed deliberately to make
him resign. He was supported by Roy Shaw, later to become secretary-
general of the Arts Council, but then an influential professor at Keele
University. The local authority sided with Peter and so did the Potteries-
born poet and novelist John Wain, though his call for local control

seemed a bit odd written from Oxford. A little more tentatively house playwright Peter Terson praised Peter's handling and inspiration of his own work. Above all, the acting company and theatre staff (about 20 people at that time) showed great solidarity in favour of Peter. The battle had been conducted largely in secret until the annual meeting of the board of Studio Theatre Ltd, Stephen's company, at which Peter and Roy Shaw were not re-elected and other members resigned in protest, leaving a small 'rump' board which put Peter on three months' notice as artistic director and manager and sent in a replacement management team headed by Terry Lane.

Eventually Peter was banned from the theatre and called rehearsals in a local pub. The publicity was terrific. A big question mark hung over which way the Arts Council would jump. At that time it provided 75 per cent of the grant and its advice on artistic matters was heeded almost automatically. Jo Hodgkinson, who had dealt with both Stephen and Peter over a number of years and supported them in other fights, made calming noises in public but put nothing decisive on the record. The *Evening Sentinel*, trying to report impartially and inclined to remind its readers of how tempestuous Peter could be, was naturally responsive to his trump card – the call for strong local leadership. But after its reporter travelled to Scarborough and interviewed Stephen on his sick-bed, it also remembered that Stephen was actually the boss (his company owned the theatre's lease) of what was still, despite public subsidy, a private concern. Newspapers don't much care for the notion of employees taking power. Just how personal it became was reflected in a sorrowful article by the *Sentinel*'s theatre columnist J.S.A. Under the headline No Happy Ending he noted that power politics were involved, not cultural differences: 'A lot said to me has not been printed.' Out of tact, presumably, or fear of the libel laws.

David Campton was secretary to the company and wrote reminding theatregoers that Stephen had also inspired writers over a long period – he himself now had a play on in Rome starring Vittorio Gassman as a result. He mentioned James Saunders, Joan Macalpine and Alan Ayckbourn; also that Stephen had been the first person to do a stage play by Robert Bolt and had rescued Harold Pinter after the London critics had 'murdered *The Birthday Party*'. So it went on. The theatre, already in deficit and playing to around 50 per cent capacity for adult shows, was in danger of being mortally wounded. Local councillors were divided. Stoke favoured Peter, but Kidsgrove thought Stoke was trying to take everything over. Biddulph delayed its grant decision: 'We have the Biddulph Players here at home,' one councillor said, content with the local amateurs. Arts Council leadership was needed as never before, but when a meeting was convened in Scarborough to thrash things out, Jo Hodgkinson didn't attend.

The fact was that Stephen was dying. Peter denied there were personal differences between them, but David Campton describes an unhappy time when Stephen always seemed to turn up at the wrong moment: 'A banner was going up to direct audiences round the coffee bar and Stephen just snapped that a steel tube wasn't straight. A woman was pushing at a door you had to pull and he complained that there still wasn't a notice on it to say so. If there was a mishap in the show he would say it was the only interesting part of the evening. Things like that.' These are petty issues which smack either of bad temper sharpened by illness or the outward signs of irretrievable personal breakdown between two strong and combative personalities, one dedicated to the proposition that after a few years a theatre company should move on or implode, the other seeking roots and permanence in a community. For all his occasional belligerence, Peter was seriously hurt by the suggestion that his work was so dull it took a mishap to make it more fun. And for all his belief in and commitment to serious and rooted theatre he is still vulnerable to (and in his less buoyant moments will endorse) a later Arts Council drama director's verdict on himself as 'worthy, but dull'.

David Campton believes that the company was in difficulty, that Stephen spotted this and that Jo Hodgkinson himself had urged Stephen to take the company back under his own leadership. Stephen, ensconced in the Drama Department at Manchester University, was reluctant to do this but had just about agreed when he went into hospital. At this point, although the seriousness of his illness was largely kept secret, his boss in Manchester had to be told. Professor Hugh Hunt was also a member of the Arts Council. Consequently Jo Hodgkinson presumably found out that Stephen was dying, and the Arts Council promptly did a pragmatic volte-face and backed Peter. David Campton's view is also that if Stephen had gone back to the Stoke company – though we have seen that his taste was for initiating things, not pursuing them to their painstaking conclusion – he would have urged Alan Ayckbourn to take over from him in due course and that Alan might have expected this inheritance. But apart from Campton's letter mentioning Alan as a playwright discovered by Stephen, the name Ayckbourn does not appear in the battle lines at all. Alan believes that for a long time Peter thought he had indeed 'been a Stephen Joseph man' and probably felt betrayed after all the support he had given Alan over *Mr Whatnot*. Emotionally and in his instincts about theatre Alan *was* a Joseph man but he didn't take sides in a struggle he hated. Although there was a coolness between him and Peter for some years, Stoke audiences had built up a great enthusiasm for Alan's plays and Peter had a practical determination to make his theatre work. In 1973 he included *Relatively Speaking* in his programme there and for a decade staged an Ayckbourn a year alongside the local documentaries which proceed directly from Peter's so-called worthy side. Nobody today would contest Peter's achievement in getting the Stoke theatre and, a generation later, the new building in Newcastle under Lyme up and running. In that new building he named the studio theatre after Stephen Joseph.

Stephen died in the summer of 1967 having lived, according to Ian Watson, a year longer than doctors had expected. It was long enough to see *Relatively Speaking* a West End hit. Lolly painted a picture for John Hodgson of an emotional Alan thanking Stephen for being the only person who could get him writing again after *Mr Whatnot*. The British theatre's debt to Stephen Joseph is enormous and largely unrecognised. Not all the theatres which have been built in-the-round have met his very specific designs and some sadly miss the point about the audience needing to be all in a single tier so that they feel as if they are in the same, intimate room. But without him we would not have had the Royal Exchange Theatre in Manchester or the new ones in Scarborough, Newcastle under Lyme or Richmond, to say nothing of so many studio theatres. Just as important as the physical shape of the theatre is the way he (like George Devine at the Royal Court) helped to return theatre production to an emphasis on the text and the actors and therefore the audience's imagination. His legacy is largely realised through others, Alan chief among them. But part of that legacy is, over and above Alan's own plays, Alan's readiness to try to allow other writers the same kind of sustained support as he had himself. It is entirely likely that in today's arts culture Alan would have been written off after, say, *Christmas v Mastermind*. Elizabeth Bell, describing Alan as Stephen's true spiritual son, also points out that Stephen was probably the first person to offer Alan something more; sustained masculine warmth. He was probably the only person from whom it would have been acceptable, thanks to their shared diffidence and undemonstrative natures. This is borne out by Alan's description of times spent together, often in companionable silence testing different theatre models in cardboard, or listening to records as Alan tried to persuade the Bach-loving Stephen of the virtues of Tchaikovsky, or drinking whisky to which Alan introduced the curiously innocent

Stephen. The latter poured it into tumblers, drank it like water and, minutes later, said: 'Ayckers, I'm completely pissed.'

Ayckbourn's response to Stephen's death, he says, was as blank as usual, but for years afterwards he would dream that Stephen had come back from the dead and they were again talking about theatre. When Stephen died he was 46, Alan 28. Alan's future had to be in his own hands.

4 : *The Sparrow, How the Other Half Loves, The Story So Far*

It didn't start very well. Less than four months after the triumphant opening of *Relatively Speaking* in London, Ayckbourn's new play opened in Scarborough. Peter Bridge and Nigel Patrick rushed up to see it. The author had directed it, taking his summer holiday from the BBC to stay in the Scarborough flat Ken Boden had somehow found in lieu of a fee. With fixed grins Bridge and Patrick congratulated everyone concerned, and then travelled back to London as fast as they could. It was called *The Sparrow*, and what Bridge and Patrick had heard was a faint echo of Ann Jellicoe's enormous success, *The Knack*. Alan hadn't seen it at the time, and when he did he thought the only similarity was the presence of a spirited heroine in a scruffy flat, but he was exposed to the fictional air by the hundreds of scripts hitting his desk at the BBC. You might as easily identify the influence of Harold Pinter in the couple playing marital games at the expense of Evie (the sparrow of the title) and Ed (the innocent lump of a lodger who brings her into Tony and Julia's flat in the first place). Tony, the flat owner, prefigures many an Ayckbourn anti-hero in being a go-getter in business who is actually much less than he seems. And the last two lines, as Ed and Evie decide to leave, once more in the rain, signal his continuing refrain:

> EVIE (*wincing at the sound of a slap and a squeal from Julia*): Ooooh!
> Here, I hope I never get married.
> ED: So do I. Come on.

The play drew full houses in Scarborough and reads effectively for its insights and distinctive comedy (particularly Tony's invention of technical language when he is supposed to be testing Evie's shorthand). It looks eminently playable. Alan has never published it or made it available for production. Many another playwright would have been pleased with it and maybe Alan thought less of it because it was rejected by Bridge and Patrick. However, it is told in a conventional way by his standards and lacks the texture of what was to come.

Pamela Craig played Evie, John Nettles, Ed, Robert Powell, Tony and Heather Stoney, his wife Julia. None of them except Heather worked with him again, though Robert Powell has become a good friend. The fact that there was a theatre for them to perform in at all was due to Ken Boden. The bluff Yorkshireman, who appeared to know everybody in the audience by name, is the unsung third hero in the story of the company. When Stephen Joseph had become ill he had decided not to carry on with theatre in Scarborough although he was still living in the house in Longwestgate with Mrs Pemberton-Billing nursing him devotedly and Hermione Gingold turning up to present him with a cat (which hated him) and to have her photograph taken. Ken and Margaret decided that if the theatre was allowed to go dark for a year they might never get it back. He arranged a season with local amateur companies for 1966 and then got the help of Alfred Bradley and Alan Plater (who lived down the coast in Hull) to keep the theatre going until the heir apparent could be lured back. (Plater promptly got involved in establishing what is now the theatre in Hull which is John Godber's base.) It would be Ken who, boosted by Alan's success in filling the theatre, would suggest expanding the company's output from a short summer season to include the winter too. And, at a very practical level, it was Ken who could supply a season's props in advance – from a bale of hay to a sofa – by using his powers of persuasion on his insurance customers.

Alan's position at the BBC was becoming awkward because he was rarely there. His secretary would tell callers he had just popped out for a minute and then ring him in Scarborough; he would ring back pretending to be at his desk. Before he finally left, the old institution enabled him to meet a *Goon Show* hero, with disastrous consequences. He was sent round to the Grand Theatre in Leeds where Spike Milligan was appearing in *The Bed-Sitting Room*, which he had written with John Antrobus. The BBC was facilitating some charity work for children and wanted Milligan to record one of his comic short poems. At first it was all shy-fan-meets-benevolent-idol. He knocked on the dressing-room door, and Milligan answered in the thick but good-natured accent of the Famous Eccles: 'Hello, lad.' Alan introduced himself rather hesitantly, explained what was needed, and set up the microphone. 'Oh, one of the little poems. Nicky nacky noo. What's it for, boy?' Still in the Eccles voice. For Save the Children, for Christmas, explained Alan. And Spike suddenly dropped the joke voice completely:

'Oh, Christ almighty! I'd do anything for kids, y'know.' Alan attempted to respond, but Spike went on: 'Do you realise how many kids are suffering in the world at this moment?' Alan didn't. 'At this moment. Millions without a square meal.' Alan conceded that this was terrible but was anxious to get the poem on tape. 'Oh yes! Oh fuck! Oh Jesus!' He did the poem. Alan left him with his head in his hands and walked back up to the BBC where he was de-spooling the tape when the telephone rang. It was the manager of the Grand Theatre, where Spike had locked himself in his dressing-room and wouldn't come out until the children of the world were fed. Two thousand people were waiting for him, so the manager had offered a donation. 'Not enough, you bastards.' A little later Alan was walking down to the bus station to go home when he passed the Grand Theatre and there were two thousand people coming out, their show cancelled.

Early in 1969, Alan's short play *Countdown* was included in a series of nine 'entertainments about marriage' in a programme called *Mixed Doubles*, produced first at Hampstead and then in the West End. The other writers were Harold Pinter, David Campton and James Saunders, also from the Stephen Joseph stable, plus Fay Weldon, John Bowen, Alun Owen, George Melly and Lyndon Brook. In *Countdown* an unnamed husband and wife, 'any evening of any week in any year of this 20-year-old marriage,' sit at the supper table articulating both the conventionally polite banalities they say out loud and their much more unkind inner thoughts. The music of a ballroom dance band points up the verbal footwork as each tries to corner the other. That year he was also asked by Alan Durband to write something to be included in an anthology of work intended for performance by children in schools. In the introduction to *Alan Ayckbourn: Plays 2* (Faber, 1998) he demonstrates his typically practical approach to the task:

> I tried to accommodate this by writing a play for a limited number of leading players and an infinitely expandable supporting cast, working on the principle that there are always three or four in any group who can do it and another fifty who just mill around eagerly but hate to be left out. Somewhat to my surprise it has turned out to be something of a success. Over the years it has received innumerable productions – probably more than any of my plays – spanning several generations of children, including at one stage both my now extremely mature sons. Rarely does a season pass without at least one actor in my company confiding to me that *Ernie* was their starting point as an aspiring actor.

Ernie's Incredible Illucinations, to give its full title, was the exception to the 20-year silence (as a children's writer) that followed *Christmas v*

Mastermind. Apart from its user-friendliness for a teacher struggling with large casts and limited talent, it invites the imagination of the audience – young or old – inside a child's mind. Imagination, Alan has said, is the magic of theatre, not 'that old claptrap of velvet curtains'. It opens in a doctor's surgery. Ernie talks directly to the audience – something that happens only in the children's plays – and explains that he has daydreams that come true; on a miserable Saturday, with his mother knitting and his father gazing vacantly into space, he was sitting at home reading a book about the French wartime Resistance when he wondered what it would be like if a troop of German soldiers turned up at the front door. And they promptly did. The doctor thinks Ernie's family has succumbed to a group hallucination. As he mutters about psychiatrists, Ernie concentrates hard and marches the doctor and all his other patients out in the guise of a brass band. It punctures authority and celebrates theatre's ability to make anything happen. Steven Ayckbourn recalls Alan coming to see it at Bryanston some years later when he himself was doing his best to avoid plays.

In that summer of 1969 the 30-year-old Ayckbourn produced for the theatre the first play to fulfil all the criteria of an 'Ayckbourn play' – at least the criteria of his early period. It is so reliably funny that actors can relax about getting laughs, which is almost a prerequisite of good comedy; it takes a very bleak view of marriage, with three wretched examples on show at the same time, but it has things to say about sex, class and power as well; and it has a brilliantly experimental narrative device which allows us to see two dinner parties, which actually happen at different times and in different places, on stage together: in fact it tends to be referred to as 'the dinner party play'. *How the Other Half Loves* has proved even more durable than *Relatively Speaking* and is a richer and a more realistically grounded play as well as being much more innovative. It made its author rich and unexpectedly unhappy.

What we see looks like a single living-room, except that it has double furnishings: on the settee, for example, are two sets of cushions, chic ones belonging to the very smart Frank and Fiona Foster, slightly tackier ones to the more middle-class Bob and Teresa Phillips. It is clear to the audience pretty early on that Bob Phillips is having an affair with Fiona Foster. But while Frank Foster is politely incurious about what his wife has been doing until two in the morning, the tense Teresa Phillips – trying to cope with a small child and the absence of proper breakfast food, while worrying seriously about the state of the world – is understandably querulous. In need of an alibi, Bob Phillips pretends to have been with William

Featherstone the night before, supporting him through his wife's alleged affair. The only real contrivance in the plotting is that Fiona Foster simultaneously invents as *her* alibi Mary Featherstone's need for support through her husband's alleged infidelity. Frank Foster is Bob Phillips's boss and William Featherstone works in the same company's accounts department. What is more natural than that each of the first two couples should have invited the Featherstones to dinner? We see both parties simultaneously, the Featherstones swivelling from the Fosters to the Phillipses and back on their dining chairs. Inevitably the Featherstones are given good reason to suspect each other and William eventually charges round to the Phillips house brandishing a monkey-wrench. The chance of an innocent couple being destroyed is one potential outcome, though even this is enriched by the fact that William is such an unpleasant man. Ayckbourn doesn't particularly go in for writing one-liners, any more than Chekhov did, or Ibsen, but William's exclamation about his timid wife – 'Do you realise, Mrs Foster, the hours I've put into that woman?' – is horribly memorable.

In gender-political terms the play is divided simply down the middle; all the men treat their wives badly. It is also subtly divided in class and character terms so that each couple is unhappy in a different way. But Mary Featherstone speaks for more than herself when she finally responds to her husband's crassness: 'It's difficult for him. He's never been wrong before, you see.'

It was at this time that interviewers started to raise the question of whether his work is autobiographical. Alan told Robin Thornber in the *Guardian* in 1970 that he 'had been drawn into the comet's tail of someone else's breaking marriage', which gives nothing away. An article by Philip Oakes in *Cosmopolitan* in 1974 said confidently: 'It is only recently that he's started to write autobiographically.' If we take that to mean that his plays tell his own life-story, he still hasn't started. But to the failure of Lolly's and Horace's relationships – two each – he could now add his own marriage as well as those of friends. His perceptions were autobiographical, but there are rarely deliberate portraits in the characters. Once he starts on a play he lives in its world. People and situations filter in via his unconscious to serve the internal needs of the drama, but he may not articulate this even to himself until afterwards when he comes to help actors in rehearsal.

Once again, Peter Bridge was pleased with what he saw in Scarborough. He had Robin Midgley (later the director of regional theatres in Leicester and Belfast) lined up as director, and he had approached Robert Morley to play Frank Foster. Of the original cast Brian Miller, as the upwardly thrusting William, and Elizabeth Ashton as his cowed wife would transfer to the West End. Alan was summoned, with Bridge and Midgley, down to the village near Henley where Robert Morley lived because the great man 'wants to make some changes'. Alan said: 'Oh, does he?' and prepared for battle, at which he says Peter Bridge replied (Alan imitates a very clipped voice): 'Don't get uptight! He's an experienced actor and a tremendous draw, darling, so we'll just go down, listen to what he has to say and DON'T GET BEADY!' It probably didn't help that Alan had taken over the part of Frank himself in Scarborough when Jeremy Franklin injured his back stepping off the kerb. Robert invited them all to the Writing Den – a shed with a desk behind which he sat and launched into a monologue about comedy and what people really wanted to see. The first argument was about the fact that Frank Foster was an unsuccessful jogger, setting himself a time to complete his run on an alarm clock in the living-room, and never quite making it. Robert thought flower-arranging would be funnier. Alan didn't. A lot of men did it, said Robert, especially in Japan. Yes, said Alan, but Frank was from Surrey. And so it went on, with Peter Bridge telling Alan to cool down and Robert eventually saying, according to Alan: 'I think I'm losing patience with this little script. I think I want to do something else.' Alan: 'Fine, you do that.' Peter Bridge tried to manage his anxiety attack as Robert went on: 'I've got a play of my own, actually, which Rosemary Anne Sisson and I have been developing and I think I'll carry on with this one.' Alan called his bluff again and Robert eventually said: 'Well, no, I don't have a lot of confidence in it.' Alan says that Robert wanted about ten changes in all – he thought his character should have a butler – and he let him have three of them but that in any case Robert changed it entirely in performance. Some of these changes he rather liked – Robert made Frank refer to lavatory paper as 'bathroom stationery' and Alan put it in the published script. Others made him 'weep quietly in the corner'. The problem was not only to do with changes to the text or business, which most writers hate but sometimes admit to be improvements, but with the sheer weight of Robert Morley's stage personality. He was a big man – you could see he might not want to jog – and he had an even larger stage presence with a very distinctive voice. A play with six equal parts inevitably became a star vehicle. He put pressure on Bridge to cast Joan Tetzel as his wife. She was American, which seemed slightly improbable for the character. Then he took against her during rehearsals. In the second cast Jan Holden took over, playing Fiona much more as she was written, and Robert complained that he wanted people on stage with him who looked as though they adored being there. But as he said at the outset: 'I've left a trail of sadder but far, far richer dramatists behind me.' He asked Lolly at a party why Alan looked so unhappy when Robert was making him so rich. She said it was just the way his face was. When he complained to Alan that he didn't 'come to see us very often', Alan said it was hard to bear, seeing all the Common Market jokes that Robert was putting in. Robert said he hadn't meant Alan should come and see the play, but he should call round to the dressing-room from time to time. One night, Alan was so upset that he was physically sick. He remembers thinking that if success felt this bad what would renewed failure be like?

It doesn't seem so grim in retrospect. He now remembers Robert Morley for his charm, the sense that he had constructed his own personality and needed to play it to the full, his sheer love of being on stage and his enthusiasm for people. And when it came to August, Robert suddenly – and reasonably – insisted on a fortnight's holiday. Since he didn't want anyone else to have a go at 'his' part in his absence, he insisted the whole cast should have a holiday. Suddenly he was the most popular man in the London theatre: 'Oh no, my darlings, you wouldn't get this with Vanessa now, would you?' He may have been a champagne socialist but Alan thinks he was genuinely left-wing, always forking out for a good cause and putting heavy pressure on others to do the same. And the show ran for two years and it did make Alan rich, not least because it would be the first of his plays to be taken up by the Americans.

A fortnight after *How the Other Half Loves* had opened on Shaftesbury Avenue Alan had opened another play in Scarborough. This pattern, with a few variations, would effectively shape his life from 1970 to the present. Looking back on a period when he was about to forge a reputation for sure-fire success, it is salutary to recognise that he now came up with a relative failure.

The new play started life in Scarborough as *The Story So Far*, was re-titled *Me Times Me Times Me* and finally achieved its greatest success in 1978 at Richmond, directed by Sam Walters, as *Family Circles*. And if you seek proof that at his best Ayckbourn is never simply technical or mechanistic, here is an example of what happens when he is. Edward and Emma are celebrating their wedding anniversary, and their three daughters have come home with men in tow. Edward says early on that we all marry the wrong person and the mechanism of the play is the way in which the strongly contrasted younger women try each others' partners on for size, while at the same time investigating if there is any truth in the rumour that their father is trying to kill their mother. With hindsight, Ayckbourn says Edward and Emma were inspired by Christine's parents, Charles and Elaine; interestingly the father of the fiancée who preceded Christine was also a lone man in an otherwise female household. The plotting is clever but somehow it doesn't quite engage you, perhaps because it promises to be a comedy of character but in the end is consciously and deliberately an ingeniously artificial construction, with actors playing their characters quite differently in succeeding scenes as they team up with different partners. In a bewildering final section they are called upon to play all three versions of themselves in short order. It suggests that all nine permutations are equally possible and equally doomed; what seem like life-choices are not much more than a lottery. It is brilliant in its way but so complicated that it is hard to relax enough to laugh. At one time Ayckbourn withdrew the production rights but later he made the play available again and perhaps it should be tried on newer, younger audiences.

Alan had, as usual, announced the play's title before he had written it, to meet the publicity deadline. *The Story So Far* covered a multitude of possibilities. His working methods still relied on late-night sessions, fuelled by cigarettes and coffee and whisky, well into the rehearsal period. One night he went to bed for a couple of hours' sleep before dawn, leaving what he had just written on top of the cooker. Christine got up a little later and blearily switched the grill on, burning the whole thing. Nothing fresh to rehearse that day. But it was at least relatively successful in Scarborough and Peter Bridge took it up and Robin Midgley directed it (as *Me Times Me Times Me*). Neither that nor a second out-of-town production by Michael Codron (directed by Basil Coleman and starring Celia Johnson again) went on into the West End. Alan was made aware again of the way the old star system was at odds with his ensemble plays. This wasn't just a producer's fixation. This was a time when stars were still applauded by audiences when they came on stage, before they had done anything. Whenever Celia Johnson was off-stage, as she frequently was, her fans simply lost interest in the play.

The Scarborough production was the first Ayckbourn play in which Bob Peck – Robert Peck on the programme in those days – appeared as a professional. Being the youngest member of the company (but always a character actor) he naturally played the old man. Peck was good at playing integrity and he was also an actor of great integrity, which is not always the same thing: he played the gritty policeman getting to the heart of a conspiracy in *The Edge of Darkness* on television, and the duplicitous Iago in *Othello* for the RSC, with equally complete conviction. When I asked him for an interview in connection with this book he was already gravely ill with the cancer from which he eventually died in April 1999, but he readily consented out of a sense that he owed Alan a favour. He gave me time, put off taking his drugs, insisted on driving me back to the station after we had finished and vowed to keep fighting, although almost his last words to me were: 'The trouble is you run out of puff.' Invited by the press to comment on Bob's death, Ayckbourn said that he'd found him acting in a cellar in Leeds and had been looking in cellars for the next 30 years without ever finding another Bob Peck. While never using such sentimental language, he had adopted Bob as a younger version of himself.

Peck was a boy from Spen Lane in Leeds who had first been recruited (through a teacher) by Alfred Bradley, for a radio play set in a school. After an unhappy spell with the National Youth Theatre at the age of 15, he returned to Leeds and became a student at the College of Art. Alan gave him small radio roles and he was involved with an amateur theatre company of which Alan agreed to be the nominal president because his secretary was also a member. When a production planned by the company fell through because they lost the rights to the play – and stood to lose a lot of money – Alan volunteered to moonlight from the BBC and direct Bob in *Mr Whatnot*, getting a BBC technician to do the sound-effects. Bob also took over a guitar-playing role in Alan Cullen's play for children, *Trudi and the Minstrel*, when another actor dropped out; men are in short supply in amateur societies and, not really being able to play the guitar very much, he had bleeding fingers at the end of the night. Alan saw that and, after Bob secured his art school diploma, offered him a job as an acting ASM in Scarborough the following summer. He also instructed him in the procedure for writing off to other theatres in the meantime (Peck was completely ignorant of how theatre was set up) and took him down to Stoke to meet Peter Cheeseman. Bob, supposedly navigating, got them lost and then a stone hit the windscreen creating the frosted effect through which it is impossible to see anything. On a bitterly cold night, Alan poked a small hole in the glass and drove on, shutting his door very gently when they finally arrived. Bob promptly slammed his door and all the remaining glass fell into the car. They had to stay the night in Stoke and Alan stayed with Peter, which meant a formal reconciliation after their estrangement in the great row between Peter and Stephen Joseph. Bob slept on another actor's floor.

To a degree Alan was to Bob Peck what Stephen Joseph had been to him, and Bob gave me some of the clearest images of Alan at the time he was making the transition from company member to leader. Alan had by now graduated to a chic black Mini Cooper and he drove Bob to Scarborough from Leeds for the 1969 season (plays by Leonard Barras, Peter Hawkins and Alfred Bradley's adaptation of a Stan Barstow novel in addition to *How the Other Half Loves*). *En route*, Alan gave him a kind of life seminar:

> I think he was conscious that I was a 23-year-old who'd lived at home all his life, got his fingers burned in London and fought shy of any city that didn't begin with L and end with S; he might have a bit of a liability on his hands in Scarborough. He wanted to liberate me a bit. So all the way there, it wasn't exactly a sex education I had but it was where the watering holes were, where I could meet birds. And lo and behold, I'd been there maybe less than a fortnight and I went into the bar at the Cliff Hotel and there was this barmaid who was five feet ten. The actor I was with told me I'd be going out with her within a week. Not only was I going out with her, I lived with her for six and a half years.

Bob lost his virginity in Alan's bed. He was convinced that Alan – who in Bob's phrase 'could laugh a different girl into bed every night' – engineered the whole thing.

Peck also recalled Ayckbourn's inventing a beach game called Buzz Flags – named after the American astronaut Buzz Aldrin who took part in the successful moon mission. The object was to plant a flag as near to the incoming tide as you dared while wearing full clothing. Alan would do everything in his power to make the company happy, taking over the nearby hotel owned by Tom Laughton – brother of the actor Charles Laughton – and giving them all a slap-up meal before, with a few drinks inside him, launching himself into a bravura performance of anecdotes and impersonations. Intriguingly, as the responsibility given to him at the BBC developed his confidence, Alan's outbursts of rage or acid comedy went into decline, but there was a price to pay: leadership meant giving up his role as company joker. When Stanley Page returned to Scarborough in 1972 he was aware that the old relationship had to be modified. Alan was becoming his own man. If his new role meant greater isolation away from the rehearsal room, so be it. He was used to being solitary, even when with people. He was also, although he couldn't know it, about to fire off an extravagant salvo of six hits in four years: a strike rate unmatched in British theatre before or since.

Chapter 5

Hitmaker to the world

1 : *Time and Time Again, Absurd Person Singular*

Peggy Ramsay had sold the rights to *Relatively Speaking* in America – eventually she sold them several times – but although Joan Fontaine appeared in a touring production it never reached New York. Part of the ambiguous favour Robert Morley did Alan was that the Americans also saw *How the Other Half Loves* as a star vehicle, and in 1971 the director Gene Saks cast the veteran comedian Phil Silvers, creator of *Sergeant Bilko*, in 'Morley's' part. Tom Erhardt, back in America after his spell working for Peter Bridge in London, got a job as Saks's assistant; it included helping Silvers learn his lines. This was no small task, since Silvers hadn't been in a stage play for many years and the double dinner party scene makes them tricky enough to learn anyway. Erhardt went back to Silvers's hotel every day after rehearsals – who knows what the gossips made of that? – and worked through the dialogue that embraces two time-sequences at once. The pre-New York tour opened in West Palm Beach, Florida, to a packed and fashionable audience conspicuously displaying its wealth; a nervous Ayckbourn joined them.

Because Silvers still hadn't been on top of the script at the afternoon dress rehearsal a hole was cut in the stage, and a hood placed over it to hide the head of Tom Erhardt, sitting with a script and torch like the old-fashioned prompter beloved of cartoonists. Silvers duly dried and Tom read out the next line. Nothing happened. He repeated it: still nothing. Then Tom heard a hoarse whisper: 'Louder, baby!' By the time Silvers eventually got the line out half the audience was prompting him. In the interval a nervous Erhardt was berated by the British co-producer of the show, Eddie Kulukundis, for prompting too loudly. But the actress Sandy Dennis defended him, saying that Silvers had become paralysed with fright and unable to take the prompt for a long time. He did learn the role as the tour progressed to Boston and Washington and when it opened on

Broadway the reviews for him and the play were good enough to secure a decent run.

Phil Silvers was a classic embodiment of the cliché about the sadness of clowns. At speaking engagements he would be introduced as one of the world's funniest men and then talk about the misery of being separated from the four daughters he adored. When every woman in the audience had been reduced to a mess of streaming mascara he would sit down. Then Silvers would lean across to Alan, due to speak next, and say: 'Now, you knock 'em dead, baby.' They became quite fond of one another when Silvers got the idea, from hearing Sandy Dennis talking about his awful old clothes, that Alan was some kind of social outcast.

In the house at Adel, there was already a map on the kitchen wall with flags to mark the countries where his plays had been produced. But what else was happening at home? Steven Ayckbourn remembers a 1930s house: art deco, according to Bob Peck, who used to walk up for a cup of tea with Chris when he was still an art student living at home in Spen Lane. It had a custom-built study, in which Alan's penchant for lighting had been allowed full rein. It also had a very fancy desk with a bar at the back and a stereo system the boys were forbidden to touch. There was a large lawn with a swing and some apple trees and room for a cricket net, and there was also a conservatory with a very large window in the long-off position. 'I think we must have hit it half a dozen times with quite high velocity and there was a sort of a DONG! And it just bounced off.' The boys used to half-try not to hit it and half-want to know what would happen if they did. Steven also remembers a wall inside the house into which they set stones gathered on family outings to the beach near Flamborough Head. The stones were only stuck on with plaster of Paris and periodically they would drop out on to the settee below. Steven thinks Alan may have encouraged Chris's father to sit there when he visited but he was never hit. While the boys called their parents by their first names, Chris called her father 'Dad' and her mother 'Mother'. Steven sensed Alan didn't really get on with his father-in-law. There had been an early holiday on the Thames near Bray with Lolly also present where the rows sowed some of the seeds for *Way Upstream* (1981). Steven remembers Lolly, perhaps surprisingly given her avowed distaste for children, taking charge of him and Philip while the others fought it out. Like a lot of people who are uncomfortable as parents, Lolly seems to have been good with grandchildren. They didn't see very much of her at this time because she was living in London and they hardly ever visited her though she occasionally visited them. She did once say something nasty to Philip but he said something nasty back and that was the end of it. You had to give as good as you got, with Lolly.

There is also a pre-echo of *Season's Greetings* in a story Philip told me about this period. Philip was the more interested in the theatre of the two boys, although both have eventually come round to working in it. If given a toy car with a figure in it, he would take the person out and play with that, whereas Steven was always more interested in the car and in building things. Philip would make shoes talk to each other as puppets if nothing else was to hand, and he devised puppet shows for the whole family to perform at Christmas for visiting grandparents. One year Alan arrived shortly before Christmas and there was no time for rehearsal. When it came to the finale of the now-forgotten show, with every puppet on stage for the big finish, Philip's puppet (a dog) got its strings tangled with Alan's. Rather than stop the show, Alan whipped both puppets away, yanked all the strings except one off Philip's puppet, gave it back and continued as if nothing had happened. Philip was in floods of tears because he had a dog with one working paw, and at the age of seven or so he didn't see any comic possibilities in this. The puppeteer in *Season's Greetings* (1980) is mainly the butt of others' jokes but he does speak up for the integrity of his art and he is given the explosive rebuttal of the man who has emerged as a low-grade fascist in the course of the family Christmas; again, no replication of real life but a distillation of experience.

The hidden significance of this story is the bit about Alan arriving just before Christmas. Like Horace during his own childhood, he just wasn't around all that much. The boys seem not to have minded – they took it for granted. Long absences are common in the theatre. They would wait by the pillars at the end of the drive when he was coming – they never really knew where from – with great excitement and anticipation. They were aware of rows between Alan and Chris but not of them being long-drawn-out. 'Each was the sort to drop the bomb and run off,' is how Philip described the arguments. Close friends testify to the fact that if there were rows, they were never seen or heard by anyone else. Sometimes the boys would be silenced on bad-tempered car journeys, but what boys aren't? Chris recalled the house – which they named The Weeds – providing much happiness for children and adults alike. Steven says his parents were right to split up in the end because they were unhappy; he has been through the same process himself. Both boys look like Alan while also looking, and being, completely different. They have also perhaps inherited the ability to get on with their own lives even while there is unhappiness around.

Heather Stoney had a flat in Redcliffe Gardens in West London, but in 1971 she and Alan finally started to share a home. Elizabeth Bell was living with the architect Harry Osborne who, as a result of a divorce settlement, was converting the house he had built in Keats Grove, Hampstead into two separate dwellings. Did Liz know anyone who wanted to buy the front half? She knew only two people who had the money. Alan was the second and he jumped at the chance. Keats Grove became home.

Lolly went to look the place over – on Chris's behalf, she said – and in due course the boys came to stay. Steven was incredibly polite, making small talk about the local shopping. Heather cooked sausages and beans as instructed. She had just had a new haircut and Alan claimed it made her look like Henry V, so they christened her Henry. Alan handled it well, she thought, by making it jokey. There was never any prospect of the boys moving in; their home remained in Leeds with Chris, but Steven would soon be off to Bryanston, and Philip duly followed him. The public school in Dorset had the advantage over Haileybury in Alan's time of being mixed-sex. Alan says that as soon as he and Chris finally agreed their marriage was over their relationship became much easier. It helped enormously that Heather had arrived on the scene after the hurtful early disappointments and infidelities. So, almost seamlessly, Alan changed from living with Chris to living with Heather. Many people notice with a certain sourness that he usually gets his own way. In the vast majority of cases, though, it is not achieved by riding roughshod over other people. To this day they all spend Christmas together in Longwestgate. Chris and the two sons have their trust funds and are financially looked after, thanks in large measure to Heather's efficiency and consideration. When Chris finally left Leeds it was to settle a few streets away from Keats Grove in Hampstead. Neither she nor Alan sought a divorce for another 30 years. For each of them, being married was a safeguard against making the same mistake again.

In America with *How the Other Half Loves* for the early part of 1971, Alan entrusted the Scarborough season to his old co-conspirator from Stoke, Caroline Smith, but in *Time and Time Again* he wrote and directed its biggest hit. When the Scarborough cast met for rehearsals the first read-through was greeted by almost total silence until one actor said: 'Well, I think it will run' – he paused for a beat – 'about 2 hours and 15 minutes.' Actors don't always know what is funny until the audience laughs, and they may not know *why* even then. Unless the author is Oscar Wilde or Joe Orton even the best comedies don't yield up their qualities to the reader either. But Ayckbourn does know what will work, within the limits of audience predictability. My theory, for what it is worth, is that a play in performance exists in five dimensions: the usual three, plus time, plus a fifth which is the physical and psychological space in which the audience itself picks up all the tone and content of the play, shared references, the apprehension of intention and cumulative effect, which draw on the other four. Alan has an unusually clear sense of this space, which is itself somehow more emphatic in the round with the audience embracing or even pressure-cooking the action. There is a small but effective example in *Time and Time Again*. Graham, a managerial bully, married to Anna, has a lecherous yen for Joan, fiancée of his employee Peter. But his brother-in-law, the feckless Leonard, manages to divert Joan's affection to himself. Outside Graham's house he persuades Joan to put her tongue out at Graham, who is on the other side of the conservatory's glass and cannot hear what is being said. This no great joke on paper – just a pretty woman teasing an unpleasant male, though it does have the virtue of being an action which demonstrates the progress of the plot. In performance, though, it can bring the house down: it's something to do with the build-up, something to do with our hopes for Leonard and Joan, something to do with the spatial dimensions in which every member of the audience has a slightly different view and perceives the event for just a second as something only he or she is privy to.

In the end nobody gets Joan. Peter, the man who won the right to ask her out by making good use of his reach in a boxing match, is sporty but unimaginative. The married Graham is never a contender. And Leonard, the first of Ayckbourn's innocent destroyers who never seem to take any initiatives at all and leave trails of misery in their wake, pulls back from a full commitment, an almost cruel withdrawal that Joan sees for what it is in good time. The play ends with Leonard accidentally injuring Peter for the third time giving a punch-line to a drama that otherwise has a Chekhovian dying fall. It is the first true character comedy – with nothing plotted for farcical purposes – of Ayckbourn's output. This, as he told the *Financial Times*, was a direct result of being inspired by a London production of Chekhov's *Uncle Vanya*, featuring Paul Scofield. In 1972 he would include the play in the Scarborough season and secure a fine performance from Heather Stoney as Sonia.

The play is set on an unkempt strip of grass (the lawn-mower is lethally jammed) between the conservatory (the first entrance) and the boundary marker of a cricket pitch (the second entrance). Up until 1976 Alan's Scarborough plays had only two entrances because that was all the Library

Theatre had room for. And one of those was the audience's entrance too; latecomers sometimes followed actors on to the set. There was also a small pond – Alan's first but far from last experiment with on-stage water. The first night went well, and afterwards there was a party at Ken and Margaret Boden's house. The last guest left at about 5.0 a.m. and three hours later Ken's telephone rang. The 'pond' was leaking and had fused all the lights in the Library itself. He put his clothes on over his pyjamas and went back to work.

Sadly Alan's relationship with Peter Bridge had broken down before the play transferred to the West End. It was in his office that Alan had read the dreadful reviews for *Mr Whatnot*; he had helped Alan triumph with *Relatively Speaking* (he had a grateful letter from the author to prove it) and his production of *How the Other Half Loves* had made Alan rich. But his own financial base had become rocky and Alan had a telephone call from a solicitor advising him not to get involved with Bridge for the time being. The shipping magnate with a taste for theatre production who had co-produced *How the Other Half Loves* in America, Eddie Kulukundis, came into the reckoning for *Me Times Me Times Me*, as the touring version of *The Story So Far* was called. Alan asked if Kulukundis would let Bridge co-produce and got a favourable answer, but Bridge angrily refused the offer. Alan thinks Bridge had a breakdown, and stories came back to him of Bridge stopping actors in the street, showing them that letter and asking how Alan could abandon him now. The friendship was eventually patched up, but it was an unhappy time. Meanwhile Michael Codron, already establishing a reputation as the leading producer of the more interesting contemporary plays in the West End, let Peggy Ramsay know that he was interested. Alan, keen to have *Time and Time Again* treated with the seriousness of high comedy rather than as a star vehicle, was happy to turn to him. The professional relationship, though not un-broken, continues to this day.

It was Codron's suggestion that the play be directed by Eric Thompson, an actor-turned-director who was best known as the voice of the children's television programme *The Magic Roundabout* until he directed a revival of R. C. Sherriff's First World War drama *Journey's End* at the new Royal Exchange Theatre in Manchester. It had transferred to London. Alan went to meet him at his Hampstead home where two small girls called Emma and Sophie were running about. Both men were nervous and trusted each other at once, coming to know each other as Big Al and Little E. Tom Courtenay was persuaded to play Leonard, not without difficulty.

Reading a play without obvious farcical laughs in it he feared that his public would think it was his fault if it didn't get laughs in performance: what Alan calls 'the star's dilemma'. Courtenay is an actor of a blazing intensity which is often associated with tragedy but he can be blisteringly funny in comedy – the only man I've ever wanted to see more of as the neurotically jealous Faulkland in Sheridan's *The Rivals*. He is also an actor whose exploration of a role never finishes; he would rather not even know when the official first night is, let alone 'fix' his performance in advance of it. This runs counter to the presumption that a clockwork precision is the most important quality for the performance of Ayckbourn's comedy; comedic skills have to be in place, but periodically throughout his career greater depth has been discovered by actors who can risk more. It keeps the rest of the cast on their toes too.

For the cricket-loving playwright the crowning triumph of *Time and Time Again* was that the Australian Test-playing brothers Greg and Ian Chappell came to see it. By its London press night (August 1972), the next play had already opened in Scarborough, and for many people *Absurd Person Singular* is, in Michael Billington's phrase, 'the big one'. Ayckbourn was writing it by night while directing rehearsals by day of a David Campton play called *Carmilla*, adapted from a vampire story by Sheridan Le Fanu. The actors made each other laugh so disgracefully during rehearsals in London and then a week of performances in the new studio theatre of the Sheffield Crucible (opened by Caroline Smith in February 1972) that they reduced the number of performances when they got to Scarborough. Jennifer Piercey was left in a coffin on stage during the interval, while the audience trooped out across the acting area making comments and tapping the box on the way. So there was a manic mood around the writing of the new play, and an element of fear. *Absurd Person Singular* was another blanket title, meaning nothing much, invented to meet the printer's deadline and originally intended for another play which didn't work out.

Alan found this play very difficult to write too. The action was to take place at three successive Christmases, with three couples hosting drinks parties in turn, the last involuntarily. In the first act Sidney Hopcroft, an ambitious tradesman and his submissive, bullied, but devoted wife Jane are entertaining an incompetent architect, Geoffrey, and his wife Eva, and a bank manager, Ronald Brewster-Wright, and his wife Marion, because of what Hopcroft hopes to get out of them. In the second, a now desperate architect returns the hospitality as he tries to hitch himself to Sidney's bandwagon. In the third, Sidney and Jane turn up uninvited at the bank manager's home to find him and his wife utterly alienated from each other and needing their visitors to bring colour as well as custom their way. The play, set in the three living-rooms, refused to take off until Alan realised that the real action was going on 'back-stage' – in the kitchens. This allowed him to dispense with two guests, Dick and Lottie Potter, altogether, although every time the kitchen door opens in Act I we hear explosions of laughter greeting Dick's jokes, and Geoffrey, the architect, tells us how he drops peanuts on to the carpet so that he can bend down and look up Lottie's skirt.

In the kitchen Jane comes into her own as an obsessive wiper of surfaces and tidier of things away; and Eva, the architect's wife, can be seen in a succession of suicide attempts inspired by her husband's lack of professional principle and determined womanising. Naturally when Eva sticks her head in the gas oven Jane goes to help her clean it. When she tries to electrocute herself the bumbling bank manager offers to help her change the light bulb and almost kills himself instead. By the end of the play, Sidney Hopcroft is completely in the ascendant. Geoffrey's buildings are collapsing and his business is almost gone. We are shown the literally freezing old house in which Ronald and Marion Brewster-Wright live and the metaphorically freezing relationship they enjoy. A brief rebellion by Jane herself has been ruthlessly suppressed. The final image is of Sidney standing on a table organising party games and forcing the rest to dance. Alan only saw what he had written at the dress rehearsal. When Piers Rogers, playing Sidney, almost screamed: 'Come on. Dance. Dance. Dance. Keep Dancing. Dance . . .' Alan 'suddenly realised it was quite a chilly ending – I hadn't thought of it that way. I decided to bring down a solo light on him and leave him in that light for just a second, a mad dictator. We re-lit it there and then and it stayed that way right through into the West End. It was like the director finding out why the writer had written it, quite funny really. I thought, phaow, don't know how they'll take this, chaps. Quite different.'

The Scarborough reviews in June 1972 were decidedly mixed but between the first and second performances Alan cut half an hour from it. As it developed speed and confidence, the breath-taking combination of comedy and tragedy was starkly revealed: the Ayckbourn trademark. A new and characteristically English category of drama had been established.

It wasn't an easy play for the actors. Jennifer Piercey, who played the suicidal Eva, struggled to 'find' a character who starts at the high emotional pitch of a Greek tragic heroine and becomes more stable and assured as the play goes on, effectively moving in the opposite direction to the dramatic norm. Alan had hit problems writing Eva too. Because he wanted to make Geoffrey and Eva identifiably bohemian, creating a three-way contrast with the ambitious Hopcrofts and the superior Brewster-Wrights, Alan had played with the idea of making Eva a nudist. But he feared it might be hard for an audience to concentrate on a play's content with a naked woman sitting a few feet away. Quite different sorts of difficulty attached to playing Jane Hopcroft. In a particularly memorable sequence in Act I, Jane, almost in tears at the thought she may have let Sidney down by tidying the tonic bottles away so successfully they cannot now be found, puts on the only outdoor clothes to hand (a man's old gardening mac, Wellington boots and a trilby hat), and slips out for further supplies. Caught in a downpour, she gets home to find she has locked herself out. She can't ring the front door bell because she wants to pretend everything has gone smoothly and she has been at home all the time, the perfect hostess. So this bedraggled vision appears outside her own kitchen door, her mouth opening and closing soundlessly. Eventually she is let in by the double-barrelled bank manager, dripping and squelching, shaking with exhaustion and humiliation. This can provoke hysterical laughter and profound anger at once, and actresses have been bewildered as to what response to play for. Ayckbourn wrote to Janet Dibley, when she sought help in preparation for a revival in the 1990s, that he only wants the truth of the situation to be played. The response will depend substantially on the audience. What he absolutely does not want is for someone to demand the laugh with a grimace or pointed move or vocal inflection.

In a memoir of that first production – published in full by Albert-Reiner Glaap in *A Guided Tour through Ayckbourn Country* (WVT Wissenschaftlicher Verlag Trier, 1999) – he says the play 'suffers from' a reputation for being very funny, and points out that it was originally played with intense seriousness 'and even a certain venom'. Further, the laughter follows from this approach and if it is actually played deliberately for laughs the comedy can wear a little thin.

Jane, incidentally, shares Heather Stoney's tendency in those days to clean up anything in sight but comes from a different social background; Marion Brewster-Wright was closer to Heather's class but her flamboyance – not her fondness for the bottle as has been reported elsewhere – owed more to Alan's agent, Peggy Ramsay. Alan's architect friend Harry Osborne recognised some of his own difficulties with the money side of the business and uncomfortable elements of a previous relationship, but his buildings weren't falling down. And Ronald Brewster-Wright's sad account of his first wife's unexpected departure from the flat above the bank reminds us that Lolly – also a drinker – had walked out on an uncomprehending Cecil.

Audiences took the play in different ways, especially post-Scarborough. The formal symmetry was too perfect for some critics. Much fun is made of the American producers, who spotted that the middle act was funnier than the final one and asked if they shouldn't be reversed. They even had researchers in the audience charting where the laughs came, and just how big or small they were, to prove their point: one tick for a titter, two for a giggle, three for a belly laugh. And they were bewildered when the author seemed ungratefully unimpressed with the results of their research and the play nevertheless ran for 592 performances, the longest by a British import since Noël Coward (that comparison again) had written *Blithe Spirit*. In fact London producer Michael Codron also regretted that the Hopcrofts weren't 'dramatically stronger than the other couples' in view of their importance to the shape of the play. Peggy Ramsay wanted the characters to develop. In Germany, however, the play was taken up hungrily and moved Ayckbourn from the boulevard theatres into his first major state playhouse, the Residenztheater in Munich; in other words, from light entertainment to art. The play has been seen all round the world: in Japan the unseen party guests all burst on at the interval; the Yugoslavs wanted folk music and dancing instead of the off-stage party games. Alan refused permission for it to be performed in South Africa in 1977. 'Blacks must be free to say No to a play about a middle-aged snob from Guildford with drink problems,' he wrote. But Slovak television saw it in 1997, the Estonian theatre in 1998.

Richard Briers played Sidney Hopcroft with relish in the West End, identifying him straight away as 'a little fascist' and investing him with all the obsessive energy of which he is capable. What nobody could know at the time was that Sidney's single-minded pursuit of his own interests would be sanctioned as the political and social norm in the 1980s, when Margaret Thatcher persuaded most of the world that getting rich and getting on were a moral duty, whatever the cost. But the play also develops Ayckbourn's persistent exploration of man's enduring inhumanity to woman: Sidney is a bully, Geoffrey a philanderer, and Ronnie is perhaps the saddest of all, a man who just doesn't get it and never will, because the terrible underlying principle of the play, turning it from comedy to tragedy in the final act, is that Things Get Worse. Time is not only not on our side, it is in league with our enemies.

2 : Falling in the Aisles: *The Norman Conquests, Absent Friends*

If *Absurd Person Singular* was 'the big one' (in Michael Billington's phrase) for the critics, it was *The Norman Conquests* for the public.

This was a different kind of revolutionary event: three plays covering the events of a weekend in a house in the Sussex countryside where the single Annie looks after her bedridden old mother. To give Annie a weekend off from full-time caring, her brother Reg and sister-in-law Sarah have come to stay. Annie is being not quite courted by a vet, Tom, who can barely choose between tea and coffee, let alone different women; the general assumption that he will take her away for the weekend hasn't even occurred to him. Annie and Reg's sister Ruth isn't expected (she is a busy executive) but Ruth's ever-eager husband Norman is entirely ready to rise to a dirty weekend in East Grinstead. Norman is a dishevelled librarian who has discovered that many women are rather lonely and will turn gratefully to a man who spots it. They are not quite simultaneous plays (that innovation would come in 1999 with *House* and *Garden*) but they show the action in the dining-room, living-room and garden over the weekend. Each play is perfectly self-contained and makes sense if seen in isolation, but there are moments – if you see all three – when knowledge of what is going on in another room steals up on you and administers a comic sandbagging rarely achieved by one on its own. When all three were performed in a single day in London a member of the audience fell out of his seat in the stalls and literally rolled in the aisle.

It happened in *Table Manners*, the play set in the dining-room, after the bossy Sarah (Penelope Keith) has insisted on a formal family dinner in spite of a great shortage of actual food in the house; she has taken ages arranging and re-arranging and re-re-arranging where they should sit, and Tom has had to sit on a lower chair than everyone else. The meal is disastrous ('Pass your plate down, Reg.' 'Ah, some more, is there?' 'No. Less.') and there is constant sniping of the kind that only families who know and loathe each other well can manage. The eruption of laughter came when Norman (Tom Courtenay again) turned in the flow of conversation to Tom (Michael Gambon), his head just appearing above the table, and said: 'Did you get that? Thought it might have been above your head.' Christopher Godwin confirms that the same line brought the house down in Scarborough, where the play had been called *Fancy Meeting You*, and led to a bad case of 'corpsing' by the cast. On paper it seems mildly amusing but unlikely to cause comic mayhem in a sane audience. But the audience isn't entirely sane by this stage. (There is also objective evidence of the volume of laughter when the plays were still at Greenwich: it blew an amp in the tannoy, the public address system that relays the sound from the auditorium to back-stage.)

According to Michael Gambon, a man not afraid of a bit of anarchy on stage, especially if he's helping to create it himself, the laughter got so fierce sometimes that the cast just had to sit very still and wait for it to die. They would also play things smaller and smaller to try to minimise it simply so that the play didn't topple under its weight. Penelope Keith's authority was particularly useful in this respect. She gave a formidable performance in that after Sarah's inherent bossiness has been registered she was able not only to get a laugh on the admission, while furiously polishing the table, that she has suffered from 'nervous trouble', but to start earning our sympathy too and make us understand – admittedly slightly less quickly than Norman does – that she is indeed lonely and vulnerable and well worth making a pass at.

Penelope Keith was particularly pleased when, after the final play, a caller to her dressing-room said: 'You made me cry.' She added: 'The fact that the house is rocking for a good part of the evening but that they're crying too – that is the peak, that is the pinnacle for me.' She had been in rep productions of *How the Other Half Loves*, sitting on a sofa next to a woman who was in another house at another time. 'Visually it's funny, and indeed vocally, but it's only truly at its funniest in the theatre. On television or films you'd just hop from house to house. On the radio you wouldn't see us sitting there. You could say, because he just takes a family, not the whole nation, to comment on that he's a miniaturist. But for an actor they are wonderful plays to work on. It's all there. Very challenging and very, very deep.' Sarah and Reg were partly inspired by Daphne and Horace Ayckbourn, but Alan thinks the relationship 'pretty common: the adult wife and child man. The more she tries, the more childish he gets.' Alan has been known to invent board games too, including a sort of theatrical version of Monopoly. He abandoned it when he realised that one of the hazards built into the game could never happen in real life, namely that you could run out of actors. The naughty old woman upstairs, who pretends to think that Tom the vet is actually a doctor so that she can insist on a full physical examination, shares her appetites with Lolly. Tom, the vet who can't commit to a human but is probably wonderful with a sick kitten, did a bit of boxing at school (like Alan) and smites Norman when he believes him to be insulting Annie by calling her 'a dried-up tea-bag'. Actually Norman is insulting his own wife, which of course is perfectly acceptable in English society. And Norman? Another aspect of Alan himself in his roving days? Alan certainly remains very fond of him and points to the character's transparency as his saving grace. 'He'll move on from one woman to another without batting an eyelid but I think it's one of my early steps in feminism that all the women know, perfectly well, what he's getting at all the time. He is unscrupulous but all the deceits and lies and trickery are so transparent that he is actually quite endearing.'

Again the characters are never simple portraits. Sarah's wish for a civilised meal may owe something to Daphne, but the moment at which she hurls a biscuit tin at Reg and calls him contemptible sounds more like something out of Lolly's drawer. And Reg's constant teasing of Annie about her salads (and how much they have taught him about insect life: 'Pass the centipede sauce') – may have reflected Horace's tastes and sense of humour but it certainly reflects Alan's too.

In her book *White Cargo* (Michael Joseph, 1998) Felicity Kendal writes of the pleasure of working with Eric Thompson, a point endorsed by Penelope Wilton who – very young – had been cast as the comically short-sighted Ruth. She remembers Alan being around, a bit nervous, but entrusting everything to Thompson who had a very light touch as a director. 'He'd suggest something in a very quiet voice and someone would say it was a frightful idea and he'd say, oh all right. But then you'd try it anyway and it usually turned out to work.' After watching the performance one night Richard Briers told Kendal how splendid she had been and wondered if she would like to read some scripts for a television situation comedy he was doing for the BBC. It might not be successful, but he liked the writing. She might be interested in playing his wife. It was *The Good Life* and it also made a star of Penelope Keith playing a part not a million miles from Sarah. The success of *The Norman Conquests* now seems a foregone conclusion but Michael Codron didn't believe audiences would turn out three times for anybody and didn't want to produce it. But once rehearsals for a production at Greenwich Theatre had started he was talked into it by Peggy Ramsay. 'She said they'd got into a buggers' muddle down there and only I could sort it out,' he remembers. By August he had transferred the whole production to Shaftesbury Avenue. It was to help audiences believe they should see all three plays that the overall title *The Norman Conquests* was found. The living-room play, originally *Make Yourself at Home*, became *Living Together*, but *Round and Round the Garden* stayed the same.

Whereas there had been an unconscious element in the writing of *Absurd Person Singular*, pure chance played its part in the structure of *The Norman Conquests*. Alan completed them in a week, writing all three plays at once: three Scene 1s, then three Scene 2s and so on. He was writing for actors he knew, and for their specific strengths. Christopher Godwin, who became something of a local star in Scarborough in the 1970s, was to play Norman but wrote to Alan at short notice to say his contract with another theatre meant he wouldn't be able to join the 1973 summer company until a week after the rest. As a result, Norman doesn't appear until the second scene and his arrival is all the more keenly anticipated. Alan spent the first week of rehearsal on the three opening scenes and then worked very hard for the next two on the rest. The plays opened at weekly intervals in Scarborough, then all three in nine days in the West End after a triumphant run in Greenwich. One London critic came right out and said the plays were a failure. The rest fell about and helped ensure their success. J. W. Lambert in the *Sunday Times* named Ayckbourn as 'the most remarkable British dramatist to have emerged since Harold Pinter'. And after years of being told his plays weren't literary enough for publication in book form, he had *The Norman Conquests* accepted by Chatto & Windus.

The '*Normans*' eventually found their way on to television, directed by Herbert Wise, and with Kendal no longer available Penelope Wilton transferred with astonishing ease to the part of Annie. Wilton makes the point that without a live audience laughing at the plays, if you sit alone watching them at home, the hidden tragedy in Sarah and Reg, and in all the relationships, comes out much more forcibly even in what is palpably high comedy bordering on farce. The plays were not a success on Broadway, despite the presence of Richard Benjamin and Paula Prentiss in the cast, which has led to the idea – sometimes endorsed by Ayckbourn himself – that the Americans have a problem with 'my stuff'. It is not borne out by the record, though he rarely makes a big killing in New York. The fact is that very few straight plays now succeed on Broadway itself, where the musical is the dominant form, but off-Broadway (where productions may be just as expensive as in the West End of London) and in the subsequent licensing of regional productions, American producers have been able to recoup their investment, show profits and win awards. It is true that Americans, who make a clear distinction between a play and a show, are sometimes bewildered by the British interest in people who are identified as failures. And comparisons with the American playwright Neil Simon haven't helped; Simon's gift for the one-liner sets up expectations for a feast of jokes – which Alan doesn't seek. But the championship of Ayckbourn by the New York critic Frank Rich and academic Albert Kalson (author of *Laughter in the Dark: the Plays of Alan Ayckbourn*) suggests we may be patronising them if we suppose the Americans are somehow disabled from 'getting' plays which, after all, work better in smaller spaces. In the off-Broadway Manhattan Theatre Club he has proved highly successful.

Because he had written all three plays together Alan hadn't wanted the 'Normans' all to reach a climax in the same place (boring for everyone, including himself). So each has a different rhythm and flavour. It is only at the end of *Round and Round the Garden*, as everyone goes home, that we realise that all the women have finally turned their backs on Norman; even being emotionally available (which Leonard in *Time and Time Again* never managed) is not itself enough. The huge event has Ayckbourn's customary dying fall, the sad elegy for human absurdity that characterises the dramatist's own broad attitude. But in writing *Living Together* Alan had made the discovery that led to the sixth of this sequence of quite different plays: in *Absent Friends*, he held an audience's attention without a dazzling plot or an innovative narrative device or a bombardment of comedy.

Never very confident, however, Alan opened *Absent Friends* in Scarborough in the summer of 1974 to muted publicity. It was, after all, a play about death. Colin's fiancée has been drowned, and at Paul and Diana's house various old friends are gathered to offer tea and sympathy. They carefully prepare what not to say when he arrives and then someone is asked if she likes her tea milky, and replies: 'Yes, but don't drown it.' The fact is that the chronically cheerful Colin is happy, even eager, to talk about his late girlfriend; his love is still alive. His good nature relentlessly exposes the death of their relationships. The dramatic action is minimal, but it is a stark reminder that the usual distinction between action and words is a false one. Just as to say 'I love you' or 'I hate you' can change everything, so virtually every exchange in *Absent Friends* pushes a knife in somewhere. Not that Ayckbourn characters usually say anything quite as simple or conclusive as that. Another experiment was to make the play happen in 'real time', i.e. the action takes exactly the time to pass that the events described would take. As Alan remarked in a letter to a student in 1990, this has the effect of bringing the audience in very close, like a camera's telephoto lens.

The distinguished critic of the *Sunday Times*, Harold Hobson, wrote that it was Ayckbourn's finest play: 'If it is the saddest and most moving thing he has written, it is also the most clear-sighted and the funniest.'

A few weeks after the Scarborough opening of *Absent Friends* Peter Hall, director of the soon-to-open new National Theatre, stepped up his courtship of Alan. This would eventually include the marvellous piece of Peter Hall moral blackmail: 'No doubt you can do very well without the National Theatre, but can the National Theatre do without you?' (which turned up, slightly recast, as a line in *House* in 1999). Hall set out his plans for new writing in the National's three auditoria and said he had laughed uncontrollably at the script of *Absent Friends*, 'disturbing several well-meaning passengers in my railway train'. He wanted to put it on at the National. But, he wondered, did the play need a climax? Alan replied: 'It's a miniature. I had to write it. It was the only play I could write following that six-hour epic [*The Norman Conquests*].' He was grateful for Hall's interest, he wrote, but planned to stick with Michael Codron for the London transfer. 'It is alarming,' he adds, 'but the more one writes, the less confident one becomes.'

Alan's very starkest plays have always aroused mixed responses and it is interesting that the wives of both Christopher Godwin, who played Colin in Scarborough, and Richard Briers, who played him in London, never really liked the play. Both the men did. Briers is very scathing about Colin as a person, who could be portrayed as rather sympathetic, even saintly, because he is forever coming out with hopeful pieties in the face of misery. Usually cast for his likeability in television comedy, Briers enjoyed playing Colin as a buoyantly self-deceiving idiot, a line Ayckbourn endorses. Generally, if an Ayckbourn character seems rather a good chap, watch out for the havoc he can cause. If he seems a monster, look for the vulnerability that has got him there. There is a slightly horrified letter from Alan to a Norwegian director planning to tour the play out of Oslo: 'Colin is certainly not the voice of the author . . . not a visiting angel but a demon king.' (Ayckbourn is influenced by Ibsen as well as Chekhov, but Colin's inadvertent capacity for revealing the truth recalls an unconscious Gregers Werle from *The Wild Duck* – and *he* wasn't the voice of the author either.) Perhaps the most illuminating response to the way *Absent Friends* confronts the death of love, and the taboo of death, came from an anonymous member of the first Scarborough audience quoted by Alan in a letter to amateurs who were reviving the play in 1992: 'If I'd known what I was laughing at while I was watching it, I wouldn't have laughed.' Some people do realise and don't laugh; a leading agony aunt once said to me of Ayckbourn's work in general that she just didn't see how people could laugh. The plays were good and true, but painful, not comic. In 1979 it would be *Absent Friends* that led the leading German critic Friedrich Luft to write: 'It is quite comprehensible that our state theatres have taken hold of the playwright Alan Ayckbourn. He no longer belongs to the Boulevard.' And in 1991, Frank Rich of the *New York Times* made a revival (with Brenda Blethyn and Peter Frechette) his top play of a year in which Brian Friel's all-conquering *Dancing at Lughnasa* was placed seventh. But when *Absent Friends* first appeared in North America, with Eli Wallach and Anne Jackson heading the cast, the tour perished in Toronto without reaching New York. Ayckbourn places it among his own favourites, marking the transition from 'the sunnier plays of my youth to the so-called darker ones that follow'.

Alan's own preoccupation, in 1974 as it is today, was to make sure there was something to go on in his own theatre. A mere ten weeks after *Absent Friends* opened in June the public and the press dutifully trotted back to the Library for *Confusions*. Encouraged by Ken Boden, the company's ambition was growing, and instead of breaking up in September and sending all the actors off to look for employment elsewhere, it launched five 'interlinked' short plays by Alan, which would extend the season into the winter. They played in Filey on Tuesdays, Whitby on Wednesdays and Thursdays, and Scarborough on Fridays and Saturdays. Then the Scarborough production would have a national tour and commercial interest could wait. The staging was different at each venue and some would need a 'proper' set. A designer (Helga Wood) was employed for the first time. There was a composer too (Paul Todd) though this was somehow less of a departure from Stephen Joseph's principles of maximum simplicity. Ayckbourn toured with it, carrying theatre to the grass-roots, even as he prepared for the biggest London date of his life.

But first he bought a house. *The* house, in fact. When Stephen Joseph died he left the crumbling former vicarage in Longwestgate to PB. His will allowed her to sell it if she wanted, but if she lived in it until she died it would revert to his family. He had done nothing to improve or even secure the house and the garden had always been so untended that, when he caught some small boys climbing over the back wall, he was able to convince them there were lions within; they fled. PB now agreed to sell to Alan at a knockdown – the word is dangerously appropriate – price so that he could afford to fix the roof. It was on condition that she could see out her days there, which Alan and Heather were happy for her to do; they camped in one room, still regarding Keats Grove as home. The 'first phase' of redevelopment in Scarborough wouldn't be completed until 1983.

The symbolic force of moving into Stephen's old house now looks inevitable. It identified as 'made in Scarborough' the great litany of hits travelling to the West End to help revive a flagging commercial theatre. From Shaftesbury Avenue (which had then lost much of its initiative to the National Theatre, the RSC and the Royal Court) they would flow back to the regional reps functioning, as Peter Cheeseman has pointed out, like a second tier of annual subsidy: *Relatively Speaking, How the Other Half Loves, Time and Time Again, Absurd Person Singular, The Norman Conquests, Absent Friends*.

3 : *Jeeves* and *Confusions*

And then *Jeeves*. 'Nobody knew what they were doing: a director [Eric Thompson] who had never directed a musical; a writer who had never written one; even Andrew [Lloyd Webber] was not that experienced. He'd never done an acoustic musical before; it had always started as a record album. It was a disaster.' Thus Alan, with the wisdom of hindsight.

Originally Andrew Lloyd Webber had planned *Jeeves* with his collaborator on *Joseph and the Amazing Technicolor Dreamcoat, Evita* and *Jesus Christ Superstar* – Tim Rice. But Rice had never written a 'book' musical, one with spoken scenes in it as opposed to one which is sung through. He had written lyrics but not dialogue. So they concluded they needed a playwright as well. Alan was approached through the producer Bob Swash, who had shown an interest in *Mr Whatnot* over ten years before. When they met up there were already a number of songs roughed out, and Alan thought there simply wasn't going to be room for the three of them to do what they did best. Tim Rice, more interested in rock opera, smartly withdrew and Alan was entrusted with the lyrics as well – 'conned into it', he has claimed. He had never written lyrics before, but his school poems scanned and rhymed, and he proceeded to construct a plot out of a number of existing and identifiable P. G. Wodehouse stories, particularly from *The Code of the Woosters*. In addition to the wealthy, idle and aristocratic Bertie Wooster himself they included his 'dragon aunts', his friends from the Drones' Club, the bullying magistrates and pillars of society who want to stop a chap having fun, and of course his redoubtable 'gentleman's gentleman', who could get you out of any scrape, Jeeves himself. He gave a script to Eric Thompson who went off to Holland to direct the Dutch production of one of the earlier plays. Alan meanwhile went down to Sydmonton, Lloyd Webber's stately home in Hampshire, and continued working on it.

They should all have known something was badly wrong when they met up in Holland to discuss Alan's new ideas – he'd cut a running chorus of Drones as too fussy – only to be told by Eric that he had started working on the basis of the original script and Voytek (whom he introduced to them there and then) had already designed the set and costumes. Which, incidentally, all seemed to be green. Lloyd Webber asked why. Ayckbourn said he thought it might be 'a concept'. Lloyd Webber said: 'Oh God.' Already the right people were not talking directly and openly to each other.

Directing a musical is like being in charge of a small battle and the first thing a director needs to do is to organise everybody's time. The choreographer wants time, the musical director and the voice coaches and the costume designer all want time. The director can end up never managing to work with the actors. When they got to the final day of rehearsals at the Welsh Centre in London, before the 'try-out' opening in Bristol, they had never run the show through. Because the read-through with music on Day 1 had taken five and a half hours, they had already been cutting furiously and it is possible the show already failed to make sense. When they decided they must run it through on that final Saturday of rehearsals David Hemmings, who had also never done a musical before but was cast as Bertie, sat on the floor after a few hours and said: 'I'm sorry. I just can't go on. I'm exhausted.' This may have been partly because, according to Lloyd Webber, he never went to bed. So they opened in Bristol without even knowing how long it was. With the Musicians' Union this matters. There was still well over four hours of it. On the first night a point was reached at which the musicians laid down their instruments and knocked off and the show carried on with a solo piano, playing rather sadly to those members of the audience who were still there.

Bob Swash called a meeting with the writer, the composer and the director. Alan argued that piecemeal cutting – a few lines here, the verse of a song there – wouldn't be enough. At least a third of the show needed taking out: an entire sub-plot and probably a whole character. Bertie's likeable aunt, Dahlia, was played by Betty Marsden, the popular theatre and radio comedienne. She followed David Hemmings (Bertie) and Michael Aldridge (Jeeves) in the billing. Who was going to tell her? Alan said he was only the writer. Eric refused to do it on his own. After a 'note' session in which there was a tell-tale absence of notes for Dahlia, they called Betty Marsden in to meet them all. Alan says it went:

> BETTY: Hello, darlings!
>
> ERIC: Erm, Betty . . .
>
> BETTY: Don't tell me, you've cut the whole fucking role!
>
> ERIC: Yes.
>
> BETTY: I don't believe it. I do not believe it. I do not f——
>
> ERIC: Well, you see –
>
> BETTY: Well, that's it! 'Bye!

And she left. They broke the news to the rest of the company that a few scenes had gone, so there were a few new little segues from scene to scene that would have to be rehearsed in short order. 'And you could see the company thinking, after the shock of losing Betty, Who's next? Nobody was safe, or could feel safe.' When the show still didn't work, Eric himself was fired, on the Friday before it was due to open in London. Why? 'They felt they had to sack somebody,' says Ayckbourn now. He had never directed in London or on any stage bigger than a living-room, but he took over the production. Critics who know they have a real loser on their hands tend to write as if they have nailed a serial killer, and the first national reviews dripped with a punitive venom which now seems as ill-proportioned as the show itself. One suggested the theatre, Her Majesty's, be burned down to spare future audiences. Later, there was a ripple of reaction in its favour. Ronald Bryden, in *Plays and Players*, was particularly pleased with the 'witty and literate' book. But it wasn't enough and *Jeeves* closed in less than a month. Eric Thompson, asked by a television interviewer if the critics had killed the show, replied gamely: 'No. The show killed the show.' With hindsight it seems obvious that Wodehouse's own talent was for brilliant, jewelled, small-scale artifice. The world of Bertie Wooster exists only in the imagination. The fact that the villainous Sir Roderick Spode is a fledgling Nazi does not turn *Jeeves* into a potential *Cabaret*. The very elderly 'Plum' Wodehouse had absent-mindedly listened to the music when the creative team had played it to him in America and seemed to enjoy it, but it is clear from letters written at the time that he had real doubts about the whole idea. The critic Michael Coveney, watching the last Saturday matinee on a date with his future wife, writes in his biography *Andrew Lloyd Webber* (Arrow, 2000) that he saw 'a muddle of scattergun plotting and mixed musical idiom scaled up beyond its potential to fill a large stage. I also saw charm, wit, quite a funny show and heard some amazingly facile and well-turned lyrics by Ayckbourn. Three or four songs were really fine.'

The failure of *Jeeves* was less bruising than that of *Mr Whatnot* had been, less personal because it was not all Alan's own work, and what was his had been relatively well received. He had established a good working and personal relationship with the volatile Lloyd Webber. And when *Absent Friends* followed *Jeeves* in three months later, in July 1975, he had five concurrent solo productions in the West End: this was and is a record. He remembers being introduced as the man with record-breaking success in the London theatre to someone (he has forgotten who) and getting the response: 'Five plays in London? You're due for a fall, aren't you?' The record was enhanced when four of the shows (the three *Normans* and *Absurd Person Singular*) were simultaneously running on Broadway. The American response was to name West 45th Street Ayckbourn Alley. Nevertheless, *Jeeves* had three lasting results: it nagged at Ayckbourn and Andrew Lloyd Webber (having his first failure too) for 20 years; for Alan it was an awful warning of what can happen when big business sets the theatre's agenda; and, much more sadly, it ended his relationship with Eric Thompson. Michael Codron loyally handed Thompson the London production of *Absent Friends*, which was to open three months after *Jeeves*, but the latter no longer really trusted or consulted Alan. Whereas on the complicated place-setting scene in *Table Manners* (in *The Norman Conquests*) he had happily said to Alan: 'Oh go on, you block it,' now he more or less told him to mind his own business: 'I know how your stuff works.' The result, according to Alan, was that *Absent Friends* was directed as if it were *The Norman Conquests* and a terrific cast – Peter Bowles, Pat Heywood, Ray Brooks, Cheryl Kennedy and Phyllida Law as well as Richard Briers – was misused in a broadly comic interpretation of a profoundly sad play. As far as I can find out, Ayckbourn didn't voice his disappointment with the production publicly until 1998 when answering specific questions put by a research student (quoted by Glaap), but the northern critics of the national newspapers had begun to notice that something seemed to be getting lost between the Scarborough and London productions. London has often assumed that this is because 'anything goes' in the clubby intimacy of a small theatre miles from any competition, i.e. the plays were not as good as the reviews said; Scarborough has assumed that the actors for whom the plays have been written must be better than the starrier names brought in to adorn the London posters. Neither is necessarily or wholly true. It took an extraordinarily long time for anyone to suggest that Alan might be the best director of his own work, even though directing was what he mostly did. It simply 'wasn't done' in the West End at that time. Peter Bridge had said: 'Only if you're Noël Coward,' and nobody had ever challenged it. Soon after *Absent Friends* Eric Thompson went down with the illness from which he died, much too young, his contribution to British theatre never properly marked. He had been one of the few men Alan could now relax with as a peer and with whom he had got pole-axingly drunk in New York. Had it not been for *Jeeves*, Alan believes they would have continued to work together happily.

Alan was by now a celebrity, or as much of one as he has ever allowed himself to be. He had been on *Desert Island Discs*, receiving the kind of really rude letter only written by the nice people who listen to Radio 4 – because he had chosen a Pink Floyd track. For the 'one luxury' he had asked for a precursor of a music computer into which he could load as many BBC sound-effects discs as possible with a view to continuing to create his own sound narratives in his island solitude. He'd posed with donkeys on the beach for the *Sunday Times* and written his name in the sand for the London *Evening Standard*. He was in *Who's Who*, had spoken to the Rotarians and judged a beauty contest at Scarborough Press Ball. He had been too busy, in the summer of 1974, with the opening of *Absent Friends* to meet the queen. The *Daily Mail* reported that he and his wife were 'fondly living apart' and that love, as a subject, was 'gelignite'. It is hard to conceive of now, but no newspaper ran a story on his relationship with Heather, although she was always present. She was still acting from time to time, but had also begun the process of turning into Alan's personal assistant and enabler. When he was nervous about doing interviews she would stay in the room long enough to make sure a conversation actually started. Still based in Hampstead, they were spending an increasing amount of time in Scarborough as the season there expanded. The *Daily Mirror* reported excitedly that with his new-found wealth he had bought a high-powered sports car, a Jensen. It didn't report that the first time he took it out the car leaped forward so rapidly when the traffic lights changed to green that he hit a milk float. Rather depressed, he went and caught the train.

Despite the media attention he had very little sense of how important he was becoming. The rehearsal room is a self-sufficient world where, for good or ill, what is going on outside – even elsewhere in the theatre world – matters relatively little. In Scarborough, in any case, real celebrities were the likes of Len Hutton and Fred Trueman and Geoffrey Boycott or stars of TV and variety. More importantly, Ayckbourn himself was always on with the next play by the time the last one got fêted in London, unavailable for fame and infamy alike.

But not fortune. Journalists were preoccupied with how much money he was making. All he really knew was that he could indulge his taste for taxis whenever he wanted, could afford fast cars and first-class transport when he had to go somewhere. He famously took all the actors in all his simultaneous London productions to a mighty dinner at the Savoy around this time but the principle of gifts and parties (arranged with a stage manager's attention to detail but a bigger budget) applies very much to the Scarborough companies too; Christopher Godwin remembers his asking the whole company out to dinner in the 1970s and giving the women £50 each to make sure they had something new to wear if they wanted to. This became a first-night custom, but ended when an actress took it for granted and asked when they were all going shopping. I have heard people say that Alan is mean. It is true that, like royalty, he doesn't carry much money around with him, but my experience of him and that of people who have been far closer to him, is that he is extremely generous and that Heather sometimes reins him in for his own good.

This phase of Alan's working life – in which he supplied hits to the nation as a writer but was still not acknowledged as a director away from Scarborough – is completed by *Confusions* and two more plays, *Bedroom Farce* and *Just Between Ourselves*. A new collaborator, Alan Strachan, directed the London productions of *Confusions* and *Just Between Ourselves*, Little Al to Ayckbourn's Big Al. Although he insisted it should go on in Scarborough first, *Bedroom Farce* was the play he finally gave to Peter Hall at the National, and Hall and Ayckbourn were to co-direct it. This opportunity was a bait Hall had dangled with typical astuteness in his long pursuit of a play from Alan. Michael Codron took longer to be convinced. After Strachan had read *Confusions* and said he would like to direct it, the go-ahead was conditional on Ayckbourn's meeting and liking him. They met at Keats Grove and got on so well that Strachan is still guest-directing in Scarborough a quarter of a century later.

The five plays in *Confusions* range from Ayckbourn's funniest writing –

Strachan regards *Gosforth's Fete* as 'probably the best short comedy ever written' – to his least typical. *Mother Figure* comes first: a woman so used to the company of children that she tells her married neighbours to drink up their drinks nicely and behave much better to each other than they are naturally inclined to do. In *Drinking Companion* we meet her husband, a commercial traveller drunkenly trying to pick up either or both of two perfume salesgirls in a hotel bar. *Between Mouthfuls* is set in a restaurant where two couples are dining; we only hear what the waiter hears as he goes to serve them, but what emerges is that the husband of one has been in a hotel in Rome with the wife of the other for the last fortnight – having given her husband (his employee) a stack of work to complete in the meantime. The three plays have steadily cranked up the comedy levels through the evening, but *Gosforth's Fete* provokes the same helpless roaring from an audience as *The Norman Conquests*: an ineffectual scoutmaster hears about his fiancée's infidelity over the erratically functioning tannoy at a church fête. And then comes the wholly unexpected *A Talk in the Park*: five barely characterised figures, their names (from Arthur to Ernest) suspiciously starting with A, B, C, D and E, are caught in a series of encounters without communication. The format mimics Schnitzler's *La Ronde* but there is no sex or any other real exchange as one-sided conversations are started on park benches, and terminated when one person walks away from what he or she is hearing to inflict his or her monologue on somebody else.

Audiences, including many of the critics, were never quite convinced that it was a good idea, after the resounding wall of laughter that greeted *Gosforth's Fete*, for the lights to go up on a bit of shrubbery and five lonely benches with dialogue as desolate as the setting. In the London *Evening Standard* Milton Shulman led the call to change the order and 'send the audience rollicking with laughter into Shaftesbury Avenue'. This presupposes that the author was really trying to write the play the reviewer wanted but didn't know how to do it. To comply would have been to put the evening's summary in the middle; the purpose of this short, formal playlet is to provide a unifying coda to what has gone before. If, that is, *Confusions* really is a coherent series of interlinked plays rather than a handful of fine short plays artfully made to echo each other. The opening play, *Mother Figure*, in which the seriously depressed Lucy owes something both to Lolly's and to Christine's experiences, had already been seen. It was in a compilation of work by different writers, intended as a sequel to *Mixed Doubles*. Called *Mixed Blessings*, it had collapsed on tour. The perfume salesgirls in *Drinking Companion* were inspired by the cigarette salesgirls (whom nobody ever called 'women') often seen in Scarborough. *Between Mouthfuls* started with a Devon hotel restaurant no longer as grand as it had been, which he had visited with Heather. The connections in *Confusions* are there, of course, because they come from roughly the same time and place in the author's head, but Ayckbourn is not a natural last-page summariser; *A Talk in the Park* rounds off an idea, not a dramatic action. Even the original beautifully balanced Scarborough company – who also toured – didn't really make it a convincing overall structure, despite the internal architecture of the individual plays.

Once again the commercial production hit problems with the sheer magnetism of the stars cast in it. The husband-and-wife team of John Alderton and Pauline Collins led a strong team: James Cossins, Derek Fowlds and Sheila Gish. Alan Strachan only had three weeks' rehearsal and must have felt jinxed when Alderton broke his ankle in rehearsals and initially had to appear in a wheelchair. Even so, the real problem was that, as the drunken commercial traveller in the second play, Alderton was simply too naturally full of confident sex appeal for the audience to believe he had no chance of getting the women into bed. In the nature of things directors rarely see other directors at work, but Strachan is able to pass on a rare glimpse of Ayckbourn's skill with actors. Having seen a pre-London performance in Bath, he suggested a less well-cut suit and more five o'clock shadow but otherwise changed nothing: 'For two days, though, he just drip-fed the occasional thought behind a line here and a line there and the performance was not transformed but re-informed, and audiences started getting the dark side to a writer they had previously seen as a boulevard jester.'

This also made the bleak final play emerge more organically from what had gone before. Ayckbourn also paid Pauline Collins the very rare compliment of rewriting some of it. Her role – a battered wife, suggesting that she might well go back to 'that bastard' – had been written for a regular member of the Scarborough company, Janet Dale, and it reflected her speech rhythms and intonation. Collins went through her extraordinary range of accents (even playing it Indian one night) and body shapes, trying to make it work for her. She tried different wigs and different coats in every town they went to. Ayckbourn gave her the rewrite in Brighton, Strachan thinks, 'and she took one look at it, said yes, she could get that to work, and from that point she was fine'. *Confusions* duly arrived in the West End in May 1976. The British public is traditionally resistant to evenings of short plays and it didn't match the success of its predecessors. Nonetheless, the popularity of the individual plays has kept it alive with amateur groups and students, and a professional revival (with Gary Wilmot heading the company) toured successfully in early 2001.

4 : *Bedroom Farce* and *Just Between Ourselves*

By the time *Confusions* opened in London there had been not one but two new plays in Scarborough: *Bedroom Farce* and *Just Between Ourselves*. Their subsequent appearance in London within five weeks of each other in the spring of 1977 is an indication of just how important Ayckbourn was becoming. Everyone wanted to gather golden eggs while the goose was laying. Ironically, Peter Hall at the subsidised National, who had always been interested in the 'dark and melancholic strain' in Ayckbourn's work, and only stops himself calling Alan the English Chekhov or Molière because he regards him essentially as the English Ayckbourn, got the lighter of the two plays then coming to London and most certainly the one with the greater commercial potential. Michael Codron (still not allowing Alan to direct) got possibly the darkest play Alan has ever written.

To his astonishment Alan was given eight weeks' rehearsal time at the National. He was used to three or four and didn't really know what he would do with the extra time. Because he was busy in Scarborough he actually missed the first week of his London debut and by the time he joined the company Hall had already worked out the basic moves and entrances. When Alan arrived they ran the show for him, a situation in which the actors had something to prove rather than the writer-director. Then Hall said he was going to pop out. When Alan asked: 'Where to?' he was told: 'Next door.' Hall had already scheduled himself to direct Ben Jonson's *Volpone* at the same time, so he had always meant Ayckbourn to fly solo. It was a classic, brilliant Hall manoeuvre that achieved the desired effect while leaving everyone feeling safe. The two men are completely different directors and far too strong-willed to have genuinely co-directed (Hall got the directing credit in the first published edition of the play). Hall's preliminary work consisted, Alan says, in asking serious questions, e.g. 'Why does Ernest eat pilchards in the middle of the night?' Because he can't find the sardines and Ernest's life is full of these little disappointments. But Hall had given the cast a realistic grounding and

Ayckbourn then worked on the jokes, looking after the production until Hall 'popped back' for the technical dress rehearsal.

Alan took to his own bed for a couple of days after writing *Bedroom Farce* at the last minute in London and then having to tear up to Scarborough by car to deliver it. The title was chosen for the printer, as usual, and the play is by no means a bedroom farce in the sense recognised by Feydeau or Ben Travers. It is not about whether anyone had sex with someone they shouldn't have done. But it is set in three bedrooms (all shown on stage together) and involves four couples. Malcolm and Kate (possibly the same Malcolm and Kate at whose party Ginny and Greg met in *Relatively Speaking*) are having another party. The unseen guests will include Dick and Lottie from *Absurd Person Singular*, Gordon and Marge from *Absent Friends* and Ken and Margaret (Boden, from the Library Theatre). The ones we do see are Susannah and Trevor, unhappily married and ready to wreck anyone else's relationship; Jan, who might have married Trevor but is saddled with the bed-bound, whining and self-centred Nick; and Ernest and Delia, Trevor's bewildered parents who are quite capable of having a bad time all on their own. There is almost a happy ending when Trevor and Susannah are reconciled, having evicted Malcolm and Kate from their own bedroom, except that Trevor drops off to sleep leaving Susannah trying to boost her own confidence by reciting a mantra to the effect that she is still attractive.

Ayckbourn owns up to being all the men in the play. Like Nick, he'd had a bad back the winter before he wrote it and had been a bad patient. He thought he blundered through his own and other people's lives like Trevor (and Norman and Leonard earlier). He has Malcolm's way of dealing with crises as if they are jokes long after this has ceased to be the case, and Malcolm's preoccupation with gadgetry which lets him down. And Ernest's weary response to the claim from Delia that he should have talked more to his son about things that matter deeply – 'Doesn't really leave much to talk about then does it?' – is very familiar. But in many ways it harks back to his earliest successes at a time when he was ready to move on. It is as if he was defying Peter Hall to do, on the big Lyttelton stage of the National with its conventional proscenium arch, a play that was all about slightly manic seaside entertainment in a tiny room above a library. For many years he even said he resented the play himself, coming when he was turning into a 'winter' playwright. But its sunny nature won him round again and he revived it successfully in the autumn of 2000 for Scarborough and a national tour.

Just Between Ourselves, his last play for the Library Theatre in Scarborough, was written at the last moment and, once again, long after the title had been printed in the publicity. It was New Year. He completed the play at about four o'clock in the morning and went out into the Scarborough night to deliver scripts through the letter boxes of actors who would be reading it more or less in public in a few hours' time. In his version of the story, he put it through one letter box and a prehensile hand dragged it away before he even let go. The actor concerned, Malcolm Hebden, who was to play Neil (and later to be associate director of the company), says he was actually lying awake nervously because he is a poor reader and wanted to have a look at the script in advance, but that he was still in bed when he heard the script plonk on to the doormat. He ran downstairs, tore the envelope open and found a covering note: 'This play has turned out much darker than expected, gone in a completely different direction, but I hope you enjoy it.' Shortly before this Hebden had come to work in a new jacket and explained that he had come into a little money. 'Somebody die?' asked Alan. 'Yes, my father,' was the reply. Alan was decently embarrassed at the time. Hebden was stunned on reading the script to find that when Neil announces to Dennis that he has some money to invest, Dennis asks him jocularly if it's because somebody has died and gets the reply that it is Neil's father. Alan later realised that he had not only lifted the insensitive moment from life but given it straight back to the person involved. When it came to the read-through Hebden 'flicked me a glance but said nothing'.

Just Between Ourselves marked the Scarborough theatre's expansion into a winter season. It was the first mature play to be physically written as the December waves started crashing over the piers below the house in Longwestgate and Ayckbourn believes he was influenced by the mood. The first scene is in February and the last the following January. In other words it starts bleak and gets bleaker (very little in an Ayckbourn play is ever irrelevant). Frequently referred to as 'the Morris Minor play', it is set in the chaotic garage where Dennis spends most of his life as an ineffectual handyman, ignoring the fact that his wife and mother are battling for possession of his soul indoors. The 'small popular car' which occupies much of the middle ground is unspecified – it was a Mini in the 1996 Scarborough revival but a Morris Minor in the original production, in the West End and then in the televised version that followed (Richard Briers, Rosemary Leach and the rest were pretty good too, in probably the most successful TV adaptation of an Ayckbourn play there has been). Initially we seem to be in for a comedy about DIY: Dennis is wrestling with the wires of an electric kettle; the up-and-over door of the garage has jammed; the pilot light on the gas stove has gone out. When Neil calls to see if the car would be suitable as a birthday present for his own wife, Pam, Dennis starts it with difficulty (going from calling it 'my beauty' to 'you bastard' in successive sentences) before it splutters to a standstill.

But within the first page or two of dialogue we have also seen him undermine Vera his wife, claiming that she wrecked the kettle by throwing it on the floor and suggesting it's part of a pattern bordering on a personality defect. In the first scene in Act II, Vera, who suspects she may be heading for a breakdown, comes to the garage, gets the bitterly rowing visitors (Neil and Pam) out of the way and asks her husband for help. Dennis, now up a ladder fixing up a little surprise for his mother's birthday, is not actually any good at the jobs he is always tackling, but they give him an excuse to play by himself all the time. 'How do you mean, help?' he asks.

VERA: From you. I don't think I can manage much longer unless I get your help.

DENNIS: Help. What way? With mother? Do you mean mother?

VERA: Partly. No, not just her. You never seem to be here, Dennis.

DENNIS: What do you mean? I'm here. I'm home as much as most men. Probably more than most men.

VERA: Yes, but you're out here, aren't you?

DENNIS: Not all the time.

VERA: Most of the time.

DENNIS: Well I'm doing things. For the house. I mean you're welcome to come out here too. There's nothing to stop you if you want to talk. Talk things over.

VERA: But we've got a home, Dennis. I spend all day trying to make it nice. I don't want to spend the evening sitting in a garage.

DENNIS: Oh come on.

VERA: I mean what's the point of my doing everything. I mean what's the point. I need help, Dennis.

DENNIS: Yes, but don't you see, you're not being clear, Vee. You say help but what sort of help do you mean?

VERA: Just help. From you.

DENNIS (*Putting his arm round her*): Yes. Well, look, tell you what. When you've got a moment, why don't you sit down, get a bit of paper and just make a little list of all the things you'd like me to help you with. Things you'd like me to do, things that need mending or fixing and

then we can talk about them and see what I can do to help. All
right?

(*Vera does not reply.*)

How about that, Vee? All right? Does that suit you?

(*Vera moves to the door.*)

Vee?

(*Vera goes slowly out and into the house.*)

Vee. Vee.

The play is set on four birthdays, in a bitter echo of the three
Christmases of *Absurd Person Singular* (Ayckbourn was writing at Christmas). Vera's failure to provide her husband with a cake on his birthday is
the turning point in her defeat by a mother-in-law who *always* made
Dennis a cake, even when his father was dying. This is the clearest
indication yet that the author's real subject is unhappiness so desperate
that it drives people mad. It seems to me, furthermore, that in the above
exchange Dennis quite wilfully fails to understand what Vera needs and
therefore at some level knows he is withholding himself from her. Isn't he
giving her and Marjorie, his mother, 'treats' as a smoke-screen to hide the
fact that he is not giving himself? If so, is it a kind of oblique confession?
Not to an excess of ineffectual DIY but to that sense of 'even when you're
here, you're not here' that everyone who tries to share the life of a creative
artist will recognise. The bumbling, withdrawn vet in *The Norman
Conquests*, Tom, admitted that he knew he was letting Annie down by not
making an emotional or even a sexual move towards her, that he could
feel himself doing it even as he did it, but that he seemed unable to do
anything differently. Ayckbourn has talked of a situation in which he had
a row with a girlfriend who then left the house. As he was already
comfortably ensconced in bed he stayed there, reading. When she let
herself back in, an hour or two later, she remonstrated with him for not
coming after her. He had known he was meant to, but just 'didn't feel up
to it'. This unwillingness to go the extra mile to sustain a relationship is
what loses Leonard the girl in *Time and Time Again*. But this is never
spelled out by a wise outsider within the text of an Ayckbourn play, and in
Just Between Ourselves characters are demonstrated entirely through action
and dialogue. The title is one of Dennis's catch-phrases, but it could be the
portmanteau title for all Ayckbourn's tragi-comic relationships: what
happens between two people? It is at the very least a highly personal play
from a man who knows what it is to have a partner and a mother

skirmishing over him. 'It is always difficult to please two women at the same time,' he points out with massive understatement.

Much of it remains funny, horribly so when Vera flips and goes for Marjorie and Dennis with an electric drill, while the deeply frustrated Pam, trying to draw Dennis into a fantasy about driving off together – in a car that can't budge – is on the verge of being car-sick. And the hapless Neil brings on Marjorie's garishly illuminated cake and starts to sing . . .

Alan Strachan again directed the West End production. He says this climactic third of four scenes was greeted with what he calls the Ayckbourn Roar, but then the final scene opened with Rosemary Leach sitting mute and perhaps catatonic, huddled in a blanket in a cold winter light and finally saying the one word 'no' when asked if she wants to go back into her lovely home. Strachan believes that as director of the play's commercial production he never quite pulled it off, despite its apparently brilliant casting. Or perhaps because of it. The late Colin Blakely, an Irish actor universally admired and much loved, played Dennis, with Michael Gambon as Neil. Strachan recalls that Blakely was excellent when he took over (from Gambon, coincidentally) in a later Ayckbourn play, *A Chorus of Disapproval*. 'But in that he played a fellow Celt, a Welshman, and I don't think he could ever quite get the sheer suburban ordinariness of Dennis.'

Michael Gambon agrees that he and Blakely were miscast, and that a point came when Blakely realised he wasn't, after all, going to bring the house down himself. A serious actor with a gift for intensity, Blakely may have thought that doing an Alan Ayckbourn play in the West End would broaden his own range and be fun. He wouldn't be the last very good actor to make this mistake if that was the case. Strachan is careful to point out that this didn't mean Blakely didn't act the part rather well, getting the big laughs available to him from the gap between aspiration and delivery in the DIY, muttering sardonically as he planned little acts of rebellion against his mother. However, the women in the West End cast were heart-rendingly good: Rosemary Leach as Vera, Constance Chapman as Marjorie, positively blossoming as she takes over Dennis's life and home again in the face of Vera's illness, and Stephanie Turner as the only character who has taken a slightly more positive approach to her own life at the end of the play than the beginning, Pam.

Richard Briers, who later played the part on television (with Leach and Chapman), offers an interesting footnote to the business of acting the play. 'I was overacting, and luckily Alan came just before we were due to record it, about two days before, and said: "Take it down." I was really going over the top, which would have been rather embarrassing on the box. I take direction very quickly, luckily, and we just patched it all up.' Briers, who had perceived Dennis as 'a complete berk', was able to play him *as he thought of himself*, a decent, helpful, kind man, who liked a laugh, asked for little and couldn't understand how other people found so much to be unhappy about. Gambon, speaking in the foyer of the National Theatre, remarked: 'Sort of play they should do here at the Cottesloe. One of those plays that really does expand in as much as the actor can take, for want of a better word, liberties with it. The actor in you does have an irresistible desire to explore all the corners. With most of Alan's plays you can't do that. You're sort of trapped, in a sense, in a machine, all the cogs going round. If you decide you're going to go way up you spoil the machine. It breaks down, stops running. The laughs stop. But I think *Just Between Ourselves* is a freer play, because it's so tragic. I think that's the reason, the laughs are of less importance.'

Audiences for the pre-West End tour seemed unhappy with the end of *Just Between Ourselves*, and the feeling spread to the cast. When it reached Richmond, Surrey, close enough to London for actors' families, lovers, friends and agents to come and see them, Alan Strachan's spirits sank: 'An agent only has to comment that it's not a very sympathetic character, dear, and the next night you'll see a completely different performance because of course the actor starts playing the agent's "notes". I found that very, very tricky.' The author, meanwhile, was conspicuous by his absence after the read-through. He saw the show in the second week of the tour and said little except to make the important point that for most of the play Vera thinks that her husband is right; because he's her husband it's his job to be right. Strachan adds: 'I think if we had done the play four years later, it would have been different. But at that time there was nothing we could do to solve the problem of the last scene. Audiences didn't want it. They resented it.' The director got rather depressed and suspects that the author knew the experience wasn't going to be all that enjoyable and therefore found himself very busy in Scarborough at the relevant time (he *was* busy, on the next play).

The commercial theatre's audiences were less practised at serious plays by now than those of the regional reps, fed for nearly 20 years on a diet which included Chekhov, Ibsen and Brecht, as well as the older classics and the new British theatre. *Just Between Ourselves* marks the point at which the 'Ayckbourn audience' ceases to be the completely dependable box office fodder that makes life easy for managers. And it didn't help that some critics thought the play was 'laughing at mental illness'.

The play doesn't laugh at it at all. It generates compassion for all the characters, even the triumphant Marjorie. But a play dealing with mental illness will always make people uncomfortable unless at least one character wraps it up with a good liberal message. *Just Between Ourselves* is a vastly better play for the fact that Ayckbourn will not even think of providing the reassuring guidance. It is because we have to interpret it for ourselves that we think hard about, rather than just laughing at, a situation seen from five directions. I am writing about it, I realise, as if it were a failure. It made nobody's fortune and it left those who had worked on it with a sense that it hadn't quite worked. But it won an *Evening Standard* Award for Ayckbourn (for the third time) in 1977, and not just for best comedy but for best play. Oddly, *Absurd Person Singular* with its downbeat third act had been best comedy (1973) whereas *The Norman Conquests*, which literally had people rolling in the aisles, had been best play (1974), as it had been for the *Plays and Players* Awards.

Ayckbourn believes this was the play – very successful in Scarborough – about which critics started to write that the work was being much better realised at home than when produced afresh in London. It would be surprising if this weren't at least partially true. The director knew the writer's work intimately, even if he sometimes only uncovered the implications of it fully in rehearsal. The actors were the ones the writer had written for and the director had long trusted. It was 15 years since he had learned the hard way with *Mr Whatnot* how a good play could be destroyed between its successful home run and the London transfer. Soon he would be in a position to do something about it. But first, he was moving theatres.

Chapter 6

Staying put, moving on

1 : Westwood Ho!

Theatre workers will put up with almost anything for a limited period, especially if they have generated 11 London hits in 11 years and are not touched by the single spectacular failure. But elsewhere in the 1970s new buildings with hitherto unimagined facilities had been provided not only in the big cities – Manchester, Birmingham, Sheffield and Leeds – but in many smaller and less expected places too: Exeter, Ipswich, Chester, Mold. Municipal pride and confidence led to the biggest expansion in purpose-built theatres Britain as a whole has ever known. Some were on a scale which now seems rash but they affirmed a belief that producing theatres represented the future: popular, and a creative heart beating in the community. The parallel boom in university building and the greater egalitarianism of comprehensive education were expected to break down the perceived class base in theatregoing. Stephen Joseph's dream of a purpose-built theatre-in-the-round was as elusive as ever in Scarborough but the town was keen to support a move out of the Library not least because it wanted the Concert Room back. By 1976 it was no longer prepared to extend the lease. Perhaps a little tactlessly, it insisted that it needed the upstairs room at the Library for 'cultural purposes'.

The first serious alternative sites were in Castle Road in 1968 (Claremont, a former Methodist church converted into a printing works) and the Crescent in 1970, an elegant nineteenth-century model of spa street architecture overlooking South Bay. Both were very central. Slightly to the south of the town centre was the small patch of green on the Esplanade where a maze and crazy golf course would have made way for a 500-seat theatre (350 in the stalls, 150 in the gallery) bigger than anything eventually built. In 1973 a moderately detailed budget (seats at 70p and 50p producing a box office income just over £25,000 a year) projected subsidy at around £19,000. It didn't happen. By 1975 the proposal was for a conversion of the former St Thomas's Church on East Sandgate; it had become a museum called Bygones and its vicarage was now Alan's house. The idea of cars and coaches from all over Yorkshire converging on the narrow, hilly streets close to the harbour has a fine comic potential. In 1976 a car park on Vernon Road, very near the Library, was considered for a purpose-built theatre, but the town council felt obliged to cash in on a more lucrative potential use. Some of these schemes (especially the Crescent) aroused vociferous local protests. Half a dozen were seriously canvassed. Many more aroused at least passing interest.

Alan had reached the point as an artist where he wanted to stretch. Staging *Just Between Ourselves* had been possible only because members of the company cut in half a Morris Minor (it wouldn't go through the Library doors), carried it up the stairs and stuck it together again inside the theatre. Plays that would go into theatres the size of the Lyttelton at the National were being created initially for a space no bigger than a living room. Alan loved the Library (he misses it still) but when he was asked the ever-repeated direct question about when he would leave Scarborough, he answered (as always) that it would be when and if he and the company couldn't do the work they wanted. For the first time it sounded like a threat and Ken Boden had to point out publicly that Alan Ayckbourn was only one fee-paid employee of Scarborough Theatre Trust and his leaving would not mean that the theatre must close.

The council, guided by chief executive Russell Bradley, genuinely wanted to build a theatre and Alan got as far as interviewing architects when yet another site came up; it now has a road through it and would have always been difficult to operate, placing the theatre bar vertically above the auditorium. But even in the 1970s, before the Thatcher government, council resources were decreasing in relation to the obligations with which new laws faced them.

And then they heard about Westwood. A few hundred yards from the Library itself, in the valley just below the station, was the former Westwood Boys' High School, closed in 1973. North Yorkshire County Council already had plans for a technical college on the first floor and in the basement, but nothing much in mind for the extensive ground-floor level. The trust put in a formal request for a lease and this led eventually to a 21-year occupancy. Local authorities move exceedingly slowly, however, and a point came when, if there was too long a gap before the company could perform again, and generate some income, it would have to be completely disbanded: not just the actors being laid off, as happened at the end of every season, but production and administration staff as well. Alan was, as always, firmly against the idea of a complete clear-out of trusted personnel to be followed by the uncertain process of recruiting new staff from scratch. Time went by and there was no response from North Yorkshire, but the trust at that time included a retired architect, George Alderson. He was in his seventies and had, he felt, been frustrated by local authorities all his working life. He had known Stephen Joseph, read his book about the workings of theatre-in-the-round and studied his very precise specifications for the size, shape, proportions and angles in the auditorium rather more attentively than other people who built theatres on the 'round' principle (particularly the Royal Exchange in Manchester and the New Vic at Newcastle under Lyme). With nothing much to lose, Alderson managed to get the keys to the building off the caretaker and simply let the builders in 'before any of the rest of us were really aware of it', according to Ayckbourn. He started demolishing and rebuilding; lorries were carting tons of rubble away. Obviously this didn't remain a secret and eventually the planning authority – the borough council – called a meeting on site.

> We all went down and sat in what had been the hall, with our solicitor and two of their legal people. We sat on very low school chairs, I remember, with a low table, so that it was like a Japanese meeting, all men in suits with briefcases but wearing hard hats. And of course builders take great delight in sizing you up and giving you a hard hat that is much too small, so we all had pinhead hats on. The noise around was deafening. They were using big percussion drills and they were into the control room area, ripping whole sections out and banging in big doors. And this man from the council legal department screamed at me: 'Have I your assurance no work will start on this building until proper documentation has been finalised?' I looked up at the ceiling and said: 'Yes, you have my assurance.' And he said: 'That's all I wanted to know. Good luck!' And he got up and left. Presumably he felt able to say at some other meeting that he had secured assurances that the work wouldn't start.

The company now had a chance of opening on the specified day in September 1976. But there was no leeway either side of this deadline, which led to one nervous breakdown in the construction team. Alan was deeply gratified when all the electricians turned up on the first night, which reminded him of the workers who came to see their own handiwork when Coventry Cathedral opened; but in fact the lighting system had only been switched on that day and they were all half-convinced it was going to blow up. The company dress-rehearsed in the afternoon (in Stygian gloom under lamps Alan had individually connected to 13-amp plugs and individually focused) and it took rather a long time, finishing less than an hour before the public were due to be let in. Rather tentatively Alan opened the doors of the auditorium from the inside to see a bar miraculously finished and full of theatregoers being shepherded away from areas of wet paint by rather anxious staff. And the show? Oh yes, just to make it more interesting, he opened Westwood with the most technically complex play he had ever written, *Mr Whatnot*.

Was it a triumph? Of course it was. There was much too much at stake for everybody – including the audience – for it not to be. In that calendar year, however, which had started with a new version of Molière's *Le Bourgeois Gentilhomme* (by Sally Pinder) and then *Just Between Ourselves* in January, the company produced *Comic Pictures*, a double bill of new plays by company member Stephen Lowe; *Mother Country*, a new play by company member Stephen Mallatratt; *The Mystery of the Lost City*, a six-part children's serial (also new) by company member Janet Dale, which was written and rehearsed on Friday afternoons and then performed in half-hour instalments on Saturdays; and *The Adventures of Dirty Dick*, a (new) roadshow devised by members of the company under the leadership of Bob Eaton. They then opened a new theatre with the aforesaid *Mr Whatnot* and went on to *The Guv'nor*, a (new) one-man play about Sir Henry Irving, performed by company member Christopher Godwin and written by him with his wife, Christine Welch; *The Caretaker*, by Harold Pinter (a nice, easy revival, this); *Robin Hood and the Magic Forest* (new) by Bob Eaton; *Dear Liar*, another revival – the letters of George Bernard Shaw and Mrs Patrick Campbell tailored into a play by Jerome Kilty; and *Scraps*, a new touring schools show by company members Malcolm Hebden and Diane Bull. They also started rehearsals on Alan's own next play, which would open in January, a few weeks before the London productions of *Bedroom Farce* and *Just Between Ourselves*.

Ten pieces of new work in a single year and only three revivals: it would put most companies a quarter of a century later to shame, including Scarborough itself. It was possible partly because people were prepared to eat, sleep and breathe theatre, none more so than Ayckbourn himself, and partly because the real value of subsidy was greater. There were problems with the new theatre, not least that the technical college put its building course students on the floor above and the noise of them tramping over the auditorium interfered grimly with matinees. A series of bitter protests eventually led to their being replaced with the quieter (and more understanding) arts students. Because they still didn't have a lease at the time of opening, the theatre trust could only spend the £45,000 that had accumulated over the years in the building fund. When the lease finally came through it made them eligible for a further £100,000 from the Arts Council, and all sorts of modifications could be made: installing a wardrobe area, improving the actors' dressing-rooms and the Green Room, converting part of an enormous space set aside for a cloakroom into a manager's office, re-siting the box office by the entrance. Eventually the café area at one end also doubled as a studio theatre and trebled as useful exhibition space for artists. It was never exactly luxurious though, and back-stage you picked your way round cables and up narrow flights of stairs and ducked under low timbers for the entire life of the theatre. The sums of money involved even at 1976 prices represented a new theatre out of the bargain basement. In 1977 Westwood took the full, if cumbersome, title Stephen Joseph Theatre-in-the-Round. The company was the county council's tenant for 21 years in all, and never in that time did it have a lease lasting more than three years.

Ayckbourn was now unquestionably at the head of his profession as a writer. Theatres that programmed a play by Ayckbourn and a play by Shakespeare every season had covered themselves with the box office and the local education authority. Had he abandoned Scarborough to live in Jamaica (like Noël Coward) or the South of France (like Graham Greene) we would have been sorry but understanding. Had the government said he should lead a big company in a big city, as would have happened in France, we might have been astonished and he would have resisted. Had the funding bodies said it was high time to give this highly creative writer-director sufficient resources in the place where he chose to work, their investment would have been entirely logical. And pigs might have formed squadrons to circle over the South Bay.

He simply carried on. The coup in opening Westwood on time had come off because everybody had joined in at the final stages of refurbishment. The actor Christopher Godwin, his wife Christine Welch and their two small sons went down and wielded paint-brushes. One 'given' about Ayckbourn's extraordinary career as the director of a theatre is that everybody will do just about anything for him. Robin Herford, who was to become one of his closest collaborators and an effective deputy, joined the company as an actor in April 1976 and offers a vivid picture of the way the company worked before and after the move to Westwood. He hadn't realised that the writer of *Relatively Speaking* and *How the Other Half Loves* also ran his own theatre until he saw a television documentary about the making of *Just Between Ourselves*. He wrote to Scarborough and got an interview; at that time actors generally returned year after year but one

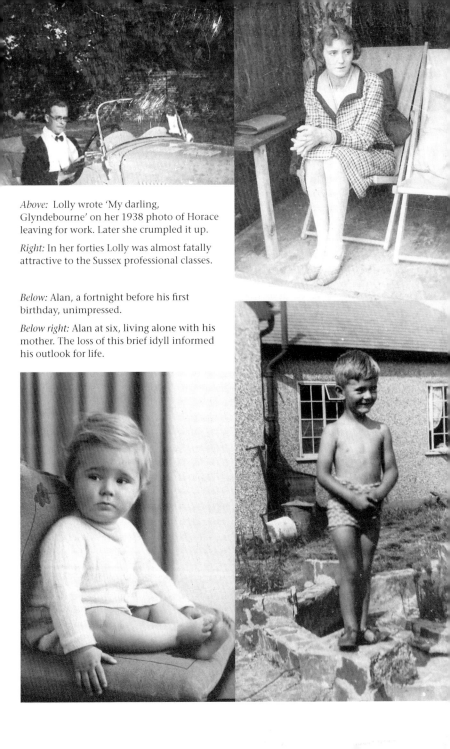

Above: Lolly wrote 'My darling, Glyndebourne' on her 1938 photo of Horace leaving for work. Later she crumpled it up.

Right: In her forties Lolly was almost fatally attractive to the Sussex professional classes.

Below: Alan, a fortnight before his first birthday, unimpressed.

Below right: Alan at six, living alone with his mother. The loss of this brief idyll informed his outlook for life.

Above: Alan and Lolly at the seaside around 1950.

Below: Alan at 15, far right, concentrating hard as Peter, attending the Nurse, in *Romeo and Juliet* at Haileybury.

Above: Cleo adored Alan; he saved her from choking on a bone when nobody else was paying her any attention. He is 14 here.

Top: 'With love to Alan for Xmas 1953, Daddy.' A father, last seen wearing flying cap and goggles, returns just in time to stop his wife remarrying in *Mr A's Amazing Maze Plays* 35 years later.

Team photograph, Scarborough 1958. Half a smile, thing in reserve from Alan (back row, second left); en Joseph is on the extreme right, at the front. o: Ken Boden)

e left: In Marivaux's *The Game of Love and Chance* (1958) made Christine Roland laugh as well as the audience. o: Ken Boden)

e centre: The Square Cat (1959). Alan's first play, written Christine Roland as by 'Roland Allen', gave him a ce to show off legitimately. (Photo: Ken Boden)

e right: The couple got married and had their first child, n, the year *The Square Cat* was produced.

: Philip Ayckbourn followed a year later. Alan pushed oys round the garden at alarming speed in a stripped-1 pram.

Above left: Stephen Joseph directing Terry Lane and Philip Clifford in *Standing Room Only* (1961). (Photo: Ken Boden)

Above right: Silver in his hair turned 23-year-old Alan into Roderick Usher with Elizabeth Bell as his sister. Edgar Allan Poe was adapted by 'Jocelyn Graves' (David Campton). (Photo: John Battison)

Left: Alan never 'got' Beckett, and briefly fell asleep during his own performance as Vladimir (with Stanley Page as Estragon) in *Waiting for Godot* in Stoke-on-Trent. (Photo: John Battison)

Below left: A disastrous West End debut with *Mr Whatnot* (1964) led to a profitable anonymous collaboration with Ronnie Barker (seen with Judy Campbell and Marie Lohr) on television. (Photo: Houston Rogers)

Below right: In *Relatively Speaking* (1967) grande dame of the British theatre Celia Johnson helped make Alan rich and the play helped make Richard Briers a star. (Photo: Houston Rogers)

Above: Robert Morley (seen with Jan Holden) left the playwright a 'sadder but richer' man with his habit of putting Common Market jokes into the script of *How the Other Half Loves*, while Phil Silvers (seen in the American production with Sandy Dennis) had enough difficulty with the script as it was. (Photos: Angus McBean and Richard S. Morse)

Clockwise, from top left: The hair got bigger with each passing production of *The Norman Conquests*. Christopher Godwin is seen seducing Janet Dale as his own wife in Scarborough (Photo: Ken Boden); Tom Courtenay with Penelope Keith as Reg's wife in London (Photo: John Haynes); Tom Conti would have seduced just about anyone's wife in the Thames Television production.

Above: Ayckbourn winning the 'best play' award from the *Evening Standard* in 1977 for *Just Between Ourselves*. Penelope Keith did the honours. (Photo: M. Fresco)

Clockwise, from right: Inspirations: silent film star Buster Keaton was one of the sources for the central character in *Mr Whatnot*; playwright Ben Travers was the master of English farce (Photo: Alec Russell); Ayckbourn was attracted by a request from female impersonator Danny la Rue to write for him; sadly the play never came.
(Photo: *Scarborough Evening News*)

Above: The power of Michael Gambon helped Ayckbourn to his best reviews as a director and the approval of the author in Arthur Miller's *A View From the Bridge* at the National Theatre in 1986 (Photo: Inge Morath). Gambon was unhappy playing in the round in *Othello* in Scarborough in 1990, but even in rehearsal and without make-up he exuded danger. (Photo: John Haynes)

Below left: The only known photograph of Ayckbourn showing explicit physical affection. 'Bolly' – short for Bollinger – was a present from Andrew Lloyd Webber. Alan even overcame his horror of needles to give the cat injections. (Photo: Clare Clifford)

Right: Keeping wicket or directing play? Ayckbourn retired from the game in 1984 but remains president of a local village side and was a proud guest of the late Brian Johnston in a Radio 4 cricket conversation.
(Photo: Alec Russell)

Below right: Julia McKenzie (right) was profoundly moving in the 1986 London production of *Woman in Mind*, Ayckbourn's most personal play to date. Martin Jarvis and Josephine Tewson were her insensitive husband and sister-in-law. (Photo: John Haynes)

Right: Heather Stoney in J. B. Priestley's *Time and the Conways*, 1980. She was also answering Alan's correspondence, organising his diary and generally acting as his personal manager.

Lost chords: although *By Jeeves* closed quickly on Broadway following September 11, Ayckbourn and Andrew Lloyd Webber had been successful with a series of American productions, including one at Goodspeed-at-Chester where executive director Michael P. Price (left) presented them and choreographer Sheila Carter with banjo frying-pans. (Photo: Diane Sobolewski)

A reflective moment with Jane Asher at the National Theatre, 2000. Ayckbourn was more than usually nervous about how the two interlocking plays *House* and *Garden* would work. (Photo: John Haynes)

had decided to move on. The initial meeting was at the offices of *Spotlight* and he did a bit of *Richard III* and 'a bit of American' by way of audition, which stood him in good stead because an American was needed for Stephen Lowe's *Comic Pictures*. He was called back for a second meeting at the house in Keats Grove, Hampstead, both men nervously talking too much after Heather had left them together. Alan had to take a call from America and knocked his coffee on to a white shag-pile rug. Robin went hunting for J-cloths, then invented a train to catch, and ran away. He was convinced he had lost the job.

Stephen Wood, now the Scarborough Theatre's general administrator, got the job of publicity officer on the strength of another long meeting at Keats Grove at which he and Alan played (very loudly) whatever anthemic rock record Wood had just bought. In his twenties and thirties Alan had come round to rock music under the influence of his sons and the attraction of very theatrical bands.

These job interviews are very like the way Stephen Joseph appointed people. David Millard, who combined the jobs of production manager and prop maker (and later designer) at the Library, introduced Alan to Wood and his wife Amanda Saunders, who was also to return to the Scarborough payroll a quarter of a century later, managing the company's touring, 'platform' performances and incoming events. Robin Herford found a genuine company of actors, but the 'family' which Alan was developing also included the staff, back-stage and front-of-house. The fact that actors were staying on – Herford's initial contract was for five months – meant that they were freed from the usual rep business of opening a play one night and then writing letters off to potential future employers the next day. Their permanence meant that the few administrative and production staff could belong to the same family, because they actually got to know the actors and the actors to know them. They even had time to get tired of each other: the family metaphor extends to the usual domestic animosities, and there were times when, for instance, Ken Boden and Alan were not speaking to each other; when Councillor Maurice Plows, a member of the theatre trust, complained at not being informed about something, Ken wrote explaining that he himself was not always told by Alan what was in his mind. Nevertheless, he did what Alan has always needed managers to do, finding little bits of extra money from somewhere so that he could after all do the project which appeared to be financially impossible. Knowing that these situations would arise, Ken deliberately tucked away money in what was called 'Ken's left sock'. Wood's task included getting proper posters produced for the first time instead of having them duplicated on the Roneo machine in Ken's 'office'. Ken took some persuading that this new-fangled publicity business was useful, but offered Wood an extra £1 in his wages for every full house, to be kept secret from the actors (they naturally believe they attract the audience). Helga Wood was the designer but Alan still did all the lighting and the sound-tapes.

At the Library the 'theatre's' rostra and chairs still had to be put in place at the start of each season. The company would rehearse in a little hall – now a martial arts centre – in the old town. When they broke for lunch in that hot summer of 1976 they would spill out on to the stone pier of the harbour and eat their sandwiches overlooking the fishing fleet. In a description that has been endorsed by a score of other actors I have spoken to, Herford says: 'I always felt an extraordinary freedom, because I felt safe, I felt secure with Alan.' That enabled him to do some extremely challenging things, from taking all his clothes off in *Way Upstream* to carrying in his head all eight versions of *Intimate Exchanges* (in which he played all the male parts). The trust that Ayckbourn creates is a two-way thing. Christopher Godwin remembers that you could 'keep throwing ideas at Alan' all the way through the rehearsal period. Heather Stoney says: 'He always had a very good sense of the whole play.' And actors were generally confident that they would get laughs, which they love. All these things give actors confidence in the area – new writing – where they are most inclined to be nervous because a new play has no track record of success. Alan was able to reassure them about this too, with his all-round theatrical sense of how to make things work. Herford contrasts the way he dealt with two of the new plays by other writers. Stephen Lowe's *Comic Pictures* was (like the writer's first great success, *Touched*) set in his home town, Nottingham, in wartime (he was 'discovered' by Richard Eyre at Nottingham Playhouse) but it mixed realism with an evocation of the dream world of the popular cinema. 'Alan really got into this and produced a wonderful sound-tape.' Stephen Mallatratt, a member of the Scarborough company who had been finding acting decreasingly satisfying, says he looked at Alan's plays, thought: 'I could do that,' put together a play with 'clear Ayckbourn types in some sort of plot that played havoc with space and time' and showed it to Alan, rather hoping to be hailed as the new Chekhov. Alan's response echoed Stephen Joseph's advice to himself: 'You're a writer if that's what you want to hear. But learn the rules before you break them.' He sent Mallatratt off to do a complete rewrite and then successfully directed the play – *An Englishman's Home* – in the summer of 1975. Robin Herford – who was to direct Mallatratt's long-running later success, his adaptation of Susan Hill's *The Woman in Black* – remembers the writing of the play Ayckbourn then commissioned, *Mother Country*. 'It was due to be the last play in the Library season and Stephen was writing it as the season went on, and one sort of sensed that it wasn't going terribly well. Alan was quite ruthless with it and kept sending Stephen away to rewrite bits, which I think was partly to get him out of the rehearsal room so that Alan could do what he knew would work. I don't write, so I don't know, but I can imagine that can be very hard for a writer to take.'

It can indeed – as Alan did know – but he was honest. If an actor came to him with a question about how a scene worked he would openly say if it didn't work 'as it is at the moment', and the actor would relax in the knowledge that Alan would use his craft to make it do so. For writers who had themselves been actors, this was perhaps easier to take than for non-actors who might understandably be caught between the need to find their own voice and the sense that it would be stupid not to take the advice of someone so steeped in the twin crafts of writing and direction. Mallatratt has always acknowledged the guidance.

Slotting into the permanent company, Herford quickly found that working with the same actors led to a kind of shorthand between actors and director as well as a trust: 'You didn't have to prove yourself every time. You had to stretch yourself every time because you couldn't keep playing the same part and Alan liked to see how you could play against type. But everything was focused towards the play and how to make each text function as well as possible. One did feel one was at the cutting edge of an area of British theatre.' Working in the round strengthened this feeling, while simultaneously enforcing a kind of on-stage democracy. Many theatres have a kind of 'hot spot', a single position from which it is easiest to dominate the audience, and if the actors are competitive enough the rehearsal period and indeed the performances can become battles to get there and stay there. The round, where anyone who tries to upstage you is by definition down-stage of you at the same time, makes this very hard. Consequently it also encourages the evenly balanced ensemble. In Ayckbourn's plays there are very few parts that are not worth someone's while to play nor is there a run of parts in which one actor can seem to dominate the company. In fact the character who 'drives' the play is not necessarily the one who gets the best laughs.

So actors wanted to stay. Stanley Page found enough to interest him between 1960 and 1979, on and off, first playing various fathers (including Father Christmas) in plays number 3, 4, 5 and 6, then returning from Australia to create the role of Reg in *The Norman Conquests* (plays 13, 14 and 15), then three more parts in *Confusions* (18) followed by more fathers in *Bedroom Farce* (19) and *Sisterly Feelings* (23). Christopher Godwin had one sustained stretch from *Time and Time Again* in 1971 to *Ten Times Table* in 1977. Robin Herford started with *Ten Times Table* and was in every new Ayckbourn play apart from the musical *Making Tracks*, *A Chorus of Disapproval* (when he was in the London run of *Intimate Exchanges*, play 29) and *A Small Family Business* (play 33, which opened at the National Theatre when he was running Scarborough) up to and including *Henceforward . . .* (play 34 in 1987) albeit in a video role rather than physically on-stage. Women have had fractionally less sustained involvement, though Heather Stoney, who is a special case, has a line of appearances ranging from Father Christmas's fairy secretary in *Christmas v Mastermind* (play 5) in 1962 to *Woman in Mind* in 1985; Elizabeth Bell was the master criminal's secretary, Angora, in *Christmas v Mastermind* (which opened in Stoke) but didn't appear in an Ayckbourn play in her native Scarborough until *The Revengers' Comedies* (play 37) some 27 years later; Lavinia Bertram, who was once described by Michael Coveney in the *Observer* as 'the quintessential Ayckbourn actress', was first seen in *Sisterly Feelings* (23) in 1979 and then in everything up to and including *It Could Be Any One of Us* (30, in 1983) – she returned for the London production of *The Revengers' Comedies* (1991); Janet Dale, known privately as Lucy, first turned up in *The Norman Conquests* (1973) and got into double figures with *Ten Times Table*. It is fair to say that although Alan sometimes writes 'types' none of these actors felt typecast. Stanley Page's fathers were all different, as evidenced by the fact that his roles were taken in London productions by actors as diverse as Ronnie Barker, Mark Kingston, James Cossins, Michael Gough and Andrew Cruickshank. I suspect, however, that Reg in *The Norman Conquests* was about the only character within 20 years of his own age. Page was not much older than most other members of the company, and audiences' readiness to accept young character actors 'ageing up' is something that has largely disappeared in the last 25 years because the ubiquitous naturalism of television gives them the real thing. In *Ten Times Table* Robin Herford, just pushing 30, played 'a grey man in his fifties'. And the youthful Alison Skilbeck played his mother who is in her eighties.

The period from Ayckbourn's assumption of the company's leadership at the start of the 1970s to his 'sabbatical' at the National in the 1980s saw the height of the 'Ayckbourn rep'. This was also therefore the height of the company as a kind of surrogate family with Alan as its genial and inventive paterfamilias; a secure place with a head whom you trusted and who usually got his way. The move to Westwood meant there was at last a rehearsal room on the premises – the room in which until the end of its life the theatre still most resembled a school. It also had a licensed bar, a blessed relief for paying customers (capacity now 300) and it began to feel comparable with other theatre buildings, to work in and to visit. With it came a change of direction from the writer.

2 : *Ten Times Table, Joking Apart, Men on Women on Men, Sisterly Feelings, Taking Steps*

Ayckbourn had become famous as a comic dramatist who dealt with unhappy couples seen in their domestic misery. Many of the critics who wrote this would insert an 'only' somewhere into that sentence. Naturally his next play ventured into the public arena and the one after had a happy couple at its centre. *Ten Times Table* was written when Britain was beset with committees planning celebrations for the queen's silver jubilee (due in 1977) and Ayckbourn has said it was 'no coincidence' that Janet Dale, playing a Conservative socialite, had her hair done like Margaret Thatcher's although the latter was still three years away from power. But the play owed most to the committee meetings that had driven him to distraction in the dash to complete the new theatre. He even told Robin Herford that his character, Councillor Donald Evans, was closely based on a member of the theatre trust but Robin elected not to meet him – bank manager Councillor Maurice Plows – until after he had made his own the first Ayckbourn role written for him, delivered as usual the night before the first read-through:

> When I first read *Ten Times Table* I thought it was all right, not that fantastic, but Alan seemed quite pleased with it. During the read-through he was nodding away and smiling. It seemed to go all right – I thought it was mildly amusing. When we actually got into the rehearsal room he began to put the flesh on the bones in the most extraordinary way. I learned so much in that production about throwing away material because there were times when he didn't want to hear the lines; there were six of us talking at the same time. They would be wonderful lines, little gems, and you thought surely some of these needed to be heard but he just wanted you to mumble, because it produced texture. He would then bring up the

spotlight on one bit of the conversation, so that was heard, and then another.

The usual ill-matched assortment of people is thrown together as a committee to represent 'a wide range of interests'. It is planning a pageant to commemorate 'the massacre of the Pendon 12', a little-known event in Labour history which a Marxist teacher is determined to make a fierce celebration of the people's struggle, leading the chairman's right-wing wife to enlist an ex-army officer to deal with the threat of international socialism to an English market town. The meetings are in the ballroom of a hotel that has seen better days. The lights keep going out. A piano and a few glitzy music-stands mock them in the corner. Much of the play lampoons the behaviour of committees, with the councillor endlessly amending spelling mistakes in the minutes, the businessmen sorting out their deals on the side, and the fun going out of the whole project as each faction tries to make the event in its own image. Quietly, though, we are also watching the teacher ('bearded and suspicious') seduce the sister of the near-fascist former soldier, while a drunken and maudlin businessman loses his wife. The final sequence is near-farce. The militia's attempt to quell farm-workers protesting against new taxes is led by the abandoned husband on a hobby-horse. His forces are armed with pretend-muskets supplied by the seriously untrustworthy Pendon Players (they wrecked *Private Lives*). The councillor has been deprived of his glasses. The workers have recruited a giant with a Russian name (but born in Slough) who – in the ensuing riot – picks up the Tory wife bodily and carries her off to somewhere they can have their way with each other. The Marxist is humiliated and rounds on both his new lover and his common-law wife, the shyly silent seamstress who has sewn most of them into too-tight trousers. And all through this the councillor's elderly mother plays her selection of hits from the musicals and misses the action completely.

Every character is pretty broadly drawn and some critics worried that Eric (the Marxist teacher) was too caricatured. Those of us around theatre's political fringes at the time recognised him all right. The other complaint, famously expressed by a cleaner in the London theatre to which the play transferred, is that 'this play starts as a comedy and ends as a farce'. Both objections are to some extent answered if you regard it as a farce from the start, or more accurately as a genre play – a satire – in which characterisation is always going to verge on the cartoon style. Looking back over Ayckbourn's career now it is possible to see that genre writing, with attendant limits on characterisation, is an important strand in his work.

However, Robin Herford confirms that there were difficulties sustaining the manic quality of the final scene.

With *Ten Times Table*, Michael Codron finally allowed Alan to direct his own play in the West End and it was a mixed pleasure. He took two members of the Scarborough cast – Christopher Godwin as the mad ex-soldier and the late Diane Bull, for whom the inaudible costume-maker had been written – into London with the show, though there is some doubt as to whether this was his idea or Michael Codron's. But the cast also included West End names: the late Paul Eddington (the faltering chairman) and Julia McKenzie as his graciously Conservative wife. They had taken over roles in his plays in the West End before, Eddington in the second cast of *Absurd Person Singular*, McKenzie in *The Norman Conquests*. Eddington was also by now the fourth star in the television series *The Good Life*, with three other Ayckbourn veterans, Penelope Keith, Richard Briers and Felicity Kendal; a number of characters in 1970s TV sitcom successes belong to a school of bitter-sweet characterisation that Alan had made his own. He also knew (and describes as 'staggeringly good' in *Ten Times Table*) Matyelok 'Puck' Gibbs, a character actress who had been in the Scarborough company in *Absurd Person Singular*, who now also had to age up to play the elderly Audrey, though not as much as Alison Skilbeck had. Benjamin Whitrow, best known for classical work, played the councillor, and Alan remembers him uttering the near-universal actors' rehearsal line: 'No, I don't think I want to do that' about some piece of business. And two actors from rather different backgrounds completed the cast: the ex-Crystal Palace footballer John Salthouse, who had just played the silent footballer in Mike Leigh's lasting hit play *Abigail's Party*, and Stephanie Fayerman. They were a complete mixture and, Alan says, they never really got on. He is always rather upset when that happens, taking the view that you don't need to be tense to act tension. The experience reinforced his very strong sense that however good actors are, they work together best 'if they come out of the same stable; you can't have heavy Method actors working alongside so-called West End actors'. Back to the family.

Actors who create roles in a producing theatre only to be replaced for the West End naturally feel some resentment of this process, but according to Robin Herford those left in Scarborough believed that to a considerable extent it was Michael Codron who insisted on star names to sell the play (a mostly accurate perception behind which Ayckbourn has occasionally sheltered) and were aware that while the stars were settling in for a long run they were already working on 'the new Ayckbourn'. *Joking Apart* opened in Scarborough, in January 1978, three months before *Ten Times Table* opened on Shaftesbury Avenue. They were indeed at the cutting edge, and they earned a steady wage, the princely sum of £45 a week. And for Alan himself there was always more at stake with 'the new Ayckbourn' too. Whatever the money, the star names, the national publicity involved, he wasn't worrying about whether the play was any good when it came to the West End revival.

But for Chris Godwin the move to Westwood was 'as if someone had cut the strings'. He had worked in Scarborough since 1971, lived there since 1973 and seen both his boys born there – 'so they could play for Yorkshire'. Now he felt he needed to move to develop further. He believes Alan was quite upset. Later Alan invited him to join the company he was forming at the National Theatre, but Godwin had already committed himself to other work, and although he did return to Scarborough in 1996 to play the lead in the première of *All Things Considered*, a fine play by new writer Ben Brown which was directed by Alan Strachan, he was left rather ruefully hoping that Alan would send for him again one day: 'He's probably the best director that I've ever worked with.'

Contented people are notoriously undramatic but Alan was determined to prove he could meet the challenge of putting them at the heart of a play. In *Joking Apart* he created a couple – Richard and Anthea – who are so happy and generous that they locate the hidden misery of people close to them and then plunge in. Their generosity to the young clergyman and his family who live next door leads the Reverend Hugh Emerson to fall disastrously in love with Anthea and destroys his relationship with his clinically depressed and finally drug-dependent wife. Richard is so instinctively good in business that his frustrated Swedish partner Sven can hardly complain that he goes his own way; Richard makes him rich (as Robert Morley did Alan). And their old friend Brian reappears in each of the four scenes – spanning a dozen years of high days and holidays – with a different but identical girlfriend (they are all played by the same actress) of whom the last is Anthea's daughter Debbie. He has grown old unable to commit himself (or even to be very nice to the women) because he carries some sort of spluttering torch for Anthea. The blissful irony is that Anthea and Richard are not themselves married. Their great success is their children, with whom they are probably much too permissive. Debbie asks Anthea almost at the very end of the play whether they have any normal friends at all. The ones we've met are 'sort of lost-looking'. Anthea really doesn't understand and perhaps this is why the play's downbeat ending, with Brian abandoned by Debbie, who dances alone while waiting for her own eighteenth birthday party to begin, feels more melancholy even than the plays about wholly unhappy people. It suggests that even the happy and good are condemned uncomprehendingly to spread unhappiness.

Each of the four scenes has a kind of ritual peg to it – Bonfire Night, the summer tennis party, Boxing Day and the eighteenth birthday – Steven Ayckbourn was 18 during the preparations for the play. These are less formal than a cycle of Christmases or birthdays but give the play its structural foundations. Michael Billington points out that you can imagine Richard and Anthea only as hosts, not as anyone's guests. Though Alan and Heather do not turn their friends into waif-and-stray vessels for their munificence, they also tend to entertain rather than go to other people's houses. Alan much prefers to be host, partly because he is choosy about food – he doesn't want the embarrassment of being offered avocado or courgettes or onions or pasta – but mostly because he can direct his own dinner parties.

The play is very funny, but whereas Ayckbourn's monsters usually reveal their vulnerability, which is theatrically likeable, Anthea and Richard's goodness and generosity form a carapace that nobody else can penetrate, including me. However, I am in a minority. At the final performance in Scarborough the audience gave it a standing ovation. Of the Scarborough cast only Robert Austin went with it to London in March 1979. Austin, a somewhat self-effacing actor much admired by Ayckbourn, played Sven, the comic Scandinavian who is such a know-all, nodding his bald head approvingly at nature as he steps out on a July morning, that we ignore everything he says. He quotes Picasso at one of Brian's girlfriends – who is sketching: 'Art is a lie which makes us realise the truth.' Ayckbourn will have enjoyed our wondering if this is intended as a statement of his own creed. Sven is also a former junior tennis champion of Finland but cannot beat Richard until they meet on a soggy court one Boxing Day. Richard has been playing left-handed. 'I see,' says the humiliated Sven. 'At least you paid me the compliment of not hopping on one leg as well.' His marriage to Olive seems loving to the point of queasiness but she is a compulsive eater and he has had a heart attack by the end of the play. Sven was the character particularly enjoyed by Peggy Ramsay.

Ayckbourn believes he didn't do the play very well in London, where the cast included Christopher Cazenove, Alison Steadman, Julian Fellowes, Marcia Warren, Jennifer Piercey, John Price and Diane Bull. Jennifer Piercey again found it hard to inhabit the psychology of Olive, Sven's large wife, and only much later realised that she should have done the simple thing and taken Alan's guidance that she was 'a contented cow in a field' and not tried to dig deeper; I quote Piercey, who speaks for a number of actors who have had this kind of difficulty, because she and her husband, Alan Strachan, are friends and admirers of the Ayckbourns and certainly not maliciously disposed. There is sadness, in retrospect, in looking at that cast because both John Price and Diane Bull died young. And, much nearer to the time, the actress who played all Brian's young women in Scarborough, the engaging and talented Fiona Mathieson, later became seriously depressed and killed herself. During the Scarborough run, PB also died after an illness.

Despite that standing ovation it is possible Ayckbourn didn't get *Joking Apart* quite right in Scarborough either. Malcolm Hebden, who played the clergyman, initially presented Hugh as a fairly ordinary young man who has, understandably but tragically, mistaken Anthea's friendliness to him for love:

In rehearsals, Alan said he didn't know whether I'd given the play a lot of thought and reached the wrong decisions, or whether I hadn't thought about it at all. But I was to come back after lunch and give him a 'comic vicar'. I protested that this wasn't what he had written. He simply said, 'You heard what I said.' I walked round Scarborough devastated. I thought I couldn't do it. But I came back and gave him very prominent teeth and made him so polite and charming it wasn't true, and Alan fell about. When we opened, I shook a tree in the garden on the set, and the leaves fell on me. The audience loved that. And one night I slipped up on a line and instead of asking if it was a good idea to put the bonfire where it was I asked if it was a God idea. Well, that finished us all. A huge success – the whole thing.

But then I got a note from Alan saying he should have trusted my judgement in the first place and could I go back to what I had been doing before? I couldn't do it by then because I was getting such fabulous laughs. A comic actor cannot give up laughs like that. In the end we reached a kind of compromise. But the honesty there! For a man in his position to drop me a note and say I was right! Many years later I did the play on radio, for Caroline Smith, and not having an audience tempting me, or a tree to shake, I knew just how to play it. He heard it and wrote to me to say *that* was it.

Hebden's feelings about Ayckbourn after years of working closely with him and being one of the few people who has ever opposed him on matters relating to the theatre are supremely mixed ('How much do you forgive him because he's a genius?'). He tells the story as an example of Alan's honesty and readiness not to rest on his record and position. He doesn't at all see why he couldn't have played the part in London, where he thought Julian Fellowes's characterisation remarkably similar to his. Ayckbourn, reviving the play in the summer of 2002, doesn't believe he would ever tell an actor to come back after lunch and give him a comic vicar. It is certainly not in character, but that is presumably Hebden's point.

After 22 plays in 19 years it was time for Ayckbourn to increase his productivity. There was a second show in 1978, a late-night musical entertainment written with composer Paul Todd. The title song might cover most of Alan's *oeuvre* to date: *Men on Women on Men*. He was dipping a toe back into the icy water of musical theatre, after the shrivelling total immersion of *Jeeves*, with a tart revue on the familiar themes of male insensitivity and female anger. There is a sketch in which a man dictating business letters suddenly switches to something more personal and lacerating. His secretary continues taking her shorthand notes:

> . . . I promise you that until you are prepared to kneel at my feet and beg my humble pardon comma that is your lot, you pigeon hyphen brained comma flat chested comma myopic comma big hyphen arsed comma bow legged two words comma intolerant cow capital C full stop new paragraph. I look forward to hearing from you in due course comma yours sincerely. Get that typed immediately, will you?

The letter is to his estranged wife. At which point the secretary goes into 'Copy Type', a virtuoso patter song, half about the bizarre layout (QWERTYUIOP) of letters on the typewriter keyboard, and half about the plight of the deskbound personal assistant (the arrival of word-processors and computers was far from rendering it out of date). The actress and singer Janie Dee includes it in her highly engaging one-woman show, *ID*.

> I'm a copy typist working for the BBD . . . C
> I type letters for a man I reckon fancies knee . . . me
> Nine to five I sit there typing
> While my supervisor's groping . . . griping.

My own favourite lines are: 'I know I am fatted for butter than this' and 'We at the BBC do what we can to avoid any lapses of toast'. The show's Big Finish does indeed celebrate 'the big finish', divorce. The BBC North Region (based in Leeds) restaged it in a television studio and broadcast it. In his twentieth year as a produced playwright Ayckbourn had extended the range of what was on offer at his theatre and he would step things up again in 1979.

But first he gave up smoking. He and Heather were on holiday near

Blenheim Palace in Oxfordshire when he went to bed one night and saw he had only one cigarette left for the morning. He usually had two before breakfast; how would he manage? He decided to give up there and then, told Heather and got a hollow laugh in response. For months he was in a dreadful state, he says, but he didn't even smoke that one cigarette. 'Because I'm really rather ill-disciplined I have to just decide things and stick to them. When I have decided, that's usually it.'

He was also about to extend his range. Again. In the year of his fortieth birthday Ayckbourn premièred his first 'multiple choice' play, *Sisterly Feelings*. Billed as a 'related comedy' – related plays, and plays about relations, it has two plot-lines, which depend on the toss of a coin, and then a further four variations, which depend on a decision by a character. It is hard to imagine a sharper juxtaposition of the elements of chance and choice in human life. The subject fascinates Ayckbourn because although he has heard himself describing his life in interviews as if it has a natural and inevitable progress he knows his only conscious career choices were to rejoin Stephen Joseph in Scarborough in 1958 and to rejoin the company again after his BBC stint in 1970. The rest, including the first season at Scarborough in 1957, had been luck or instinct. A further influence on the play – and many that follow – was the move into a building where he could do much more with the space itself. So when the Scarborough audience first trooped into the auditorium they found that one of the four seating blocks which normally surrounded the stage had been replaced with a steeply sloping grassy hill down which, in due course, an actor would come careering on a bicycle.

The play is set on a corner of Pendon Common (not far from the Reading road, so we're back in Berks) and – in line with Alan's predilection for the formal and ritual occasions that mark out our histories – starts just after a funeral. The septuagenarian Dr Matthews has just buried his wife. With him are his daughters Abigail and Dorcas, and his student son Melvyn. Melvyn has a girlfriend (Brenda) and her bronzed and athletic brother Simon is also in the party. It is when fighting over the right *not* to take one remaining space in a car returning home, but walk back with Simon instead, that the women stake everything on the toss of a coin . . . this in spite of, or perhaps because of, their current attachments: Abigail is married to a slightly older, uncompromisingly materialistic businessman, Patrick, and Dorcas has an unkempt and disappointed-looking young would-be poet, Stafford, in tow. Whichever sister wins the toss also has a moment of choice at the end of Act I, when the actress has to decide for herself whether to stick with Simon or return to the husband/boyfriend.

But the final scene in the play is always the same: back to the status quo. There is, of course, more going on. When we hear Abigail and Dorcas discussing which of them their increasingly potty father should live with we are inevitably put in mind of a comic *King Lear*. And the dead woman's brother is a policeman who embodies Alan's distaste for those who arrogate to themselves the moral welfare of others. In a further practical innovation, Ayckbourn asked his resident composer, Paul Todd, for musical themes for Abigail and Dorcas, which could be played together and separately. He started describing Abigail as a little bit flighty, ethereal and even fly-by-night and Paul Todd responded: 'You've just said "flute" to me.' Dorcas was to be more methodical, in a way earthy, with a lower emotional pitch. She became an oboe. The exchange was fast – almost telepathic, according to Todd – and effective, the kind of detail barely noticed at the time but conclusive to the production.

What the play also explores is an issue that is always live in the rehearsal room. The increasing knowledge of psychology in our time has led to the idea that you can predict how a person will behave in any given circumstance. Few now adhere to a full-blown determinism, but you often hear an actor (especially one who is not entirely confident of a play) argue: 'No, I don't think my character would do that. No, I don't feel as though I can really say that here.' Playwright-directors in particular may be tempted to howl back: 'Yes, your character jolly well would do that. I made it up and I know.'

Sisterly Feelings is more tactful and less certain than that. Even if it had a clear message, it would have been undermined by the play's own history. The first two Scarborough performances were 'rigged' – naturally Ayckbourn wanted to test both Abigail's and Dorcas's versions in front of an audience straight away. The next night the coin was tossed 'for real' for the first time, and it managed to land on its rim, roll off the stage, out of the auditorium and into the foyer where the actors dutifully followed it and, out of sight, could have taken the play in whichever direction they chose. When it transferred to London (back at the National Theatre), naughty actors did indeed take a hand in it. Stephen Moore was playing the handsome but disappointing Simon, whose job it was to toss the coin. Michael Gambon was playing Patrick, Abigail's crass but suffering husband. They both preferred doing the version in which Abigail won the toss, partly because they had taken a great shine to Penelope Wilton, who played Abigail, and partly because it involved rather less running up and down the big hill at the back of the set. Also, Gambon could miss out on a rather hectic quick change in the wings between entrances. At Moore's suggestion Gambon, who is an engineer, turned to his home lathe: 'I put a penny on the lathe and cut it in half. Then I did another one and sweated the two together so that eventually we got one penny with two heads and one with two tails. Steve tossed the coins, so he always had them. We had to obey however it fell on stage but we would decide beforehand what we wanted to do. Some nights we'd say "Oh, be fair," and let it just happen. Other times, if we didn't want to run up and down too much we'd just make sure Penny Wilton went on.'

Moore adds: 'When you look at the number of performances that we did, and the various different versions, it all evened out in the end anyway, which is very odd.' This was partly because when Penelope Wilton found out what they were up to she lied about the way the coin had fallen anyway. If the boys had put out their clothes according to what they 'knew' was going to happen next they had to go and make some very hurried adjustments, which served them right. Anna Carteret, playing Dorcas, did get rather suspicious and insisted on checking the coin one night, but she only checked one side, having wondered if Moore was simply lying about how it fell. The other element that stopped it all being pure chance is that a certain number of performances of each version had to be guaranteed in advance so that theatregoers could attend twice and be sure of seeing the alternatives. Afterwards Moore insisted (Gambon was less certain) that they should tell Alan what they had done. Practical jokes are no good unless their victims are aware of them. They cut holes in a postcard, stuck the coins in and sent them off to him with a note to the effect: 'We took no chances. From the tosser and the welder.' Alan never responded but he has worked with both men since to good purpose.

Alan was still not allowed to fly solo as a director at the National. He was teamed up this time with Christopher Morahan, and they literally took turns with the actors. Their approaches were completely different – Morahan taking the usual interest in characters' motivation and history outside the plays, sometimes presiding over slightly depressed rehearsals as a result – whereas Alan knew the tragic undertones would emerge anyway and cheerfully orchestrated the cast in the brilliant picnic scene in which they are all competing clamorously for sandwiches. Stafford is a vegetarian, which allows Patrick the immortal line as the food runs out: 'All right, own up, who's eating Stafford's nuts?'

Penelope Wilton identifies a huge part of the attraction in appearing in an Ayckbourn production of an Ayckbourn play when she says that sometimes that scene worked so well that 'you wanted to applaud, even though you were in it. You know if you play what is written in the way it is written, this series of hugely enjoyable treats will come your way'. And she doesn't think there is really very much difference between playing Ayckbourn and playing Chekhov (she had recently completed a highly praised *Cherry Orchard* for the RSC when we spoke), and Pinter and even Beckett: 'If you say it right, it will deliver. But it has to be said, it has to be looked after. If you start to change it around it doesn't work.'

The critical verdict on *Sisterly Feelings* can be summarised as praise for the ingenuity but a reservation about the balance of the two narratives. The fact that Abigail is married is held to mean that much more is at stake in her story. Certainly there is a terrific scene between Abigail and her husband, Patrick, when she is preparing for a night under the stars with Simon and he behaves with impeccable grace and heartbreaking suppressed emotion. When Simon finally turns up and is very far from the adventurous bohemian for whom she wants to dance naked on the Common we feel a mixture of smug satisfaction and dreadful disappointment. At some level perhaps Gambon and Moore were seeking out the stronger dramatic development by concentrating on Abigail's version, but it may be that as a result of their intervention Dorcas's story never quite got the same energy. Reading the play now, I guess that Robin Murphy (in Scarborough) and Simon Callow (in London) never had quite as much to play against in the character of Dorcas's lank poet, Stafford, as the turbo-charged Gambon found in the supposedly dull Patrick. It's worth revisiting, I suspect.

In 1978 also came the farce *Taking Steps*. This time, the writing took until the last conceivable moment and beyond. There had been times in the past when an idea for a play led nowhere and had to be abandoned. But that usually became clear fairly quickly and Alan would pick up another idea instead. Sometimes plays changed their nature unexpectedly, as with the developing darkness in *Just Between Ourselves*. Alan had done his initial work – pencilled ideas, dialogue and diagrams (much too rough, he says, for anyone to reconstruct the play if he'd been run over by a bus) and began dictating it to Heather. He often came up with the actual lines as he went along, as if he was improvising. This could be good fun for both of them. But *Taking Steps* got completely stuck when most of the play was written. This time it wasn't finished the night before the read-through. The cast started to worry – Robin Herford's richly understated memory is that it was 'quite frightening'. Alan was darkly frantic. More than a week of rehearsal time had gone by and there was still no script. Publicity had gone out. Tickets were sold. The atmosphere was becoming corrosive.

And then, says Heather: 'He did the classic thing of going to bed. He always sleeps a huge amount, unless the writing's going really well and then he'll get up early. But he deals with problems in life by sleeping, which is a great art. He woke up in the morning and it had all happened. He just carried on and finished it.' What this confirms – and Alan endorses it – is that for all his enormous brain, for all the craft which even his greatest critics applaud, Alan is fundamentally an instinctive writer, putting deliberate faith in his unconscious to come up with the right material and not analysing too much either the ideas or the technique, except perhaps some time afterwards for the benefit of interviewers or students.

But the read-through was almost catastrophic. One member of the company read his role (rather badly, Alan says), and then said he didn't much like it. There was a white-faced confrontation and the actor left. A replacement was found in Jeffrey Robert. The play is another exchange in the continuous dialogue that runs along the lines of: 'What is it impossible to do in the round?' Answer: To show a house on three levels simultaneously. 'Then let's do it . . . you'll see, it's even funnier.' We are invited to imagine that some of the characters on-stage are on the ground floor, some on the first floor and some in the attic; although we can see them all, obviously they can't see each other if they are on different floors. We are also invited to imagine the two staircases that lead between the floors. A carefully plotted farce exploits the visual device to the full.

The house in question is an ancient Gothic barn in serious need of renovation, which an extremely rich bucket manufacturer (Roland Crabbe) may decide to take off the hands of a somewhat shaky builder (Leslie Bainbridge). He is attended by a stand-in lawyer (Tristram) who is unable to complete a sentence in such a way that any other rational human being might comprehend it. Meanwhile the businessman's wife (Elizabeth) is a former dancer trying to get out of the marriage to resume her career. The wife's brother (Mark) bores for England and has brought his submissive fiancée (Kitty) to the point where she faces a choice between jilting him and simply committing suicide. And the house has a reputation as a former brothel and is home to a female ghost.

Taking Steps is dedicated to Ben Travers, the author of *Rookery Nook* and godfather of the English farce. The curtain to Act I falls as Kitty hides in an attic cupboard only for Roland to jam a bed against it, trapping her inside for the night and launching into the Anvil Chorus from Verdi's *Il Trovatore*. A repentant Elizabeth climbs into another bed from the foot end in the belief that her husband is in it and only discovers the next day that she has slept with the bumbling innocent Tristram. He in turn is terrified at the thought that he has been visited by the ghost of Scarlet Lucy. One actor, working with Alan for the first time in a revival of the play, asked what happened when the two were in bed together. Alan asked what he thought happened. The response was: 'What, *that*? I didn't think those sort of things happened in your plays.' Oh yes they do.

As with *The Norman Conquests* in Greenwich, the laughter of the audience on the first night of *Taking Steps* overloaded the tannoy system and it cut out. Thereafter the actors, led by John Arthur as – in Ayckbourn's memory – the definitive Roland Crabbe, had to go from a silent back-stage to the tumult of the auditorium and were frankly a bit unnerved. It is a graceful homage to Ben Travers but it goes far beyond the older man's understanding of what farce can do. One moment we are all laughing at Roland's drunken teasing of Tristram as he contemplates signing a deal on the house and the next he reads Elizabeth's note saying she has left him; he breaks down in tears and we are left utterly becalmed between wind and water. As we teeter on the verge of weeping for Roland he then spells out precisely why Elizabeth wanted to leave. He says he gave her a share in 'practically all my worldly goods, pretty nearly'. She offered 100 per cent of everything she had, comparatively little though that seems to him. At the end Kitty and Tristram (who have also slept together by now, but only in the literal sense) decide to leave together and pool their inability to communicate; Elizabeth is left dithering in indecision on the threshold.

Because *Joking Apart*, directed by Ayckbourn himself, hadn't done well in the West End, Michael Codron brought in Michael Rudman to direct *Taking Steps*. Alan's policy of gradually introducing Scarborough actors to London was over, at least for the time being. Rudman, Peter Hall's deputy at the National Theatre, had also had great commercial success with the comedies of Michael Frayn, *Donkey's Years* (set at an Oxbridge College reunion) and *Alphabetical Order* (in the cuttings and reference library of a newspaper office). I admire him enormously but he wouldn't be my first choice for this play of Alan's. It is not simply that his background is so different (his grandmother was, he says, 'the only Jewish communist Russian immigrant in Texas') but that his interest in rigorously pursued psychological truth didn't really chime with a farce which, for instance, glosses over the fact that Mark seems unable to recognise his fiancée's handwriting. Dinsdale Landen was cast as Roland, an actor who, in Alan's words, is 'like a runaway truck in comedy. You have to jump on board and get hold of the handbrake.' Landen gave a bravura comic portrayal of a serious drinker but seemed to make very little of the basic gag that when his wife was limbering up ('or lumbering. Some say limbering. I say lumbering') for her dance exercise, supposedly in the room upstairs but actually on the same stage as himself, it is the way the downstairs actors look worriedly not at her but at the ceiling which gets the laugh. The question should be raised, however, as to whether the basic conceit of the staging lent itself more to the round than to the proscenium arch. Although Alan has revived the play himself twice – satisfying himself of its ability to make an audience laugh until it hurts – he hasn't had the opportunity to make it effective in a proscenium theatre. Not yet, anyway. Michael Gambon, who was brilliantly effective in the last revival in Scarborough but loathes acting in the round, longs to have a go at it behind a proscenium arch somewhere, with Alan directing.

Ayckbourn was in attendance only occasionally for rehearsals of *Taking Steps*, having long since decided that other directors needed to be left alone after the read-through. He did, however, decide that Rudman was nervous about farce and wrote him long letters about it. After watching a run-through he gave Tom Erhardt a long critical memo to pass on. Erhardt had joined Peggy Ramsay after nursing Phil Silvers through the American production of *How the Other Half Loves*, and Ramsay was furious with Alan for absenting himself in Scarborough 'directing a play that anybody could have done'. In fact he was writing and then rehearsing another play of his own which would open in Scarborough three weeks later. But on the London opening night of *Taking Steps* the Act I curtain arrived to almost complete silence, in contrast to the aching roar greeting it in Scarborough, and things were not much better at the end. Alan was aware of the sound of Heather sobbing beside him. 'She was more upset than I was. I just went out into the night,' he says, but I suspect his upset – as on other occasions before and after – was simply buried at once. There is a story of his being so distraught at the misdirection of one of his plays by someone else that he injured his hand, pounding on a window; and then had to go back-stage and tell the actors how good they were with his hand wrapped in a towel. Nowadays scouts are sent ahead to report on shows – Heather, Tom Erhardt or Alan's casting director Sarah Hughes – and only if there is enthusiastic approval does he go himself.

Alan had wanted to direct *Taking Steps* but Michael Codron had overruled him; from now on, however, he resolved that first London productions of his own work would always be directed by himself. What was clear, as 1980 came to a close, was that Alan was no longer a sure-fire

West End hitmaker; the first of that year's new shows in Scarborough would not make it to Shaftesbury Avenue at all (the first time this had happened for ten years) and the second would take 18 months to get there. Shakespeare's output was confined to 20 years. Had Alan shot his bolt as a writer? It's a question which gets asked at least once a decade and the rumble grew louder as 1980 gave way to 1981.

3 : *Suburban Strains, Season's Greetings, Way Upstream, Making Tracks*

Neither Ayckbourn himself nor his collaborator Paul Todd had any real expectation that *Suburban Strains* would go to the West End. After a series of late-night and lunchtime music theatre offerings they had decided on a full-length musical; although to say they would 'work together' would put it rather strongly. Usually book-writer and composer agree on a broad outline of a show's story, pencil in the places where songs will appear, and come to an agreement about who writes what first, words or music. Alan just gave Paul Todd the title. As usual, this was announced and the publicity printed, before anything at all was written. 'All I knew,' says Todd, 'is that it was set in suburbia.' Todd shut himself in his office and started writing songs. On a good day he can manage three songs: he has a rule that if the first he tackles is in 4/4 time and the key of G, the second must be neither of those things, and the third must not repeat anything that applies to the first two. Consequently after a few days he had a wide range of material for the writer to listen to. He put the songs on to a cassette, called 'Todd's Doodles' (Toodles eventually became his nickname), and a terse message back came in numbers: 'Quite like number 15. Could 22 have a slower section?' and so on. Eventually he was summoned to the house in Longwestgate to look over the lyrics and check that there was nothing too impossibly tongue-twisting to sing, so he found out a little about the characters and even the likely order in which songs were sung. But he didn't see the 'book' until he offered to help Alan collate the pages of the script the night before the read-through and glimpsed some of it in passing.

Alan was determined to create a musical which was thoroughly rooted in its book and its acting well was more important than its singing well. Lavinia Bertram, who had joined the company in 1978, had gone to the house in Hampstead to audition, absolutely bursting to perform, and saying: 'I can sing, I can sing,' only to find that all Alan wanted to do was talk. She had played the stolidly happy girlfriend of Abigail and Dorcas's brother in *Sisterly Feelings* – not a big part; she just unites the sisters in distaste – and then had practically burst into tears when she got the script of *Taking Steps* and found she was playing the almost silent Kitty who hides in a cupboard for much of the play. 'We're all so insecure that you stupidly thought you were only in it at all because he felt he had to write you in. And throughout the rehearsals there was this sort of half box, for the cupboard, which you just had to sit in all the time while everybody else did all the acting. And I thought: "Oh God, he doesn't think I'm any good" because I'd only got these tiny parts.' In fact, Kitty is pivotal in *Taking Steps*, but when it came to *Suburban Strains* 'I suddenly had this mammoth part, and having longed for a big part I was so nervous of doing it'. She was the only real singer in the company.

On press night the critics were greeted by Stephen Wood with the usual invitation to interval drinks. Then he added: 'I may not be able to join you because I may have to go and help work the "revolve".' There were three concentric circles on the stage, and two of them revolved. In different directions. At the show's only preview the set had not worked, the various bits of scenery had not met up and a table full of crockery had crashed to the floor. Bertram was in such a daze that she lost the words of the final song and repeated the first section over and over again. It was called 'I'm an Individual' but for a few minutes she sounded like an automaton. In the event the press performance went perfectly but the reviews were lukewarm. Critics have to judge shows in the light of their own ambitions for them rather than the authors' and something which plainly satisfied the Scarborough public was interred with faint praise. The subject matter was recognisably Ayckbournian: Caroline is a teacher who has just ended one relationship (with an actor) because she has caught him with her pupil; she is immediately pressured to start another one by interfering friends. The new man is a smug doctor who wants to improve her, to the extent that her self-esteem – never very robust – is 'unravelled, like a jumper with a loose thread'. She reverts finally to the actor, who at least lets her eat chocolate, because she would rather have a thin relationship than none. This downbeat conclusion mysteriously led some critics to argue that Ayckbourn had copped out with a happy ending. Possibly it felt more upbeat than the text suggests because it finished with a clinch and the climax of a song. As usual, there were other things going on: the 'revolves' signalled that the narrative moved backwards and forwards in time (another first, casually integrated into a musical) and a strong central number emphasised the difficulty, with polite people who feel they should never make a predatory move, of ever knowing what another person wants of you.

Alan learned a lot, he says – both what to do and what not to do. There were too many places where a song arrived simply because it felt like time for a song. Having a live five-piece band on stage posed huge problems in the round, where there is nowhere an on-stage band doesn't come between the action and part of the audience, and although the show's technology was ingenious some of it was too primitive and cheap (the radio mikes, for example) to allow the show to proceed serenely through the run.

It opened in January and was followed in September (three weeks after the London opening of *Taking Steps*) by *Season's Greetings*. This is one of Ayckbourn's most-revived plays now, but it went very stickily for a time. It was another Christmas play, which meant Peggy Ramsay wouldn't like it, and after *Taking Steps* Michael Codron didn't want to produce it either. Alan still wanted to direct his own plays in London, ideally with the Scarborough cast. It must have seemed a good idea at the time to join with the splendidly maverick producer Thelma Holt who was then running the Round House, a converted engine shed in Chalk Farm, a little way up the railway line from Euston station. The Round House was, for a start, round. It had also played host to the distinctive Glasgow Citizens' Company as well as visitors from abroad. But it hadn't necessarily drawn huge crowds to an unfashionable (code for middle-class fears that their cars would be stolen) part of North London. For Holt, collaborating with Ayckbourn was a chance to develop the audience. For Ayckbourn it was a space in which the Scarborough work could be showcased without star names unbalancing it or other directors not understanding how to do it. In 1981 the Scarborough productions of *Suburban Strains* and *Season's Greetings* transferred in their entirety. But Westwood was small and intimate and the Round House was vast. Alan says:

> We tried to shrink it. We got a lot of curtains hung around and we moved the seats in as far as we dared. But *Suburban Strains* was completely lost in it. It felt as though the voms [an entrance tunnel to a thrust stage or a theatre-in-the-round stage is called a vomatorium] were 100 yards long [90 m] so all the entrances went for nothing. Your voice came back to you on the public address system. The revolve sat in the middle looking like a sort of pimple.

It was terrible. We tried again with *Season's Greetings* and that wasn't much better.

Nor did Alan enjoy the restaurant-free ambience of Chalk Farm in February, or share Thelma Holt's enthusiasm for the overseas work there that he characterises as 'an actor hanging on a rope for 40 minutes spouting French', though he got on well with the dynamic Holt herself.

In April he wrote to Alan Strachan, now the artistic director of Greenwich Theatre: 'We didn't have an awfully good time at the Round House with *Suburban Strains*.' He blamed himself for neither mounting completely new productions nor running in properly the ones he'd got. 'As it was "*Greetings*" got okay-ish notices, hardly any audiences and now it appears no one wants to do it because it's already been seen. Well, I say no one. Let's say Michael [Codron] is being very beady about it and saying, what's the point of him doing it now?' The Round House experiment had failed. In the West End 'frankly, the last two or three haven't been the happiest of events'. He would be happy to go without a London showing at all, he adds, were it not that foreign markets needed the seal of approval of London. The letter has an underlying tone of self-doubt and pessimism, and it leads up to Alan declining to bring a Scarborough production to Greenwich. However, 'Would you consider the possibility of my directing *Season's Greetings* for you there some time early on next year in a new Greenwich-based production?'

Well, yes, Strachan would. There is hardly a theatre in the land that hasn't at some time wondered if Ayckbourn wouldn't come and direct his own play (or the telephone directory if that's what he wanted) for them, only to be politely rebuffed. But this was the route that had taken *The Norman Conquests* into the West End in the face of Michael Codron's unwillingness to produce all three. Alan liked the theatre itself, he trusted Alan Strachan, and he had a point to prove. He was in any case bringing *Season's Greetings* back that summer in Scarborough and had persuaded a reluctant Michael Codron that it might just be worth his while having another look at it. But as he was also aware: 'People were generally assuming I'd finished.'

The pessimistic tone was enhanced by the fact that the Scarborough company of the time was particularly enduring and close to Alan. Now that any theatre which keeps a company together for a few months trumpets its commitment to an ensemble, it is worth remembering that Robin Herford and Lavinia Bertram worked together from 1979 to 1985, virtually without a break; John Arthur and Alison Skilbeck had been

creating Ayckbourn roles from 1978 and 1976 respectively; Robin Bower-
man joined from 1979 and carried on until 1982. So when he started
writing his next play in autumn 1981 he needed to prove himself as a
writer to keep faith with an acting company with whom he was intimately
involved – and of course to fill his own theatre.

Alan once wrote to Michael Codron, apropos of something else: 'When
you're in a corner, the only way forward is the centre of the room.' The
schoolboy boxer came out fighting. The result: *Way Upstream*.

There was only one audience entrance to the auditorium at Westwood,
and if your seat was in a block on the far side it was commonplace to walk
across the acting area. Indeed disgruntled patrons, or those in urgent need
of the lavatory, sometimes used to leave the same way in the course of the
action (one elderly woman being taken for the ghost mentioned in one
production). But when you arrived for *Way Upstream* and turned right by
the box office, you looked up a short flight of steps towards what appeared
to be a river-bank with the top of a boat just visible beyond it. As you
climbed the steps you saw a stretch of water the size of the acting area
with a cabin cruiser moored on it. You picked your way to your seat along
a narrow towpath of worn grass, noticing that the water inches away was
of a quality recognisably opaque to anyone who's done much messing
about in boats. In one corner of the set there was a wooden bridge.

Alan started writing the play about ten days before it went into
rehearsal. He had joked for some years about setting a play on water and
now he called in his production manager Trevor Smith and designer
Edward Lipscomb and told them he would need a cabin cruiser. For once
they had the opportunity to get started while he was still finishing the
play. They commissioned a local boat-builder to provide a cruiser with no
bottom, so it didn't require deep water to float in. They experimented
with the idea of making it move by pulling it with ropes but in the end
used an electric motor of the size that would normally drive a lawn-
mower. Swimming-pool experts recommended a very firm, bolted wooden
frame and a flexible polystyrene liner. So that the water was believably
opaque – and so that the audience couldn't see the underwater workings –
a patented substance called Murk was dropped into it. Murk was made in
Manchester and nobody ever found out what went into it, in spite of
sending it sent to a laboratory in America for analysis. It clouded the water
without eventually sinking to the bottom, unlike everything else they tried,
or causing ill-effects for people who had to breathe near it or step in it.

The other technical effect Alan demanded was rain. In a proscenium
arch theatre you persuade an audience that the whole stage is undergoing

a serious downpour by showering the front of it with water, so that the action is seen through it. The wide-angled shower-head that was rigged up at Westwood sprayed the whole stage and – sporadically – some of the audience as well. This was less of a problem (since Yorkshire audiences often get wet on their way to and from their places of entertainment anyway) than the way it tended to go on dripping after the rain was supposed to have finished abruptly. The solution to this was extremely hi-tech: a yoghurt carton on a piece of string, painted black to be invisible and tugged into place at the end of the storm.

The boat is the *Hadforth Bounty*, and around midnight (due to a train crisis) two couples are starting their joint holiday. The men run a business together: Keith knows he is a natural leader, and Alistair knows he is a natural follower. It is easy, says the acting edition, 'to see how pleasant a man he is to know and how infuriating to live with'. Their wives match them well: June, attractive, positive and in a filthy temper about the late start, and Emma, pleasant, nervous, unflamboyant. One of June's complaints is about the size of the boat, but the four climb aboard and eventually settle down for the night.

Although the boat starts near Pendon Bridge (suggesting the usual Home Counties location) the target for the boating holiday is the upper limit of navigability on the River Orb, Armageddon Bridge. These names are the first hint of the play's allegorical weight. Keith is spoiling for a fight with the trade unions back at work. Alistair won't get involved but runs the boat aground. The party is only rescued with the help of the river-wise Vince, who happens to be passing. He pilots them to the next lock and arouses the intense sexual interest of June (perhaps inspired by Lolly, Ayckbourn often identifies sexual adventure with independence of spirit and even anger in a woman). Vince (whose name means 'conquering') is a kind of modern pirate. He brings his girlfriend, Fleur, aboard and they take over the boat. Keith is locked out of his own factory and deposed as skipper. Vince and Fleur plan to have their way with June, to maroon Alistair on an island and finally to make the timid 'lover of the great indoors', Emma, walk the plank. It is this last that finally stirs Alistair to action. He offers to fight Vince, although he knows he is both weaker and lacking in aggression. But, bloodied and hurt, he wields a tin of baked beans with timely force and Vince is put out of the fight. Alone, unable to manage the boat, pursued by the vengeful anger of the righteous Keith and unrighteous Vince, Alistair and Emma reach Armageddon Bridge and the final crash. Blackout and end.

In one sense it is possible to identify just about all the sources of this play. The potential for misery of a river holiday, especially between married couples, had been long familiar to Alan from holidays on the Thames with Lolly and his in-laws. There had also been trips on the Norfolk Broads during which Alan and Christine and the boys had endured or enjoyed a number of adventures: Steven Ayckbourn remembers how he and Philip as little boys were sent 'below' when the boat was carried downstream on what he thinks must have been a fierce tide allied to the current, until there was a mighty crash, the fridge door flew open and the contents spilled out, and the boat came to rest after a prolonged scraping along the bank or quay. A large chip was taken out of the bow. That, if you like, is the most local source. The more general one is the fact that in 1979 the Conservatives under Margaret Thatcher had been elected to the most right-wing government for over 40 years partly on the back of popular disaffection with the trade unions and the association of the outgoing Labour government with the so-called 'winter of discontent' in which the results of industrial inaction reportedly included the non-burial of the dead by striking municipal workers. There had even been industrial action at the National Theatre, causing Peter Hall to vote Conservative for the first time. Although the great confrontation with the miners led by Arthur Scargill had not occurred when Ayckbourn was writing *Way Upstream*, the polarisation of politics into radical extremes had already begun, and the Labour Party was fragmenting: Roy Jenkins, David Owen, Shirley Williams and William Rodgers became leaders of the new Social Democratic Party. The degree of hatred, not only between right and left but also between left and breakaway centrists, was bewildering to anybody less engaged in politics than the activists. I recall a conversation at the time in which Alan bitterly resented the suggestion that *Way Upstream* was a 'kind of party political broadcast' for the SDP: 'I think one can do rather more than that.' It had been made by one of his most consistent supporters, the northern critic of the *Guardian*, Robin Thornber, a radical Liberal whose party was being flooded with defectors from Labour. Ayckbourn acknowledges a 'very English' dislike of the extremism he saw on both sides of the political divide. But because he hates anyone telling other people how their lives are to be organised, however much he personally believes in the objective of a fair society, he will never write a play with a party political message. 'Political theatre is usually too much politics and too little theatre,' he argues. *Way Upstream* is a moral, political and social play but the *Hadforth Bounty* is as much a 'ship of fools' as a 'ship of state'.

The characters of Alistair and Emma were so fully informed by Robin

Herford and Lavinia Bertram that to see anyone else playing them comes now as a surprise. Bertram's gift for the shrinking violet had been exploited in *Taking Steps* and *Suburban Strains*. Herford's ability to embody ineffectual English niceness has been an enormous resource to Ayckbourn. And as ever, all the characters – even Vince – come from Alan himself; none more so than the decent, pacific non-interventionist who has to decide when to take up arms (or tin of baked beans) in defence of what is right.

When Alan handed the scripts to the cast there was a note for Robin Herford. In the final scene Alistair and Emma were to remove their life-jackets and the rest of their clothes and to continue their dialogue naked, until their final jump into the river. The note promised Robin another option if he felt unhappy with what was written.

Rehearsals got under way, with an arrangement of chairs marking out where the boat would be. In practical terms this reduced an already small acting area to a tiny and sometimes treacherous surface. When it was time to rehearse the end, Alan excluded from the rehearsal room everyone except Eric Lumsden, who was the stage manager 'on the book'. 'The hysterical thing,' Robin Herford recalls, 'was that when we finally did it we were all so busy looking at each other's faces that Alan actually started giving us notes while we were still standing there naked. Eventually I asked if we could just put a pair of knickers on.' Because the dialogue between the strip and the jump took an embarrassingly long time Alan agreed to move it forward so that it would take place before they had stripped off completely. When, well into the rehearsal period, Robin got slightly cold feet – if that is the phrase – and enquired about the alternative, it seemed mysteriously to have disappeared. Ayckbourn told him it no longer seemed quite as convincing. Now he cannot remember what it was. Did it ever really exist?

The boat itself looked like causing major problems as rehearsals reached their climax with the 'tech', the technical dress rehearsal at which everything – sound, lighting, costumes, set – is finally put together with the actors more or less walking through. Alan, as everyone who has worked for him testifies, normally has the smoothest and slickest techs in the business because he has done all the relevant jobs and knows precisely what he wants. They generally take only a little longer than an actual performance (other people's can take days). On this occasion the tech kept being cancelled because the motor failed to move the boat. Finally there was one run-through with everything working on the afternoon of the first performance in front of the public. It finished at 7.05, with the public show due to begin at 7.30 (nobody got the break demanded by their union agreements). Herford recalls:

> Normally Alan exudes incredible confidence about his own work, in rehearsal, for the benefit of his actors. But one realised he was shitting himself, for a number of reasons, on a number of fronts, as director and as producer and as writer. Would this be the play that closed the theatre or what? This time he didn't watch it. He was watching on closed circuit TV, I think, but he couldn't be in the auditorium. And he didn't come round to wish us luck beforehand and you got the sense that he was wondering if he'd finally overstepped the mark this time.

That first performance was for an audience that included almost everybody who had ever worked on it, particularly the technical side. Never have I sat in the theatre wondering so hard what a set would actually do as in the minutes after 'daybreak' at that first performance. The entire company was wondering much the same. There was one deliberate, teasing false start, then the boat's engine roared into life. A spat betwen Keith and June, some jargon-loaded instructions to Alistair, and when the boat edged away from the river-bank on cue there was a sort of half-suppressed cheer as if the queen had been present with a champagne bottle. Only after the performance did we start to realise that Ayckbourn had been *far* more adventurous in terms of his content: at the start of the most selfish, materialistic and confrontational decade in living memory he had written about good and evil, a moral fable. The ending is, in narrative terms, an evasion: we have no idea what happens to Alistair and Emma. But as an image it is profoundly moving and therefore more positive than we are accustomed to with Ayckbourn.

When the show opened to the press it duly produced a headline about nudity in the *Scarborough Evening News* and during the run there were occasional problems with the boat but by now one of the expert advisers had become so committed to the cause that he was permanently on call in case of emergency. There were times when the audience was kept waiting in the foyer while he took off his socks and shoes, rolled up his trouser legs, and performed an instant on-site repair before the show could take place, but it was never cancelled. The only concession made to its difficulties was that it did not play in repertoire with other shows, which would have meant taking the whole pool and boat away in the middle of a week and reconstructing it in the middle of the following one. It had an unbroken run, following the summer season, opening to the press on 2 October 1981.

While *Way Upstream* started its run in Scarborough, Ayckbourn was advising Alan Strachan and Michael Codron, who had become interested in the play again, on casting *Season's Greetings* in Greenwich, and writing a new musical with Paul Todd. *Making Tracks* opened 11 weeks after *Way Upstream*, and featured a producer who doesn't know how his studio works. He's making one last desperate attempt to create a hit record to pay off his debt to the gangster who financed the studio in the first place. Unfortunately Stan's protégée Sandy Beige (Lavinia Bertram) is not quite the artiste he thought the night before, but the gangster's new girlfriend is. She is also Stan's own ex-wife.

As artistic director of the Stephen Joseph Theatre-in-the-Round Alan also took overall responsibility for a production of *Twelfth Night*, which Robin Herford was directing. That summer had also included new full-length plays from three other writers, Brian Thompson's *The Conservatory*, Paul Copley's *Tapster* and Peter Tinniswood's *You Should See Us Now*, which he directed. Oh, and a 'fringe' of shorter pieces including his other engaging collaboration with Paul Todd that year, *Me, Myself and I*, in which three actresses embodied the Ego, Superego and Id of one woman, each actress commenting with delight or horror on the bits of her behaviour for which one of her colleagues has been responsible. The conventional wisdom is that anyone doing so much must be spreading himself too thin, and there is some evidence that a year or two later Alan looked back on this period and took the same view. *Making Tracks* was relatively poorly received by the critics – especially when it followed *Season's Greetings* to Greenwich in 1983 – and it depends on an old stand-by for plotting purposes. One singer moves away from the microphone but the sound carries on because another, much better, singer is hidden away (out of sight of her thuggish lover) actually providing the rather impressive volume we are hearing: shades of Debbie Reynolds and Jean Hagen in *Singin' in the Rain*. The growing relationship between Sandy Beige and the diffident studio engineer Rog is pleasantly predictable but not much more. Likewise, the running gag about what you can hear from a soundproof studio depending on whether the microphones are open or not is well-trodden territory, not least by Ayckbourn himself in *Confusions*.

Professor Albert-Reiner Glaap of Heinrich Heine University in Dusseldorf in Germany – the closest academic student of Alan's plays – regards *Way Upstream* as the second 'dividing line' in Alan's career – the first having been *Absurd Person Singular*. You can see why: it is the first play to raise so explicitly the issues of absolute morality as opposed to insensitive personal behaviour. But for the regular theatre audience who had just seen

Season's Greetings and would watch *Making Tracks* next, such clear definitions were less easy to make out. *Making Tracks* was funny, enjoyable, had another happy ending and one terrific number. But it was for Christmas, not for life. It did astonishingly good business, in Scarborough and Greenwich (97 per cent of seats filled), but the consensus is that any hopes it would follow *Season's Greetings* from Greenwich into the West End were killed by the critics. It also brought to an end the full-scale musical collaboration between Ayckbourn and Paul Todd.

But that was still 15 months away at the end of 1981. First at Greenwich, *Season's Greetings*, the play that 'nearly got away' in its short, unhappy time at the Round House, was brilliantly salvaged by Alan Strachan with a cast that included Peter Vaughan, Bernard Hepton, Gareth Hunt, Nigel Havers, Barbara Ferris, Marcia Warren, Diane Bull and Bridget Turner. Ayckbourn himself directed, and though Hunt and Havers left the cast, to be replaced by Bryan Marshall and Brian Hall, when the show transferred to the West End, it seemed to reassure a public which had not enjoyed *Taking Steps* that Alan still had his direct line to the collective psyche of British marriage. The play's Christmas setting is wryly established with the protagonists watching television, and exploits its season hysterically when the bored housewife Belinda attempts to have sex with a visiting writer only to set off the elaborate sound-and-light show that her ingenious husband Neville has rigged up on the Christmas tree; he is another man who spends too much of his time playing with his screwdriver. Also in the house are Belinda's sister Rachel, supposedly not interested in sex but a quiet martyr to loneliness; the novelist, Clive, is her guest. There is Neville's sister Phyllis, who is a sort of drunken Fury in the kitchen. Harvey, Neville's uncle, is a near-fascist ex-security guard given to awful warnings about the world's descent into chaos; he tries to shoot Clive. And then there's Bernard, Phyllis's husband, a self-confessed failure as a doctor, whose annual puppet show for the children is the butt of everyone else's jokes. If we are looking for autobiography, of course, Bernard's ringing refusal to compromise his standards by putting a bit of sex and violence into the Three Little Pigs for the unseen children is Ayckbourn saying aloud but bathetically what he would be more likely in life to keep to himself; and the point at which Bernard's show starts to go wrong and he turns into a raging obsessive, bullying his recalcitrant helpers mercilessly, recalls the young father who reduced his son Philip to tears when a puppet show went awry by shouting that 'fun' was only for amateurs. But when Harvey intervenes by physically attacking the wolf and the little stage itself, it is Bernard who rounds on him (and us, if we have been mocking Bernard too) with an angry tirade against Harvey's safe negativity: 'You've never made anything or done anything that anybody can criticise. All that they can really say about you is that you're a snob, a bigot, a racist, a chauvinist, an ignorant, insensitive, narrow-minded, intolerant, humourless wart.' Invective is usually exhilarating; it is hard to believe that this speech wasn't settling a few scores. There are no happy endings in this play and, with a cast of nine, it is partly the universality of the despair which takes it further than previous explorations of domestic unhappiness; and being played out over one Christmas rather than the three of *Absurd Person Singular* it seems to describe a permanent state of misery in the Bunker family, steadily uncovered by the narrative, rather than a plot-led descent into it. In a programme note written much later for someone else's production Ayckbourn explains that he wanted to return to Christmas because he wanted to write about 'the log fires, Christmas trees, excited children's faces, candlelight, the holly and the mistletoe'. But the children getting over-excited and fighting over their toys, clamouring for attention, bullying, sneaking and crying, are those aged between 25 and 70: 'Just an average family Christmas. And looming over the proceedings in true pantomime spirit the shadow of two eccentric uncles, the good angel and the bad one' (the note is quoted in full by Glaap).

So, at the start of 1982 *Making Tracks* was playing in Scarborough; in the spring *Season's Greetings* opened in the West End. In August Alan was due to open *Way Upstream* with a new cast at the National and in September he was to revise *Making Tracks* for its transfer to Greenwich. Where's the new play? Due to open in Scarborough in June, and not one new play but several, all recalling a very English childhood. But their story starts abroad.

Chapter 7

A mad world

1 : *Intimate Exchanges*

Texas. A young white woman visiting from Britain, dressed in the durable but nondescript clothes of a stage manager, seizes the opportunity given by a short break in a very tight working schedule to nip out and fetch something to eat. She sees the golden arches symbol of a McDonald's restaurant close to the theatre and goes in. Bewildered to be on the receiving end of some hard stares, she looks round and realises everyone else in the establishment is black. This doesn't faze her particularly but their open hostility does. The fast food cannot come too fast. Remarking on her reception when she returns to the theatre she is told she went into a 'black' restaurant. There is no segregation in the American South in 1982 of course, just some places you don't go. Houston is a rich and civilised city, with the full set of opera and ballet companies and a symphony orchestra, as well as the theatre. But it is not a place you walk to work.

The Scarborough company was already justifiably jumpy. A few days before they left home, the general manager of the Alley Theatre (where they were due to play) had been strangled in her office. It took some time for Ayckbourn to reassure his team that it was safe to go; he wasn't all that reassured himself, though everyone realised such a murder could just as easily happen in London or Manchester. The police had stated confidently that it had all the hallmarks of a 'gay killing' though the victim had been a happily married woman. Half the theatre's staff were gay and were therefore potential suspects. In fact the killer turned out to be a vengeful ex-employee who had beaten a murder rap in another state; his background had not been investigated when he had got the job because it would have been deemed an intrusion under American law unless his new post required him to carry a gun.

An invitation had come from the Alley Theatre – a theatre-in-the-round that had been known to Stephen Joseph – as a result of contacts Ken Boden had made with amateurs in Texas. They liked Alan's work, they

said, and would he bring some over? After recent unhappy experiences on
Broadway (where his own National Theatre production of *Bedroom Farce*
had won good reviews and nominations for Tony awards but not been a
success) and with the commercial theatre in London, this had seemed a
very attractive idea. Alan warned Houston that his work had moved on a
bit since the early plays with which they were familiar and that *Way
Upstream* contained full frontal nudity from both sexes. Houston went
quiet for a while but eventually gave the go-ahead, and after further
anxiety as to whether they would be allowed the water for *Way Upstream* if
there were to be a drought in Texas, they set off.

Houston was racier than Scarborough but not necessarily more sophisticated. Lavinia Bertram was dismayed to find pornography in her
apartment in the block they stayed in, and when their much-loved
production manager Trevor Smith later contracted AIDS, from which he
died, they assumed that must have happened there. Alan's fear of urban
chaos sometimes seems wildly exaggerated, bordering on the paranoid,
but it was certainly nourished by Texas.

Reactions to the play were extreme. One woman let out an involuntary
scream at the nudity. One man ran at the stage tearing up his ticket at the
end. The actors, dazzled by the lighting, thought he was leading a
particularly demonstrative standing ovation since American audiences are
known for these. He was angry, he explained, because his daughter might
have seen the nudity, although she was actually in another town at the
time. But one of the most perceptive remarks ever made about the play
came from a retired military man after the first night: 'I have the
impression I've just seen the Bible backwards,' he told Alan. The play does
indeed yearn for a return to paradise and chimes in not so much with
Alan's vague and self-parodied idea that we should all have something
bigger than ourselves to believe in as with his conviction that life is
naturally good and relatively easy to manage but that human beings
wilfully 'bugger it up', especially their own relationships. The plays to
come included a couple of references to the devil and a couple more
innocent heroes, crusading for good against evil more knowingly than
Alastair and Emma but with less clear-cut results. None of this adds up to a
developed moral philosophy but Ayckbourn retains an (unfashionable)
sense of good and bad which ties in with a remark to the cast of *House* and
Garden in 2000 that the unpleasant characters 'in my stuff' generally get
punished.

Alan stayed with the company in Houston through the initial run of
Way Upstream in the early spring of 1982 because, during the day, he was

rehearsing them in the revival of *Absent Friends*, which was to join it in the repertoire. His plan was to return to Scarborough and prepare the summer season there. This would bring *Way Upstream* back (it had only run four weeks the previous October and November), with *Absent Friends* (unseen since the Library Theatre production of 1974) and the musical *Making Tracks*: three existing Ayckbourns in the repertoire and a new one. Before he left he invited Robin Herford to dinner one night. It was a day when there had been two performances and the second finished after midnight, but this is no bar to getting a good dinner in America. They were joined by Heather and Trevor Smith, and Alan started to order some very good wine. When they had drunk quite a lot of it Herford thought he had better ask Alan what was on his mind.

Alan had had an idea about writing a two-hander. He had hinted at this in the past, making his actors rather nervous because it meant that all but two of them would be out of work. Now, all but two actually wanted a breather. Alan explained that although it was a two-hander it was more than one play. It was four. Actually it might have eight endings. Two actors would play a variety of characters and was Robin interested in being one of them? Robin is a slow study – he takes a long time to learn the words – and he remembered that Anthony Shaffer's two-handed thriller *Sleuth* had been a bit of a slog. He mentioned this but Alan promised him the whole thing well in advance. In fact he was off to write it now. Robin's final question was about who the other actor would be. Alan confessed he hadn't asked her yet, but he thought Lavinia Bertram, the other company member who hadn't signalled a wish to leave. She and Robin had been appearing together in Ayckbourn plays since January 1979. Robin agreed, and went to bed at about three o'clock in the morning, fell asleep immediately and then 'woke up about half an hour later. I *knew* I'd made a mistake. I just didn't have the stamina to do it. My youngest son had just been born – he was four months old – and I thought: "I've got a young family. I can't do it. I've got to tell him now." But I couldn't remember which room in this awful apartment block Alan was in. I padded round the apartment looking for the number, couldn't find it, hadn't got it written down anywhere, so I went back to bed.' The next night Alan took Lavinia out to dinner. She agreed, Robin felt he couldn't back out and the next day Alan left for home and writing. From the tumult of Houston he immersed himself in the life of a Sussex prep school; weak men and women, certainly, but not monsters.

Herford had become Alan's associate director in Scarborough. On his return home he went straight to London to hold general auditions for the forthcoming season. He was there for a week, and when he got back and went to report to Alan he was sent up to the eyrie at the top of the house in Longwestgate where Alan was writing. He was shown a chart on which a pyramid shape was made of lines connecting a series of little circles: it is reproduced in the published edition of *Intimate Exchanges*, though it now looks more like some as-yet unidentified sea-creature than a pyramid, and it shows not four plays with eight endings but eight plays with sixteen endings. Some of the great moments in twentieth-century British theatre history involve Alan and someone else *not* having a confrontation, and Robin is, if anything, even more politely restrained than he is. So after 'Right' and 'Well, cheerio' they parted. But Robin was, in his words, 'fuming': 'it felt as though I'd been asked to run a marathon and when I'd doubtfully agreed, been told it was actually going to be two.'

Each play is in five sections. In the first, Celia Teasdale, wife of the headmaster of a failing prep school (Bilbury Lodge), takes a breather from clearing out a loft in which is the unseen figure of her maid, Sylvie Bell. The scene is five seconds long and what follows depends on whether or not she breaks her own rule and has a cigarette before six o'clock. Either she is visited by the gardener, Lionel, who is walking out with Sylvie but seems to have other aspirations, or by the chairman of the school governors, Miles, who is seriously worried about her husband (Toby) and his running of the school; though no more worried than she is about his conduct in their private life. Each of these scenes also leads in two possible directions, four scenes altogether which happen five days later; and the eight scenes which occur five weeks after that form the bulk of each play and give it its title. Finally, each has a kind of epilogue when the protagonists meet up again after five years at a series of formal church events – weddings, funerals, a christening, a harvest festival and so on. There are ten characters in the whole saga, and each actor plays five, including one who is a parent of one of the others. The scripts total some 400 pages in the two volumes in which Samuel French publishes them, compared with the 80 or so for *Season's Greetings* and *Way Upstream*. At the first read-through just three and a half of the eight had actually been written and Alan says he was not at all sure that in the end he would be able to sustain his invention for the planned cycle, but that he was prepared to announce only (only?) three plays and allow himself a year to explore possibilities for the rest. What the actors got, as usual on the Sunday before they started, was one play, *A Cricket Match*, which they read on the Monday morning and started rehearsing that afternoon. At the end of the day they got a second play, which they took away to prepare for a read-through on Tuesday morning before returning to rehearsals of *A Cricket Match* in the afternoon. The third script was handed over that evening. By Thursday they were both hoarse.

They had three and a half weeks to get the first two plays on: five characters, five costumes, wigs, even complexions. Herford had to exit as Toby the drunken headmaster with his schoolmasterly tweeds and unhealthy floridity and reappear seconds later, from the opposite direction, as Lionel in gardening clothes with a good outdoor tan. And there were a great many lines to learn. And then there was more. Because Alan had to go off to rehearse the National Theatre production of *Way Upstream* with a new cast, they had to get the next pair of plays – *Events on a Hotel Terrace* – ready in ten days. In this, Celia has taken Toby off to some dreary seaside resort to convalesce after he has fallen down at a school assembly. Lionel turns up, now apparently a waiter, and while Celia has a long, bewildering series of scenes uninterrupted by any of the other women, Toby and Lionel are on and off like demented wasps in pursuit of Celia or each other, and Lionel has to do some sustained business with a tray of tea which has to be got right each time he appears. It was while rehearsing this that Robin Herford finally snapped. He broke down, saying he couldn't do it, the lines wouldn't go in. He had been getting up at seven o'clock, learning from seven until one o'clock, cycling to the theatre from his home in Scalby, just outside Scarborough, rehearsing from two until six o'clock, working without the script on the 20 pages he had learned that morning, having a tea break, getting ready at seven and doing that evening's play, cycling home and settling down to a further hour and a half's study before he went to bed. If he didn't learn 20 pages a day he would have to make up the difference the following day, because time was finite and the words had to be in the bank.

Alan quickly assured him that performances could be cancelled, the introduction of new plays delayed and things generally made to work. 'Did we hell!' recalls Robin. But the reassurance was just enough. 'He got his second wind,' says Alan, 'and he never had another problem with it.' It is any director's instinct to try to reassure his actors in these circumstances – knowing that it is confidence that makes things possible – but Alan concedes that he himself didn't really know if it was possible for the human brain to hold all the information required to make it work. He himself had eight endings 'of this stupid, long, long play' in the bag a week after the first ones opened. *Intimate Exchanges* eventually ran, on and off, from June 1982 as scheduled in Scarborough (where in the very last two weeks of the run all eight plays and sixteen endings were performed) until February 1985 in London after a new producer, Ray Cooney of the Theatre of Comedy, joined in transferring them to Greenwich and finally presented them at the tiny Ambassador's Theatre in the West End. The remainder of the plays had been added gradually in Scarborough around other events. The last to be performed was *A Pageant* almost a year after it had all started. The campaign had been conducted by a tiny commando force: the writer/director and his two actors were supported throughout in particular by Eric Lumsden, the stage manager 'on the book' – responsible for keeping them on the right script – and the dresser, Tracey Blacker, a young Scarborough woman who had never worked in theatre before but whose off-stage dependability made her into what Lavinia Bertram calls the third character: 'We insisted on taking her to London because we couldn't bear the thought of teaching somebody else. What to do. Where to put everything. And in what order to put it.'

Ayckbourn's cunning, and gift to the actors, was to provide them with one character to whom they would respond quite quickly and easily and one other which he knew they would find hard, plus some very enjoyable near-caricatures. So Robin got on well straight away with Miles, the self-deprecating chairman of the governors, but initially disliked the drunken Toby. Lavinia found Miles's wife Rowena – 'I'm what they used to call in the bad old days a nymphomaniac. Now known as a perfectly healthy woman' – complete with extravagant wig, much more difficult to start with than Celia, whose character may have been based on the headmaster's wife at Wisborough Lodge but whose sentence structure is reminiscent of Bertram's own. After a rather painful rehearsal process each delivered a stunning characterisation. Robin remembers the whole process now as agony at first but a joy once he was on top of the characters:

> You knew that behind you was this huge body of work. You've seen Toby at his wildest and you've seen him at his most pathetic and you can call on both of those to play whatever's in front of you at the moment. It was almost an orgy of acting. The wonderful thing was that one knew one could be profligate. It was not the kind of situation where you have 40 lines in a play and you know there are four good laughs and you've got to get them every night. You've got hundreds. Hundreds. And you could just fly a bit.

In the nature of things *Intimate Exchanges* is rarely revived, though a small group of the plays was produced in Leeds in 1999 to mark Ayckbourn's sixtieth birthday. Its unfamiliarity means he would love to do it again himself if he could find the actors who would devote themselves to it. And it divides opinion: Heather Stoney believes it contains some of his very best writing while others regard its intrinsic worth as less than its status as an event. Nothing like it has ever been achieved in the live theatre and one of its great qualities is that it has some of the wide-ranging and appetite-filling scale of a novel, without losing the importunate passion or the public intimacy of theatre; the extended comedy of the television sitcom without forever having to contrive new situations. It also makes a very fair case for the random element in the nature of human existence, in that Celia can end up quite credibly as either a highly successful businesswoman or a cramped and lonely housewife according to the different routes the action takes. Alan himself derived two incidental but telling pleasures from it. Sir Lawrence Byford, the Yorkshire policeman who undertook the inquiry into the John Stalker affair (the senior policeman forced out of work in Northern Ireland), told him 'going to see what Lionel and Sylvie are up to tonight' got him through the 'most miserable time in my life'. And the only filmed version of any of his plays that Ayckbourn really has any time for is that made by the veteran French new wave director Alain Resnais in two parts under the title *Fumer/Non Fumer*. There is no real point in filming *Intimate Exchanges* because in the cinema you can have as many actors as you want and quick changes can be done at your leisure between takes. But Resnais, who observed that Alan liked to make plays as filmic as possible, decided he wanted to make films that were as theatrical as possible, and this pair (one scripted from the men's point of view, the other from the women's) has a kind of weird internal logic of its own. Resnais has become a personal friend; a subsequent film, *On Connaît la Chanson*, offers a fleeting glimpse of a Scarborough souvenir tea-towel as a token of affection. Even more dramatic was his telephone call to the Ayckbourns in early 1999 to be at Scarborough Register Office on the following Saturday. Resnais and his partner, the actress Sabine Azema, chose it for their marriage. That summer Sabine appeared in the double play *House* and *Garden*, enabling Alan to realise a long-held ambition and have a French character entering through french windows. Thus it was sometimes possible to see the venerated director of *Hiroshima Mon Amour* and *L'Année Dernière à Marienbad* pushing a bit of sticky English pudding round his plate in a Scarborough café. Though this may have been less exotic than Stephen Sondheim's quizzical look at the mushy peas offered with his fish and chips in Wackers some years before. The world comes to Scarborough for Alan.

Astonishingly the two actors never slipped into the wrong play during any of the versions of *Intimate Exchanges* and Alan told Robin he need never be nervous about his ability to learn lines again. And Robin told Alan he wasn't sure if he wanted to act any more, and has since concentrated on directing.

2 : The Flood

While *Intimate Exchanges* was an epic on a shoe-string which worked, albeit sometimes painfully, because of the collective will to make it work, the National Theatre with its resources of manpower, technology and experience assumed that it could easily achieve what little Scarborough had done with *Way Upstream*. When the NT workshops intimated to Alan that he could and should leave to them the business of making the boat and the river work, he willingly stepped back: one thing fewer to worry about.

A 'complex but ingenious' new set design by Alan Tagg was handed over to the production department where, so Ayckbourn remarked, the metalworkers were less busy than the carpenters. Accordingly they set about the metal inserts that were to strengthen the wooden structure to hold the tank of water. For some reason there was twice as much metal as wood and the structure weighed tons more than it should have done. Instead of the tough but flexible polythene pool-liner, they opted for a rigid fibre-glass tank. This was fatally brittle: one crack from the boat itself was enough to split it right across, which led to gallons of water pouring down into the electrical switch room.

And there were problems with the boat. Tagg had put it on a kind of pendulum which would allow it to do much more sophisticated things than the boat in Scarborough: to rise and fall, swing and turn. It was designed to hold six actors, but staffing agreements at the National meant that at any one time there might be 12 people in it: dressers, props people, stage crew – full staffing gets things done quickly and effectively and all theatres would love it. But Amanda Saunders, who had been working in Scarborough through the production period of *Way Upstream*, was brought in with an independent production company to manage the period between the play's scheduled opening in August 1982 and its eventual press night on 4 October and she counted 52 people on stage at one point doing an interval set change that had been managed by precisely one person in Scarborough. Rules meant that props staff didn't touch anything that was stage crew's job; stage crew didn't touch anything that was an electrician's job; electricians were different from lighting department; and so on. In the interval new clothes and props had to be set on the boat so everybody was queueing up on the 'river-bank' to get aboard. To make matters worse, the people inside the boat throughout the show – there to operate its movements – started to get disorientation sickness after more than three hours in the pitch dark. None of this became clear until they reached the technical rehearsal on the stage of the Lyttelton Theatre, the proscenium arch auditorium named, ironically, after a former associate of Stephen Joseph.

The hardest thing about *Way Upstream* for the actors was the terribly confined space, and the threat of a ducking or injury if they slipped on the boat's roof, but their rehearsals had gone beautifully with a strong cast (which included Jim Norton, Julie Legrand, Susan Fleetwood, Tony Haygarth and James Laurenson) and Alan had left the production side to its own devices. Now the production side seemed unable to deliver what had been designed and wanted to do it differently – but to do it differently he would have to re-rehearse some of the show. Peter Hall was away and Alan refused to send the actors on until the set was fully ready, so he kept cancelling previews. Eventually he took the heartbreaking decision to do it without the water, but even then he still had to go out and tell the assembled audience three times that the show would not go on. There was much laughter on the first two occasions but the audience started to mutter on the third. 'By the time it opened it could never have been a success because it had just turned into a *cause célèbre*. The play was forgotten under a whole welter of jokes.' The difficulty the National Theatre had in getting it on without flooding the building was gleefully described and the late Jack Tinker, critic of the *Daily Mail*, turned up to the much-delayed press night wearing his Wellington boots. In Scarborough the anxieties had at least been compressed into a shorter time-scale.

Alan now believes it was too long (it ran three and a quarter hours) but it was, after all, a long journey. Reviews were mixed, and subsequent productions have found it difficult to make the play's points while maintaining the author's lightness of touch. Surefootedness is essential in every sense. But more than any other play, *Way Upstream* demonstrates Ayckbourn's belief that the 'where' of a story is often as organic an element in it as the 'what' and the 'who' and the 'how'. He says:

I can never quite comprehend people who write plays and give you no sense of place at all. I think it informs a lot of other things. There are plays where you don't need it, but in a lot of plays where it is just, say, Jack and Joe talking and the rest is just left to the director, you mustn't bellyache too much if you suddenly find the actors are putting up a tent or something. They're not spoiling your play, just trying to finish it off. It's a bit boring, sitting here for two hours, however interesting the dialogue is. Something's got to be happening. Otherwise it's radio. Otherwise why waste light?

This time at least the National had the heavyweight play in *Way Upstream* and Michael Codron the more obviously comic *Season's Greetings*. Alan found it ironic to see a large neon sign outside the latter proclaiming it as his 'best play' when it had been all but buried a year before at the Round House. *Intimate Exchanges* was gathering stories in Scarborough and would come to London two years later, and *Making Tracks* was on the way in Greenwich where, he wrote to Alan Strachan, he wanted to take all his work in future. To keep his own theatre busy, at the end of 1982 he also added his own version of Sheridan's *A Trip to Scarborough* to the repertoire for Christmas. Because there is still quite a lot of Sheridan in it, Ayckbourn doesn't list the play in the official canon of his work, but it is much more interesting than the slight comedy around which it was woven: Sheridan had in any case pinched the story of John Vanbrugh's 1696 play *The Relapse* and cleaned it up a bit for the less adventurous tastes of 1777. Vanbrugh's original was itself a sequel to and parody of a play by Colley Cibber, so there was nothing very sacrilegious about tampering with it further. It was the first time since *Love After All* that Ayckbourn had set anything in the past, adding a time-strand from the 1940s as well as one contemporary to the 1980s. The location was inspirational in a rather different way: the three narratives were linked by a porter and manager of Scarborough's Royal Hotel, which belonged for many years to Scarborough Theatre Trust's longstanding chairman, Dr Tom Laughton. The theme that had got Ayckbourn going was the changing nature of the romantic hero. Vanbrugh's Tom Fashion, in search of sex without responsibility, was bowdlerised by Sheridan, but Ayckbourn matched him in the 1942 story-line with fighter-pilots billeted in the town, fractured heroes surviving on alcohol-fuelled nervous energy, and in 1982 with conference delegates out for a good time, no matter how sleazy. For a minute at the end the three time-zones merge in what has become a mixture of comedy, drama and thriller. *A Trip to Scarborough* is unpublished and has only been produced at Stoke, apart from Scarborough itself. Alan hankers after doing it again, believing it to be a rather well-kept secret. It doesn't depend on its Scarborough 'relevance' any more than Sheridan's original did. But his production did involve three on-stage musicians; amazingly the theatre in 1982 could afford them in addition to carrying an acting company of 12.

In the record books 1983 goes down as a not-very-successful year. *Making Tracks* was condemned by the critics, at Greenwich. There was another 'musical entertainment' with Paul Todd back in Yorkshire, titled *Incidental Music*. And the new play for Scarborough was *It Could Be Any One of Us*, a whodunnit inspired by the board game Cluedo, with the possibility of alternative endings built in once again so that patrons were told they could happily tell their friends who the murderer was – it would be someone else another night. Unfortunately whodunnits are always pretty arbitrary (they have to be, to keep us guessing) so having alternative resolutions didn't add very much. As a writer essentially of character comedy Ayckbourn never quite came to terms with the fact that everyone in a thriller has to be nasty enough to be a murderer, or to be murdered. Although he has returned to the play since, it hasn't achieved an extended life. He had wanted to emulate, or improve on, the ingenuity of Anthony Shaffer's *Sleuth*, produced in Scarborough in 1977, and a play famously more rewritten than written. But the cast was strong and the Scarborough public faithful.

3 : *A Chorus of Disapproval*

Peter Hall had not been put off by the fiasco of *Way Upstream*, nor did he want Alan to revert to co-directing. He was calm enough to spot the difference between a flood (forgive the pun) of adverse stories in the press and real disaster. *Way Upstream* had brought in an audience and given them an experience which exerted the grip of a film. Alan was willing to give him another play, but as with *Bedroom Farce*, he wanted to produce it in Scarborough first. *A Chorus of Disapproval* was actually a rather watered-down version of what he had originally intended. A play about a local amateur operatic society, it was to have involved 20 real amateurs who would initially have been planted about the auditorium, springing into action one by one to create an opening dialogue between the audience and the stage where the Pendon Amateur Light Opera Society (PALOS) was putting on its production of *The Vagabond King*, an operetta chosen mainly because Alan fancied the title. He got hold of a libretto on which someone had marked out all the chorus moves on one particular song, something along the lines of 'Man 1, Man 3 and Man 5 stride forward making threatening gestures with their right fists. Man 2 runs round the back of Women 7, 8 and 9 and appears the other side with arms extended.' Alan's idea was that a Welsh director – he had to be Welsh – was working on *The Vagabond King* with half the chorus missing, so that Man 1 also had to be Man 3 and Man 5 and possibly stand in for Woman 2. Unfortunately the Rudolf Friml estate refused permission for the composer's masterpiece to be sent up, claiming a major revival was in the offing, for which I think we are still waiting. At the same time Alan realised that Equity would be unlikely to sanction the use of 20 unpaid performers. He was getting rather dejected when he remembered *The Beggar's Opera* and a maxim of his own, that you should always work on something you admire rather than something you are inclined to sneer at. John Gay's 1728 mixture of political satire, parody of Italian opera and showcase of popular English melodies was something he loved, and now the political element pointed him towards the comedy potential of amateur opera combined with a satire on small-town society.

Pendon took a dramatic leap Yorkshirewards and Ayckbourn's ambiguous relationship with Scarborough came close to being the subject matter. Most Scarborians who know anything about him acknowledge what he has done in raising the town's profile, providing fun and bringing in business. But there is also a Yorkshire suspicion that he must be on to some racket. He tells the story of trying to convince a man in the amusement arcade business that actually he rather liked Scarborough and he certainly believed in the theatre and here he had the best conditions anyone could ever hope for to go on doing what he liked best. The man was frankly disbelieving until he heard that the plays went round the world and earned more money without Alan having to be there: 'Even I have to turn up to empty the machines,' he said – in open admiration. I am not saying that the crass councillor and businessman who has pensioned off his 92-year-old mother, or the partner-swapping couple always on the look-out for a fly business deal, or the former actor who's turned dodgy lawyer, are based on real individuals in the town. If there is a trait here or a turn of phrase there it wasn't enough for anybody to complain, let alone consult a dodgy lawyer of their own. The powerful young stage manager with a punch to lay out any man is the first in a long line of terrifying women who may be inspired by a stage manager who did indeed punch actors who put props down in the wrong place, but she wasn't a Scarborian. What *A Chorus of Disapproval* does is echo a small town mood, with everybody consumed with dislike for almost everyone else and trying to put something across everyone else; the competition is sexual, commercial, physical and social. There is something very close to Alan himself in the way it affirms the importance of art while simultaneously deprecating it. The Welsh ex-actor who has become the director of PALOS productions, a passionate man who persuaded his mother to leave home on the same day that he did, is given one of Ayckbourn's occasional arias:

> ... nobody really cares. Not in this country. Anything you want to mention's more important than theatre to most of them. Washing their hair, cleaning their cars ... If this was Bulgaria or somewhere we'd have peasants hammering on the doors. Demanding satisfaction or their money back. This place, you tell them you're interested in the arts, you get messages of sympathy. Get well soon. Well, maybe they're right. Why beat your brains out? Every time I vow I'm just going to have a ball. I'm not going to take any of it seriously. It's just a play, for God's sake ... And every time it gets like this. Desperate. Life-and-death stuff. Look at me. You'd think I was in really serious trouble. While all that's happened, in fact, is that a play might not happen. That's all. But of course the irony is that outside these four walls, in the real world out there, I actually am in serious trouble and I couldn't give a stuff. Now that really does raise questions, doesn't it? If I were my psychiatrist I'd be worried that all was not well. And I'd be right.

Making the character a Welshman gives him the *hwyl*, the power and the licence to express himself in much the way Alan does if he lets himself off the leash. What he says, and the way he undermines what he says with jokes, are both true to him. We don't really know what trouble Dafydd might be in, outside those four walls. His wife is cuckolding him, but he doesn't know that, nor that she is doing it with the very man to whom he is talking. Guy is the company's new recruit, who has worked his way up from playing Matt of the Mint via Crook-fingered Jack and Filch to Macheath himself, the romantic lead, thanks to a series of catastrophes in the company. Guy, whose very name is a kind of cipher, is one of those innocent people who by the end has wrecked everyone else's little game and taken the starring role, not because he meant to but because he never said 'no' – and all their schemes have rebounded on them. Did Alan feel himself in trouble? He had become seriously involved with another actress, installing her in a flat in London, which obviously threatened his relationship with Heather and made other actors uncomfortable. But all the evidence is that it is not current experience that he uses in his plays.

He has said that writing itself 'was becoming a bit of a slog' so we can identify some personal despair in the speech, especially in the remarks about the respect given to artists, but we should also remember that if Dafydd comes from Alan, Guy does too.

This was the first play that Alan wrote on a word-processor, and he was late with it. For the first few days of rehearsals the cast had to work on the songs with Paul Todd. He rewrote the above speech over and over again, partly because he could. In the end he was relieved to get back to something like what he first thought of: 'You can hone a speech to a point where it's actually better, but in the end you don't believe it – it's too clever, sort of joke-planted all the time; it's always possible to make things funnier. But you can see the truth running out of the door.'

A Chorus of Disapproval is funny all the way through and rather sad all the way through. There is a wrenchingly tragi-comic scene when Dafydd is lighting the set with the unseen Raymond, who has renumbered the jackfield without telling anyone. Dafydd asks his wife, Hannah, to stand in a series of key places with Guy so he can see whether the lighting works. They are trying to find a dark corner to sort out whether or not they are ending their affair, but every time they come to the point a light flares around them. When the show was revived at the National, Alan's regular lighting designer, Mick Hughes, asked him to inspect a special effect the electricians had prepared for the scene, a lantern which exploded. He was delighted, partly because it was a very good effect, but also because it meant the LX department had watched and enjoyed the scene enough to want to share its creativity – a rarity akin to camera crews laughing at the television comedy they are shooting. Although Ayckbourn sends up amateur operatics mercilessly and the play's theme is ubiquitous betrayal, it is also a great celebration of excellence and the worth of playful creative activity. Towards the end, Dafydd finds out that Guy has betrayed him too, in the most hurtful way, and he briefly vents his misery on him – and then wishes him luck for the performance. It is a comic, perhaps pathetic moment, but also a serious affirmation of the value of what they are doing, simply in getting work on. The show has a formally happy ending, just as *The Beggar's Opera* has. And it admits that such an ending is false, as *The Beggar's Opera* does.

The on-stage musical director in *A Chorus of Disapproval* is the 'small, intensely shy' Mr Ames. He was played in Scarborough and London by the small but not quite so shy Paul Todd, who was a founder-member of the theatre cricket team. Michael Gambon played Dafydd in London, following Russell Dixon in Scarborough, each in quite different ways offering a splendid combination of cutting edge, self-indulgent braggadocio, soft centre and artistic ambition. Stephen Moore, the tosser to Gambon's welder on *Sisterly Feelings*, was in the company of another production in the National's repertoire whose costumes were from approximately the same period as *The Beggar's Opera*, but whose start in the Lyttelton auditorium was 15 minutes later than that of *A Chorus of Disapproval* in the Olivier. Moore conceived the bright idea of slipping on to the Olivier stage, in costume, during the opening chorus from *The Beggar's Opera*, just to give a gently energising shock to his friends in the cast. He told Michael Bryant, who could see no reason why the whole of his company shouldn't join in. It is something of a National Theatre tradition and Dame Judi Dench once turned up as a rather chubby little pirate in *Peter Pan*. For one night only, Pendon Amateur Light Opera Society was amplified by more than a dozen distinguished members of the profession who had, however, jumped ship by the end of the evening. Alan makes light of it now but the consensus at the time was that he wasn't pleased. Nor was Bob Peck, who had been reunited with Alan after nearly 14 years to play Guy.

When Peck first read the play he thought the part of Guy had been based on his own progress through the ranks with the amateurs in Leeds (also Guy's home town) and then as a novice professional in Scarborough; when Ayckbourn said it wasn't, Peck came up with the more probable notion which he didn't put to the author – namely that Guy was Alan himself: 'There is a sort of Everyman figure in his plays, the innocent or naive interloper who doesn't want to do anyone any harm but manages to get caught up in their lives.' Now the 'big name', Peck had taken over from Lennox Greaves who had originally created the part. Greaves came to watch Peck at the Olivier and afterwards told him: 'I can't believe Alan let you do that.' Peck remembered how (when he was a young member of the Scarborough company) Robert Morley's larger-than-life performance had unbalanced *How the Other Half Loves* in the West End, and he could scarcely believe it himself. He describes Alan's guidance to actors in Scarborough in 1970 as 'play detailed, small, real. And I was someone who prided himself on being a low-key realist. And here I was hamming it up, as big as I could get. I nearly broke a swing hammock, leaping in and out of it. I think because I was playing in the Olivier it had just run away with me, my performance got bigger and bigger.' But Ayckbourn didn't object, perhaps because he was coming to terms with the scale of the Olivier stage and auditorium himself: 'That place is a barn for us small comedy writers,' he wrote to Alan Strachan that summer. But *A Chorus of Disapproval* did well there, winning more 'best comedy' awards than any other Ayckbourn play before or since and ending something of a drought since *Joking Apart*'s share of the *Plays and Players* Award in 1979.

By the mid-1980s, he could afford to be relaxed about winning awards or even commercial success. In that same letter to Alan Strachan, who was mounting a revival of *How the Other Half Loves* in Greenwich, he says he doesn't really mind whether it transfers to the West End or not:

> I've made this new resolution – which I really should have made 15 years ago, only it's an easier one to make when one has a certain financial independence – i.e. that no show in which I have any control should (a) go ahead unless it's at least possibly going to be good, (b) that the show should never be stretched beyond its own natural length of run. No more under-directed, undercast takeovers redone in ten days.

He has never begrudged being a milch cow for the commercial and subsidised theatre alike – obviously the plays never earn money without rewarding him and working for audiences: he enjoys success – but after the disappointments of the early 1980s he had realised he didn't need a commercial hit every year as much as the commercial theatre needed him.

Nor was he particularly interested in getting his plays filmed or televised, though he chose films for his own enjoyment as a child and has now built a cinema in his much-extended house. It is to do with two different kinds of trickery. He told Albert Glaap: 'I don't believe anything that happens in films. But on stage there are no tricks except the tricks you see. The tricks are the actors and actresses persuading you of what they are.' Because it was possible, on film, to graft Marlon Brando's head on to a thinner body for *Apocalypse Now* it wasn't interesting to do. Although Terry Johnson (a playwright who acknowledges Alan's influence) had directed a strong version of *Way Upstream* which darkened the evil still further, there was no reason to suppose the boat wouldn't work; had it faltered, filming would have stopped and they'd have done a retake. Consequently the element of risk was lost.

So Ayckbourn wasn't particularly enthusiastic when Michael Winner wanted to film *A Chorus of Disapproval*. But Winner is persistent and Peggy Ramsay thought it time Alan made the transition to the screen and he consented. Winner wrote a screenplay, and Alan tried to rewrite it in a day. Winner turned up at the London flat hoping they could work together and was sent away. But still he persisted and when Alan and Heather went on holiday to the West Indies Winner took some very famous actors (Anthony Hopkins, Prunella Scales, Jeremy Irons, Sylvia Syms, Patsy Kensit and Jenny Seagrove among them) off to Scarborough and started work. Alan returned to find some very disgruntled actors who had thought he would be around for discussions about their characters. The film is a great disappointment and when Winner, plaintively describing himself as 'a lonely Jew in Shepherd's Bush' according to Alan, asked to film the play Alan had started in the West Indies, *Woman in Mind*, he was told enough was enough.

4 : *Woman in Mind*

The strongest argument for suggesting that Ayckbourn had explored himself more directly than ever before in *A Chorus of Disapproval* is the play which followed, arriving between its Scarborough and London openings. *Woman in Mind* is not confessional – an instinctive writer rarely adopts the confessional mode, by definition. But it goes further, deeper and more bleakly into a single psyche than any other Ayckbourn play, and illuminates the plight of the trapped, unfulfilled woman more thoroughly even than *Just Between Ourselves*, not least because the new play opens with the central character, Susan, and invites us inside her mind straight away. We observe Vera's desperation in the latter play, initially at least, with the bewildered gaze of her husband and the appalled anger of the visiting Pam. Ayckbourn first started playing with the idea of it on holiday in the Virgin Islands, when he was attracted by the essentially cinematic idea of telling a story from the point of view of an individual who remained more or less unseen until the final frame. The precise trigger was the 'film noir', *Dead On Arrival*, in which we finally discover that the story-teller is actually dead.

But Alan had also been reading Oliver Sacks's book, *The Man Who Mistook His Wife for a Hat*, and when he began the play it was about a man. 'I wanted to take the audience inside a mind that was being overthrown. I had this notion of someone inventing an imaginary family and out came this play. It was going to start with a bloke but, as so often happens with my plays, it turned into a woman rather rapidly as soon as I started to work on it.'

This metamorphosis is rather hard to imagine:

They [the characters] get formed – not sexless but without any particular identity. You start thinking about them and voicing them very gently, not necessarily with specific dialogue, and it just seemed to me to be a woman's voice for some reason, seemed to be an easier way to write it. Sometimes there are parts I feel much more comfortable writing about as a woman rather than a man. Obviously there was a tiny element of my mother in there although, looking at it now, I know there were faults on both sides. But she did have a marriage with a man she felt didn't appreciate her.

His mother didn't have a son who had joined a cult which forbade him to speak to his parents. 'No, I didn't do that. I think I felt guilt that I wasn't there more. And Gerald, her husband, although he is a monster, he is also a very bewildered man. He does try, but he doesn't understand her at all. He tries, but he is very conventional.' Gerald is a vicar and Susan is, or has been, a good vicar's wife. Her husband seems to need her less and less for anything; even gardening, she says, is something else she now has to do on her own, and it is just about explicit that she means sex is the other thing. Gerald is given terrible, self-sacrificial support in parish and home by his sister Muriel, a woman who mistakes Earl Grey tea for the *fines herbes* when making an omelette. Their son, Rick, eventually breaks his silence, only to call in and tell his parents he has married but he is not even going to introduce them to his wife; in fact he is taking her to Thailand.

In order to cope with her misery, Susan has invented a much more satisfactory family which begins to get more and more real in her psyche, and it is at the point where she thinks her wonderful imagined husband Andy may in fact be the devil – in fact that she is 'making love to the devil' – that she begins to crack up so visibly that even Gerald has to take notice. Gerald's incomprehension is obviously inspired by Cecil's bewilderment at Lolly, a fact confirmed by Alan's 'note' to Martin Jarvis – who played the part in London – telling him about the spoonful of the mashed potato descending on Cecil's head. Alan wanted to convey the way in which Cecil/Gerald rolled his eyes towards the heavens in a 'Father, forgive her, she knows not what she does' kind of manoeuvre. I wonder if Cecil was actually quite so piously condescending. Is there a hint of Steven Ayckbourn in Rick? Steven was in a community in California and did get married there but, as he points out, there was no literal silence or complete non-communication on his part. Steven's absence in California, however, may have been enough to remind Alan of his own absence during Lolly's breakdown.

The play opens with Susan regaining consciousness following a minor accident in a suburban garden – with a rake; she is disgusted to realise that even her accidents are banal – and an incompetent doctor bending over her (Bill Windsor, the incompetent doctor who was mentioned but never seen in *Intimate Exchanges*). Mildly concussed, she can't understand what he is saying but it sounds like 'squeezy cow, squeezy'. She believes she has died and gone to somewhere they don't speak English, and when she does start to understand and recognise the doctor her first instinct is that he is dead too. He knows he's not much of a doctor but doesn't believe he's actually dead yet, no. All this is very funny in the playing, but in the first page or two Ayckbourn has also hinted at her fantasy life – 'My garden's . . . five times the size of this' – and her sense of herself as nothing more than a nuisance who simply shouldn't be around any more. No playwright is better than Ayckbourn at sowing these seeds without appearing to give formal exposition. By the end of the play it is Susan herself who is speaking gibberish: 'December bee?' she asks, as she waits for the ambulance which will take her away to deal with something more serious than a bump on the head, 'December bee?' Which is not only the heart-breaking 'Remember me?' but also a perfect image of a creature out of her place and time. In between the writer has done something unforgivable according to his own lights; he has invited us to follow the play through Susan's experiences and then told us she is a fantasist.

> The play sets off with all the known parameters of playwriting, with a central character you hopefully associate with. The other characters are portrayed, if not unsympathetically, at least at arm's length, so you have her as a companion. Then you create a major inconsistency, which as one knows from teaching young playwrights, you never do. You say: 'For God's sake, don't break your own rules.' Here I was saying: 'Oh my God, we're with someone we can't trust, whose perceptions are not to be relied upon, and we've spent quite a lot of the evening believing they are.' You could feel the audience sometimes go 'oo-er' at this point. And after that you spiral into a sort of comic nightmare, with mad races going on, a bride turning up in strange headgear . . . there is also no clear time-frame, and I think if that happens it should always be the dramatist's conscious decision.

Actually, Susan's situation is so well charted that we don't exactly cease to trust her; it just becomes a different kind of trust. She has been drinking (a charge levelled at Lolly in darkest Sussex) and she and Gerald have been bickering over whose fault Rick's alienation is (it turns out he was sent off to 'that piddling little public school' at Gerald's insistence) when Susan's fantasy daughter appears in pale, flowing clothes, bearing champagne, asking how her book is going and bringing the news that her (fantasy) husband is in the kitchen where he has prepared salmon and summer pudding. We *know*, obviously, that this is fantasy, but there is also much we can't be sure about as Susan and Gerald swap scandalous claim and counter-claim about their son.

I first saw this brilliant, poignant, continuously tragi-comic play in Scarborough in the early summer of 1985, Russell Dixon and Ursula Jones playing Gerald and Susan with the real cutting edge of people who have been unhappy together for much too long. Jones in particular conveyed an intelligence which was turning destructively inwards because there seemed to be no outside demand for it. Heather Stoney was the unfortunate Muriel, forever trying to get in touch with her dead husband and cooking poisonous meals.

In the London production in September 1986 Martin Jarvis played Gerald. In his entertaining memoir *Acting Strangely* (Methuen, 2000) he gives a wonderfully recognisable account of his first proper meeting with Ayckbourn – over breakfast, the morning after *A Chorus of Disapproval* had transferred from the National Theatre to the West End. Jarvis asks the usual questions about the character: might he wear rimless glasses? Open-toed sandals? A sleeveless cardigan? To all of which Ayckbourn offers: 'Mm. Yes. If you like.' It is only as Jarvis is leaving that he volunteers: 'Thing about my stuff – it all happens in the niches. Bits in between what people say.' Jarvis describes Gerald as a 'complete bastard' and had to learn not to make him overtly cruel to his wife.

The casting of Julia McKenzie as Susan was inspired. She had made her reputation in musicals and was in danger of being pigeon-holed accordingly when Alan and Michael Codron employed her to take over the part of Ruth in *The Norman Conquests*. She followed this with *Ten Times Table*, and then the television version of *Absent Friends* in which Alan had especially enjoyed the opening ten-minute duologue (with Maureen Lipman) between two rather distraite women.

Nevertheless the invitation to do *Woman in Mind* came like a bolt from the blue: 'I knew it was a great part but I was very frightened. And we don't speak about those things, Alan and I, don't speak about fright and that sort of thing, but he knows because he's frightened. He sensed it and held my hand, really, throughout the entire thing.' Of Susan, she says: 'The whole thing is real to her, so there wasn't any great jump into believing (the fantasy element) because that's who she was. This other family was her family and they all belonged to her. It is so beautifully written that the dream family is as natural to her as cleaning her teeth.' She and Jarvis seemed to me to bring out the 'ordinary' side of the couple, the suburban familiarity.

McKenzie has a fund of stories of audience reactions to the play: the woman who sat with her son in the front row and just cried quietly and couldn't leave at the end, her son shaking her and murmuring 'Mum, Mum' over and over to her; the man who wrote saying his daughter was in a bad marriage but had walked from the theatre in silence, far apart, until they had sat down to a glass of wine in a pub and started to talk of things they had kept silent about for years; the actor who had come round to congratulate her and after ten minutes in the dressing-room had simply started to cry and cry and cry. Ayckbourn himself has a similar account of waiting outside the theatre – not really wanting to go in – and hearing two women as they left boasting competitively with their accounts of how accurate the play was in describing their lives. And yet the play also produced gales of laughter and the actress had to remember to be a comedian as well as a tragic heroine. Jarvis, on the other hand, had to be urged not to keep doing more (and getting disruptive laughs) as the run continued. Ayckbourn revisited the show a number of times; usually actors don't see him much after the first night. Plainly he got on unusually well with the cast but perhaps he was also unusually attached to the play.

McKenzie's gift from Alan was a 'December bee' brooch, to add to the cherished glasses he had given her for one of the earlier performances. She says his gift for writing for women comes from his own feminine side, and I am sure this is true; it is a side developed in those childhood years when he learned to perceive the world through Lolly's experience. He also said in 1998 that *Woman in Mind* had been influenced by Ibsen's *A Doll's House* more than he realised when he wrote it; thoughts of what would have happened to Nora if she had stayed with Torvald and her children, perhaps.

I do not doubt this, but I think there is more. The fright that Julia McKenzie mentioned echoes Margaret Boden's observation about frightened genius long ago and I recall him telling a story about a mutual acquaintance's breakdown – itself both funny and sad – and ending it with: 'And I thought, there but for the grace of God . . .' I think it is significant that the central character started out male and that the ambiguous grammar of the comment on feeling 'much more comfortable writing about as a woman' may be significant too. On the other hand Susan's situation is not in the least like Alan's, and he certainly never encouraged Ursula Jones or Julia McKenzie to think of the part as autobiographical. How would they have played it if he had? Both actresses, he said later, were more than usually inclined to turn into their character. Eventually the play triumphed in New York when Stockard Channing gave an award-winning performance at the Manhattan Theatre Club and in California when Helen Mirren played Susan.

Did he really mean that line about 'there but for the grace of God . . .'? He seems never to have reached the point of clinical depression but there is a capacity for frustration and despair close to the heart of his creative self. Although the proportion of his life spent actually writing plays is very short, there is a part of him always at work on one. If this process, never switched off, is crowded with what to everybody else are the thoroughly important matters of daily living but to him at that moment feel like irrelevancies, he will 'get a long way down'. Small obstacles will look insurmountable, a shortage of taxis on a London street will provoke an arm-whirling public outburst, and – most damaging – he will be unable to produce anything. Being alone exacerbates this and the solution is to find company. He accepts there may be much that he doesn't know about his own psyche but also insists that there is a lot that he does; he spends his working life excavating it and values what is there, not least the fact that his instinctive responses are rarely politically correct, because he can use them dramatically. Far from being a kind of computer, as people sometimes guess, his mind is like an Aladdin's Cave where the treasures are characters, experiences, emotions of unknown provenance; they have never been catalogued or put in order. Many creative artists – and scientists of genius for that matter – have something of the autistic's inability to turn their attention to others when preoccupied with what is going on in their own heads. Ayckbourn is unusually good company most of the time, and few people get close enough to him to be aware of this side of his nature or his occasional spells of what Heather calls 'the blue meanies'.

If, in his mid-forties, Ayckbourn felt himself to be threatened by personal crisis, as lines in both *A Chorus of Disapproval* and *Woman in Mind* may suggest, he responded in the classic manner of a driven man by working harder. In 1984 and 1985, when those two plays were written and produced, he also wrote *The Seven Deadly Virtues* with Paul Todd, unconsciously inspired, at most, by Kurt Weill's *The Seven Deadly Sins*. It has seven through-composed sections about the destructiveness of virtue and is a piece whose interest would bear further examination. The virtues in question were Faith, Hope and Charity; Fortitude, Prudence, Justice and Temperance. Hope had actually surfaced before, as a short piece called

'Petra and the Wolf', which appeared in *Incidental Music*. He described *The Seven Deadly Virtues* as 'the best we've done so far'. And there were lunchtime entertainments, *The Westwoods* and *Boy Meets Girl* and *Girl Meets Boy*. There was also a revival of what had been called *The Story So Far* in 1970, then *Me Times Me Times Me* and was now *Family Circles*. In 1986 there was no Ayckbourn première in Scarborough (though there was a revival of *Time and Time Again*) but during the year he did write another major play, which had to be submitted to another producer for the first time since *Relatively Speaking* had been posted off to Stephen Joseph in 1965. Peter Hall had firmed up an offer he had been dangling for some time, for Alan to go to the National Theatre, form his own company, and do a play in each of the three auditoria. He could choose what he wanted to do on condition one of them was a new play of his own. 'Presumably Peter thought that if I buggered up the directing side at least he'd get a new play out of me.' On the principle that it is best to tackle whatever is most fearful, he elected to write a play for the Olivier and sent off *A Small Family Business*.

It was really the chance to have his own company at the National that swung it; he wouldn't have left Scarborough for anything else. The board of Scarborough Theatre Trust, he thinks, assumed he wouldn't be coming back; this was the common view in the wider theatre world where what keeps him in Scarborough has never been fully understood. Just in case, the town took the opportunity to grant him the freedom of the borough in 1986. He took Robin Herford to London on the train and, typically, broached what was on his mind more or less as they were getting off at King's Cross. Would Robin like to run the theatre while he was away? On balance, yes, he would, if he could run it his way. And so in due course Alan said his temporary farewells. He and Heather had, inevitably, recently taken the decision to sell the house in Keats Grove because they were almost never there. Needing somewhere quickly they found a flat in Wapping, in a Docklands warehouse conversion. It has almost as good a view of the river as the house in Longwestgate has of the South Bay. It is near a river police station and when the taste for the macabre is on him he can watch the bodies of the drowned being brought ashore.

5 : *A Small Family Business*

In February 1987 he was invested with the CBE (Commander of the Order of the British Empire) by the queen. She and the queen mother are known to have enjoyed Ayckbourn plays. The queen mother saw many of them at the local rep in Windsor and enquired, after watching *Time and Time Again*, what would happen to the garden gnome when the production finished. 'Bernard' duly made his way to a better place. Alan believes the queen knew his early work and enjoyed it but had been less keen to see the darker plays, and had been gently discouraged from going to see *Woman in Mind*. Probably wise.

As he waited his turn at the ceremony, he was suddenly aware of a Palace official walking purposefully towards him and expected to be told it was all a dreadful mistake and would he please go home. In fact the official wanted his autograph on a programme. When his name was mentioned somebody else in the queue said: 'Oh, are you Alan Ayckbourn?' and also produced something to sign. When Alan's ego was sufficiently inflated his name was called. Or rather an Alan Aitchbone's name was called. He went forward anyway.

He was accompanied to the Palace by Lolly, now retired to Scarborough. She had worked as editor of the John Lewis house magazine and for a publisher as well as continuing to produce the occasional short story. Alan had given her a subject when he saw a young man holding his girlfriend's clothes as she ran naked into the sea late one Scarborough evening. He thought this quite raunchy but she turned it into a decorous romance. I remember her at a press night in this period coming over to a knot of critics enjoying our free interval drink and asking what we thought of Alan's latest play. Without waiting for an answer she added: 'Not very good is it? Not up to his usual standard.' She liked to stir things up a bit. She fell into Alan's front door one night after one of her regular drinking sessions with two other women, and eventually moved into the basement at Longwestgate before moving to a top-floor flat on the Esplanade.

Like most writers, when Ayckbourn sends someone a play he hopes for an instant response. Peter Hall was in Los Angeles, but a fax arrived saying *A Small Family Business* was everything he'd hoped for. Alan put together a company which reunited him with Michael Gambon plus a number of Scarborough veterans, including Paul Todd as composer, John Arthur, Marcia Warren, Polly Adams, Russell Dixon, Elizabeth Bell, Diane Bull and Michael Simkins. The newcomers included the late Simon Cadell and

Suzan Sylvester. Cadell's agreement to play the character of Benedict Hough in *A Small Family Business* was something of a coup. The actor, a consummate light comedian of a particularly English type, was most widely known at the time as the gentlemanly, out-of-his-depth manager of an anarchic holiday camp in the television series *Hi de Hi*. His character in the new play was a private detective in a wholly corrupt society; down its mean streets went a man who was, alas, himself mean. Alan picked up the play with more than his usual nervousness, not so much because it was at the National but because there had been a gap of a year between the writing and the playing. Normally he finished the script on a Sunday and by Monday afternoon was beginning to move the actors around the rehearsal room floor, still on a roll of excitement from the writing and with no vacuum in between for a writer's fearful paranoia to seep in: would he still like it?

He treated it as he would somebody else's play and 'just followed the author', but it took him the first two weeks of rehearsal to get back into it; fortunately he had seven weeks at his disposal. *A Small Family Business* had two starting points, one visual and the other narrative. Ever since the designer Voytek had given him evocative green abstractions for *Jeeves*, he had hankered after a complete house with the back taken off so that the audience could see upstairs and downstairs at the same time. Alan Tagg now provided him with a sitting-room, kitchen (with a hatch providing glimpses into a dining-room), hall and front door downstairs; upstairs there was a landing (not as extensive as Alan had hoped, which meant some re-plotting) with doors leading into the (visible) main bedroom and bathroom, and two more unseen bedrooms. The stairs were also visible. All this was in part a direct response to the physical challenge of the Olivier, a plan to make the on-stage presence so strong (and tall) that the audience would be drawn in and fused into the single unit that the Greeks and Stephen Joseph always wanted but the concrete divisions of the Olivier rarely allow. But showing action taking place throughout the house was also essential to the content of the play, which demonstrated a whole family – and through it a whole society – imploding morally and emotionally.

The narrative starting-point had been a Green Room conversation in Scarborough about what sort of 'fiddling' was permissible and what was real fraud. The play opens with a scene as funny as anything Ayckbourn has written. Businessman Jack McCracken, with a background in fish fingers, has just been given control of his father-in-law's furniture firm and he comes home with the express intention of celebrating by having sex with his wife. He heads upstairs, casting off clothes and giving vent to a rough Viking fantasy, but his wife lures him instead into the sitting-room. When he reaches it, his trousers round his ankles, and snaps on the light, he is greeted by ten people, family and business colleagues. Surprise!

When Jack recovers himself he announces, hubristically, that the firm is to be incorruptible. Everyone who works for him is 'family' and must be completely incorruptible; no smuggling out office stationery (Lolly had been outstandingly successful at this), no private telephone calls, no slipping a few extra quid on to the motoring expenses. The party is broken up by the arrival of a private investigator, Benedict Hough, seeking to confront a shoplifter. Although the sum involved is only £1.87 Jack has to agree when Hough says, 'Theft is theft is theft,' even though the criminal is his 16-year-old daughter Samantha. The sinister Hough worms his way on to Jack's payroll and uncovers a sliding scale of corruption: minor sins on the part of his wife and other daughter, a sister-in-law having an affair with an Italian business rival, the least of whose vices is industrial espionage, and eventually a drugs racket involving that great defender of the family, the Mafia. Hough dies when he is confronted by the women in the bathroom and cracks his head. The play ends with another party, celebrating the seventy-fifth birthday of Jack's near-senile father-in-law, the firm's founder. As it begins, Samantha locks herself in the bathroom in the half-light, huddled, blank-faced, drugged; everybody else toasts a family business in which Jack himself is now complicit in drug-dealing and his daughter has been broken on the wheel of his moralising.

This cocktail of blackmail, murder and drugs – the evil of *Way Upstream* now made shockingly specific – was convincing because it was realised visually and because he got edgily realistic performances from a strong cast. Michael Gambon, as Jack, changed clothes and shape during the performance, from the comfortable, slightly shambling decency of the new boss at the beginning to the sharp-suited Mr Big of the climax. But just before the press night, a great shriek was heard from back-stage. Many thought Gambon was larking about but he had tripped and seriously injured an ankle. Understudy Alan Mitchell took over, very effectively, and to fill the gap left by postponed reviews Ayckbourn gave an interview to the BBC Radio 4 arts magazine *Kaleidoscope*, making it clear that the play expressed his feelings about Thatcherite Britain, that a culture of enterprise at all costs was being sanctioned in the name of an individual citizen who was being involved without being consulted. The notion that he wrote 'boulevard' comedy still lingered and some critics assumed that anyone who was commercially successful must also be conservative, with a small or capital 'c' – if not both. But in 1999 Mark Ravenhill (author of the streetwise hit of the late 1990s, *Shopping and Fucking*) argued, also on Radio 4, that *A Small Family Business* had been *the* political play of its time because it targeted the twin values of family and business. The play is larger than Thatcherism or topicality, though. In connecting the queasy human aspiration to perfect innocence and the selfish ambition to be better off than average, it touches most of us.

Its physical scale led to two problems. One is that very few people can afford to produce it, and where they can (e.g. Broadway, where it flopped) they may not like what it has to say. The other was that during rehearsals it became clear to Alan's regular lighting designer Mick Hughes that the Olivier didn't have the resources to light the whole house properly.

Hughes long ago endeared himself to Ayckbourn, when asked if he could achieve a particular lighting state, by replying that his lamps were all whores and would cheerfully do whatever they were asked. So when he said something was impossible, he was believed. They formed a small delegation to David Aukin, then the executive director of the National Theatre, and told him the problem. Aukin asked what the solution would be and was told a new lighting bar across the ceiling at the back of the Olivier auditorium, which wouldn't cost much, and a lot of new lamps to hang on it, which would. How much? There was a lot of rather technical elaboration. Aukin just wanted the figure. Hughes cleared his throat and said the total (as far as he can now remember) was £38,000. There was a short silence. Then Aukin said: 'OK.' They left, wondering if they should have asked for more. Later, Aukin stopped Ayckbourn in a National Theatre corridor and said he had been meaning to tell him that the box office take for *A Small Family Business* had just passed £1 million. It had paid for the lighting bar.

Partly no doubt because it hasn't been widely produced, Alan remains very fond of the play and points out that moving into a more social and political kind of drama is only really feasible if you can command a decent-sized cast: 'If you've got two or three people, you do tend to go down the "I love you" and "No you don't" route. Sexual politics. That's also good but one's done quite a lot of that. I rather want to go back to the big canvases. That's what the National gave me, and that's what I've missed in the last few years.'

It is also, of course, what he gave the National. No other new play has yet quite achieved the audience engagement of *A Small Family Business* in the institution's largest auditorium. It won the 'best play' Award from the London *Evening Standard* in 1987.

In the event there were four productions from the Ayckbourn company at the National, including his own play, and he stayed slightly longer than the two years originally estimated. The others included *Tons of Money*, a veteran rather than vintage comedy (1922) by Will Evans and Valentine, which he had just tinkered about with and directed in Scarborough, but which seemed suitable for the proscenium arch Lyttelton Theatre; the Jacobean tragedy *'Tis Pity She's a Whore*; and the one which made everybody beyond Scarborough wake up to just how good a director he is, Arthur Miller's *A View From the Bridge*.

Ayckbourn had directed the same author's *The Crucible* in Scarborough in 1979. According to Paul Todd he blocked this anti-witch-hunt modern classic, as if he were a cricket captain placing his field. He got the most out of the wintry central relationship between John and Elizabeth Proctor but he also handled the near-biblical language with great fluency and above all he found the great beating heart of the play. Which is what he now did with *A View From the Bridge*. The contemporary and local nature of this play deals with an immigrant community in 1950s New York, scrambling for a living and trying to avoid being sent home to impoverished Italy. The eternal nature of it juxtaposes an illicit passion and corrosive pain against two kinds of justice. The hero, Eddie Carbone, is so over-fond of Catherine, the niece he has brought up as his own daughter, that rather than let her go and marry the popular (but illegal) newcomer he has also sheltered, he informs on him to the immigration authorities, thus defying the ancient and harsh code of Sicilian loyalty and honour. Elizabeth Bell, playing Eddie's emotionally and physically neglected wife, Beatrice, was particularly well placed to describe Ayckbourn's approach: 'He did work very, very deliberately against the tragedy, and held it off and held it off until it was inevitable, until it couldn't *not* happen. Until then we had to play a family who were very happy together.' A dozen years later, when he revived Ibsen's *A Doll's House*, Ayckbourn did something similar. Each play is a tragedy – which is to say, a story with an unhappy ending that is memorably and upliftingly moving rather than simply sad – only if there is a possibility that it could turn out differently. Each story may have the power to shock us, like the news on television, but not the power of art to move us so that we mysteriously feel better, not worse, for watching it. But if the Helmers and the Carbones are ordinarily happy when we meet them, the darkness which emerges is all the more powerful.

There was no room to rehearse in at the National to begin with. They trooped off to a church hall with the dialect coach, Joan Washington, and all gave poor imitations of Robert de Niro in *Raging Bull* – watching it had been part of their preparation for playing Brooklyn Italians. Bell is an actress of great intelligence and passion but Ayckbourn had spotted something about her work that she hadn't been aware of and that nobody else had ever expressed, namely:

> I am very much on the balls of my feet as an actor – until I know what I'm doing I can't settle on the ground. And the very important thing for Beatrice is that she is earthed. I kind of circle somewhere above the ground until I know what I'm doing and then – gradually, gradually, gradually – I can settle. But he made me settle very early on, just by pointing it out. I had a huge body suit because I'm quite slim and on stage you look thinner anyway and I would have looked too like the girl. It gave me 44-inch hips and I had it from early on in rehearsal because he insisted. It changes everything about the way you use your body. And he knows, with me, that I'm much better if I'm doing something, so he had me setting tables, clearing tables, carrying food, playing the scene from in the kitchen where I was washing up. Always doing something, so that the acting gets incidental.

Bell says that Michael Gambon, who was to win just about all the available Best Actor awards of 1988 as Eddie Carbone, is also a 'light actor in a heavy body'. Carbone is a longshoreman, a docker, and from early on in rehearsals Gambon wore docker's boots, giving his fighter's walk a heavier tread. Towards the end of the play, when the illegal immigrants are arrested, the young man's bigger brother Marco names Eddie as his betrayer. Unless Eddie can secure an apology, make him 'give me back my name', nobody in the community will speak to him again. Eddie's confrontation with Marco takes place in the street outside the Brooklyn living-room where we have seen most of the action. Ayckbourn told Gambon he didn't want to have to bring stage crew on to shift the table and chairs between the scenes and break the tension; was there some way he could get rid of it himself? A couple of days later Gambon came into the rehearsal room and played the scene leading up to it. At some level the brooding, bloodshot Eddie already knows his doom. Suddenly Gambon kicked the chairs off stage. With gathering violence he picked up the table and hurled it after the chairs. The furniture fell in a heap just short of Bell and Suzan Sylvester as the girl, Catherine, who cowered in the face of this volcanic and completely unexpected explosion. Gambon turned back to Ayckbourn: 'Something like that?' he grinned.

This became an unforgettable moment in the production. Interestingly, Gambon and Ayckbourn each gives the other credit for the idea, and

Gambon was quoted at the time as saying that Ayckbourn was his favourite director because of that familiar quality: 'he makes me feel so safe.' Recalling the production in 1999 Gambon said simply: 'I've never had such a creative fun time in my life.' That unforgettable moment came partly from a simple need to clear the stage without breaking the tension. But because the purpose was not to break the tension, the solution was to increase it.

A little earlier in the play, their relationship already ruined, Catherine tells her uncle/adoptive father Eddie that she is moving out and will marry Rodolfo; Eddie begins to cry. In rehearsal Gambon did what virtually every other actor playing Eddie has always done: he turned up-stage, away from the audience, and let his back do the acting, heaving with what appear to be sobs. Alan, educated in theatre-in-the-round where there is no upstage, said: 'Wouldn't it be nice if you cried right at us?' Gambon replied: 'You bastard,' gave him a look and stomped off. But two days later when they got to the scene again, Alan said:

> He just did it, and it just took your head off. And he turns round and says: 'Something like that?' with a big smile on his face. Sometimes you take an image with Gambon and he'll just run with it. I remember saying I thought that at the beginning of his final scene Eddie was trapped in his own prison because his family has stopped giving him respect, like an injured animal. And he started walking round the stage on his own, waiting for the others to arrive, making these extraordinary noises at the back of his throat. Chilling.
>
> I think people sometimes treat Gambon as somebody you can't go near. He does give the impression of that when you're working with him. He's not a bit spiky but he is a bit bearlike. [Ayckbourn gave an illustrative growl.] He needs great input, but if he doesn't like it he just discards what you say, not rudely, it's just as if he'd never heard you say it. But he's a man who loves to work and he's actually very practical so that he likes challenges that involve something physical as well. He's very intelligent but he's got a great emotional bearing as well. I think I once described working with him, and a few other actors, as like being allowed to drive someone's Lamborghini for the afternoon. You get a bit of open road and put your foot down on their emotion pedal, and you realise the harder you put your foot down, the more they'll give you. There's still more under the bonnet so it's you that has to ease back. Meanwhile there are other people beavering up the hill just to give us even the vestige of a little cry. And even if you do make them do it big, you wouldn't believe a word of it.

We reveal ourselves in praising others. Ayckbourn is at his very best, as writer and director, when working with actors of that power and intensity. They bring out his daring in the face of what they are frightened by. Some years later, in 1994, the American Judd Hirsch appeared in Scarborough in Herb Gardner's play *Conversations with My Father*. The explosive energy he brought to Ayckbourn's production was a reminder of Gambon, and a reminder of how much power there can be in Ayckbourn's work when it is played with the kind of force that British actors – with notable exceptions – often have bred out of them.

But Ayckbourn's achievement in the Miller play was as formidable with Michael Simkins as Marco, the strong and silent Sicilian nemesis. He was known in Scarborough as a very English Ayckbourn comedian but here he revealed a dark stillness and power. At no point does Elizabeth Bell remember Alan 'saying anything very deep and mysterious about the mood of the play apart from not playing the tragedy'. In the final week of rehearsals, the company was back in the National, padding about the corridors in rudimentary costumes, going into the canteen and being made to shriek with laughter by Alan, who by now was keeping up a constant flow of jokes and mimicry (his Pinter, Stoppard, Michael Winner are terrific vocal cartoons). The other companies seemed a bit envious. People were beginning to say they'd 'heard it was terribly good' in hushed voices. The technical rehearsal was as ever (not counting *Way Upstream*) pretty painless and then they did the first preview. Bell says they were half-way back to the dressing-rooms when they heard the sound of stamping from the audience, the rumble of an incipient ovation. 'Something special had happened which we had no idea of.' Arthur Miller was to endorse it as a definitive production of the play and it transferred across the river for a profitable run in the West End. *A View From the Bridge* won Alan the 'best director' section in the *Plays and Players* Awards for 1988.

Tons of Money was a success without making the critical impact available to the more heavyweight play and *'Tis Pity She's a Whore* was rather more coolly received, with some people taking the view that Ayckbourn was simply out of his depth with a Jacobean classic. Ayckbourn was grateful to discover that Ford was capable, if unconsciously, of finding comedy in a tragic moment. But there was one other achievement at the National. *Mere Soup Songs*, yet another musical entertainment with Paul Todd, had been written for Scarborough but it was also given a series of late-night performances in the foyer on the South Bank. One night Thelma Holt, the producer who had run the Round House but was by now on the National's payroll, physically dragged Peter Hall along to see it – an achievement worth watching in its own right given their relative statures. Through much of his time at the National, Hall was contending with some very difficult industrial relations with what he regarded as stroppy technicians: it was no longer as bad as it had been in 1979 and much of the problem derived from the wider political and historical climate, but there was perceived to be a gulf between unions and management and technicians and actors at the National at the time. Now he arrived in the bar to find the 'techies' buying champagne for the Ayckbourn company for the end of a show. 'Look,' said Holt, catching hold of Hall's jacket. 'They're doing something right here. Learn from it.'

6 : *Henceforward . . .*

April, 2001: an appeal to a Sky Television agony aunt: 'I'm a DJ and my girlfriend recently finished with me because she discovered I had taped our sex sessions and then sampled her moans and groans on my tracks. I don't see the problem but she says it makes her feel sick.' The advice was that he would go far in the music business but he would go alone.

Fourteen years previously Alan Ayckbourn had reached a similar conclusion in the play he had promised for Scarborough when he went off to London for his stint at the National Theatre. *Henceforward . . .* was his first play set in the future since *Standing Room Only*, with which he had so nearly made his commercial breakthrough in the 1960s. That play had responded to Stephen Joseph's anxiety about over-population with a cheerfully libertarian humanity. Now the future reappeared as a place where both the technology and the people fail to function in the way they were intended. *Henceforward . . .* was funny all right but it was also an addition to the literature of dystopia, like Orwell's *1984* or Huxley's *Brave New World*. The real 1984 had seen pitched battles between striking miners and reinforced police. Poll tax riots were still to come, but the politics of extremism, Alan's Houston experience and living in London for an extended period seem to have intensified his natural wariness of the urban jungle and impulse to stockpile tinned food in case the general level of disorder escalates into civil war. The science fiction also serves an established comic theme in its suggestion that some men would be better off living with personable robots since they cannot relate to real women

properly. Ronald Brewster-Wright in *Absurd Person Singular* would sub-
scribe to that. The play explores a quite different part of Ayckbourn's own
psyche but is in its way as much about himself as *Woman in Mind*.

The central character is Jerome, a composer who lives with a defective
robot designed to be a Nanny but ineffably clumsy and in a complete
muddle with her bedtime stories. Jerome is separated from his wife, about
which he seems quite happy, but wishes to have his daughter Geain to
stay ('Geain . . . is that Gaelic?' 'No. Just pretentious'). He needs to employ
somebody to pose as his new girlfriend so that he can convince the
Department of Child Well-Being he has a suitable home for Geain to come
into. This is why Zoe, an out-of-work actress, turns up for interview.
Unfortunately she has been attacked on the way by a female gang, the
Daughters of Darkness, and she arrives with her crisp shirt and business
suit in shreds.

Christine Ayckbourn had joined Alan and Heather in Scarborough as
usual one Christmas and friends had come to visit her from one of the
north's post-industrial towns. One, a man, lived at the top of a tower
block in an estate on the edge of town and the other, a woman, said,
jokingly, that she was no longer going to visit him there because it had
become completely lawless. The man said that he was staying on because
civilisation was such a fragile thing that if *he* left a little light would go out.
Alan was instantly suspicious of this altruism and made Jerome a
thoroughly obsessive and self-preoccupied character whose great ambition
was to write the definitive electronic musical composition. It was to be
something called 'Desperandum' when Alan embarked on it but he
spotted the greater dramatic potential – and savage irony – of having a
solipsistic hero apparently seeking to have the last musical word about
love. Hitherto this man's only claim to popular acclaim has been a
television commercial which features a troupe of babies made to appear to
sing. Zoe, a plucky and cheerful girl to whom we instantly warm, is not
immensely bright and rather blots her copy-book by wondering why he
doesn't write more stuff like that, even offering one or two hints for
improving it. But he needs her to pose as his girlfriend and she needs the
work, so they strike a deal and then find they are actually quite attracted
to each other.

It's when she discovers that he records every sound she makes,
including the little cries she utters during sex, to put through the super-
computer on which he composes, that she realises just how self-absorbed
he is and walks out. The first act ends with him playing back her final
outburst and dismissing it as lacking in truth. He cannot recognise the real

thing. By Act II he has reprogrammed his old robot with Zoe's voice (so the same actress simply continues in marginally more mechanistic vein) and faces his ex-wife and the man from the Department of Child Well-Being with equanimity: the machine can be his partner. The surprise is Geain, no longer the tender, loving, feminine nine-year-old on Jerome's video but a monster to rival the Daughters of Darkness – at 13 she has tried to turn herself into a male, to join the Sons of Bitches. She is rather quicker to realise that the supposed new girlfriend is a robot than her mother or the official and is happily impressed with it. Corinna, her mother, is in fact desperately lonely (she is also a bank manager) and she eventually confesses that she still loves Jerome and persuades him to come and join her and Geain in their rather more secure home. They leave and Jerome is about to follow when he just plays back Corinna's repeated cry of the word love. He's found it at last. Not love in the sense of the real thing but love in the sense of the word expressed with painful beauty, the essential ingredient for his masterpiece. With the Daughters of Darkness bombarding his front door he triumphantly completes his composition, only to realise how thoroughly alone he is at the end. For a central character, Jerome is pretty unsympathetic. He is getting regular messages on his video answering machine from an old friend, falling into ever more desperate circumstances. He ignores them all.

Alan Ayckbourn is much less self-serving and misanthropic than Jerome; the character is pushed to extremes by the needs of drama. But like all creative artists Alan gets his material where he can, always from people he meets rather than research, sometimes tactlessly, usually unconsciously. There is a tough, self-centred streak in anyone who can get on with creating art despite the 'distractions' of daily life with friends, colleagues and family. Alan indicated to Barry McCarthy, who played Jerome in Scarborough, where the play opened in July 1987, and on the five-country British Council tour which followed, that there was something of himself in the character. Jerome's flat is described as revealing his contradictions: immaculate and lovingly kept technical equipment, but a living area heaped with discarded clothes, food, coffee mugs – 'the signs of someone who lives alone and has stopped caring much'. Alan's living conditions are in beautiful order, but maybe they wouldn't be if he lived on his own.

In London Jerome was played by Ian McKellen, possibly the finest interpreter of Shakespeare's dramatic poetry in his generation. On paper his alliance with the most successful contemporary dramatist of his time looked ideal, but it didn't work out. McKellen and Ayckbourn have very little in common as personalities and, more damagingly, their working methods are entirely different. When Ayckbourn faces a problem he can't solve he seems to cut himself off from anything other than the basic formalities of a relationship and McKellen became more and more frustrated at being unable to uncover a part in the way that he was used to, digging for more meaning in the text and searching for a key to the character. On one (unspecified) line in particular, he recalls, he was asking Alan for more and more help of the kind he cannot give until eventually Alan said the preceding line would get such a big laugh that the line in question was only there to bridge the gap until the next line the audience really needed to hear. When I spoke to him McKellen had just finished playing Garry Essendine in Noël Coward's self-portrait, *Present Laughter*. He added: 'I just thought that if it had been a play by Noël Coward that line would still have been a gem anyway.' Ayckbourn was simply bewildered by the difficulty being encountered with something he knew to work. Each man has remained commendably reluctant to criticise the other. Jane Asher, in her first Ayckbourn role as Corinna, is very close to both men: McKellen is the secular godfather to her daughter and she 'would do anything with Alan'. She points out that it *is* difficult to come into a play in which there are other actors (e.g. the very funny Serena Evans as Zoe) who have been in it before and already seem to know exactly how it works. In addition, Jerome is one of those central characters who is the most important person in the play but doesn't get the laughs. This can be hard for an actor in a comedy to bear. The insecurity built into the profession inevitably makes you wonder if it's your fault. If it isn't, is everyone else conspiring to make you look bad? The two men would not or could not confront each other but innocent bystanders got hurt as rows blew up over costumes and props and, inevitably, the way the play had been done before. There were tears.

Paul Todd was given the daunting job of finishing the play by supplying Jerome's music. He had been wearing green trainers to rehearsal and was slightly alarmed to see McKellen wearing the same one day. Was Jerome based on himself after all? No, but this suggests an ever-more-despairing actor trying to find his own route (and root) to the character. Todd's music, incidentally, was composed for the rare and expensive Synclavier computer and was in no sense 'satirical' – the task was to make it as good as it could be, which apart from anything else is another light on the character. For the West End, Ayckbourn insisted on a slightly bigger finish, a response to the larger and more formal space as much as to the showier expectations of a West End audience.

When the cast changed Martin Jarvis took over from McKellen and quickly sorted out the mixture of high comedy and psychological exploration of a creative solipsist but took longer to act convincingly that most difficult proposition, an artist at work who has to 'play' Jerome's composition while his wife and daughter are left to the mercy of the Sons of Bitches and Daughters of Darkness. Jerome only communicates with the outside world via technology, and looking as if they can work technical equipment doesn't come easily to many actors. Eventually Jarvis got a friend to video Paul Todd as he played it and followed it slavishly for three weeks until he convinced himself he was 'playing'. Alan, of course, loves his new technology, except when it doesn't work; in which case it becomes one of the few things that still provoke open displays of rage.

The point about *Henceforward . . .* is that while the author had obviously rooted around in his own psyche again for the character of Jerome he had also found something essential to say about the state of the world. Margaret Thatcher won another election in the year the play was first seen, and the social endorsement of individualism was more or less complete. The play predicts not only the DJ cited at the beginning of this section (assuming the quote is genuine) but the selfishness of an era that is still with us. People talk about life imitating art but sometimes art predicts life. Ayckbourn wasn't finished with the moral trends developing in the 1980s and with each passing year his next play gets more topical. By the time *Henceforward . . .* opened in August 1988, he was back in Scarborough – much to the surprise of those who had knowingly said London was where he really wanted to work: didn't everyone?

Chapter 8

Changing patterns

1 : *Man of the Moment*

A changed Ayckbourn returned from his two-year stint at the National Theatre, and to a changed theatre company.

When Alan had mumbled to Robin Herford an invitation to think about taking over the Scarborough theatre for a couple of years, Herford knew that if he wanted to direct, it would be crazy to refuse. Ken Boden had decided to retire at the same time, sadly when he and Alan were barely speaking (the worst job in the theatre is telling an artistic director what he or she cannot do), but Heather did get Alan along to Ken's leaving 'do'. Five years later, when Ken died, Alan was able to pay the warm tribute he unquestionably deserved to 'the last person ever to call me lad'.

Ian Watson, who had been Ayckbourn's stage manager on *The Sparrow* 20 years before, came in as administrator and appointed the short, hirsute and volatile Russ Allen to an up-graded post taking responsibility for publicity, marketing and press relations. In the tightly-knit little company that had operated virtually unchanged for ten years this marked real change. The acting company was also mostly new, and to a programme still based round a new Ayckbourn play (promised for each year) Herford introduced a wider range of contemporary writers. Most notable among them was Yorkshire-born John Arden whose grimly poetic anti-war play *Serjeant Musgrave's Dance* (1959) has a large cast and has rarely done well at the box office. It had a redoubled resonance and sensitivity at a time when British squaddies were dying in Ireland, but Herford's memorable production reminded Scarborough of the range of drama Stephen Joseph had thought possible. There were only two new plays in his second season but they were *Henceforward . . .* , which included his own last appearance (thus far) in a new Ayckbourn role (the ignored friend on video, appealing to Jerome for help), and Stephen Mallatratt's dramatisation of Susan Hill's ghost story, *The Woman in Black*, which transferred to London and was still running there 15 years later. Watson and Herford had inherited a deficit of £20,000 – relatively small even by the standards of the time, but a shock and a rarity for this theatre – and they wiped it out. Watson introduced new income from sponsorship and Herford kept strictly to a budget of £27,000 for eight shows in the 1987/8 season – less than the cost of the extra lighting alone for *A Small Family Business* at the National.

At this point the Arts Council introduced the 'parity' policy under which national subsidy would do no more than match local authority grants. Potentially disastrous for a small town, and a classic 1980s example of giving to the rich and taking from the poor, the policy nevertheless had the desired effect of levering extra money from many local authorities. It was grasped with real courage by Scarborough and subsidy increased relatively painlessly. Ayckbourn has suffered from the (usually but not always unspoken) assumption that if things get really tough he can always get out his own cheque-book. The suggestion, outrageous in a public service, is probably encouraged by the assumption that he sometimes does it. Nobody thought Robin's cheque-book (or Ian Watson's) were comparable. Negotiations were probably easier as a result.

Financial recovery was matched by critical approval and a healthy box office. But away from the stage and the rehearsal room the theatre was less happy. Paul Todd, working with Alan's company at the National, got a telephone call during the show one evening from BBC Radio York: did he know that the Sunday music concerts he had carefully built up over the years had been stopped? He did not. The reasons, like much else during this period in the theatre's history, are hard to unpick, but it seems likely that the concerts were caught between the theatre's artistic aspirations and administrative needs. The fabric of the building was suffering and theatre technicians didn't have the time to service the concerts and the play performances: something had to give.

Alan and Ken may have had to negotiate through go-betweens but the theatre still functioned effectively and outsiders were impressed by the appearance of unity and goodwill. Somehow, with Alan away and after Ken had retired, a local Inland Revenue officer was given, or took, offence; the Midland Bank became wary of the deficit and the theatre's account had to be taken elsewhere (to Barclay's in the nearby town of Driffield, where the manager, David Fowler, was a good friend to the company); the two part-time clerks who constituted the accounts department both left and the company's auditors had to come to the rescue; stories appeared on the front page of the *Scarborough Evening News* and in *Private Eye*, not always accurate but giving the theatre an unlooked-for notoriety. Ian Watson decided to leave 'to concentrate on his writing' after three years in the job. A passionate and able advocate of Stephen Joseph and theatre-in-the-round, he had not only attracted new sponsors but developed an international role for the theatre, partly through the British Council. Unfortunately, the Scarborough Building Society, a major sponsor attracted by him, was alienated after he left by the alleged rudeness of a senior member of staff. The theatre did a very poor deal over *The Woman in Black*, which might have earned the theatre a useful income for more than a decade, because nobody – including Alan – thought it was going to be lucrative enough to pursue; Stephen Mallatratt has, I gather, voluntarily paid the theatre a proportion of his own royalties in addition to the maximum of £5,000 specified by the original contract.

Ian Watson now says simply: 'I fell foul of three millionaires – Mac McCarthy, John Downe and Alan Ayckbourn.' Charles McCarthy CBE was the thoroughly energetic chairman of the theatre trust and the man behind the spectacular growth of the frozen chips and pizza manufacturer, McCain's. The Right Honourable the Viscount Downe was vice-chairman. When the Midland Bank became aware of the deficit it had asked the three men to sign guarantees that they would pay off future deficits, which the three had quite rightly refused to do: the personal liability of directors is covered by legislation and any bank with an understanding of theatre finances and the processes of subsidy of a public institution would not have made the request of just three members, though nobody disputes the bank's right to withdraw overdraft facilities. Future requests for more general guarantees met no objection. Russ Allen had promised to get a 'theatre story' in the *Scarborough Evening News* every day for his first six weeks but this wasn't the kind of story – splashed on the front page – the trustees wanted to read. For a small organisation in a small town the diverse personalities at large on the administrative side of the theatre were simply too volatile to be contained.

When Alan returned he brought Keith McFarlane back to the theatre as financial administrator. McFarlane had been introduced to the business as a very young man working for a Scarborough accountancy firm in 1965. Before that Stephen Joseph had kept the books himself. Having worked on the privately owned Futurist Theatre's books and those of its sister theatre in Llandudno, McFarlane was regarded as the firm's theatre expert and sent up to the Library to interview a big man wearing turned-down fisherman's wading boots who only lasted about five minutes of questioning before he had to get up and pace about: Stephen. This relationship with the theatre continued until the move to Westwood in 1976 when the Arts Council insisted that there be an accountant on the staff. Ken Boden offered the job to Keith in a roundabout way; he took it, with a small cut in wages and a small increase in holiday. He had left in 1985 when the Arts Council began its process of delegating clients (including Scarborough) to the new regional arts boards (or associations, as they were initially). He had no problem with delegation but was shocked by the Arts Council's decision that all institutions to be delegated would have their deficits paid off. McFarlane wanted to know what reward would go to someone who had worked hard for nine years to avoid having a deficit? Er . . . nothing. Feeling cheated and disgusted, he left the industry. On his return he was straight away involved in a successful application for one of the Arts Council's newest schemes, Incentive Funding, with a plan to extend the theatre's sales drive to Humberside, Teesside and Leeds. It became McFarlane's job to have the difficult conversations with Alan when the theatre cannot afford to match his imagination and work-rate. 'He does kick the furniture a bit but I remind him not to shoot the messenger.'

Alan offered Robin Herford the opportunity to stay on, acting and sharing the directing. But after 13 years in one theatre, and knowing that he would not enjoy watching Alan switch back all the procedures he had put in place, Robin decided to leave. He is in considerable demand for directing Alan's plays – about which he is evangelical – around the country. Paul Todd, on the other hand, turned up in Scarborough after his stint with Alan at the National to find that his office had just been knocked down. After an unenlightening interview with Alan, he caught the train back to London. They remain in touch at the Christmas card level and are in regular contact, usually through Heather because Alan rarely speaks on the telephone, on the subject of the music Todd wrote for so many plays. But they have met in the flesh only twice since then: the London opening of *Man of the Moment*, when Todd recalls Ayckbourn suddenly rushing across the theatre bar to give him a (very uncharacteristic) hug; and in 1999 at the sixtieth birthday gala when Todd was a welcome contributor, accompanying those four (of the six numbers incorporated) which were composed by him.

Ayckbourn had taken a conscious decision not to go down the same road as Peter Cheeseman's company at Stoke, seemingly almost unchanged for decades. His policy is to have a mixture each year of people he has worked with before and newcomers refreshing the company and himself. However, like a lot of people who manage most of their relationships really well, once he has taken an uncomfortable decision he is less likely to change it or even mentally revisit it than people who operate more clumsily as a general rule. Withdrawals are final, and Todd is not the only formerly close associate to feel bewildered and discarded.

The biggest change in work patterns was that the new Ayckbourn no longer left it until the night before a scheduled read-through (or later) to complete a script; he had submitted *A Small Family Business* to Peter Hall like any other playwright and he had given Scarborough time to prepare the video of *Henceforward . . .* He had also tasted the benefits of writing first and casting afterwards, getting the actors you wanted for particular parts rather than writing the plays around whoever was available in the permanent company. From now on he would have his own casting director (Michele Tidy to begin with), whom he paid directly so that she didn't add to the theatre's costs. Artistically, there is always a risk in going back that you will also be going backwards. Instinctively (of course) Ayckbourn avoided this by finding a new creative direction. He would write for children, though he had to mount his new play for adults first, and that would bring something of London back to Scarborough too.

Crossing the River Thames on his way to work at the National Theatre, if he forsook his usual taxi, Alan used to pass the flower stall run by Buster Edwards, the Great Train Robber who – after serving his term of imprisonment – became something of a celebrity. His life-story was eventually filmed with musician Phil Collins in the title role. Another robber, Ronnie Biggs, had become a kind of hero because he had regularly outwitted the police. At the same time John McVicar, having served a prison sentence for violent crime, had used his time to secure qualifications enabling him to work as a writer and journalist. In contrast to the attention paid to these men, not all of it dishonourable, Jack Mills, the driver of the train robbed by Edwards, Biggs and company, had received injuries from which he subsequently died, his plight largely ignored. Ayckbourn's new play pushes the idea of a glamorised criminal a step further. Vic Parks has served his time and become such a successful media personality that he has his own television show and is in demand for visiting sick children in hospital. Douglas Beechey, on the other hand, is the man who tried to stop Vic's bank robbery 17 years ago and for all of a year was a hero. Now he's not only an unknown but that hopeless case, someone who has nothing to say to the media. Years later a television series called *Their Paths Crossed* reunites them at Vic's luxurious Spanish villa. This is how Jill Rillington, its ambitious producer/presenter, describes Doug:

He's about as lively as a sheet of laminated chipboard. I've just spent four days interviewing Mr Beechey. In his home town of Purley. I think I've got about 20 seconds of usable material. And those are the shots of Purley . . . Oh, he talks. It's just that he never says anything. You know, when I first started out with the BBC as a radio interviewer, I went on this course and they warned us that one day we'd all of us find ourselves interviewing the uninterviewable. I thought, after ten years, I'd managed to escape. And then along comes Mr Beechey.

It's a hell of a build-up for one of your leading characters.

Ayckbourn himself has never been hounded by the media but while he was at the National Theatre he did witness the press pack at close quarters. Peter Hall left his third wife, opera singer Maria Ewing, during this time and set up home with the present Lady Hall, Nicki Frei. She had been working in the National's press office (with Alan's former and future Scarborough colleague, Stephen Wood). Hall had told Maria Ewing in the morning that he was leaving, and by the time he got to the theatre the newspapers already knew. Within the hour the building was under siege from the photographers. He got out hidden in the back of a car and lay low first in Scarborough and then in Wapping. Stephen Moore looked out of his window one day and saw the designer Alison Chitty (who was working with Hall) heading for his block. He shouted out: 'Sir Peter Hall is not here!' thinking he was inventing the idea that Hall *could* be there. The truth was ahead of the fiction.

There is plenty of input from Ayckbourn's own experience into the detail of the play. He had, after all, been sent on a radio production course himself 20 years before, and he had by then been interviewed in all branches of the media: and he misses nothing. But the themes are drawn from his observation of the wider world. You have to look quite hard to find elements of himself in the characters of Vic and Douglas: Vic has the star's freedom not to have to be polite to anybody, and never to confront what he doesn't want to; Douglas voices a resistance to the accepted wisdom that conflict is a necessary part of entertainment, and has Alan's skill at avoiding uncongenial subjects. But both are forced to face up to the past and each other in the resolution of the drama. The play is quite close to being played in real time. Even the interval is signalled by the one word: 'Cut!' and although the play ends in what we must suppose is a much later reconstruction of the whole encounter the join between the 'real' and the 're-creation' is smooth and seamless.

In the incident 17 years beforehand Vic was charged, head-down, by

Doug, and his gun went off in the face of the woman cashier whom Doug had regarded as beautiful but unattainable. Scarred for life and rejecting the company of other suitors she has since agreed to marry Doug but has never recovered her physical or mental poise. Hers is an unseen tragedy. Vic turns out to be every bit as nasty as we might expect but not without a farouche magnetism. He mercilessly teases the fat girl who looks after his children and is besotted with him until, in one of the most memorable pieces of almost on-stage business seen in the theatre in the twentieth century, she stands on him in his own swimming pool so he is very satisfactorily drowned. This gives a splendid ending to Jill Rillington's TV documentary, albeit an untruthful one in the filmed reconstruction. As Vic had said, 'This is TV. It's all fiction.' The play is partly about the cynicism – and ignorance – of the media and the corruptibility of a society that lionises a criminal with charisma and forgets the 'little people' who are his victims. It is one of the very few plays that is able convincingly and interestingly to show television in action. It is also a revisiting of Ayckbourn's theme that eventually nice people do stand up for themselves, however ludicrous they seem to us and to themselves; Doug does in fact once again lower his head and charge Vic. But there is one more thing. Although we never see the disfigured Nerys, we know Doug's life with her has not been the happy-ever-after of the original fairy-tale the media reported 17 years ago; but he isn't the bitter figure that Jill Rillington expects him to be at all. He isn't even mildly unhappy. He arrives at the Spanish villa, pleased to be paid for by TV, and is happily impressed at the luxury in which Vic lives. And then he has a speech of such simple, affecting clarity about how much better his life is than it was, that Vic's wife, to whom he is talking, first kisses him on the mouth and then bursts into tears. It is, inevitably, funny too: Nerys was engaged to someone else when the bank robbery happened, a double-glazing salesman, and Doug left the bank for the double-glazing industry in the ridiculous hope that she liked the type. But the point was, Doug says, that Nerys's first fiancé had 'treated her as only a handsome man can treat a beautiful woman. If you know what I mean.' Trudy knows exactly what he means and that is why she cries and is then prepared to collude in covering up Vic's murder a few minutes later. His speech to Trudy is of course the interview that he will never give Jill Rillington. The truth is too important and too simple to be wasted on her.

All of which moves the play a bit beyond what would otherwise be a very effective satire on modern life into something more hopeful, a kind of hymn to humble decency. Condensing the narrative makes it seem more sententious than it really is. The inside knowledge about the workings of the media, and useful advice from Vic on how to use them to your advantage, are part of a rich if cynical knowingness that runs through the play. But the 'how' of the narrative is also important; the television documentary has some of the force of a play within a play, and enables the author to pull us back from the main narrative at the last moment to see a wider picture, and this distancing device – 'like putting a strange chord in a symphony' is how he describes it – is part of the conception. Michael Holt, the drama lecturer and designer who was responsible for the Scarborough staging, has written an excellent short study of a selection of Ayckbourn's plays for the Northcote House/British Council *Writers and Their Work* series. He argues that the way in which the play ends up in the television studios as a reconstruction 'indicts us all as accomplices in the television scam'. Theatre audiences who perhaps assume they are superior to television audiences (at home or in the studio) are made very uncomfortable when they are bullied into applauding by the floor manager. Television is only the most powerful and vivid expression of the media generally, and that is why Ayckbourn has not only tackled it but, uniquely I think, made it realistic on stage. He quoted to Albert Glaap, at the time of the original production, the case of the radio arts producer who had come to record an extract from the play and revealed that she had left news journalism because her colleagues had celebrated with champagne the fact that their crew had been first to get to the Zeebrugge disaster.

The Scarborough cast was headed by two more trusted regulars, Peter Laird as Vic, Jon Strickland as Doug. When the play reached London in February 1990 they were replaced by stars, the suavely dangerous Peter Bowles and Michael Gambon. Having asked him to cry for real and then clear the stage in *A View From the Bridge*, Ayckbourn was asking Gambon for the near-impossible again because finally it is the impossible that is really interesting to the professional inventor: he had to make a nonentity captivating. Gambon somehow transformed himself again into a collection of large, flapping hands and feet. He wore a knitted jumper and tie under his sports jacket (pens in the breast pocket) under the Spanish sun, and for the first few moments his only utterances as he gazed round Vic's villa were a repeated indeterminate vowel sound before his first line: 'Isn't this glorious?' It was, and so was he. The two men's roles commanded most of the comedy. There is a third driving part that doesn't get so many laughs: Jill Rillington (Lynette Edwards in Scarborough, Samantha Bond in London) is on stage for much of the time, and she starts and finishes the play with some good jokes. But she cannot be a sympathetic character however much we understand the cynicism bred by a career in the media. Trudy (Lesley Meade and Diane Bull) is altogether more likeable now that she has seen through Vic's charm, but there are plays in which the plight of the women is not absolutely central to the drama and this is one of them.

In the *Guardian* Michael Billington welcomed the play as 'Ayckbourn at the peak of his powers, using comedy to say harsh, true things about our society'. In the summer of 1999 the *Observer* newspaper devoted a page and a half at the front of its cultural 'Review' section to an enthusiastic feature on a 'hard man' now reportedly looking for a career as a columnist and chat show host: not a tabloid, you notice, but the quality Sunday newspaper of Kenneth Tynan. Art had predicted life again.

Ayckbourn had started the 1980s with a sense of crisis about what was best to do with his plays after Scarborough. Unhappy with West End productions directed by other people, he had not found the Round House an appropriate substitute, but Greenwich under Alan Strachan had provided some of the same integrity and expertise as Scarborough while being able to draw on the pool of actors who felt famous enough not to leave London. (Sadly, Strachan's ten years at Greenwich came to an end in 1988; the wisdom of his board and its relationship with the funding bureaucracy can be best judged by the fact that in another ten years the theatre would be on the brink of closure.) Michael Codron had, at length, recognised that he was the best director of his own work and the National Theatre under Peter Hall had let Londoners know what Scarborians had understood for years, that he was a first-class director of other people's work too. He had enjoyed a decade as a major public playwright, provoked by the sour culture of the times. After the minor crisis of the start of the decade, he emerged a stronger and more confident public figure too. A man who at one time had had to be accompanied into press interviews by Heather or a press officer – just to make sure a conversation occurred – was now practised and skilful at giving journalists what they needed without making himself too vulnerable. He had won more awards – both *Henceforward . . .* and *Man of the Moment* were 'best comedy' for the London *Evening Standard*; *Henceforward . . .* went on to win the Critics' Award in the tough theatre town of Los Angeles – and he had been honoured by Scarborough, the queen and the first of the eight universities to have given him the academic distinction he had turned his back on 30 years before. His friends noted more flamboyant clothes (terrific silk waistcoats) and a much more confident public manner. He would need that in the following decade, as the running of theatres became more and more subject to the stresses of local and national government, business practice and the particular bureaucracy of the arts.

2 : Children's Hour

So why did he turn to plays for children? *Ernie's Incredible Illucinations*, written for children to perform, had been written in 1969, and *Christmas v Mastermind* way back in 1962; one had been a more or less continuous success ever since, the other had been a complete disaster. Apart from his natural appetite for something new, Ayckbourn was aware that some parents were bringing their children to his plays anyway and that they seemed to pay close attention. He thought they should have work written especially for them but also believed he was 'not good with children'. He tells a story about seeing a small boy sitting in a cardboard box, an expression of deep concentration on his face. When the boy saw Alan, he scowled. Alan suggested the box was a car. Silence. A boat? Silence. A plane? Silence. What was it then? The boy sized him up and then said: 'It's a cardboard box.' But putting himself in 'childlike mode' in terms of subject matter proved distinctly liberating both for the 'family plays', as he prefers to describe them, and his adult work. It cannot be coincidence that he started to write more filmically at this point – the plots more adventurous, constructed in sequences of short scenes in exotic locations – perhaps prompted by memories of what excited him as a small boy.

The immediate prompting of *Mr A's Amazing Maze Plays* was the need to build up a children's audience at Christmas in 1988, but what is fascinating is the way, as he approached 50, he casts a little more light on his own childhood, albeit through a female central role. Suzy has lived alone with her mother since her father took off in a balloon race and went on going up instead of coming down. Remember Horace's choice of a flying cap as he careered around the country in fast cars? Suzy's only friend is a very large dog, Neville. Remember Romulus and Remus? And worst of all, Suzy's mother looks like remarrying, not a bank manager but a Mr Accousticus, who steals sounds: the song of the birds, Neville's bark, mother's voice. Every child knows what it is like to be silenced. The great invention of the narrative is one which puts the story partly in the hands of the audience, who are allowed to choose which room in Mr Accousticus's Gothic villa is to be explored by Suzy and Neville next:

multiple choice with a vengeance as there are some 25 possibilities, though each lasts barely a page. Suzy and Neville find Accousticus's stolen treasure, a Cabinet of Sounds, alias a radio effects disc collector's dream; every time a drawer is opened one sound after another pours out only to be silenced when it is hastily pushed shut. Neville briefly swallows a man's voice saying: 'Hello, hello, hello old boy' and Suzy swallows a chicken's cluck. But they put them back. At the denouement, Suzy's father's balloon suddenly reappears and lands on the villain and happiness is unalloyed, although Suzy's mother must have some explaining to do. Ayckbourn believes in happy endings for children: 'Don't shut the door on them in terms of options,' he told Albert Glaap in 1992. It is just possible the next generation will solve some of humanity's difficulties, but not if we have remorselessly told them there is no solution.

The set, designed by Michael Holt, principally to accommodate a production of *The Turn of the Screw* which was playing at the same time, consisted entirely of different levels and steps. Ayckbourn has said that he wanted to introduce children to the magic of theatre, not in the sense of red velvet curtains, which he didn't have and didn't believe in, but of what can be created in the imagination through the complicity of the audience with skilled actors. An elaborate diagram in the acting edition of the play bears testimony to what actors and audiences were able to keep in their heads: where the flights of stairs were, where the scullery, the music room or the cellar. He once said that the first performance was the most nerve-racking he had attended, but he has never looked back. *Invisible Friends* was to follow in the winter of 1989. Lucy, like Susan in *Woman in Mind*, has a dreary family who take no interest in her – another kind of loneliness – so she invents a set of dream friends that rapidly turns into a nightmare. But unlike Susan's fantasy family, Lucy's invisible friend Zara is a kind of idealised *alter ego* and Lucy has the strength of will to defy Zara and re-enter reality. Next summer he produced a double play, *This Is Where We Came In*, for alternate Saturday mornings where they had to work on the set of whatever play was on in the evening, so it featured 'a group of strolling players lost in a strange abstract landscape'. There are echoes of his old enthusiasm, Pirandello, in the opening exchange between Fred, waiting patiently by a sign saying 'STORIES TOLD HERE,' and Nell who is rather scornful of him for not knowing who invented him or what story he is in. It gets a good deal more specific than *Six Characters in Search of an Author* as it goes on, but it is evidence that Ayckbourn very rapidly learned not to worry about what children will follow. They would follow almost anything as long as there *was* a story and he kept to whatever rules he told them he had set. *My Very Own Story*, which followed in the summer of 1991, a similar kind of framework. There are three story-tellers – Percy, Peter and Paul – and each turns up in the others' stories as well as his own. 'Some adults said they couldn't follow it,' Alan said later, 'but as far as I know no children did.' But by then there had also been another Christmas show, *Callisto 5*, about a boy lost on a space station with only a robot, a vocal computer and a sister in some kind of permanent suspension of consciousness for company; the happy ending here is entirely about being reunited with parents and the restoration to health of the sister. I do not wish to make too much of this preoccupation with loneliness – it is, after all, the quickest way to show children that you have some idea of what is really going on in their minds – but Alan was particularly good at tapping into it without mawkishness. After a gap of 20 years, there were five children's plays in four years, not counting *The Inside Outside Slide Show* (1990) which entertained children for 30 minutes with a partly photographic account of Victorian life and some clever technical effects to get characters in and out of the screen.

Two of these plays went on to the National Theatre – *Invisible Friends* first, in 1991, and then *Mr A's Amazing Maze Plays* in 1993. The new director of the National (from 1990) was Richard Eyre who introduced a long overdue commitment to the production of theatre for children. He seemed to prefer Alan's work for children to what he was now writing for adults; his taste was for the earlier plays with less ambitious aspirations rather than the big public plays or remorseless explorations of the psyche that had followed in the 1980s. Eyre was a brilliant commissioner and director of new plays and a superb leader of the National Theatre and the theatrical profession at a difficult time. But although he seems to have been keen to retain Ayckbourn's relationship with the National, and later embarked on a nominal co-production of another children's play (*Two Weeks with the Queen*, adapted by Mary Morris from Morris Gleitzman's book), the two men were too wary of each other to combine comfortably. Maybe, as Alan suggests, he was simply too closely associated with Peter Hall's time at the National for comfort. When Hall left the National and set up his own company, with the backing of the producer Bill Kenwright (the man who was stage-managing the tour of *Two for the See-saw* which had ended Alan's acting career almost 30 years before), Ayckbourn agreed in principle to direct some productions for him, not instead of but around his commitments in Scarborough. It fell apart, amicably, in a lack of time and resources.

3 : *The Revengers' Comedies* and *Body Language*

The parting from the National, at least as far as adult plays were concerned, came in 1990 with *The Revengers' Comedies*. Ayckbourn described this as a fiftieth birthday present to himself, a two-part play which – unlike *The Norman Conquests*, *Sisterly Feelings* or *Intimate Exchanges* – makes sense to an audience only if both parts are seen in the right order. It starts on Albert Bridge in London, where Henry Bell is loitering with miserable intent at midnight when he hears the cry of a woman just below him. Karen Knightly is suspended above the water with her coat belt caught on the ironwork. Having effectively saved each other from suicide, they undertake to carry out each other's revenges; he has been fired from the job into which he put everything after his wife left, and she (who really meant to be on Chelsea Bridge) has been betrayed by her married lover. Ayckbourn has acknowledged the inspiration of Alfred Hitchcock's 1951 film *Strangers on a Train*. In that, only one man takes the idea of the deal seriously, and the other, more sympathetic character is unwittingly involved in murder. Here too one of the partners is much more aggressively engaged: Karen is rich, used to getting her own way and almost psychopathic, but Henry is merely a useless, middle-aged, middle-class male. We know how much damage the feckless as well as the determined can do in Ayckbourn.

The plays career round the country (like a film) and have a Gothic quality. Karen's lover, Anthony Staxton-Billing, challenges Henry to a duel, which the local police (somewhere near Salisbury) are perfectly content to allow. Henry has never fired a gun in anger (or even mild irritation) before, but wins by accident and at once is received into the dead man's social circle where it turns out nobody liked Anthony anyway. Fatally, for Karen's grand plan, he falls in love with Imogen Staxton-Billing, the bounder's widow, and now has a reason for living rather than simply carrying out his half of the bargain. The plays end with Karen determined to blight Henry and Imogen's future happiness in the only way she can conceive of: by killing herself. Once again they meet up on Albert Bridge, but Henry and Imogen walk away together. Karen jumps again, with a cry of 'Revenge!' This time we hear the splash. Unlike most of Ayckbourn's previous adult plays, *The Revengers' Comedies* are constructed in a series of fast-moving short scenes with some characters whose brief appearances are essential for plotting but do not require any exploration in their own right, such as servants, a fireman, a motor-cyclist.

Either Karen or Henry is in almost every scene, so that we also get an unusually specific perspective on the action, itself a feature more of cinema than of theatre. Revenge has been a great staple of adult drama but 'getting your own back' is above all a preoccupation of childhood. In which case *The Revengers' Comedies*, though adult in their content, are of a piece with the work for children.

The plays were successful in Scarborough, with Jon Strickland and Christine Kavanagh in the leading roles. The resolute could see both plays together on certain days, a five-hour marathon with a decent break in the middle during which the little theatre café attempted to feed 300 people. Alan gave in to long pressure and agreed to be interviewed by satellite on Terry Wogan's BBC TV show – he still looked furtive – and Frank Rich appeared in the first-night audience. The analysis of 'the butcher of Broadway' is worth quoting because, despite regular visits to British theatre, he took less for granted than his British colleagues. He points out that 'the playwright never lost the rapt attention of an audience widely heterogeneous in age and class' – compared with Broadway, I suppose – and calls the plays

> an immensely disturbing vision of contemporary middle-class England poisoned by the rise of economic ruthlessness and the collapse of ethics . . . Karen cannot let go of the game, and, in Part Two . . . the game has become synonymous with the national sport of hostile corporate takeovers, wholesale job 'redundancies' and industrial destruction of the countryside . . . With a subtlety beyond the reach of many polemical English play-wrights, Mr Ayckbourn does not shy away from presenting the alternative to good as pure evil.

The home critics had recently seen Ayckbourn being much more overtly political in *A Small Family Business* and *Man of the Moment*. And 'pure evil' is not how Ayckbourn himself thinks of Karen according to a letter addressed to an actress who had not found enough in the character with which to empathise. He does, however, endorse Rich's view that the play is about what has happened to society itself. He describes Karen as a child in an adults' world, probably neglected by her parents, certainly spoilt, and continues (in a letter replying to criticism that Karen was neither sympathetic nor believable):

> I know many people for whom life is a game. I know several who are obsessives. With the collapse of any generally recognised moral consensus – certainly in this country – most of us make up the rules to suit ourselves.

Karen, he thought, in the kind of analysis he brings to his characters only after he has done the work, combined her own ethics with an emotional isolation that bordered on the autistic. He ended by saying that he remained very fond of her. So did the actresses who played her, Christine Kavanagh in Scarborough and Lia Williams in London. The latter thought Karen 'had an insanity about her, she was crazy, but the audience would cheer as she did bad thing after bad thing so they loved her – loved to hate her'. The author's cunning makes us all cheer her vindictive justice before we realise what we are endorsing. Karen has a child's psyche and an adult's deadly weapons.

Alan had hoped that the National Theatre would take the plays as they were. Richard Eyre did not believe London audiences would come on successive nights, or even nights a week apart, to see both plays, but he was prepared to stage them if they could be condensed into a single major event. Ayckbourn dug his heels in for a repeat of the Scarborough experience. The argument was being conducted through third parties, and Stephen Wood, Alan's once and future employee but then still working in the National Theatre press office, remembers the language becoming acrimonious on Alan's side, more reserved but determined on Richard's. When they communicated directly with each other – by letter – they made hopeful noises, even as Ayckbourn was pulling out. He wrote: 'I do know what I'm doing – even if what I'm doing turns out to be wrong.' He said he didn't want to damage the relationship. Eyre replied: 'I'm very sorry you want to withdraw. I should have kept my mouth shut. I do very much want you to work here.' But there wouldn't be an Ayckbourn play for adults on any National Theatre stage for a decade. Michael Codron eventually produced the two plays in full at the Strand Theatre two years later. He had his doubts about their commercial potential but may have seen it as something of a loyalty test. The Gulf War and economic recession made matters worse.

Commercial producers never really admit to making or losing money, but Michael Codron will say he got off relatively lightly in the end with *The Revengers' Comedies*. It didn't run successfully in the West End (which for Richard Eyre proved that it wouldn't have worked at the National and for Alan reinforced the view that the National should have done it because nobody else could) but Codron's deal-making kept losses to a minimum. The shows were designed in Scarborough and London by Roger Glossop. He and Alan had worked together on and off since *Woman in Mind* (in London), and Glossop had designed the great drum set (conceived by Alan) used on the Olivier revolve for *'Tis Pity She's a Whore* at the National, but now for the first time the author had said: 'I don't know how to do this. Please read it.' Codron liked using Glossop because at that time he would not only design the show but build it, with his firm in Sheffield, much more cheaply than Codron could have got it done in London. But *The Revengers' Comedies* was never going to be very cheap in London. In-the-round in Scarborough you can suggest the Albert Bridge with a bit of parapet and some atmospheric Mick Hughes lighting and the sound of a river-boat or two – the audience supplies the rest. But in a proscenium arch theatre you need to build the best part of a bridge. There were 43 more scenes, all to be changed with the speed and fluidity of a film. Three moving tracks, like airport travelators, were built which could be loaded and ready in the wings to move each new set into place.

The cast was led by Griff Rhys Jones and Lia Williams. He was a 'name', though mostly from television, and she hadn't yet starred in the London productions of David Mamet's *Oleanna* or David Hare's *Skylight* which would make her reputation. And at that point nobody had quite realised how seriously good Joanna Lumley (who played Imogen Staxton-Billing) could be, although Jennifer Saunders saw her as Imogen and cast her in the television comedy *Absolutely Fabulous*. People did sometimes see Part Two first, either through carelessness or because they just never understood what kind of a package it was – and they were justifiably baffled. Among letters of passionate approval, particularly from theatre professionals, Alan received complaints about not always hearing, not always seeing, not understanding. One ends: 'Please accept this criticism in the spirit it is given. PS You have a winner if some changes are made.' Once again he was starting a decade with some demoralising experiences.

The other had been *Body Language*, which had premièred in Scarborough in May 1990, an extraordinarily daring play about a very topical public subject, the relationship between women's bodies and their identities as perceived by others and by themselves. A woman reporter who has 'let herself go' with cigarettes and chocolate turns up at a private clinic in the English countryside to interview a surgeon (who has recently left his Eastern European homeland) about his questionable innovations in transplant techniques. At the same time a model is in the clinic having a small blemish removed from her bottom. She is also being pursued by a tabloid photographer, who was once the reporter's boyfriend, and by her own husband, an ageing rock star who flies his own helicopter – badly. When there is an accident, both women are decapitated by the helicopter's rotors and the surgeon seizes his opportunity to sew the heads back on: unfortunately on to the wrong bodies. Although the story has echoes of Thomas Mann, Ayckbourn didn't know this at the time. The idea had come to him in a Green Room conversation: an account of a terrible accident on the road to Leeds, when a car had driven under a low-loader lorry and it looked as though the people in the car must have been decapitated, had reminded him of the death in a car crash of the American film star Jayne Mansfield, more famous for her big breasts than her acting ability. Speculating on what it must have been like for the traffic cop who had found the world's most famous torso separated from the part of her where we usually assume the personality resides, Alan made the remark, as he often does when dealing with something unbearable, in the form of a black joke. At this point the actress Frances Jeater drew attention to a scar on her own neck: she had once gone through a car windscreen. This was one of the rare occasions when, as Alan puts it, 'It was like the clock striking and a little cuckoo coming out,' and he felt he was being offered an idea for a play. But something much less conscious was going on too. His own press officer – following the departure of the mercurial Russ Allen – was (and still is, happily) in a relationship with a photographer; had been on the *Scarborough Evening News*; and is a big woman. Ayckbourn didn't realise what he'd done until the read-through when he saw Jeannie Swales staring at him with blank incredulity. Her hurt would have been greater still were she not a fundamentally different character, a cheerful woman who was demonstrably good at her job. What he had done unconsciously did not go unremarked; if Irving Wardle, writing in the *Independent on Sunday*, was correct, the surgeon's 'ruthless addiction to playing with people evidently represents the playwright's *alter ego*'.

Body Language represents the furthest a male playwright has ventured into the minefield of a major feminist issue. Is it possible to write at all about women's bodies without inviting criticism or causing hurt somewhere? Probably not. Is it desirable that major playwrights should avoid the most sensitive subjects of our times? Certainly not. In 1999 Ayckbourn directed a new version of the play in which the long second half was substantially cut, revealing that the photographer's role in the earlier version had been artificially enhanced because he wanted to provide a long part for the established actor playing it. He felt no such obligation to Danny Nutt, the relative newcomer playing it in 1999. But *Body Language* is also a personal play. In 1990, according to the *Yorkshire Evening Post*, Ayckbourn had lost 10 inches (255 mm) from his own waistline. He had known what it was like to be very thin and then to put on a substantial amount of weight when he gave up smoking. He would go through the cycle again. My problem with the play is the resolution. After two hours of political incorrectness he doggedly contrives an ending which makes both women equally independent of what anybody else thinks of them: he likes both these women in both their physical states. It feels like wishful thinking.

The production, designed by Roger Glossop, is another tribute to the Scarborough team's ability to solve problems and perform the seemingly impossible. Two actresses of sufficiently like build – Lia Williams as the model, Tam Hoskyns as the reporter – were kitted out with astonishingly believable 'bodies', including the normally giveaway hands and feet, so that both could appear like chocolate addicts or compulsive exercisers. Lia Williams recalls:

> The bodies were absolutely astonishing. The arms and the legs and the feet were hand-moulded and then made, exquisitely, even to the fingernails and the hairs on your toes. Then we had padded bodies and silicon breasts with detachable nipples. We fitted these into bras which we put on when we changed the characters around. They were fantastically believable because they moved with you, you could even still have a bare midriff.
>
> It was really interesting the way people changed their reaction to you, even though they knew you as Lia Williams the actress, their perception would change depending on what costume I was wearing. Some of the stage hands would be slightly fancying you, slightly sort of leering when I was Angie the model with the whiff of 38-inch C-cup breasts, and then slightly frown and curl their lips when I was being Jo, the big thing.

There is another sensitive element in the content: the surgeon either believes, or pretends to believe, that his assistant/interpreter is a lesbian and that this is a considerable joke. He is such an identifiably disgusting old man that in conversation with Alan some lesbians who went to see the 1999 version had no problem with this in itself but did complain at the use of the word 'dyke' as a term of abuse when, they said, some of them were trying to reclaim it as a badge proudly worn. To complicate matters, a lesbian in the acting company said she didn't want to be called a 'dyke' at all but she had no problem with the play. Some women certainly disliked the play, but the frustrating thing about the very mixed reviews it got (full of cheery puns on flab and the need for cutting) is that all the ones I've read are by men who overlook the tenderness emerging from the initially hostile relationship between the two women. What they complain about is very often Ayckbourn's failure to resolve the issue he has raised. Unlike, say, *King Lear*, which comes up with a ten-point programme for dealing with that aged parent who is beginning to behave a bit irrationally but still values his own dignity.

The revival didn't do such good business as Keith McFarlane had hoped, perhaps because the author's need to test it again outweighed Scarborians' need to see it again. But Alan took comfort from watching the audience one night, as is his custom, and seeing a big woman sitting next to her (male) partner, smiling nervously from time to time until they took each other's hands and from then on laughed freely. The play is still flawed, but richly complex in its signals, risky in its content and generous in its intention.

The plan in 1990 had been to transfer the play to London in the original production, straight from Scarborough and before *The Revengers' Comedies* went in. In rehearsal it was obvious the shape of the play was a problem but Alan didn't want to cut. After the press night, according to Alan Strachan who was staying in Longwestgate while rehearsing another production, Ayckbourn stayed at home and scarcely moved from his armchair for two days while playing very loud rock music. Some cuts were put into the show eight days later with more following two days after that. 'Cast rather tense', says that night's show report. By the end of the run in September the second half was still half as long again as the first; imbalance is better the other way round if you are going to have it at all. There is some excellent comedy in the play – not least as Alan plays with language again, giving the surgeon speeches in what John Peter of the *Sunday Times* cleverly dubbed Sado-Croat (a Hungarian by birth, Peter plainly knew what was coming in the Balkans). But the transfer was first postponed and then dropped by Ayckbourn and Michael Codron together. And there were relatively few enquiries about it from elsewhere. American film interest was discouraged when it was realised they wanted to Americanise it. A theatre in Odense, Denmark, wanted Alan to go and direct it himself, as did Matthew Francis at Greenwich. At one point Alan sent it to Andrew Lloyd Webber who had been casting around for subjects for musicals. The mind boggles.

On the back of a West End revival of *Absurd Person Singular* John Peter wrote that Ayckbourn was 'still not recognised for what he is [. . .] Of course, when [he] is safely dead, things will change. He'll be seen for the domestic political dramatist he really is, and his social insights will be compared, quite rightly, to those of Jonson or Congreve.' This production at the Whitehall was also what prompted Michael Coveney in the *Observer* to describe Lavinia Bertram as 'the quintessential Ayckbourn actress: sad, blinkered, victimised, radiantly normal'.

But 1990 had started disappointingly and got worse. Ayckbourn achieved a real coup in persuading Michael Gambon to lead a Scarborough cast in *Othello* and a revival of *Taking Steps*. And it was a good company: Ken Stott as Iago, Claire Skinner as Desdemona, Elizabeth Bell as Emilia. Naturally, they did terrific business but it was an unhappy experience all round. That two major problems were not resolved before they started must, ironically, be something to do with the amount of mutual trust involved; maybe there was too much of it. First, Ayckbourn had adapted *Othello*; he thought the play repetitive, as if Shakespeare, or the printers, had left the rewrites in; and sometimes the order felt wrong. Much of Iago – a longer part than Othello in the original – disappeared in the tidying process and so did some of the subtleties. Elizabeth Bell praises the version and wishes Ayckbourn would tackle the entire Shakespeare canon, but Gambon apparently thought he was going to do the whole play and concluded that Alan simply didn't like Shakespeare very much, which is not far from the truth. The second, possibly even more fatal, problem was that Gambon hates acting in-the-round. He told me:

> I just couldn't cope with it. I walked on that stage and I just gave up before I even started. You're faced, whichever way you look, with a pair of trainers and a different kid wearing them. And if you do look at anyone, you've got other people behind you. It denudes the player of his secrecy, his ability not to be seen. That's just as valuable, isn't it? There's a moment when you don't want anyone ever to see you. Just see your back, that's as valid as being seen. And I think theatre-in-the-round destroys that.

This of course is heresy in Scarborough, although not everyone who has worked there, reasonably happily, signs up to the complete gospel of Stephen Joseph. Around the theatre, Gambon's feelings were well known. Ken Stott, his part truncated, joined Gambon in an angry Celtic silence. On stage the play was terse and immensely gripping. Gambon's proximity as he prowled the small area in which he felt both caged and exposed was thrillingly dangerous. You wanted to reach out to Desdemona and say: 'For God's sake look after the handkerchief. Don't mention Cassio again.' Gambon's anger took terrible forms: one night he walked off-stage, gave an animal howl and came back, apologised to Stott and got on with it. Waving his scimitar in rage he would take chunks out of the set, uncomfortably close to where some innocent Scarborian was sitting. And then the mischief-making side which takes effect as soon as he gets bored came into play. Michael Holt had designed a small Venetian fountain on the set and towards the end of the play Othello tried to drown Iago in it.

As he thrust his head in the water those close to him could hear him mutter: 'Short back and sides?' And Iago's reply: 'Shampoo and set!' When Alan remonstrated that the audience had paid good money, Gambon was unimpressed. This was precisely the kind of thing Alan himself would have done as a young actor, and now hated most.

Elizabeth Bell probably speaks for the company when she argues that Ayckbourn didn't give them enough attention, especially after the production opened. His response was that this was the only space he had in which to write his next play. This was true, but he had also withdrawn himself – as is his custom – from actors with whom he seemed to have lost contact and a play in which he had lost confidence. He still doesn't really 'get' Shakespeare and now entrusts him to companies visiting Scarborough, but there are such exciting possibilities in matching his sense of the shape and meaning of a play with Shakespeare's language, wit and tragic sense that I hope he does it again.

Taking Steps followed and was much happier. Gambon had the time of his life putting on pebble glasses, having most of his hair shaved off, jamming a big cigar in his mouth and acting the drunken businessman as Roland Crabbe. He had much less trouble with the round in what he still thinks is the funniest play he has ever been in. And when he left Scarborough at the end of the run of the two plays it was with cordial handshakes all round and never a cross word actually exchanged between the two of them. Elizabeth Bell had had a few, but that is the privilege of old friends and very frank women (and she and Alan didn't speak for some years). The plan to transfer both plays to the West End was quietly and unanimously dropped but other members of the company claim they were kept in the dark about this for a heartless length of time. Alan is not actively cruel and when he withholds himself it is to avoid inflicting or enduring pain. But it does hurt.

4 : *Wildest Dreams, Time of My Life, Dreams From a Summer House*

In the spring of 1991 Ken Boden died, ending another link with the roots of the company. He had been the last of an old breed of general manager. Alan's tribute to him was once again a mini-autobiography. He recalled that when he had first got a job at Scarborough as stage manager he hadn't even known where it was, let alone how to sort out props for four different plays from 250 miles (400 km) away in London. In desperation, he contacted his predecessor:

'Scarborough?' she said. 'Oh that's a doddle. A summer holiday. Listen. Write down all the props you need, right? Then write down all the furniture you need, right? Then write down anything else you need, right? Then put it in an envelope and post it to Ken Boden. B-O-D-E-N. Right?'

I arrived in Scarborough to find the set and props for *The Glass Menagerie* and *An Inspector Calls* piled up in the middle of the Library Theatre dressing-room floor. 'There you are, lad,' said a big, gruff, genial, every-Southerner's-idea-of-what-a-Yorkshireman-should-look-like Yorkshireman. 'It's all there. If you want anything else give me a call. Boden's the name.'

The sheer energy and time he devoted to that tiny, virtually unknown theatre was remarkable. In fact it is, of course, a matter of record that without Ken there would probably be no full-time professional theatre in Scarborough today.

For almost 15 years we worked side by side, administrator and artistic director. His ability in times of economic crisis to conjure up extra money from nowhere . . . his care never to interfere with the artistic decisions but nonetheless unfailingly to support them – for these things and more, I shall remember him with gratitude.

He finished by revealing that Ken had appeared in one of his lesser-known one-act plays, and Alan had appeared with him. To the maxim, 'Never work with animals and children', he had quietly added the name of Ken Boden. After Ken, he thought, nobody would ever call him 'lad' again. Although there had been long periods when they hadn't got on, Alan meant both the factual tribute – actually delivered by Malcolm Hebden – and the affection. When the new Stephen Joseph Theatre was opened in 1996 the meeting-room-cum-hospitality suite would be named after Ken Boden and his picture – bluff, genial – watches over it. Joan Macalpine, Stephen Joseph's lorry driver, manager and playwright, wrote to Margaret Boden that Ken was a rare combination of total unpretentiousness and achievement in the artistic life of Scarborough, and through Scarborough of the country as a whole.

Just at that moment those achievements were beginning to look as though they might be finite. *Body Language* was the first adult play not to go to London since the Cluedo thriller *It Could Be Any One of Us* in 1983. *Wildest Dreams*, which followed in the summer of 1991, is an exploration of the relationship between the actual characters of a group of people who meet regularly for dungeons-and-dragons-type games and the personae they adopt: Alric the wise, Idonia the mystic who can speak with tongues, Xenon the half-animal stranger and Herwin the warrior. Alric, for example, is the gentle, ineffectual schoolteacher, Stanley. Rick, a small and undernourished woman in her twenties with a permanent cold, is Herwin, who also has a woman's body and a man's name; it is not altogether surprising to discover that she is a lesbian who wishes she could change her gender and that she was abused as a child. In addition to these harmless fantasists there is a very cocksure VAT inspector, a man you wouldn't expect the author to like, who is Stanley's brother-in-law. We meet, or hear of, various parents, but the catalyst for the play's action is Marcie, a likeable and open new member of their circle who charms them all but seems to want to improve them. The play was eventually picked up by the Royal Shakespeare Company, and Marcie was played by Sophie Thompson, younger daughter of Alan's one-time West End director, Eric. It performed well enough at the box office but remains one of his least-known works.

The Scarborough family was in any case not at its happiest. Alan had been spending a great deal of time with an actress who claimed he was commissioning her to write a play (he never confirmed this to Keith McFarlane and no money changed hands) and the company was frankly jealous: she was keeping Alan from them. And one other strange little episode rebuked him in the summer of 1991. A local property developer had decided to name a housing scheme after him; the units in Ayckbourn Chapters were duly advertised. Michael Gray, writing in the *Guardian*, was very hostile to this and blamed Alan, first for allowing his name to be used and second for not selling it for enough. Alan hadn't sold it for anything. The name had been suggested in a competition and Alan had simply given his permission.

It wasn't until *Time of My Life* in 1992 that Michael Codron picked up another play for a West End run with any confidence, and even that feels like 'one that got away' in the sense that its run was not long and that its technical innovation and harsh comic vitality remain undervalued. Its structure is dictated by a series of meals in a restaurant of some strange Southern European provenance (Albanian perhaps? Bulgarian?) all of whose waiters over the years are played by the same actor – Terence Booth in Scarborough and London – heroically serving improbable delicacies. It opens with a big family celebration. A businessman, his wife, their two sons, a daughter-in-law and a girlfriend are celebrating the mother's birthday; she's a woman who appears to be merely the foil and support to her astute entrepreneur of a husband but turns out to be as quite as tough as he is and much more honest. In the course of their night out some serious scores will be settled. Meanwhile the narrative of their philandering elder son and his betrayed wife goes forward in time, in the usual way. But the third strand, involving the younger son and the rather 'unsuitable' – i.e. lower-class – girlfriend that he has brought along to a family 'do', goes backwards in time, getting heartbreakingly more innocent as the evening develops. The overall effect is a fascinating and, though it encompasses the death of the father, funny family portrait. The subject is Ayckbourn's old favourite of the relationship between men and women, but the three stories are so varied but intertwined (the parents having made the sons what they are) and the narrative is so ingenious that it doesn't feel like old ground.

Heather Stoney now realised that she had given up acting without noticing. When Alan remarked that she could play Laura, the wife, her heart sank. She preferred to devote herself to Alan's career and wasn't available for work elsewhere. The part was played by Colette O'Neil in Scarborough, and Russell Dixon was the husband, Gerry. He brought his customary edge and she was rather more mellow in contrast. The commercial production was the other way round, with Gwen Taylor not suffering in the least from the star's disease of wanting to be liked while Anton Rodgers made Gerry into a charming but ineffectual old buffer whose firm might very understandably be on the slide. In neither case were they quite accurately matched. It was not a great success.

Had Alan taken his eye off the ball? There were distractions. The company had outgrown Westwood. Furthermore, Yorkshire Coast College, as it now was, wanted the ground floor of the old school back. In 1990 the Odeon cinema just up the hill, opposite the railway station at the entry point to the town centre, had come on the market. A group of the wealthier board members – including Alan – bought it immediately rather than wait for the mills of bureaucracy to grind out another scheme, by which time the building could have become a supermarket. From 1990, at least part of his attention was devoted all the time to the conversion into something near the purpose-built theatre that Stephen Joseph had dreamed of. Alan hadn't laid the ghost of his musical ambitions, and with his new collaborator John Pattison, he wrote a 'comedy with music', *Dreams From a Summer House*. They went on a joint 'holiday' to Majorca to do it, working together each day after Alan had had enough sun. The play acknowledges its debt to *Beauty and the Beast* by having fantasy characters called Belle and Baldemar, and all the characters in it have to learn to stop hiding their beauty from themselves, but the central love story –

facilitated by Belle – is between an unkempt tomboyish 17-year-old woman and the much older ex-husband of her permanently angry big sister. Robert is an artist – Belle comes to life out of his painting – and he has the most virulently misogynist speech in the whole Ayckbourn *oeuvre*, addressed to his brother-in-law:

> . . . in a perfect world [. . .] there'd be only perfect girls with vast chests and unfailingly sunny dispositions. Girls who are there solely to whisper, 'I love you, I love you, I love you. For ever and ever and ever.' But the world isn't perfect, I'm afraid, is it? Instead it is filled with lean, mean, narrow-eyed, suspicious, sanctimonious, flat-busted women with lantern jaws and the light of sexual battle eternally in their eye. Women who mean us all harm and humiliation. Who take the bread from our mouths and snatch the bottle from our lips. Women who argue with us just for the joy of putting us down. Who laugh at us just for the sheer pleasure of watching us grow smaller and smaller by the minute. And they, Grayson, they eventually inherit the earth. Not us. Not you and me. For they are the stronger sex. Not, you understand the better sex but the stronger one. And you and I will be crushed to dust beneath the platform heels of their aerobic, biodegradable trainers. For lo and behold, it is writ, blessed are the titless – for they shall inherit the earth.

When Griff Rhys Jones delivered this trumpet call of chauvinism at Ayckbourn's sixtieth birthday gala in 1999, completely separated from any redeeming context, it got a burst of applause that suggested to me, at any rate, that it wasn't being taken entirely satirically. It forces us to qualify the description of Ayckbourn, coined by Michael Billington and widely endorsed, as an instinctive feminist. It is a mistake ever to identify a playwright with the sentiments expressed by just one of his characters, but equally 'the real Alan Ayckbourn' will remain elusive if we deny any of the characters who 'all come out of me, really'. Sometimes when (in life) he expresses similar attitudes he may, as he says, be test-running a character. Sometimes he is doing it out of the devilment of a good joke. Sometimes he means it. He has a deep well of sympathy for the unhappy and ill-treated, and in the world he describes these are mostly women. Jane Asher, asked this very question by a member of the public at a National Theatre 'platform' performance for *House* and *Garden* in 2000, did not accept the use of the word feminist, preferring humanist. This is a complicated issue: Ayckbourn writes the best parts available to women, but one reason why they are so enjoyable to play is that they show flawed and sometimes nasty characters, not a parade of saints and martyrs.

There was to be no London production of *Dreams From a Summer House*, largely because it proved impossible to find an actor to play Robert. He had to combine the starry reputation necessary to sell the show to a commercial producer with the ability to sing music which exposes any uncertainty mercilessly: a combination of Hugh Grant with José Carreras with balls, is how Ayckbourn expressed it to Alan Strachan who, now running the Theatre of Comedy, was a possible producer. It did get produced in Seattle, however, and Arizona. In the same season Ayckbourn also directed two new plays by other writers. Peter Robert Scott's *One Over the Eight* is in not dissimilar territory to John Godber's *Up 'n' Under* in dealing with a male sporting outfit – a rowing eight – being coached by a woman. It was slick and enjoyable but Peter Robert Scott has had less attention for better plays. Alan cast a black actor, David Harewood, as the most sexually aggressive of the men, flying determinedly in the face of the then political correctness of either 'colour-blind' casting or the provision of what white liberals would regard as positive role models for black people. He had of course been equally 'incorrect' in casting a white actor, Michael Gambon, as Othello, but this was less of an issue in Scarborough than it would have been in a town with a black population of any significant size; had it gone into London it might have been another matter. In fact the charismatic Harewood scored a personal triumph in *One Over the Eight* partly because his well-muscled physique impressed a lot of women, but also because he played the character to the hilt. The other new play – which did find its way to London after being revived at Nottingham Playhouse – was Tim Firth's comedy *Neville's Island* about four men marooned as part of an 'outward bound' type of course designed to test their management potential. Brought to Ayckbourn by the theatre's then literary manager, Connal Orton, Firth had two more full-length plays produced in Scarborough, *The End of the Food Chain* and *Love Songs for Shopkeepers* which showed great promise without especially setting the box office alight. But despite his more lucrative success in television he wrote Alan a fourth play for production in 2002.

5 : Professor Ayckbourn

In 1992 Alan Ayckbourn followed Stephen Sondheim and Ian McKellen as the Cameron Mackintosh Visiting Professor of Contemporary Theatre at the University of Oxford. He was so flattered to be asked, he says, that he agreed to do it before he thought about it. With no specific brief and no experience of university he prepared a slightly defensive opening address.

He began by repeating his concern that comic dramatists do not get taken seriously; that only when you are dead do you merit serious academic study and then it is mostly devoted to explaining why such-and-such a joke was funny *then* but isn't *now*. In fact, of course, his presence there as a professor and the attendance of a couple of hundred people in the big hall at St Catherine's – the college to which the chair was attached – indicated that he was being taken seriously; but perhaps he had grown out of being a comic dramatist. He had also devised a thoroughly structured pair of short courses, one on playwriting and one on directing. Apart from lecturing he arranged for his students (ranging from under-graduates in their late teens to a senior Fellow in his seventies, with some Oxford housewives in between) to travel to Scarborough, sit through a first read-through of *Time of My Life*, meet all the departments of a working theatre, attend some rehearsals including the 'tech' and watch the opening previews. He also promised to direct a production in the Old Fire Station arts centre in Oxford of a student play, if anyone came up with one that was suitable. One did, and Malcolm Hebden – who joined him in the work – remembers Alan sitting in the audience urging the play on in his familiar rocking and shifting style just as anxiously as if it were a Scarborough opening of his own latest play. He was impressed at how much Ayckbourn cared. But the writer in question, Daniel Chambers, when encouraged by Alan with the suggestion that he might write something else, decided that it would be more interesting to work as a researcher in television. This was in itself something of an education for Alan: other people on the course had striven much harder to write a play, whereas this young man had just 'written it on the back of an envelope, practically, and slung it at me'. He was frustrated with the one-to-one sessions with writers who, he felt, weren't prepared to take the responsibility of making things happen in their plays. But Chambers's *Selling Out* was revived in Scarborough the next summer, directed by Malcolm Hebden this time.

The parallel course for directors had two five-strong groups, and more people from this have used at least some of what they learned in their subsequent careers, even if these have not been in the theatre. He provided four professional actors for them to work with. Each student drew a piece to direct out of a hat (he had to explain who J. B. Priestley was), worked on the piece for a couple of hours with the actors and then had an hour of discussion about it with them and him. Again, he was disconcerted to find that some of the students used up half the short time available shaking hands and warming up instead of getting on with the human and written material. It sounds as if the students didn't want to be caught doing anything wrong. But he cherishes a memory – at one of the meals he habitually laid on for them in a good restaurant – of the voice of Stephanie Turner rising above the hubbub of dinner-table conversation, saying to a student director: 'And if you ever, EVER, do that to a professional actor again . . .' before it tailed elusively away. His year, according to students, was wonderfully pragmatic and congenial, and the result included televised master classes. He came away with some impressive anecdotes – he claims to have seen one don in earnest high table conversation suddenly secure the undivided attention of his colleagues by setting his beard on fire, another bang the gavel on the table for grace only to see it shatter in small pieces, and a third at the all-female college of St Hilda's get into a splendid confusion about the Chippendales when Alan meant the male strippers and she meant the furniture. He also had considerable admiration for the wine cellar at St Catherine's, whose then Master, Brian Smith, has become an enduring friend. His commitment to students is real. The Scarborough Theatre hosts the annual National Student Drama Festival and Ayckbourn is an actively engaged patron.

At Cameron Mackintosh's urging, he also met Stephen Sondheim, first in an Oxford café, then in a Scarborough one. The idea was that the two cleverest creative minds in contemporary theatre might wish to collaborate. Each man does far too much to allow space for the other in a collaboration of equals, and it came to nothing. Each man also has great difficulty in making eye contact with whomever he is in conversation with; they gazed at ceilings, floors, windows and food – and never quite met.

Looking back at his time at Oxford, he says: 'I think in the end, I'm not the best person to teach. I'm a good person to talk to at the level of Tim Firth, someone who is robust enough to take out of it what he wants.' When he directed Firth's play *Love Songs for Shopkeepers*, a play much better than the response to it suggested, their discussions often included practical questions such as how to get people off stage so that the next scene can happen, or the slimming down of scenes to clarify them and make them more effective (most people – aware that a scene has a problem – will write more). Following discussions during rehearsals Firth would take himself off to Ayckbourn's office and rewrite a scene while the cast worked on something else. The Oxford undergraduates were not far enough down the road to benefit from this sort of thing.

So what can you teach about writing? Ayckbourn says that when he gives his talk on playwriting he thinks most of the people listening to him do not want to have the problems identified and addressed. They want to be told how easy it is. Many people want to be writers. Few want the graft and craft of actually writing. There is a suspicion that success, if it is not to do with whom you know, is to do with how big a margin you leave and how you set out the stage directions. But there are practical steps you can take towards writing better plays. One of the things Ayckbourn gets very impatient with is the idea that somehow plays write themselves. He blames Harold Pinter for allowing himself to be quoted as saying (he supplies the deep Pinter bass): 'I just write "A room". And then I see who comes into it.' He thinks this must be Pinter covering his tracks. Many of his Oxford students never got beyond page 12 because they thought the characters should somehow write the play, and often not much had actually happened. Ideas will come into the writer's head once he or she starts making the character do things, but it is his or her head, not the character's. So, the writer has to take the responsibility and the initiative. The writer has to get the structure clear, has to decide what the time-frame of the play is, has to think about what the space is in which the play takes place. None of this means it has to be completely realistic; just that the writer has to be in charge of the material. For an audience the feeling that a writer is not quite in control of what she or he is doing is generally disabling. The writer also has to decide whereabouts in the story to start telling it. To begin at the beginning and carry on until the end sounds like good advice, but can be ponderous. Alan's rule is to start as late as you can without leaving the audience terminally perplexed, which is a trick clearly understood by Sophocles in *King Oedipus* and approved by followers of Aristotle as 'unity of time'. The writer, above all, has to decide about the relationship between narrative and content.

Alan describes *Absent Friends* as almost narrative-free, since it is all confined to a tea party where the most extreme thing that happens is that someone gets a jug of cream poured over his head. But the structure allows five characters gradually, and through interaction with the sixth, the catalyst, to expose their emotional sore points. Barely a line goes by without generating laughter or wincing. The other thing that he teaches through what he says about his own work is the need to have more than one idea before you start. With him it is usually at least one big idea about content, the 'what' of the story, and at least one more about the 'how' of its telling. 'Where' and 'when' are important too: people behave differently in summer and winter, at dawn and midday. And if you are writing character drama, every person in it needs to be a full character with his or her own wants, even if you are not going to make much use of them; sometimes you see or read a play in which there is no indication even what the gender of the character is beyond the name on the cast-list. But when he was asked how he built a character, at the National Theatre 'platform' in 2000, he replied that he didn't really know. He certainly didn't watch people in restaurants or make notes. He leaves it to his unconscious.

And then there are the very practical details. How to get characters off stage is one; on television (which is where most people see their drama most of the time) the camera simply goes away to another scene, but the theatre audience cannot do that. The craft which Alan cannot teach because he seems to do it so effortlessly himself is exposition: how to get the background information across to an audience without the audience feeling it is being formally filled in. Alan's view is that the actual dialogue in the meat of the play is the easy bit. Not for everybody, it isn't. Most new writers write too much for the modern audience's taste, which is why he gave the advice to Tim Firth to simplify a 'muddy' scene, and why he sometimes gets writers to test out a piece of work by inviting them to remove one half of the conversation in an exchange between two people, to see if it exerts more grip rather than less. It is a very illuminating exercise. And then there are issues like giving characters time to change their clothes if they leave one scene on Tuesday in winter and reappear on a Wednesday in summer.

It is possible that the single most useful preparation for writing plays is to be an actor. But it is a useful substitute to watch plays, and many fledgling playwrights don't seem to have done that. Ever since Chekhov's 'invention' of sub-text we have been conscious that something more happens in a scene than the stage directions or words alone make explicit; actors and directors have to discover what this is to perform it and writers need to examine it as intensively. Alan's final step, when a play is finished, is to read it through as all the prominent characters in turn, so that in addition to establishing the overall architecture of the play he has a sense of the shape of each character's progress through it. Structure is the word that he – and other directors – come back to time and again. It is not an assertion of the importance of form over content but a recognition that form gives expression to content.

It is comforting to believe that natural talent will out, but – by definition – we never find out about the natural talent that perishes unfulfilled. Ayckbourn, aware that it was only with his seventh play that he achieved real success, believes the right to fail is essential for fledgling writers and that theatres must therefore be able to give them a sustained period of support. But the fewer productions of any kind that you do in a season, the greater the risk if any one of them is a box office disaster. It is entirely possible that Ayckbourn himself would not have matured under the policy he has had to impose on his protégés recently, which can be summed up as 'three strikes and you're out'.

No new play by Alan Ayckbourn was premièred in 1993, the first time this had happened since 1968 when he was still working at the BBC. Frustrated at not being in his new building, as he had hoped, he revived *The Norman Conquests* to celebrate its twentieth anniversary. This became famous within the theatre as the last time Alan shouted at one of his cast. He and the actress in question drastically failed to communicate; he took the view that she had been repeatedly asked to be less 'theatrical' but wasn't responding, and that this in turn was putting unfair pressure on the rest of the company. According to Malcolm Hebden, back at the theatre effectively in Robin Herford's old role, directing some productions as well as acting occasionally, she felt she had taken her performance down to a complete minimum as requested. In the end Jane Maud – playing bossy, punctilious Sarah, the 'Penelope Keith part' – was quite as good as anybody else in it and the three plays packed the theatre all summer long. But the company was not a happy one. Alan hates confrontations of any kind and will go to considerable length to avoid them. 'They leave me wobbly for days afterwards,' he says, and they usually mean something has gone irreparably wrong. He also believes that if a relationship with an actor hasn't worked out 'it is at least 50 per cent my fault'. The season showed him at his most inventive in decking out a lightweight romantic musical – *Love Off the Shelf* – to good effect, and a first production was given to another author who would in due course write a play with commercial potential: Vanessa Brooks, whose *Love Me Slender* would be produced in Scarborough in 1997 before going on a national tour. At Christmas he revived *Mr A's Amazing Maze Plays*, prior to a transfer to the National Theatre.

6 : *Communicating Doors*

If he shared his colleagues' anxiety at a period of relatively low achievement, without a real hit since *Man of the Moment* premièred in 1988, it didn't show. I saw a good deal of him at the end of 1993 and beginning of 1994 as a result of making a radio documentary about the production process of the play that swept him back into the West End, had a successful run in New York and eventually convinced even the French of his talent. He was hospitable and good company, and seemed relaxed and confident.

Communicating Doors had been written in advance; its title reflected its content. The first draft, to get the whole story on paper, had taken three days. A further four had been spent shaping and refining it. Even so, it wasn't the play which had originally been announced. This was something called *Private Fears in Public Places*, inspired by an image of a man forever saying farewell to a woman at an airport or a railway station; it may be written one day if only to frighten Alan's master carpenter, Frank Matthews, with the task of building an escalator. *Communicating Doors* had a hotel location (inspired by the Savoy, where he and Heather had lived while work was being done on their house in Keats Grove) but came out of a preoccupation with time that dates back at least to his work on the plays of J. B. Priestley in the 1950s. It is set partly in 2014, partly in 1994 and partly in 1974, and the dramatic premise is that when you pass through the (usually locked) doors which connect suites at our grander hotels, you slip backwards or forwards two decades as well. It depends on the premise (implausible to one critic) that hotel fixtures and fittings stay the same.

Although Heather no longer has to type the script of a new play, she is the first reader, followed by Roger Glossop (the designer nobly took himself off to the Savoy to research the real thing) and Alan's new casting director, Sarah Hughes. He had at least conducted formal interviews for this job when Michele Tidy left to get married but maintained the instinctive tradition established by Stephen Joseph almost 40 years before by appointing a woman who had been recommended by somebody he trusted (Caroline Smith), shared his sense of humour and brought none of the 'baggage' of experienced casting directors. Hughes had been working as a secretary at the Regent's Park open air theatre and was prepared to go anywhere to watch actors. Ayckbourn gave her his usual idiosyncratic thumbnail sketch of each part as well as the script. He likes to say things like 'Not a bad part for Jack Nicholson' or 'If this were a Hollywood film, Glenn Close would play this'. Hughes then draws up a schedule of meetings with actors rather than auditions in the traditional sense. Actors may be asked to read from the new play, with Ayckbourn himself often reading another character in the scene, but they won't then be told to try it again differently. Essentially he does not want the performance to be already in place; for that he can go to the many actors he knows already. In trying to make sure that each company has some new blood in it, he is really looking for people he (and everyone else confined to Scarborough) can get on with, characters he can lead out through the play, performers he can imagine physically embodying the roles required, actors who are unselfish. Each gets half an hour and a 'good chat'. There is unlikely to be any 'colour-blind' casting. Alan takes the view that with his plays audiences will reasonably want to know whether there is some family history they should be watching out for if some of the actors are black and others white. He has never yet written a black character, and so he has very rarely employed black actors. He likes actors to look distinctive and different, and Robin Herford may be right in thinking that being tall and thin helped him get a job in 1976.

The cast for *Communicating Doors* – covering 40 years of action – also had to be able to look older or younger at very short notice. Although this was partly achieved by clothes – allowing us all to enjoy flared trousers once again for 1974 – it was also cleverly suggested in other ways including the casting itself. Nick Stringer, playing an obtuse and self-important hotel detective with dreams of having his own sea-going cruiser, has been almost bald for much of his acting career. To cut his age by 20 years the simplest thing – but a false one – would have been to give him a full wig. Instead he was given a Bobby Charlton-style strand across his pate. This was infinitely more convincing (and cheaper; these things count in rep). John Hudson did need a wig to appear both as a 30-year-old honeymooner and a seriously ill 70-year-old: but in the flesh his own age was hard to tell. He played Reece, a businessman who believes himself to be dying, as the play opens in 2014. Wanting to settle his conscience he needs someone to witness his signature on a confession, undetected by his villainous partner; his solution has been to send for a 'dominatrix' prostitute, Poopay Dayseer (try saying it with a French accent). For the latter Adie Allen, clad mainly in leather, and as the villain Richard Durden (an old Haileyburian) didn't change much at all. Nor did Liz Crowther, who led the company as the hero's former wife, who doesn't survive into

2014; when Alan had been a teenage actor and stage manager 35 years before, her father Leslie had appeared in variety in Scarborough. Sarah Markland was cast as Reece's apparently dizzy, social climber of a first wife. A great deal of black veil made her believably 20 years older.

When the cast assembled just after the turn of the year, four of the six were new to Scarborough. Durden articulated a newcomer's first impression: 'There's a great feeling in the building, isn't there, that they've all been together a long time, and he's completely without side. They all treat him like he's Joe Bloggs; occasionally he writes and the plays sometimes go to London, but only if he's lucky. It's quite a strange atmosphere.'

Read-throughs in Scarborough, and at many theatres now, are so democratic and open that they are practically performances. It makes sense to have everyone present, from box office staff to wardrobe supervisor to administrator, because they all have to 'sell' the play, but it makes what might otherwise be a first private exploration a public ordeal. Alan believes in the general principle of open rehearsals and he was ebullient, a cross between a schoolteacher leading a particularly enjoyable outing and a host at a party at which everyone confidently expects to be happily drunk. But he was very brisk, perhaps nervously. He didn't introduce the play: 'Not much point in talking about it. It's impossible to explain. Better just read it.' And they were off. Actors do what they can with read-throughs; some of them are as nervous as they will be on the first night. They don't really want to expose themselves at this stage, in front of the assembled staff, but nor do they want to seem dull or stupid. They get their tongues round the words but hold back on energy and interpretation. So it was with this company but there were some gratifying laughs – Big Frank Matthews, the master carpenter, is British theatre's northern area heavyweight laughing champion – and Alan nodded and grinned a lot. He didn't say much more afterwards but allowed Roger Glossop and Christine Wall to divert some of the pressure by displaying the model set and costume ideas. Nick Stringer was sporting a beard at the time, and Glossop thought this might make it difficult to make him look younger. 'Fear not,' said Stringer, 'the beard will go next week.' There would be nothing 'Star Trek' about the clothes for 2014. There was no mention of potential problems. This was a moment for reassurance. As soon as he had got everyone else out of the room, Ayckbourn simply started again at the beginning, 'putting the play on the floor' and letting the actors walk through rather than just read through. And that is his basic rehearsal technique. Obviously he concentrates on individual scenes much of the time, but fundamentally he goes through the play over and over again, so that everyone always has a sense of the overall shape and rhythm of it lodged in his or her mind. Actors try out their own ideas, and good ones go in. The play grows by a process of accretion and letting go, the script itself gradually sticking to the actors. A few days in, Ayckbourn reported: 'It's going very well. The first few days are always finding out more about the actors I haven't worked with before, how they work and at what speed they work. We've got the usual mixture of fast and slow.' Robin Herford told me Alan *chooses* a mixture of fast and slow workers, of actors who just get on with it and others (often the women) who want to be led into discovery of the character. Alan himself thinks that mixture just happens naturally. But he is genuinely bewildered when actors tell him that in rehearsals with other directors they sometimes spend the first week or two just talking about the play. He reaches his understanding of the play by playing it, not the other way round.

I heard him give one direct piece of advice to an actor about a scene (I suspect he may have been laying it on a bit because he knew we needed some rehearsal 'actuality' for the radio) and even that involved a simile. Adie Allen, as Poopay, had escaped to 1994 and, having met Ruella (Liz Crowther) and explained her own predicament, was astonished to find that the other woman was not simply preoccupied with the idea of escape but that things should be put right. For Ruella, due to be thrown off a balcony that night according to what Poopay already knows, there is a moral imperative not just to save herself but to act to save her husband from himself. Poopay, an orphan whom nobody else has ever helped to be better, cannot believe that she has got to go back to 2014 to do *good*, at great personal risk to herself. For the play to proceed, the actor has to play a switch in motivation. Ayckbourn said: 'This is a funny moment because it's the first time plans are being made. The whole play up till now has been about what to do next, to get away from Julian, to witness Reece's confession, with no time to think. They've actually not talked to each other very much. I think, Adie, the way into it is to be very, ultra casual about it. It's like a teenage daughter who's gone upstairs in a tantrum and slammed the door and is lying on the bed. She's in a mood where she could just kick out or clam up. Shall we do that once more before lunch?'

John Hudson told me: 'He gives you clues about the character, but he does it in a rather sideways way.' Ayckbourn had told him: 'He's a sort of "the milk's boiling over" man – the sort of man who stands in the kitchen and says, "Darling! The milk's boiling over!"' Liz Crowther (Ruella): 'He knows. He's got pictures of it all in his head. He'll illustrate things with different stories. But sometimes it's quite hard to work out technically what you have to do.'

Half-way through the rehearsal period the actors were perplexed to find that the director sometimes talked about the writer in the third person. A kind of anxiety crept in that is always present when you rehearse comedy. There are few surprises left after repeating the comic business for a couple of weeks and you start to wonder if any of it will seem funny to an audience. You know that the writer has had 40 or so acknowledged successes, and if this play doesn't work it may be your fault. You restrain yourself from doing what most actors do with most new plays when you reach this point: 'You're a bit more cautious about saying,' said Nick Stringer, who had worked on a lot of new plays, 'this is a load of rubbish.' As rehearsals came towards the end of the third week, actors found they more or less knew the lines but weren't fluent. What is natural under these circumstances is to embellish rather than to hesitate (and stop the flow). Actors often embellish anyway, putting in 'ums' and 'ahs' and adding or telescoping words to make them sound more natural. Ayckbourn managed not to wince at this, but as Adie Allen said: 'He doesn't start picking us up yet, when people drop the odd word, but he will, I'm sure. He writes it in when somebody fluffs or somebody hesitates, so there's no room to do it yourself. It's there.'

Ayckbourn: 'The big danger is that you come to rehearsals as writer/director as if you had some great big sealed holy book out of which the actor reads, observing the underlined bits and the pauses very carefully. I am pretty obsessional about getting my dialogue right, but I try always when I'm directing to give images, reflections of what's happening.' He had been quoted in 1993, that fallow year, as saying he thought about one in every five or six of his plays was a dud. Although he tries never to show the actors, there is usually a point in rehearsals when he wonders if this is the one. The impression actors get, that he knows exactly what he wants and it is all in the script, is only half the story. In the same season Connal Orton had been directing Tim Firth's *The End of the Food Chain*, and Ayckbourn had felt a little mixture of depression and envy when he saw Orton and Firth walking off together after rehearsal, thrashing out any difficulties.

> I just thrash it out with me, really. You can't sit down and tell the cast that you have a severe doubt about the script. That is sort of catastrophic. But one does. You do see a run-through, or a scene put together for the first time, and you think, 'Oh my God, this isn't going to work.' But of course a lot of the ingredients aren't yet working and, God bless 'em, the actors

come up with a bit more energy and a bit more speed and start to do the things you asked them to do two weeks before, and gave up ever expecting them to do.

One of the things making it harder for them to get there was the more than slightly ridiculous nature of rehearsing a scene where (in 1994) Ruella is to fall from the sixth-floor balcony and Poopay (on the run from 2014) and Jessica (the honeymoon wife of 1974, now married to an Italian aristocrat and vainer and sillier than ever) have to try to pull her back, using the bedspread she has managed to catch hold of. They tried it first of all using a bench and then a temporary block the same height as the balcony would be. The first discovery was how extremely rough and painful this could be on an actress's front. Ayckbourn was 'leaning gently' on production manager Alison Fowler to get the real thing in place ahead of the technical rehearsal. Taking the edges off the balcony, and covering it with cushioning topped by marble-effect lino, reduced the rough edges and the friction. Fowler and Roger Glossop also had to solve the question of how to make Ruella invisible when she falls; it's easy enough beyond a proscenium arch when nobody sees where Tosca lands (unless it's on a trampoline and she bounces back up, as in the famous story) but in the round some members of the audience are looking straight down on wherever she goes. The solution was to get Mick Hughes – by lighting everywhere else – to plunge this spot in darkness; everything there would be black in any case. And there was a mattress in place on which Ruella could lie out of sight. Even more, perhaps, the cast were waiting to see the communicating doors themselves, to give 'reality' to the moments when they move a couple of decades in time. They needed a precise event to which to link the metamorphosis, as opposed to the vague process of miming a door and making the kind of noise you think it might make. But the door was presenting another challenge. The only place it could go, in the tiny theatre in Westwood, was in the area used by the audience to enter and leave the auditorium. The fire officer would refuse to let the play go ahead if the audience could be trapped by the set. Glossop made the door hinged on one side only. If you pushed the other side the whole thing would move out of the way: just like any emergency exit, really. And then there was the bathroom, which had to have running water so that a credible drowning attempt could take place. Plumbing water in was no problem, said Ali Fowler. The difficulty was getting rid of it. The hi-tech solution was to have someone suck very strongly on the end of a pipe.

Meanwhile, in the corner of the beige and white rehearsal room, John

Pattison had been sitting, thumping away at a silent keyboard, trying out embellishing music only he could hear in his headphones. When he settled on an idea he started to let bits be audible, including the screeching chord from Hitchcock's *Psycho*. Alan would catch his eye, nod at some things, shake his head at others, almost imperceptibly. A score was developing alongside the text. As usual Ayckbourn earned his actors' gratitude by having a strict rehearsal timetable. He worked out how many pages he needed to cover in each session and rarely deviated from his schedule. He always finished on time, without ever being seen to look at his watch. When rehearsals were over for the day, he would be out of the building and gone before anyone noticed.

The twitchiest time for everyone is just before they go in front of an audience for the first time. As an observer I wondered if Alan had fleshed the part of Ruella out enough in the writing for Liz Crowther to play it. Liz had started to denigrate herself and play up her nervousness; was she wondering the same? Richard Durden was anxious about carrying the weight of making the play a thriller, the solitary fright-inducing factor. In an interview for a national newspaper he described the process as like the way theatre worked 20 years before, the moves all 'blocked' in the first session. Alan tends to do this anyway, in the knowledge that he can change things later, but on this occasion the layout of the set made it essential. But he was uneasy; he didn't want to be thought too old-fashioned.

This is also when actors started to moan about wigs. It is easy to be scathing about actors' anxieties (you wouldn't know, from what journalists and politicians say about 'luvvies', that there were other vain professionals on television) but looking right is part of getting it right. The costumes looked promising: miraculously, Poopay's tarty fur coat was already available in Christine Wall's theatre wardrobe – made of wolfskin – and Harold's suit was supplied by a firm that did indeed kit out security officers, so it was the real thing. Jessica's negligee for the honeymoon scene started as the real thing but had to be lined so that it wasn't completely revealing under theatre lighting. The set, complete with doors, plumbed-in bath and balcony, was ready and the scent of Mick Hughes's pipe announced that a lighting designer was at hand. This is the point at which Alan got 'the whole train-set'. He was in his element. Then just as they were wondering if anyone would ever laugh at material they had long ago ceased to find even mildly amusing, there came the question of what to do if the audience did laugh, uncontrollably. There is an exchange between Ruella and Poopay, by now good friends, when the older woman asks the prostitute if she makes lots of money at her trade. It's not the business it was, says Poopay. Too old-fashioned in 2014. She just gets the older clientele. There are three possible laughs in the line that follows. She says: 'The rest are into VS [simmer]. Virtual sex [temperature rises]. Sitting at home, mouse in one hand, joystick in the other [boils over].' You can't really slow things down to accommodate three laughs in one line of dialogue. It is a question Ayckbourn is used to:

> I always say to actors, if they need telling, don't stop unless you have to. Don't jump on laughs and kill them and metaphorically glare at the audience. And of course, if there's a lovely belter, then obviously wait for it. But the thing about my stuff, they never come at the same place. Often there'll be a completely different set of laughs on any two consecutive nights. I always say at the last dress rehearsal before we go before the audience, a sort of traditional note, 'Keep your innocence,' and that's an innocence where you neither demand a laugh nor expect a laugh. Laughter is a little bonus we get on a straight play.

The characters don't know they are funny, so the actors mustn't either.

Between the last dress rehearsal and the first preview of *Communicating Doors* a technical crisis blew up. That pipe taking the water from bath to human suction pump had sprung a leak and there was a wet patch on the brand-new carpet of the hotel bedroom. It had to be got rid of because the audience will look at the wet patch on a carpet in an Ayckbourn play and wait to find out its significance in the story: blow-heaters were pressed urgently into service.

The acting company had other worries. One said: 'The first time you put it in front of an audience you shake for the first half hour, don't you?' At five minutes to seven, the 'half' was called by stage management, half an hour before the point when the company is expected to be ready to go on. These last 35 minutes, later in the run, will be a relatively calm time for simple preparation. At the first performance there were final encouragements from Alan among the cards and flowers and then the actors were left to their own kind of holy terror. And the author? 'When I was writing but not directing I never went anywhere near the auditorium. I used to just sit in the bar. Now I direct as well I have to stand on the bridge with my chaps.' In fact his whole psyche was with the actors and the play even as he appeared in the bar, greeting the few friends he asks to first nights and saluting board-members, influential citizens and, with the minimum smiling acknowledgement consistent with politeness but not ingratiation, representatives of the media. No alcohol now or in the interval. Knowing that his tendency to rock to and fro, as he wills the cast on, can be seriously disruptive, he had got in the habit of using an area in the theatre at Westwood reserved for late-comers to slip into and stand, unobserved, until there is a suitable moment for them to take their seats. Sprinting into it once, a little late, he hit his head on the doorway, and everybody knew he was there. By 1994 plenty of people knew where to look for him anyway, especially the cast, so that unless he lay on the floor – not unknown – they would clock the faint light reflected on his forehead just once in a show as a kind of talismanic reassurance. You could no more tell what he was thinking, however, than interrogate a brick wall.

Afterwards, he did drink. There was no real sense to me at this point of just how well or otherwise the show had gone. Well enough, certainly. There was no question but that the audience had enjoyed it, swept along with the thriller element as well as the comedy. I knew I had enjoyed it, although the laughs hadn't always come where I had expected. For instance, in the opening few minutes Poopay duly goes into her dominatrix routine for precisely the wrong man (Julian) who claims that she reminds him of her mother. The laugh I expected here was subdued, for the perfectly valid reason, I guess, that the element of menace in Julian and the possibility at the very start that we might be in for an evening of sado-masochism made the audience more edgy. When Reece appears very soon afterwards and remarks of the hall porter that he can never get you a taxi when you want one but he has no trouble supplying a woman, the joke is more familiar and it feels more like 'Ayckbourn country'. The audience relaxed and laughed. Towards the end I was astonished to find that even though I knew every word of the play by now I still got a lump in the throat at the tender parting (in 1994, with a promise to meet in 2014) of Ruella and Poopay: there was an unfashionable but hugely effective amount of 'heart' in a play that, more than most, had seemed at first reading to rely on a clever narrative device. The cast afterwards had that excitement and relief that comes from a sense of first having 'got away with it' and then earning warm and sustained applause: a success, certainly. But I doubt if anybody thought, as Alan went through the first-night ritual of hanging the framed poster for the show in the bar, of future runs and awards in London, New York and Paris. The party moved on down to a boathouse on the sea-front. I left before it got out of hand. Alan was in attendance, but by this time he was actually rather depressed: not about the play but because that was the end of his intimate relationship with the production and the people in it. A part of him had already said goodbye.

The reviews, when everybody got round to reading them much later, reflected the evidently rather bewildering mixture that the play itself represented, openly contradicting each other over even the relatively minor question of whether hotel rooms actually change or not in 20 or 40 years: Irving Wardle (*Independent on Sunday*) thought they would have done; Jeremy Kingston (*The Times*) was pleased to have his belief that they do not confirmed. You think: Is this the point? The author's asking you to accept the notion of time-travel and you're worrying about the need for redecoration? Wardle, John Peter (*Sunday Times*) and Alastair Macaulay (*Financial Times*) found the characterisation too sketchy to permit real involvement and Kingston also found the play without 'substance to take home afterwards'. Charles Spencer (*Daily Telegraph*) thought it lacked the depth of Ayckbourn's greatest plays but that he had rarely written anything that offered more pure fun. Michael Billington enjoyed it for *Country Life* but wanted Ayckbourn to return to 'charting the absurdity and desperation that underlies our social behaviour'. In the *Guardian* Robin Thornber noticed flat spots, scenes when credulity was over-stretched, an evening 'of gentle smiles rather than guffaws', but found the theme fascinating. John Peter wrote his review as a conversation between a critic and a reader, a device also explored by 'AN' in the *Scarborough Evening News*, where the dialogue involved a Mature Scarborough Lady and an Angry Young Man; she saw a play which offered something for everyone and he – enjoying the punch-line of the review – one which had not quite enough for anyone. This, in fact, was the most hostile review of all, and when it came out at lunchtime on the day after the press night (3 February) it was potentially a serious depressant. The next regional voice followed an hour or two later with the arrival from York of the *Yorkshire Evening Press*, where Charles Hutchinson – pointing out the connection with *Psycho* and Robert Zemeckis's film *Back to the Future* – seemed to relish a play which 'keeps women in suspenders and the audience in suspense on a night for being scared wittily rather than witless'. Other Yorkshire reviewers were all substantially favourable. Of the nationals, it was Paul Taylor in the *Independent* who most fully explored the play as it was, rather than a play Ayckbourn had written before or a play the critics expected him to write now. His was the kind of good review which also smacks the author a couple of times for perceived past transgressions. Taylor had enjoyed the new play as a refreshing change whose contrivances you were prepared to forgive for the 'beautiful and mysterious change in mood' of the ending. He also contrasted the way time is played with in *Time of My Life*, in which the author, according to Taylor, imposes his three time-sequences on the story-telling method, with the scheme in *Communicating Doors* in which the time-travellers (or some of them) are as aware as the audience of what is going on. And, most importantly perhaps, he pin-pointed the moment when Ruella decides to enlist the help of Reece's first wife to change the future (rather than using the magic wand of time-travel) as an Ayckbournian 'thumb-print' on the play, a reminder that the play was by the same author 'as the excellent *Woman in Mind* and other works of powerful, if unassuming, feminism'.

Many of the critics referred to a recent theatre survey (by the Little Theatre Guild) which showed that Ayckbourn and Shakespeare were now performed with roughly equal frequency (after a period in which Alan had been slightly outscoring Will) at the head of British theatre. Almost all of them pointed out that this was his forty-sixth play and looked forward to the half-century. And Charles Hutchinson remarked that the feeling usual on an Ayckbourn first night, that the theatrical 'centre' had moved from London to the Yorkshire coast, was further enhanced on this occasion by the presence of members of the House of Commons select committee on Heritage, led by its chairman, Gerald Kaufman.

Some actors, writers and directors genuinely never read the reviews. Some devour them as soon as they come off the presses, even waiting for the early editions (of those newspapers that still print overnight reviews) in the manner prescribed by showbiz mythology. Alan had gone through that with *Mr Whatnot*. The sanest thing, if you can manage it, is to read them when they no longer threaten to blow your performance off course through extravagant praise or devastating criticism. Alan says the critics never tell him anything he hasn't already spotted and that he knows if the audience 'feels that you have just given a party which isn't quite as good as other parties you have given in the past'. He can usually predict who will like what. However, the occasional remark of surprised pleasure when he thinks they have liked something and understood what he was on about suggests that there is also a vulnerability to bad reviews that he would like to have ironed out long ago. Jeannie Swales, his then press officer, thinks that even now he can be stung by reviews; even if he doesn't read them himself, others do. If it is the habit of those closest to you to congratulate you on the good ones, you can hardly fail to notice the deafening silence if they have nothing to say. It is very hard to keep out of the theatre a general raising or lowering of the mood if they are all good or all bad. What annoys Alan most, according to Jeannie, is when the local paper sends someone along, in the absence of the regular critic, with no knowledge of or interest in the work, as happened with *Wuthering*

Heights all those years ago. The happiest thing about the reviews for *Communicating Doors* was that all the doubts expressed related to the play; everyone acknowledged expert production and every member of the cast found at least one favourable mention somewhere; nobody took a personal battering.

Only Adie Allen and Sara Markland retained their roles when *Communicating Doors* went to London 18 months later. Although, as is often the case with Ayckbourn's plays, there is no star role, Alan's established collaborator Julia McKenzie came in to play Ruella, so that there was a 'name' for the commercial production. This was bitterly disappointing for Liz Crowther, who had been generously commended in almost all the reviews. There was no longer the compensation that the old cast was by then well on with the next Ayckbourn play or even the next but one. However, the original cast did travel to an international theatre festival in Chicago with the play. The West End production duly ran for a year.

It also ran, off-Broadway, in New York and gave Alan long-awaited success in Paris, where it won him his first Molière nomination (and one of his actors took the award). The cast also included Zabou Breitman who would reappear in *House* and *Garden* at the National Theatre in London three years later. She made the perceptive remark that the French were suspicious of serious plays which were also funny and that the English were suspicious of serious plays which were not. The French like art with an idea in the foreground. Very few plays succeed in London, Paris and New York.

Chapter 9

Waiting for the Odeon

1 : *Haunting Julia* and *A Word From Our Sponsor*

A month after *Communicating Doors* opened, Ayckbourn went into rehearsals with his first play written for an end-stage or proscenium arch theatre. He had expected to have one by now, in the second auditorium of the converted Odeon cinema. When that auditorium was finished first, he toyed with the idea of opening it up while keeping the theatre-in-the-round running down the hill at Westwood. The audience would have had to pick its way across a building site at the Odeon and sooner or later an usherette would have been killed crossing the main road, so he dropped the idea. But he went ahead with *Haunting Julia* anyway – and it still worked, if you sat opposite the place in the set where a door in the wall of a student flat was supposed to be. It was an interesting play if you sat elsewhere, but its principal *coup de théâtre* – the moment when a doorway that is supposed to be bricked up opens, and we believe a ghost to have swept through – had to be taken entirely on trust. The marginally lesser effect of a patch of blood appearing in her empty bed was still powerfully effective. The play was revived early in 1999 in the now-finished McCarthy auditorium of the new theatre and toured the country very successfully. It has, however, not been seen in London. This is Ayckbourn's second play in 'real time' and ideally it should be played without an interval (as it was in Scarborough). When other managements insisted on one because they needed the bar takings, Alan made the best of it by stopping the play at a suspenseful moment and then, after the interval, restarting it on the line before the stoppage, so that it felt uninterrupted.

The plot is driven by the desire of Joe to discover why his brilliant and much-loved daughter Julia has committed suicide. She was a musician and a composer, and he has turned her old bed-sitting-room into a kind of shrine and study centre. Here he brings her student boyfriend, Andy, and a psychic, Ken. The narrative feints to go in a number of different directions – and reveals that Andy had given Julia up just before her death.

But the outcome is presaged in the title. It is not just that Julia is haunting anyone else, although she briefly seems to; it is the pressure of a father's love and the sense of an overwhelming amount of music in her head that have combined to deny her the possibility of living an ordinary life. Alan was keen to explore the plight of the adolescent who thinks nobody sees her as herself, and therefore Julia needed not to be so extraordinary a figure that the teenage girls who came to see (and identified with) the play thought she was outside their experience. He also had in mind the parents who push their children to almost impossible feats of performance, competing through them. He deliberately didn't do that with his own sons but the sheer weight of his reputation must have had some effect, conscious or otherwise. Both boys did in the end go to drama school as mature students. Steven has been working in the marketing department of the theatre in Scarborough; Philip takes English drama to French schools. But *Haunting Julia* is also a play about gifted people who are hard to live with because they have no concept of the needs of others, 'like a slight autism'. Did he include himself in that? 'Slightly. I hope I'm not in the bracket of the monsters. There is a feeling sometimes of somebody telling me the most terrible news and I'm drumming my fingers because I want to be off writing.' And he connected this with Jerome in *Henceforward* . . . There must be some significance in the fact that both plays feature music – Alan's main non-professional artistic interest and his father's profession.

If Alan is all his characters these must include the psychic, Ken, who looks as though he is going to be a caricature and then most certainly is not. Does this mean Alan believes in ghosts? Well, he was conscious of his father's presence beside him in Scarborough some years after the latter's death. This play 'started as a ghost story – at least that was an ingredient in what I wanted to write – but I became more interested in why we need to believe in ghosts, why some people are happy with that and others reject it. It's obviously a sort of assurance of our own immortality. But also some people are genuinely obsessed with contacting people after they've died. It's like they have a feeling they haven't finished talking to them, or there are things that are left unsaid. I really don't have a strong view on whether any of it is genuine. All I know is, it's like the rules of science fiction, it's completely prescribed what ghosts do and don't do, like the supposed rules about what flying saucers are meant to do. It's been around for a very long time, certainly before Shakespeare.'

By horrible coincidence the musical which followed *Haunting Julia* involved a real death. Its impact on Alan completely contradicts his otherwise deserved reputation for reticence or emotional coolness.

With John Pattison, the writer of 'Julia's' music, Alan had written *A Word From Our Sponsor*, a satire on the relationship between art and sponsorship in which he rather blunted his anger by dressing it in a nicely sung love story. Arts organisations had endured a decade or more of being told they should find more subsidy from private sources. Even at the National Theatre Alan had experienced the difficulty of attracting a sponsor for *'Tis Pity She's a Whore*: classic or no classic, the title wasn't perceived as good for corporate images. Since 1990 he had been seeking support for his new theatre, only to find the general public readier to throw coins into a bucket when he or Malcolm Hebden went in front of them with an appeal before each performance than big business was to make larger donations, though eventually some sort of sponsorship came through for most sections of the building. The play, set in the future, concerns a church nativity play whose last (and dodgiest) potential sponsor disappears when a local night-club burns down. The vicar is in despair when an inter-continental train makes an unscheduled stop at the local station and the passenger who disembarks offers him everything he wants. It is, of course, the Devil: him again, and in this case her again too, because the cleverest stroke in the play is that the Devil is beautifully male or female depending on who is to be tempted. His/her price is that the nativity story should undergo a trendily commercial exploitation: Mary should become Herod's unfaithful wife and the baby should be a girl called Jasmine. Ayckbourn himself was never satisfied with the piece, but it did pretty good business as a spring entertainment in Scarborough, with a mildly *risqué* relationship between the vicar, who was already married to a woman whose career has taken her out of reach, and Gussie, the downtrodden companion of a bullying wealthy parishioner.

It was due to open in Chichester, at the smaller Minerva Theatre, when the actress playing Gussie, Sophie Winter, was suddenly taken ill and died within a matter of hours. She was pregnant, and delighted to be so, but nobody had realised that the pregnancy was ectopic, that the baby was in the wrong place. Theatre people are notoriously sentimental on these occasions, of course, but everybody really did love Sophie. She had joined the company initially to appear in a play directed by Malcolm Hebden, who recalled:

> She was raw when I first worked with her. She'd been a singer and dancer and had got quite weighty at that point but she was adorable-looking and

just heaven to have around. She had a unique quality: she could portray innocence on stage. Not many can do that these days, and Sophie in many ways *was* an innocent. And then Alan put her in something and she got better and better and better. He found something in her and he was looking forward to many, many years of working with Sophie. It was flattering to him, to have something to mould, although the quality must have been there to start with. Alan moulded and polished that, and she was wonderful.

Heather Stoney confirmed that Sophie had been the latest in a line of actresses whose talent was drawn out by Alan over a sequence of roles and that he had felt there was much more to come. Alan explained: 'There are certain people you work with who have bottomless resources and you relish the thought of working with them again because you know they are going to respond. Sophie was also a natural clown who had great warmth as well as talent, and she sang and danced. And was completely barmy as well, completely off-the-wall sense of humour and wondrous to look at.'

Alan himself broke the news of her death to the company in Chichester and the tears in the room included his. The cruellest thing was that, for the show to go on, a substitute had to be recruited at once, and he immediately set about the task with Sarah Hughes. He wrote an obituary for Sophie and later led a memorial event in Scarborough, speaking the tribute himself. Mick Hughes, who lives just outside Chichester, confirms that on this occasion anyway Alan really felt the punches. Alan's phrase now is the classically understated agreement that Sophie's death 'took the fun out of it', but fun is close to being a synonym for life in Alan's book. He cancelled a trip to Singapore involving some lucrative lectures, helped Mick sail his boat to a new mooring in Chichester Harbour, and didn't write or direct anything else until he left the theatre in Westwood for the new building. It was two years before a completely new adult play would be seen from him. He wouldn't return to the musical form until tempted by a collaboration with Denis King several years later. Amid all this he did spot that he and John Pattison had taken a pounding in the reviews of *A Word From Our Sponsor*. Plans for a tour of *Dreams From a Summer House*, produced by the Theatre of Comedy, were quietly dropped.

2 : Almost a Purpose-built Theatre

The Scarborough Odeon is a rather splendid 1930s art deco cinema opposite the station and at the crossroads where the A64 from Leeds and York turns into the town's central thoroughfare of Newborough. Apart from a laughable absence of parking, it could hardly be better placed. Its auditorium had seated 1,700, a much bigger capacity than any small-town or even large-city cinema would now be expected to put in front of one screen. It had finally closed as a cinema in 1988 and Scarborough Theatre Development Trust – effectively Alan himself, his chairman Charles McCarthy and vice-chairman Viscount Downe – acquired the lease of the council-owned building with their own money. The eventual cost of converting it to a theatre with two auditoria, dressing-rooms, workshops, offices and a restaurant was put at £5.2 million. The development trust raised over half of this from the private sector, with an appeal launched in June 1993. Malcolm Hebden, taking his turn to rattle the bucket before a performance of the family Australian play *Two Weeks With the Queen*, began: 'I would like to make it clear that I am not the queen in question.' Rarely have appeals been so entertaining.

The European Commission, the Foundation for Sport and the Arts, and the Arts Council Lottery provided the rest of the money, but because the lottery system only came into force after fund-raising (and building work) had started, its contribution at £1.5 million was a much lower proportion (under 30 per cent) of the total cost than is the case with most lottery-funded arts institutions. However, the Arts Council, through the lottery, was still in a position to impose conditions for its support, and these included the development of services such as an education department. What it did not do – as it would have a year or two later – was to insist on quality architecture. Ayckbourn had been consulting his friend Harry Osborne (who was also supervising work on the house in Longwestgate) throughout the years he had grown impatient with the limitations of Westwood. They had wandered into the Odeon to look at the possibilities long before the lease came on the market. Harry had thought there was 'a tremendous case' for it and encouraged the quick move to buy what was otherwise surely destined to become a supermarket. There was strong local opposition to the plan to convert it to a theatre, but the local authority, knowing Westwood had to return to its educational calling, supported it.

Then Charles McCarthy discovered that the firm of Shepherd Design and Build, by not employing a separate architect, could offer a significantly cheaper price on the conversion. Mac had no ties with Harry, and as a hard-nosed businessman would not have let them sway his decision even had they existed. Alan had to recognise the force of the financial argument. And Shepherd Design and Build did do the job cheaply. Because they had never built a theatre before, mistakes were made: a steel beam was put in place only 5 feet 6 inches (1.6 m) above the mouths of the voms – which would have meant using very short actors or allowing for very bad headaches. Although Harry Osborne says he pointed this out on the plans, nobody took any notice and once built, it had to be cut out. Alan, who visited the site every day, says he had to stop a wall being built across a thoroughfare. Osborne regrets the loss of some things he had hoped to provide – including an area where the story of the country's art deco Odeons could have been told – and he believes that the site was treated as an industrial unit rather than an organic development. He gives Mac credit for telephoning him personally rather than writing a letter to tell him Shepherd Design and Build had got the job. He even admires the skill with which Mac beat him down when he went to claim payment for all the work he had done in advance, storming across the room and picking up the telephone to cancel the opening ceremony when Harry wouldn't agree to cut his fee still further: 'A wonderful bit of play-acting. The climax for me was that on the last of the series of "first nights" at the new theatre, he introduced me to his wife (for about the twentieth time) as the architect who had turned the theatre down. I ditched them! And he said it with such aplomb and conviction I just stood open-mouthed.'

The relationship between Mac McCarthy and Alan Ayckbourn is an interesting one. Ayckbourn unquestionably profits from Mac's drive, money and business contacts. It also helps that Mac likes his plays. Their mind-sets are so different that they drive each other mad sometimes, but Mac, capable of a good rant himself, is unfazed by Alan's outbursts. His techniques aren't subtle but he gets on with things. The strength of their relationship is reflected in the fact that the 400-seat theatre-in-the-round and the 165-seat end-stage theatre (named after Mac) both opened on time, with plays ready to go into them. The weakness is that they had not achieved the breakthrough in revenue funding – the annual subsidy for play production – that would have made it possible to run the theatre at full throttle for its first year. Nor did they do so in 2000–1, despite a gradual improvement and the promise of a further increase as a result of the Arts Council's theatre review in 2002.

The history of lottery funding for the arts in Britain is a sorry story of a five-or six-year period when money was available to put buildings up but not to run them. Almost everybody knew this would happen but nobody had the will or the power to do anything about it until a couple of years after the change of government in 1997. The Conservatives basically didn't believe in subsidy coming from taxation. The arts community for years resisted the replacement of state funds (which it thought could be guaranteed) with lottery funds (which could not).

The situation was made worse because companies with new buildings were invariably being asked to do more than in the old. In Scarborough it wasn't just a matter of a new education programme. At Westwood the café/bar area had been used as a makeshift studio theatre. Lunchtime and late-night performances had been staged with minimal decor and effects. A larger main auditorium (a third bigger than Westwood) and a purpose-built separate theatre would need more actors, more stage management, more front-of-house staff, more production staff. All this, according to finance director Keith McFarlane, was flagged up four years before the theatre was due to open. When Stephen Wood (by then heading the National Theatre press office) returned to Scarborough to be interviewed for the post of general administrator of the new theatre he asked the interviewing panel if the money was in place to run the new operation. The regional arts board said in effect: 'Oh yes, no problem.' This is not denied by the board, now called Yorkshire Arts. For the last year in Westwood, the grant from Yorkshire was £211,200. The initial offer for the first year of the new theatre was exactly the same, increased after what Keith McFarlane calls 'a bit of arm-twisting' to £236,000. The arts board says it signalled that it always intended to increase the grant, though 'clearly not enough in relation to the scale of change'. Scarborough Borough Council and North Yorkshire County Council also made increases, slightly larger ones in percentage terms, so that the total subsidy towards running the theatre, as opposed to building it, increased from £397,410 to £447,700. To run both auditoria through the year would have needed at least £750,000 in subsidy (the theatre argues it should have had more). Ayckbourn was furious at what he perceived as a simple betrayal and openly stated that he would run the theatre 'at full throttle' from April until October, as he had about half the money he needed, and then if it had to close the funding bodies would be clearly to blame. The regional arts board saw this as irresponsible blackmail and no immediate progress was made. Stephen Wood decided to appeal over the head of the regional arts board to Alan's former producer at the Round House in London, Thelma Holt, now chairing the Drama Panel of the Arts Council of England (ACE), and to the drama director of ACE, Anna Stapleton. Holt and Stapleton worked with the regional arts board, uneasily at times, to come up with a formula which drew attention to the lottery's relatively small contribution to the building cost of the theatre and persuaded ACE to make £325,000 available from the lottery to that year's running costs. This of course broke all the principles of keeping lottery money and revenue funding separate, though there was an attempt to disguise this by calling it Capital Enhancement. Relations were, to put it gently, delicate between the Arts Council and all ten English regional arts boards, which were committed to achieving as much executive power within their regions as they could while acknowledging ACE's overall strategic responsibility. Roger Lancaster, chief executive of the regional arts board, and his chairman, Sir Ernest Hall, were in their different ways now quite as angry as Alan, Mac McCarthy, Stephen Wood and Keith McFarlane. The theatre had been kept open for the time being, and its total subsidy in its first year of £772,700 made a benchmark for the negotiation of future funding. But the scheme introduced by Holt and Stapleton would provide extra money from the lottery only for a further two years. When it ran out, the regional arts board most certainly worked towards increasing its own contribution and increasing the contributions of Scarborough and North Yorkshire: in 1999–2000, Yorkshire Arts allocated £410,000 to the Stephen Joseph Theatre, Scarborough £211,616 and North Yorkshire £51,500. This totals £673,116, or almost £100,000 *less* than the eventual, not-quite-adequate total for that first year. But this is a better situation than seemed possible when the big crisis came in the winter of 1996, six months after the new theatre had opened. North Yorkshire proposed to cut all its arts funding altogether, protesting to the Conservative government that its public spending cuts were imperilling North Yorkshire's good reputation for education. The same winter, when Alan's latest children's play, *The Champion of Paribanou*, would deliver its Arabian Nights-style charm and excitement to thousands of local children, one councillor in Scarborough prompted an unforgettable newspaper headline, 'Luvvies or Lavvies', by suggesting it was better to close the theatre than a public lavatory. Fortunately the council as a whole did not see this as an either/or issue, and the regional arts board came into its own with some aggressive negotiation with North Yorkshire; but the county's subsidy was only restored to just over half what it had contributed before. By the first week in January (with the new financial year only 12 weeks away) it was clear that support would continue in both councils, with overwhelming backing emerging from the Scarborough vote. But by then, having mounted a buoyant 500-plus performances in the season so far, Alan had been forced to take the decision to close the theatre for the last quarter of the financial year. From the beginning of January until the end of March, he wrote to Alan Strachan, 'sadly there will be no more pattering of Thespian feet'. And for the next year, 1997–8, the 13 productions he had originally planned would have to be cut down to 8, one fewer than he had mounted in the old theatre. 'Why move, I ask myself.' The question of funding is one that can still turn his face dark and get his fingers drumming on whatever surface is to hand.

The case against subsidy has always been threefold. Extreme Conservative ideology argues that it is bad in principle. Cash-strapped individual authorities argue that the money they are allowed to raise covers only their statutory obligations, so little or nothing can be spared for 'inessentials'. And some people who accept the principle of subsidy say the arts are so inefficiently managed that they don't deserve help while others complain that they are not popular enough or of high enough quality. These are complex and sometimes contradictory points of view, and it would be a nimble administration that was able to refute all of them all the time. But there is also confusion about what subsidy is for. When a North Yorkshire councillor asked: 'How do we know these theatres [Scarborough and Harrogate] are being run properly?' they sent in PriceWaterhouse to investigate; the theatre got a clean bill of health, but the question was indeed asked, based on the figures, 'Why don't you just do the plays of Alan Ayckbourn?' Because that's not what it is paid to do. Subsidy exists to help institutions provide precisely what market forces do not. The job is not to make and distribute a cash profit but to enhance the cultural life of the community, while respecting the demands of accountability in the use of public money and breaking even overall.

The Stephen Joseph has a pretty good record on this, rarely going into deficit and providing extraordinary value for money, partly because its resources include an extremely popular playwright-director but also because its financial controls are strict and its small staff is committed and talented. There are figures to support this. To fill a 400-seat theatre from a population of around 40,000 requires that 1 per cent of Scarborians attend every night. The same proportion of paying customers in Leeds or Sheffield would fill a theatre seating 5,000, in Manchester or Birmingham 10,000 or more. Each performance in the opening year at the Stephen Joseph was subsidised to the tune of about £1,500; each performance that year at West Yorkshire Playhouse in Leeds, widely regarded as a model of good and exciting practice in regional producing theatre, was subsidised at more than double that rate. Scarborough played to 80,000 people that year, twice the population of the town, and increased its box office income to nearly half a million pounds (double the final year at Westwood); West Yorkshire Playhouse – acknowledged as setting high standards – attracted almost 180,000 against a Leeds population of half a million.

Meanwhile Yorkshire Arts worked hard to rebuild the relationship with its most famous client, although its officers plainly felt they had been misunderstood and both sides felt misrepresented. The timing of the lottery application (when the appeal designed to raise money privately had stalled) led to a too-speedy assessment of it. The relatively low cost of the conversion gave a misleading idea of the likely running cost: energy costs, for instance, were got badly wrong (a point from which Harry Osborne might derive a certain wry satisfaction). The business plan was, in their term, 'underdeveloped'. In fact the lottery cash had been needed urgently to stop the builders leaving the site after two thirds of the work had been done and the privately raised money had run out.

Yorkshire and Humberside Arts had six producing theatres to support – three of them in serious difficulty, and the other three at least registering anxiety by 1996. To find money for Scarborough would have meant taking it from elsewhere, and for a newly empowered organisation it sometimes seems frankly boring to use your limited resources to support the most established artist around. Ayckbourn also suffered from a trend in arts funding away from judging quality (which was deemed a subjective issue by the bureaucracy) in favour of seeking out more measurable criteria: accessibility, social ambition, conspicuous innovation, business plans agreed with funders, coherent policy-making. These are all desirable in themselves but as the servants and enablers of art rather than the key objectives. They are also more obviously applicable to large urban centres. And they involve additional staff to devise and monitor appropriate policies. As I write, the role of the regional arts boards is being streamlined by the entrepreneurial new chairman of the Arts Council, Gerry Robinson. The series of hoops that a succession of bureaucrats has devised for artists to jump through is being dismantled. But what other criterion can a creative artist have than the work he wants to do? Government new money for the regional theatres has not been matched by new resources for local authorities who are struggling to meet the responsibilities imposed on them. Scarborough Town Council has made the theatre the cornerstone of its cultural strategy from 2002 but had to be dissuaded from cutting its grant again, along with everything else.

It is widely known that Ayckbourn dips into his own pocket to help the theatre. He takes an annual salary of £25,000, then uses it as a contingency fund to help out individual productions during the year. For example, the false bodies used in the revival of *Body Language* in 1999 cost £14,000, with a further £11,000 for spare limbs ('They go through arms and legs,' Keith McFarlane told me). He pays the salaries of some staff. He supplies gadgetry, paying for expensive stage equipment for his Christmas 2000 family show *Whenever* which now belongs to the theatre. He also entertains at his own expense and has invested his own money to provide congenial accommodation for guest directors. When he wins prizes he gives any cash involved straight to the theatre. He has made speeches to conferences and – after a lifetime of subjecting marriage to savage comic scrutiny – given his blessing to couples who get married in the theatre; all boost the theatre's income. In 1999 he estimated his total contribution at around £75,000 a year, but it can be argued that some of this expenditure would not be thought necessary by other cash-starved organisations – although it adds to the attractiveness of the theatre as a place to work and a place to see plays. Some of it goes on work which is very specifically for him rather than the theatre, such as casting his West End productions. A more serious argument is that this supports the line: 'Oh well he can afford to bail out the theatre himself if it's in difficulty.' A letter to the *Scarborough Evening News* at the end of 1996 began:

> It's high time Alan Ayckbourn and his ilk realised that not many people, rightly or wrongly, want to watch live theatre and if he still insists Scarborough should have a theatre, then let him pay for it as the rest of us have to. Otherwise close it down.

The fact that Alan's plays, produced in London and around the world, are a bigger 'industry' than the Stephen Joseph Theatre may militate against its getting taken as seriously as it should be as an organisation. A very successful week for the touring revival of *Bedroom Farce* in Guildford in 2000 almost wiped out that year's mounting deficit. No other theatre except perhaps John Godber's Hull Truck (which is in a much larger city) operates in comparable circumstances and funding bodies don't really know how to handle or appraise a theatre which, they think, might not be viable without one man; they could make it so. A Scarborough opposition councillor argued in 1999 that the Stephen Joseph was a commercial operation, a kind of development workshop for Alan's commercial enterprise. It would be very foolish of Ayckbourn to use it this way. There are many bigger workshops where he could earn more. He has never been short of offers. But the criticisms from within Scarborough that occasionally hit the newspaper headlines are usually from minority sources. Alan gets cross when the borough fails to include the theatre in its tourist brochures, but he generally gets pretty solid local support.

3 : *By Jeeves*

In spite of the cash crisis, Ayckbourn was personally buoyant when the company moved into the new theatre, seven years after the idea of buying it had first come up. The actual timing was the traditional close-run thing, with the theatre licence coming from the Town Hall two hours before the first performance. Because the last play at the Library Theatre had been *Just Between Ourselves*, Alan decided to close Westwood with it as well, with Malcolm Hebden playing Neil again, 20 years on, directed this time by Robin Herford. On the last night, Alan staged the opening of *Mr Whatnot*, the play originally written for Stoke and crucified in London, which he had revived as the first show at Westwood. This sentimental journey was intensified by the knowledge that Malcolm Hebden was leaving the company after almost seven years as associate director, having been in Scarborough for another spell before that as an actor.

Hebden's relationship with Ayckbourn was intriguing because the discord in it was that of two creative men. Hebden has had the longest working association with Ayckbourn of anyone, thus far, apart from Heather Stoney. In the heyday of variety they would have made a fine double act, bound together in a mixture of love and loathing, reconciling their opposite natures for the duration of the performance. Alan is tall, Malcolm short. Alan is enthusiastically heterosexual, Malcolm always says he is a (sadly) inactive homosexual. Alan is public-school-educated middle-class and the child of artists, Malcolm working-class, his father a chemical lavatory salesman and his mother a barmaid. Alan remains a southerner in speech and manner, Malcolm is audibly northern. Malcolm hates cricket and rock music and sometimes enjoys a miserable persona: 'Smile, Malcolm,' someone will say, noticing his down-turned mouth. 'What's there to smile about?' comes back in a deliberately flattened Lancashire accent. Even his cat is miserable, perhaps because Alan's cat used to beat it up. The critical personality difference is that while both are loyal in practice, Malcolm is open and very forthright in his criticisms and disagreements, whereas Alan is more inclined to go silent until his feelings erupt – and, when he has disgorged verbal lava on the surrounding slopes, the earth closes over again and he does not, certainly in public, return to his complaints and criticisms. What unites them is a fundamental belief in full theatres, a sense of the seriousness with which theatre should be created and executed, and the importance of giving audiences value for money; which is why they both condemn actors who 'corpse' or make others do it. Not that this stopped Alan teasing Malcolm for his puritanical work ethic. As a character actor Malcolm blossomed in Alan's work (in which, apart from the genre plays, all the parts are character parts) and as a director he complemented his boss well. In 1984 when Alan's energies were taken up with putting *Intimate Exchanges* into the West End, Malcolm intermittently ran the theatre, supervising the run of *A Chorus of Disapproval* and directing J. B. Priestley's *The Linden Tree* as well as playing *The Last of the Red Hot Lovers* by Neil Simon, a fine Malvolio for Robin Herford in *Twelfth Night*, and the title role in Simon Gray's *Butley*.

He adds some very specific detail to the picture of Ayckbourn's qualities as a director: 'If you have a problem, you can guarantee he'll try and make you solve it yourself, because that's always the best way, but if you're really stuck he always has the answer, he can always do it for you. And he will always explore the alternatives, which is a terrific thing for a director to do, because by the time you've finished you've explored every aspect of it.' But working in Ayckbourn's shadow can be curious. The 1990 children's play *This Is Where We Came In* was 'blocked' by Alan and then Malcolm was told to get on with rehearsals; actors who had been ready to try anything became a bit more recalcitrant the minute Alan was out of earshot. In the course of the show Cecily Hobbs had to carry a very stocky frog – Timothy Kightley – upstairs to the Princess's bedroom. One Saturday morning her back gave way and Malcolm telephoned Alan to ask what to do. Alan simply said: 'Well, get the frog to carry her then.' In the performance, the story-teller said that the maid would then carry the frog upstairs. Hobbs took a look at Kightley and signalled 'No way', then she climbed on a table and on to the frog's back and he carried her upstairs. Malcolm says: 'It was a wonderful laugh. Actually it was much better. Not only had it solved a problem, but it had added something.' He also recalls Alan responding to a polite 'How are you?' with 'Oh, I wish I could get in a cupboard and jump out and surprise myself', in which you seem to hear the bored child speaking. Then in the next breath, Malcolm told me: 'He never imposes a way of working on anybody because he has the maturity to know that, to get the best out of somebody, you've got to let them come along at their own pace. He directs by stealth.' But Ayckbourn's style and Hebden's diverge sharply at the end of rehearsals. However badly you feel you want to talk to Alan at the close he is gone; Malcolm, Alan thinks, talks to the cast too much, but Malcolm sees it as part of a director's role to be something of a social worker to his company. Alan really wants nothing to do with all that – other people's love affairs, abortions, nervous breakdowns, bereavements are a horrible embarrassment to him. So Malcolm would be hospital-visiting, arranging for flowers to be sent, providing sandwiches. When a London cast fell out with each other in a big way, Alan wouldn't go down to sort them out. Malcolm would, and he was rewarded by being allowed to stay at the Ritz. (When he called the company to a meeting, they sat miles apart from each other all over the stalls. Malcolm tried to jump on-stage, failed; failed again; and again. When he was eventually lifted up bodily by a big stage manager, they all burst out laughing: problem at least half solved.)

But Malcolm was one of the very few people who would stand up to Alan on matters other than budgeting and they had terrible arguments. Sometimes it was over the choice of new plays, when Alan – anxious to keep up the commitment to finding new writers and giving them a chance to develop as well as doing new plays by more established ones – would sometimes unilaterally choose an inferior play and then make Malcolm direct it. Malcolm is also committed to new plays but believed some of them simply shouldn't have been done. In one case he threw a chair at an actor (who threw one back) in frustration at being asked to do what he thought was the impossible. He says now he should of course have thrown it at Alan. After they had both cried a lot, he and the actor made it up when, a few minutes later in the rehearsal, the actor had a line of dialogue asking someone to sit down and there wasn't a chair to be seen. Eventually the company suggested to Malcolm that he stay away from rehearsals and they do the show on their own, and he agreed. He doesn't believe Alan ever found out.

At the beginning of 1995 they had an unusually spectacular row. Alan may have been on edge because he was about to go into rehearsal on *A Word From Our Sponsor* or, more likely, because Keith McFarlane had just returned from heart surgery. Alan, true to form, had never visited him, though of course Heather had. At a management meeting they were discussing how to market David Mamet's ferocious response to militant feminism and political correctness in American universities, *Oleanna*. Alan wanted its 'selling' to an adult audience but because it was set in a university Malcolm (who was to direct) volunteered to give a talk to older students. According to Malcolm, Alan thought he was interfering with the marketing department and told him to mind his own business 'and do what you're paid to do'. Malcolm said all right, he would – he wasn't paid much anyway (£12,000 a year) and stormed out. It is very possible that Alan was only defending his marketing staff – 'You either defend people or you get rid of them,' he says. The issue hardly seems big enough for a major, arms-whirling, white-faced row between artistic director and associate director. Once an impasse is reached, Ayckbourn doesn't have the managerial resources to sort them out. Naturally anti-authoritarian himself, he can be rather clumsy if his own authority has to be imposed. Mostly he gets his way because he has the best ideas and he has created a mood of confidence and consent.

The move to the new theatre in 1996 was seen by Hebden as an opportune moment to depart, as he was also anxious to look after his ailing mother. He does not, in fact, admire all Ayckbourn's plays, disliking anything (by anyone) set in the future, and he voices heretical thoughts about theatre-in-the-round. But he also regards Alan not only as a genius but a man whose generous belief in the right to fail allowed him (Hebden) to try himself out as a director. This of course is Ayckbourn's maintenance of the great tradition in which Stephen Joseph allowed him the right to fail a generation before. At their contrasting best they did work well together and Hebden, like Robin Herford, has not achieved the 'profile' in the wider British theatre his talent deserves because he has spent so much of his career in Scarborough, and probably thought he would stay for ever. Alan couldn't understand how somebody who had done so much of the hard work didn't want to stay for the fun of the new building. He even admits to being disappointed when Hebden decided to leave, and 'rather hurt'.

So there were bitter-sweet feelings that last night at Westwood. Alan had wanted to lead the whole company up the hill, past the station and across the road into the foyer of the new theatre for a glass of champagne. This idea was blocked by Mac McCarthy so they stayed down at Westwood and all got very drunk until Mac fell over a trayful of glasses.

Part of the excitement of the move was to do with the sense that Alan was finally laying a ghost. The official version was that Andrew Lloyd Webber had pestered him to revise and revive their joint disaster, *Jeeves*, but Ayckbourn had long suggested doing it again to prove that in a small-scale production it could work. In fact, *By Jeeves* – the new title – was also a substantially new show. Alan's book dispensed with actual story-lines from the original Wodehouse and instead provided a new story of a recognisably Wodehousian nature for identifiably Wodehousian characters.

Alan had persuaded Andrew to collaborate on some new songs. His method with the lyrics was to draft a dummy version, establishing the scansion and the rhyming pattern, which Andrew would then set and return for Alan to refine and polish. He recalls giving Lloyd Webber the title phrases of the stomping chorus 'By George! By Jove! By Jeeves!' and the composer responding to them at once with a thumping little tune, singing them over and over again at dinner to the growing impatience of his wife Madeleine. Andrew came up to Yorkshire, nominally for rehearsals, but actually to indulge his passion for Victorian churches while Alan got on with the work.

There was a whole series of 'first nights' as groups of different degrees of importance were invited to see the dream-made-reality. The press night was 1 May and I doubt if any other theatre has opened to more media goodwill. This is partly a tribute to the affection with which Ayckbourn himself is regarded, partly to the good-natured efficiency with which Jeannie Swales actually dealt with the press, and partly to a physically welcoming building: brave new neon outside, peach-coloured walls within. True, you had to climb a lot of stairs (though there is a lift for the disabled) and cross a bridge over an atrium to reach the larger theatre. And some thought it too cosy, the finish less intricate and subtle than an ideal realisation of art deco. But it reflected the essential warmth and potentially intense environment for the theatre experience sought by Alan and the man after whom the theatre is named. The large auditorium had been designed to meet as closely as possible the specifications laid down by Stephen Joseph: even the very front row of seats is raised a few inches above the acting floor, the rest are raked more steeply than in the stalls of a proscenium theatre but not at such an angle or distance that you see only the heads of far-off actors. The sense that all members of the audience are part of a single unit isn't sustained when the house is not very full and we seem to be dotted about the auditorium like the first meeting of a singles' dating group. But when it is full – as it was then – you sit down with a sense of anticipation which is unique to theatres where your fellow customers reflect your excitement back at you.

There is some very sophisticated machinery below the stage, in theory permitting a full set to be whisked down and stored while another is put in place, making a speedy change of play in repertory much more feasible, and cheaper. But for the unbroken run of *By Jeeves* which opened the theatre this was not relevant. *By Jeeves* opens with what looks like a child's cardboard toy car. All that money spent and they can't afford a decent set and props, we thought. But of course the car (which was actually rather more cunningly made than it seemed) was Alan's way of reminding us from the start that theatre is about the collective imagination of actors and audience. Similar devices included the seemingly simple ladder with which Bertie Wooster had to burgle a country-house bedroom. Rather than have him disappear up into the state-of-the-art lighting grid, the ladder performed a controlled tip forward on a fulcrum as he got towards the top so that he played the scene safely and visibly just above the stage. It wasn't universally well reviewed, but the vast majority of the audience patently had a good time. Andrew Lloyd Webber had stopped just short of pastiche and the essential unseriousness of the story – in which Jeeves arranges for Bertie to play a completely silent banjo – was well reflected in it. Stephen Pacey (Bertie) and Malcolm Sinclair (Jeeves) were well matched and, though rather better-looking than one imagines the originals, utterly sympathetic to be with.

The show moved on almost instantly to the West End and then reappeared in a new production in America. After its opening in Connecticut in October Ayckbourn wrote to Alan Strachan: 'We had a great time. The cast were super (as people and performers) and worked like mad and came up with a *By Jeeves* which was overall every bit as good as the British one.'

The McCarthy Theatre opened immediately afterwards with Robin Herford's production of *Forty Years On*, by Alan Bennett, and was also now fulfilling its function as a specialist cinema, partly to carry on the Odeon tradition and partly to meet a need (the town had no other cinema). Because nobody really knew about cinema projection, the films got off to the least technically efficient start, the first few resembling, according to Alan, some sort of Hall of Mirrors. As a shape, the McCarthy has a conventional end-stage which is rather wide for the size of the auditorium and rather shallow: there are times when the audience's heads turn in unison from side to side as if watching a tennis match. But of course this is just the right shape for a cinema and it is far from unserviceable as a theatre – just a 'very tricky space', according to Ayckbourn. Between them the two auditoria presented an interestingly mixed programme of plays that first season. It also included Chekhov and Goldoni (in free versions by Michael Frayn and Robert David MacDonald), revivals of two contemporary plays by writers who might be thought of as belonging to the Royal Court stable in Stephen Jeffreys and Martin Crimp, and the première of Vanessa Brooks's *Love Me Slender*, the third and most commercially successful play by a writer who had developed thanks to the theatre. Ayckbourn also revised and revived his Cluedo whodunnit, *It Could Be Any One of Us*. This was another revisiting of a less successful piece to find out if it was any good. It transferred to Chichester where Charles Spencer wrote in the *Daily Telegraph* that if audiences listened very carefully they would hear the sound of Alan Ayckbourn scraping the bottom of the barrel. He urged Alan to take a rest and recharge his batteries.

The hydraulic lift under the stage of the Round Theatre was also presenting problems. It was 18 months after the theatre's opening before the company felt confident enough about its operating properly to programme the repertoire season for which it had been planned into the building, enabling visitors to Scarborough to see a number of plays in the same week or even over a weekend. The problem was chiefly with its safety devices, although a fail-safe mechanism meant that it never endangered anyone; it simply stopped, and the nearest specialist engineer was 100 miles away in Sheffield.

The restaurant – also close to Alan's heart – likewise got off to an uncertain start and remedial action had to be taken after a year. It now pays its way and business holds up even when the theatre is less well attended. But the change of Scarborough theatregoing habits needed for it to make a substantial contribution to the theatre's budget is comparable with that initiated by Stephen Joseph's opening of repertory theatre in the Library in 1955. Ayckbourn's life in producing theatre has covered a period when the job of running one has changed from being 'just' a matter of inspirational artistic leadership to heading a multifarious organisation whose functions include finding a menu for a marketing officer to sell.

In one small but significant detail, however, Alan has found a management device for at least retaining the sense of a tightly knit 'guerrilla band' that Stephen created then. If you want a cup of tea or coffee as a member of the company at the Stephen Joseph Theatre you *have* to go to the Green Room to make it. No kettles are permitted in offices or workshops. And will you please see to your own washing-up? Apart from the sociability implicit in this, there is a practical advantage. When people from different departments of the theatre meet regularly, everybody knows what everybody else is up to, and the chances of something being built the wrong shape or painted the wrong colour are lessened. This is one of the minor secrets of Ayckbourn's technical rehearsals going so smoothly. Everybody knows as much about what he wants as he does.

On 11 February 1997, Alan Ayckbourn was knighted by the queen 'for services to the theatre'. Heather and the boys went with him. Nobody got his name wrong this time, ten years to the day after his investiture with the CBE, but nobody in this slightly more exalted company asked for his autograph either. He was the first playwright to be knighted since the man suddenly eclipsed by the revolution in British theatre in the mid-1950s, Terence Rattigan, though Tom Stoppard and then David Hare followed soon afterwards. John Major's government, in its last months, seems to have heeded the recommendation of John Hodgson, who kept a copy of his short letter urging the honour. A newspaper article suggesting that Tom Stoppard was knighted before him is one of the few things Ayckbourn has ever written to the press to correct.

Chapter 10

Still new places to go

1 : *Things We Do For Love*

In 1997 Alan came up with an irrefutable argument for not accepting the economic argument for closing the little McCarthy auditorium and pouring all the Stephen Joseph Theatre's resources into the larger Round Theatre. His own new play could only be performed in the McCarthy.

Things We Do For Love was only the second play he had written for an end-stage (*Haunting Julia* had been the first) and typically he latched on to a staging opportunity which the Round couldn't give him but which had appealed for a long time: the chance to show three different levels of a house at the same time. He had done this in the context of farce in *Taking Steps* for which the audience is invited to imagine the three floors; now he wanted to use the realism of a triple-decker set for a play which was also more emotionally naturalistic. *Things We Do For Love* marks out new territory for Ayckbourn yet again: instead of exploring the unhapppiness and casual, unconscious cruelty into which most of his married characters have slumped, he confronts the start and finish of relationships. This is, uncoincidentally I think, the first time the word 'fuck' comes into an Ayckbourn play and the first time physical domestic violence breaks out.

Most of the play takes place in the sitting-room of Barbara's house, and this occupies most of the set. But below it we can just see the ceiling of the bedroom of the basement flat beneath her. And above, the floor of the bedroom of the flat upstairs. It is part of Stephen Joseph Theatre lore, and probably true, that when some punters took their seats and found they could see only part of the attic and basement they insisted on being seated elsewhere – only to discover the view was no better from any other seat. Barbara, fortyish and a woman who has devoted her life to her work and, even if she barely acknowledges it, her boss, is a woman virtually without sexual experience; there was something messy and unpleasant with the caretaker's son at boarding-school and that was it. Her life is very neat and so is the flat. When the play begins she is about to let the upstairs flat for a few weeks to her old schoolfriend Nikki and the man Nikki is about to marry, Hamish. Nikki has been in serious relationships before, and they have tended towards disaster, with her being beaten up or locked in cupboards. In the basement is Gilbert, postman, handyman, amateur painter and passionate admirer of Barbara, whose old clothes he is supposed to collect and take to the charity shop from time to time. In fact, as we eventually discover, he wears them; and on that ceiling we can just glimpse, but Barbara never sees, he is painting a huge mural of Barbara in the nude. When Hamish arrives, he and Barbara take an instant dislike to each other – he is a vegetarian for a start, and Scottish (she is equally prejudiced against the Welsh and Irish. And the French) – but it is such a palpable feeling that you guess slightly before they do that it is there to hide a quite different kind of passion. When they do eventually kiss we recognise some familiar Ayckbourn theatrical language because Nikki is in the bath and we can hear her singing the jolly old school song. They rush upstairs and have extravagant sex, but what we see is only four legs on a bed as shoes and clothes are discarded and loud moaning noises ensue. The innocent, infinitely betrayable Nikki is by now substituting extremely rude words for the original song. The savagery of the irony is extended to the scene where the guilty pair sit down – at Barbara's insistence – to tell Nikki they are having an affair: she has been happily digging out the old photographs of school, where she idolised the older Barbara. Nikki charges upstairs and cuts up all Hamish's suits and ties before leaving with her small suitcase. Gilbert also reveals his little secret and, while drunk, falls from the scaffolding he has in place for painting the ceiling. Barbara and Hamish get into their fist fight after he has flung the photograph album away and demolished the shelving she had put up herself (an effect that didn't work the night I watched, causing mortified fury for both Ayckbourn and Roger Glossop) and they finish only when both are quite badly hurt. By the last page, although they agree it is best to go their separate ways, it is as though too much is at stake now to give up. Ayckbourn has said that we shouldn't really believe they will make much of a go of the relationship – both are too used to having their own way and their own space, and I don't think we like either of them as much as poor Nikki and Gilbert – but it is hard not to hope for the best for them as the lights fade.

Where did this all come from? Ayckbourn is so specific about the way Nikki reacts to Hamish's confession that he is now in love with Barbara – shallow panting, followed by doubling up as if she has been punched in the stomach, then short staccato cries of pain, growing in volume and intensity – that you think he must at least have witnessed something of the sort. As for the cutting up of clothes, Caroline Smith's sister had done precisely that to the wardrobe of a departing husband in a case rather well covered by the newspapers and certainly discussed by Caroline with Alan. But apart from these details, the explicit nature of the whole play and its directness in dealing with subjects that Ayckbourn had previously seemed too diffident to confront suggest a real change of attitude. Was he at last ready to use the more visceral material from his own occasional 'flings' years before? The play opened in April 1997 shortly after his fifty-eighth birthday, with Joanna van Gyseghem (Barbara), Sally Giles (Nikki), Cameron Stewart (Hamish) and Barry McCarthy (Gilbert). In the London production which opened in March 1998, Jane Asher played Barbara, Serena Evans Nikki, Steven Pacey Hamish; McCarthy remained as Gilbert. The play won the biggest playwriting prize there has been in Britain, the short-lived Lloyds Private Banking Playwright of the Year award, and also went on to tour very successfully with Belinda Lang leading the cast. It was an unusually tiring show to perform, according to Jane Asher, because (apart from the fighting) it was openly emotional. Crying is always exhausting, she points out, whether it's your job or your life. There was also much rushing upstairs. One night the door to Barbara's flat jammed solid and Hamish and Gilbert had to ad-lib their way in through the bathroom. The London listings magazine *Time Out* hated the play, arguing that it said that domestic violence was amusing and that a man had only to beat up a difficult woman to make her fall into bed with him. This criticism naturally made Asher very anxious but these last two events actually happen the other way round and the fight was painful for everyone. The general press reaction was that Ayckbourn had at last 'returned to form'.

In a manner highly satisfying to the middlebrow tabloid newspapers (he has never really interested the 'red tops', the *Mirror* and the *Sun*) *Things We Do For Love* provided a neat label for the next episode in his private life. He was still technically married to Chris after 38 years. However, most people by now assumed that Alan and Heather were man and wife. For the *Daily Express* the biggest story of the day was the news that Alan and Chris were to divorce. Chris, 'door-stepped' by a reporter, said she was letting Alan go because she loved him; she had offered him a divorce many times before that, but he had always replied that he didn't think he'd get round to marrying again. Heather felt no great need to marry but the knighthood had made the difference. As she saw it: 'I suppose you get to a certain age and it starts to seem silly not to tidy things up.' Because the divorce followed the knighthood each woman could, in due course, call herself

Lady Ayckbourn. Neither, *of course*, takes the title seriously, but just occasionally it might help with a restaurant booking. Heather remains content to be called Heather Stoney, but certainly prefers Lady to Mrs Ayckbourn.

There was never, she recalls, a very romantic proposal, any more than there had been any starburst of emotion when they first got together, and that was over 30 years before. Such things had never really happened in the plays either until *Things We Do For Love*. Alan says their relationship was always based more on a shared perception of things and people, linked humour, mutual respect. 'We neither of us go in for huge rows and slamming doors. We've had a few spats, but nothing major.' Now he said something along the lines of: 'I think it's about time we regularised this,' and Heather replied: 'Well, all right, if you want to sort it out.' He wrote to Chris, who agreed, and the divorce came through by May 1997, which is when the newspapers, by now bored with Labour's election victory, put it on the front pages. Alan and Heather got married in September. A week beforehand Alan thought he might have a bit of Friday off, and wouldn't Roger Glossop and his wife, Charlotte Scott, be nice as witnesses? The Scarborough company was playing at Roger and Charlotte's theatre, the Old Laundry (in Bowness on Windermere), which replicates the layout of Westwood. One of Alan's ways of relaxing is to stay with the Glossops and go for walks. So Heather started ringing round register offices to see if anyone could fit them in. Kendal was too busy but Penrith had a space, so Penrith it was.

On the day, a white limousine turned up, ordered by the Glossops. Other members of the Scarborough company who were staying at the house knew nothing of all this and left, still ignorant. Roger, who habitually fears the worst (he's supported Sheffield United all his life), thought Alan might take one look at the showy white car and stomp off, but he didn't. Heather didn't stop smiling all day. They set off for Penrith and the woman driver took them rather a long way round. Glossop began to wonder if she knew where they were going. They got to Penrith with about ten minutes to spare and the driver certainly didn't know where the register office was. They asked at a garage and got directed across the town but couldn't find it; asked at another, recrossed the town (it isn't big) and were still lost. Roger and Charlotte smiled as if everything were perfectly normal. Alan and Heather smiled, perhaps a little more nervously. And then they spotted a bride marching along the street, with her mother holding up the train of her wedding dress, and they followed her to the door. The ceremony, with just the four of them in the room with the registrar, was very moving, according to Glossop. Ayckbourn, for all his theatrical exploitation of marriage as an institution, was happily posing for the traditional photographs of the signing of the register, saying the words he must have satirised a hundred times, sitting in the car again beaming at people who were looking on not because they knew who he was but because they were in an eye-catching car. The wedding breakfast was in the Sharrow Bay Hotel on Ullswater at a table by the window with a stunning view of Glen Ridding. As Glossop noted, the day had mixed elements of Ayckbournian comic disarray with an unusually happy mood.

2 : *Comic Potential, The Boy Who Fell Into a Book, Gizmo, Cheap and Cheerful*

In the 1997 season Ayckbourn had for the first time included a play by his East Coast writer-director neighbour, John Godber. *Lucky Sods* – about a couple torn apart by the 'luck' of a lottery win – provided the platform for a more active collaboration between the two men the following year, and one of Alan's most ingenious solutions to the problem of limited resources.

One of the attractions of having a permanent company for a whole season is that you can have the actors rehearsing one show while performing another for a single wage packet. The acme of cunning planning would be to use every actor, if possible, right up to the limits allowed by Equity before you have to start to pay overtime. Alan's scheme for the summer of 1998 was a Ten by Ten by Ten season which did just this: ten actors, ten plays, ten writers. Three of the plays would be full-length productions in the Round: his own new play, one by John Godber and one by Tim Firth – a varied comedy programme which was also likely to do good business. The other seven plays included lunchtime, late-night and evening performances in the McCarthy. Five of them were new and the other two very little-known. To give himself and his colleagues the best chance of strong casts, his own play was to have all ten actors in; many more people will commit themselves to a summer in Scarborough if they are to appear in the new Ayckbourn than if they are not. Some of these were playing small parts or doubling them, but he also planned the season so that each had at least one strong part in another play. With ingenious use of the computer, he eventually came up with a performance schedule which meant that only once in the season did the theatre have to pay for an actor to do one performance more than the Equity rules permitted. New Equity rules might have meant there was considerable difficulty in getting the rehearsal schedule to work as effectively, but the actors agreed to waive these, as allowed for in the Equity agreement. It was, moreover, a happy company which worked absolutely to the limit all summer long and delivered a fine season's work.

Alan was in his element devising the schedule and writing and directing his own new play, *Comic Potential*. In its assessment of present trends in the creative media it was in the same genre as *Henceforward . . .* but it also explored the nature of comedy and the way in which our sense of what is funny reflects on whom we can love and what we regard as the kernel of our humanity. It is set in the near future in a television studio where it has become unnecessary to employ actors at all. Carefully programmed robots, known as actoids, can easily perform the limited range of dialogue, expressions and actions required of the average soap opera: the process is comfortably demonstrated in an opening sequence involving a doctor, a distraught mother and an immobile young man in a hospital bed. They may not do it better than actors (the dramatic irony is of course that we watch actors pretending to be more mechanical than they are) but they certainly do it cheaper and without complaint. Another blow has been struck against the trade unions, also ironic in view of the way the Scarborough company had agreed to co-operate in making the season possible. The man reduced to 'directing' this material – effectively giving simple instructions to two technicians with cameras – is a great American film director named Chandler Tate who has fallen foul of studio bosses and is therefore in the double exile of Britain and television. Into his studio comes a young man (innocent Adam Trainsmith) who is the nephew of the television company's owner but also an admirer of the director; he seeks to restore the great days of film-making when the length of a drama was dictated by its content, not the 'slot' it has to fill. And it is this young man who spots that one of the actoids responds to a joke without being programmed to do so. In other words Jacie Triplethree (or JC 333) is at least partially human, sufficiently human to be fallen in love with. On the grounds that this makes it (her) unsuitable for work as an actoid the order is given for her (it) to be melted down. The couple go on the run, taking refuge in – among other places – a brothel. But the play has almost a happy ending when the media magnate, a cross between Rupert Murdoch and Howard Hughes, in a wheelchair, decides to put her in charge of the company. Almost happy, because she learns the language of media 'product' at once and tells young Adam he can make his film but only at the length she prescribes. She has long since overridden her own initial agreement that a sense of humour is a 'fault' in a logical machine, and the strength she now derives from it will enable her to take over the whole show.

The play begins and ends, therefore, as a satire on the business of television in particular and the growing domination of life by computers in general, suggesting an exaggerated future for trends which are already evident, but has a middle section which is a love story and something of a 'road' thriller. Sadly, Jacie tells Adam that she isn't built for actual sexual activity, so there is a limit to how far *Comic Potential* can be pressed into service in support of a theory that Ayckbourn is now writing more overtly about sex than before, although his passing interest in lesbians reappears with due lack of political correctness in the television studio. It does, however, demonstrate a link between sex and comedy and the way in which they form an alliance against the forces of mechanistic logic, whether these are the computers themselves or the people who use them in the vain belief that the world can be sensibly planned. Ayckbourn's own note on the play – quoted in full by Glaap in *Ayckbourn Country* – suggests that it is not so much predicting a future in which machines inherit the earth as trying to catch a moment of change.

The play remembers his own long-ago use of a wildly inappropriate double take, includes a kind of master class on how to do the custard pie slapstick gag and exploits Jacie's discovery of her own voice (out of anger, that other antidote to rationality) by having her scream the ill-understood words she has heard in the television studio: 'Fuck dyke!' But the play is also deftly conscious of the most fundamental contradiction within the human psyche, Ayckbourn's recurrent theme: our longing for paradise and our capacity for spoiling it. It echoes the Pygmalion story in Adam's relationship with the robot, but also the Garden of Eden when he teaches her to read via the opening sequence of the Bible, the only reading material in a hotel bedroom. They start with the Creation and get up to the curse on Woman after the Fall, upon which theological base the male supremacism of Judaism and Christianity is founded: she is given the blame for persuading Adam to eat the fruit of the Forbidden Tree. In the play this is a light and passing moment without discussion, but it allows the audience a lightning-flash glimpse of Adam as Adam and Jacie as Eve, and with that the sinking recognition that the innocent idyll of their love will not be allowed to last. This is not only a classic instance of Ayckbourn disguising the depth of what he has to say, it sums up what I might call the cheerful despair that emerges in the later plays when a fundamentally good-humoured writer addresses the way the delight of new love is poisoned or wears out. There is just a hint of this way back in the relationship between Ginny and Greg in *Relatively Speaking*, but on the whole the first swathe of hits dealt with relationships which were already failing when the plays began and out of which nobody escapes. This is perhaps why they are able to be funnier than plays in which we have, as audiences, hoped for happiness with and for the lovers; it was Ayckbourn's revolution that allowed us to care about as well as laugh at fussy, vulnerable Sarah in *The Norman Conquests* but now he invites us to care first and join the journey to human disappointment.

The critical response, in Scarborough in May 1998 and then in London in October 1999, treated the play partly as a prediction about the future of television (the common mistake, with Ayckbourn, of mistaking the location of the play for the subject) and partly as a vehicle for its actors. Janie Dee, as Jacie, was deservedly named Best Actress in the 1999 *Evening Standard*, Olivier and Critics' Circle Awards for a heartbreakingly comic performance which charted the waters between the machine and the human quite beautifully. The play itself won no awards, despite thin competition, partly because (I think) the critics missed its disguised depth and partly because there is an awkwardness about the change from the satire of the television studio to the tenderness of lovers on the run. This is enhanced by the drawn-out nature of second-half scenes that Ayckbourn enjoys (in a brothel, for instance) but which hold up the narrative energy. He cut a couple of minutes between the Scarborough and London runs but his recent work has only been subjected to the severest script-editing when it has, by his standards, failed on its first outing, whereas in the early days it had to impress a lot more people before it went on in London. But I find it much harder to draw a distinction between the play and Janie Dee's performance than those judges.

Dee is an actress who made her initial reputation in musical theatre, being nominated for an Olivier Award for her supporting role in the National Theatre's production of *Carousel*, and in 1997 had taken the leading female role in *They're Playing Our Song* in Scarborough. But a great hunger to improve and to stretch herself as a 'straight' actress (resenting those jobs, especially in television, where she is only asked to do what she can already do easily) took her to Scarborough in 1992 to play the furious, non-singing ex-wife in *Dreams From a Summer House*. She first thought of Ayckbourn as a kind of guru who might impart to her the kind of wisdom she felt was just waiting to be unlocked. In her first season in Scarborough she had dreams about him, and according to her all the other women in the Ten by Ten by Ten season told her they did too. 'We all fall in love with him a bit,' she says. More confident in her working relationship with him and perhaps more aware of his own lack of confidence, she plucked up the courage, just before *Comic Potential* opened in Scarborough, to ask him what it was about and then she just got the answer: 'It's about a lot of things really.' Between the Scarborough run and rehearsals for the West End she said: 'He doesn't want to answer your questions. He informs you when he chooses. He gave me loads and loads of notes but he doesn't want to discuss character. He tells his stories, anecdotes, parallels and there is a lot of laughter. You're free to experiment – the last thing you should do is to ask permission. In fact it is helpful to be ignorant of certain things to play this part. He wants me to be innocent and very open. After seven months I've begun to feel a bit more clued up.'

Stanislavsky and the 'Method' – teaching that you need to know all you can about a character to play it with the same knowledge and the feeling that the character has of itself – is not much help with robots, and eventually Alan recognised Dee's appetite for learning and gave her the reflections of the American playwright David Mamet to read as a counterbalance to the Russian. Dee responds to the closeness of the Scarborough theatre to its public, in the physical and metaphorical sense. She is moved by Alan's love of theatre rather than of money, even more so by his constant striving to get things right and asking more and more of her. She believes him to be sensitive to character in person and therefore easy to talk to about serious things, which is probably a privilege her own openness and persistence won from him. It would round things off nicely if the part of Jacie had been written for her and the Pygmalion element in it reflected the relationship of audience and star, but it wasn't; her extraordinary ability to give the robot different voices was a bonus he didn't know he was going to get.

Comic Potential ran for nine months in the West End with the American David Soul, a former television star (*Starsky and Hutch*: he was the blond, blue-eyed Hutch) playing Chandler Tate and Matthew Cottle from the British situation comedy *Game On* playing Adam.

The coincidence that Alan Ayckbourn and John Godber, the two most popular writer-directors in Britain, should be running companies only a short (though often tortuous and snowbound) drive apart through the Yorkshire Wolds did not bring the men themselves together very quickly. Both their lives were wrapped up in the places where they lived and worked, apart from occasional forays with transfers of their own productions. They probably first met as a result of a media-arranged symposium.

But they get on rather well, though Alan was once rather fazed to get a note signed 'John G' until he identified the author as Godber rather than Gielgud. Their work is so different that it is possible for them to respect each other without too much fear of comparison. Each feels, with some justification, slightly undervalued: that people think what he does is easy and therefore not worth so much. After Godber had agreed to supply a play, *Perfect Pitch*, for the Ten by Ten by Ten season, however, it seemed to Ayckbourn that the younger man then offered him every opportunity to call the whole thing off, as if not quite believing it was wanted or nervous of the inevitable comparisons: 'Better make it a good one, as it's at your place,' he growled to Alan at one point. There was no sight of a script until the first read-through; Alan could hardly complain about that, but he did take the precaution of working out a half-decent idea for a play with the same title, should it fail ever to materialise. In the event the story of a repressed middle-class couple, a teacher and his wife, pitched next to a noisily expressive miner and his girlfriend on a Scarborough caravan site, demonstrably entertained an audience the Stephen Joseph may have missed till then. Godber himself is an ex-teacher, comes of mining stock and has bought a caravan. He uses his own life much more directly than Alan in his plays, and when he is accused – usually by middle-class critics – of patronising the working class in his writing, he gets justifiably bitter: if he shows the working class as ill-educated and culturally deprived, it is because he is angry on his own behalf about a system that seems content to keep them that way, and as an 11-plus failure who was eventually accepted to read for a Master's degree at Leeds University (thanks to drama) he has a strong case to be heard. He writes plays he thinks his own family might want to see, and when you see them in his own small theatre in Hull, it is like attending a cross between a raucously good-natured party and a needle sporting encounter in which the home side always wins, fierce good fun.

Before 1998 was over Ayckbourn had written three more original shows: *The Boy Who Fell Into a Book*, *Gizmo* and *Cheap and Cheerful*.

The Boy Who Fell Into a Book was the Christmas family play. Kevin reads long past the time he is supposed to put his light out and dreams of getting involved with one of his heroes – Rockfist Slim, who has a dangerous predilection for shooting his way out of every crisis – in a series of adventures which change as he falls out of one book into the next. *Gizmo* was Alan's response to a commission to write a short play for the BT Connections scheme in which companies of 11- to 18-year-olds from schools or youth clubs are offered a choice of ten plays to produce in competition with each other. Thinking he couldn't understand what teenagers talked about half the time, he took his old route of setting something in the future, on this occasion because it seemed like neutral ground. A barman has been traumatised – paralysed in fact – by witnessing a gangland killing, and the 'gizmo' of the title is a little gadget strapped on to a carer's arm, connected to an implant in the patient's brain, which activates the brain sufficiently to make the paralysed sufferer able to mimic the movement of whoever's wearing the 'wrist-watch'. The result was a combination of science fiction, a murder thriller and the excuse for young actors to play a favourite game – copying the actions of somebody more powerful and, when accused of taking the mickey, affirming that they can't possibly help it. And *Cheap and Cheerful* was the parody of a failing variety night which provided more or less adult entertainment to go with *The Boy Who Fell Into a Book*.

And, if those four premières weren't enough, his adaptation of Ostrovsky's *The Forest* opened at the National Theatre. This was the fourth in his 'collaborations' with dead writers which had started with Sheridan's *A Trip to Scarborough* and continued with *Tons of Money* (Will Evans and Valentine) and *Wolf at the Door* (which started life as *Les Corbeaux* by Henry Becque). For the latter, as with *The Forest*, he worked from literal translations by other people, David Walker and Vera Liber.

Apart from *Comic Potential* and the opening of *Things We Do For Love* in London and on tour, none of these made a huge impact with the media or with the commercial audience. *The Forest* was a disappointment in production but the others all fulfilled their functions and created genuine enjoyment in the theatre: the exchange of pleasure between audience and performers which Ayckbourn sees as his daily task. The national critics were sadly absent from his production of Ibsen's *A Doll's House*, the best production of the play I saw in a decade which saw many higher-profile versions. As with *A View From the Bridge*, he held the tragedy of the play back until it had to happen. The play is now widely perceived as a proto-feminist work in which it is inevitable and right that the caged and patronised young wife and mother, Nora, should walk out on a husband who – like so many of Ayckbourn's own husbands – has no real conception of or interest in her aspirations or potential. Consequently modern actresses often play the knowledge of this from the start and the final slamming of the Helmers' door as she leaves simply confirms something we already know about domestic relationships, albeit some-thing important and still relevant. Ayckbourn had played Torvald Helmer as a young actor in Stoke and, although Peter Cheeseman, who directed him then, does not remember or believe it, Alan found comedy in the play: not laughs triggered by funny lines or business as such, perhaps, but the constant bubbling of humour that informs the life of a young and happy family that by no means realises that it really ought to be in despair. Claire Carrie and Richard Derrington showed us a couple who teased each other a lot, each of whom believed in her or his innate superiority to, or need to 'manage', the other, who loved their young children and whose mistakes were derived at worst from insensitivity or not thinking enough. As an audience, you wanted them to be happy ever after. But as Nora turned, in Torvald's presence, from one kind of doll, pretty and pampered and apparently inactive, into the physically rigid woman who can no longer respond to the physical embrace of the husband she has been forced to see as insufferable, we knew not only that her departure was inevitable but that – in one of Alan's favourite phrases – 'there but for the grace of God go we'. This surely is the reality of the play as written in 1879, but even if it is not it is a more powerfully disturbing reading of it than one which simply portrays a woman tyrannised by a near-monster of a husband; and we let ourselves off the hook if we think of him as no more than a product of his time. The essential point, in terms of understanding Ayckbourn, is that Torvald was seen, not from the outside as an exemplar of a certain kind of flawed husband, but as an individual; the audience should feel his emotions and aspirations, even if not absolutely identify with them. The same applies to his own character plays.

Carrie's performance as Nora was pivotal to the production and revelatory. Derrington, a well-established actor (once the 'boring' Mark Hebden in the Radio 4 soap *The Archers*) and something of a Scarborough regular, metamorphosed comfortably into Rockfist Slim, the fictional detective with jutting jaw and itching fists in *The Boy Who Fell Into a Book*, and then the psychic in *Haunting Julia*, a clerical worker of a ghost-hunter with a row of pens in his breast pocket. In the auditorium for which it was intended and with John Branwell as the possessive, possessed father, and Bill Champion as the dead woman's student boyfriend, the play was more effective both as a ghost story and as a human tragedy; making my glib distinction between the character plays and the genre plays a little harder to sustain.

After a management meeting in February 1999, nearly three years after the new theatre had opened, Alan reflected that it was at last running more or less as intended. There had been 20 different promotions in January, ranging from meetings of writers' groups to Gilbert and Sullivan one-night stands to a cookery demonstration by the technical college; all this in addition to a children's play, an adults' play and a revue written by himself. 'At least it's being used, and by the community as well as us. All I would like is to increase our own share of the space a bit more.' And as he headed towards his sixtieth birthday in April, struggling with budgets which were making it harder and harder to generate the sheer volume and scale of activity he sees as the theatre's job, he 'felt it in my bones that it was time we had another of our big events'. This was the month in which Lolly died. The news came through at 10.30 p.m. and Alan was in bed. His reaction was barely noticeable. In about ten years' time, when he discovers what he felt, we may find out too.

3 : *House* and *Garden*

His 'sixtieth birthday present to myself' followed *The Revengers' Comedies* in being two plays, but instead of the action of one following the other, they would be simultaneous, happening in two theatres with a single cast commuting from one to the other; *House* would show the events indoors, and *Garden* would show what was happening outside. *House* would be in the McCarthy, *Garden* in the Round, and audiences would have to book twice but on selected days they could watch *House* and *Garden* as one – in either order – with a meal in the restaurant in between.

Just before *House* and *Garden* went into rehearsal came *A Chorus of Approval*. On the Sunday evening before his sixtieth birthday on 12 April, Alan went into the theatre knowing that something was afoot but not precisely what. The Round auditorium was completely packed with people who had paid up to £100 a seat for an event designed to raise money to support the production of new plays in the theatre, and when the lights went down the voice of Griff Rhys Jones was heard in the darkness beginning the speech from *A Small Family Business*, when Jack comes home intent on having sex with his wife but runs slap into a surprise party. With his trousers round his ankles. The device of *A Chorus of Approval* was that a small committee had been set up by his wife to honour Pendon's most famous inhabitant, a distinguished playwright whose name nobody could ever quite get right. The socialite, the borough councillor and the representative of the local media – Alison Skilbeck, Robert Austin and Robert Powell respectively – were sitting in the dark in the hope that Jack would go away. When he found out what they were up to he very quickly did. Within this framework – roughly inspired by the committee to celebrate the Pendon Ten in *Ten Times Table* – some 50-plus actors presented spoken material extracted from 24 plays plus six songs. Martin Jarvis and Julia McKenzie reprised the West End production of *Woman in Mind* and the entire cast of *Confusions* re-created a substantial helping of *Between Mouthfuls* 25 years after they had played the parts in Scarborough; the playwright Stephen Mallatratt, playing the waiter, hadn't acted for more than a decade. There were moments of sublime brilliance. Stephanie Turner, who directed the whole event, and the actors had had the theatre only from the middle of Saturday to rehearse. Many of the actors had worked on their material at home before they arrived, because once on stage they only had about ten minutes to work on each extract. Adam Godley and Jennifer Luckraft were playing a scene from *Time of My Life* in which a young man and his girlfriend decide to go home from the restaurant and have each other for pudding. They were stopped a few minutes into their first and only rehearsal by Stephanie Turner and, before restarting, introduced themselves to each other: they hadn't met before this, but when I spoke to Alan afterwards he thought they had played the scene superbly. Robin Herford and Lavinia Bertram, now something like the age they had acted in *Intimate Exchanges*, put the infinite eight-play tragedy of Toby and Celia Teasdale into a few short lines. Janie Dee sang the pert and plaintive 'Copy Type' and the romantically beautiful 'I Am Sleeping' (with Bill Champion); Michael Maloney and Marcia Warren gave a comedy master class as Greg and Sheila in *Relatively Speaking*; Anton Rodgers felt his way like a rambler without a map through the minefield of Ronald Brewster-Wright's incomprehension of women from *Absurd Person Singular*; Stephen Pacey brought back Bertie Wooster's innocent incomprehension of the real world, leading the title song in *By Jeeves* after Malcolm Sinclair, as Jeeves himself, finally told the self-appointed committee why they should celebrate the Pendon One, in spite of his anarchic distrust of all pillars of society and his apparent readiness to celebrate sex outside marriage. The household names and the incredible infantry of British theatre all did it for no fee and in many cases no expenses. For every actor who took part there was another who had to withdraw because of filming commitments. The theatre's staff and production team worked their own miracles and I think even Alan, who hates watching his own work, was moved by it. I had done the hacking about of his plays which left them in bleeding but bite-sized chunks in a show which was only to last two hours overall and, typically, he was grateful that we had moved on from each play before he got bored with it. The event, organised by Amanda Saunders with Heather Stoney and Stephen Wood, raised some £16,000 for new plays.

House and *Garden* set records for the new theatre in the summer of 1999, with both theatres together playing to 90 per cent of capacity, although the Round had been restricted to the audience size of the old theatre at Westwood (302) to lessen the imbalance a little between the two auditoria: if everyone who saw *Garden* in the Round also wanted to see *House* in the McCarthy there would have had to be twice as many performances of the latter to fit them in. Between them, the two plays reached an audience about 40 per cent larger than Keith McFarlane can normally expect to budget for. In other words, the 'event' factor drew more people than two unconnected plays would have done. Also each put a cast of 14 on stage and allowed the writer to combine public and private dramas in a way that is now normally out of reach of a new play. All these things may be connected.

The plays are set inside and outside a large country house where Teddy Platt's philandering has become so serious that Trish, his wife, has decided to pretend that he isn't there at all, entering rooms in which we see him to be present and declaring to a third party what a shame it is that he or she has been left on his or her own. This is the day when the annual garden party is being held for the local yeomanry and a smooth apparatchik of an unnamed political party has arrived to persuade our man to enter politics for the sake of the party and the Prime Minister. I say the party is unnamed, and the smooth bachelor who arrives to spin him first in and then out of candidature led one punter to warn Alan: 'Peter Mandelson will sue.' But of course the home reeks of county Toryism and Alan had thought of this character, played with oily conviction by Terence Booth, as at least half Jeffrey Archer. The truth is that Ayckbourn finds none of the main political parties interesting enough to be worth a play on its own. Two years before, in the year of the General Election, he had told Albert Glaap:

> You have to comb to find a difference between the Labour and the Tory Party [. . .] They're obsessed with taxation, both parties [. . .] Hospitals and schools are in a shambles. The infrastructure is crumbling. They need money. The Tories have allowed this country to run down [. . .] Labour joined the same wagon. There is no clear, radical left wing any more, it's very sad. Having said that, there are a lot of people with a lot of money in this country. They've made a lot of money and don't want to let go. We're a very middle-class country that clings to its property. Theatre is caught up in

a very political maelstrom.

In 1999 he quoted with approval someone else's remark that there was no sense in being disappointed in the Blair Labour government: 'What do you expect if you elect a PR firm?' The old allegiance of the arts to Labour was disappearing now that you had to read through 30 pages of the party's manifesto to find any mention of the theatre, he said. The government's attachment to the concept of 'Cool Britannia' was simply part of the public relations image. There was a rumour that he had in fact broken the habit of a lifetime by voting Labour in the 1997 election. It isn't true. He did vote in a local election, for an independent candidate known to him but with no chance of being elected.

So *House* and *Garden* satirise the squirearchy in alliance with New Toryism. But it is mostly fun. The garden party is to be opened by an alcoholic French film actress. This allowed Ayckbourn to employ Sabine Azema (who is also Alan Resnais's wife) and to satirise the theatre he grew up in by having a French character enter the stage through the french windows of the 'summer sitting-room'. (The house in Longwestgate now has a sitting-room for the appropriate season too.) The Archer/Mandelson figure is called Gavin Ryng-Mayne (the ring-main in BBC premises allows everyone to tune into BBC output at his or her place of work or to hear a pep talk from the Director-General; it has faint overtones, therefore, of Big Brother).

House and *Garden* is not so much two plays as one long play which happens in two places and in which – as in life – the characters cannot all see or know what is going on all the time. Nor can we, as the audience. One of Ayckbourn's avowed intentions was to reflect on the way, at any given moment, we may be only tangential figures in other people's dramas even though our own stories seem all-consuming to us. The sense of a whole community at large was enhanced by the involvement of 16 local children, in two teams, as maypole dancers, and the presence in the foyer of genuine stalls (the Women's Institute selling first-class jam) and imaginary ones like the members of the stage management team forming a kind of live fruit machine.

The scenes as written are timed with great skill so that an actor could rush from *House* to *Garden* without breaking a stride in the characterisation; only one of them actually had to run, but this was Barry McCarthy who had suffered a heart attack while appearing in the London run of *Things We Do For Love*. He came through splendidly as the ineffectual Giles, husband to the teacher who has been having an affair with Teddy

Platt. In addition to the careful timing of writer and director, the shows' technical smoothness was the responsibility of the two deputy stage managers, and it helped immeasurably that Fleur Linden Beeley and Lucy McEwen had worked together for the previous year; in fact five of the six members of the stage management teams had worked together, a direct product of the continuity that Ayckbourn encourages. The DSMs had timed each page of the script separately so that they would know at once if they were slipping adrift of the schedule. They were in constant communication during the show on an open telephone line and thus able to make sure that each scene started at the same moment as its parallel scene in the other auditorium. Any discrepancy at the end of the scenes could be made good by extending the black-out for the scene-change, covered by music from John Pattison. The variation in running time was virtually always to do with how many and how long the laughs were. On a couple of occasions the mayhem of *Garden* provoked outbursts of hilarity which coincided with a particularly stolid audience response within the formality of *House*, and they threatened to lose their synchronisation.

The production period was more tense than usual. The workshops had to have two sets ready at the same time: the lavish interior of a big country house, a garden with another pond, and 14 costumes. The actors were less inclined than the previous year's company to waive the new Equity regulations on working hours. Alan threatened them all with blanket calls instead of his usual readiness to let them go whenever possible before the union acknowledged that the rules were not really aimed at reps in the first place. Alan felt disappointed that he wasn't being trusted as an employer by people who had worked with him before, but maybe it is no longer possible to manage simply by creating a family atmosphere. It all got a little fraught when the time came for technical rehearsals of one play then the other, in each case with the parallel play being quietly run through in the Boden Room.

Ayckbourn told Lyn Gardner of the *Guardian* that when he had announced the project there had been a bit of a silence and then the production manager had said, Well, that was the kind of thing that made her stay in Scarborough. As Ali Fowler remembers it, he never actually announced it to her at all but slipped it into the middle of another conversation. Nor did she actually say what was attributed to her. But yes, that is why she is still there ten years after her arrival in 1990. So the story is true without ever having actually happened.

House and *Garden* offer few crumbs to the psychological detective. Trish has something of Heather's demeanour as well as being the daughter of a high-ranking officer. Ryng-Mayne pinches a line from Peter Hall's courtship of Alan for the National Theatre. There may be half-remembered jokes behind the exchange between him and Teddy about not bringing up their shared schooldays, when Teddy was known as Penelope. But when Ayckbourn rewrote *Callisto 5* for Christmas as *Callisto #7* it had fewer echoes of his own childhood than before. Generally, I would suggest, there is less suppressed fury in his work or his public presence over the last decade. When a couple, teachers probably, approached him in the bar at Scarborough and generously offered him feedback about the Christmas revue *Cheap and Cheerful*, citing their regular attendance at West Yorkshire Playhouse as critical credentials, they told him exactly what they thought had worked and not worked. And when a small boy who had twice seen *The Boy Who Fell Into a Book* demanded to know why Alan had moved the set round between the two performances, he certainly wouldn't have it that he had been sitting on different sides of the theatre. Alan is a sitting duck for these approaches; it goes with the job, or his interpretation and enjoyment of it. He grinned and said: 'Thank you very much.' Maybe he is controlled enough even to tackle the front-of-house job now.

There was some box office 'resistance' to *Callisto #7*, possibly because teachers thought they were being asked to bring children to an old play. Those that came seemed gripped by the adventures of the boy marooned in space with another robot charged with the task of keeping him sane but with some deterioration in his/her own circuitry. Given his own resistance to repeating himself, Alan can hardly object if Scarborough tells him that new plays from him are its priority, though he might reasonably expect them to trust him by now not to serve up the mixture as before. But the fact is that in spite of all the public money invested, all the public and critical acclaim, all the dedication of the people who have worked there, the institution he leads is as frail as when he started – since 1957 the company has always managed eight productions in a year – and the pressure on his own next play is much greater than it was in the insouciant days when he and Christine wrote *The Square Cat*.

4 : *Virtual Reality* and *Whenever*

There was no holiday in 1999. He wrote *Virtual Reality* in the week after *Comic Potential* opened in London. It is thoroughly contemporary in that the latest technology in communication weaves contrapuntally with a group of human beings who fail hopelessly to communicate personally. Alex is a computer wizard who supplies pubs with 'virtual reality' figures named 'Mr MacGregors' after Beatrix Potter's *Peter Rabbit* gardener. They go through the wholesome motions of tending the herbaceous and vegetable plots outside. A very clever illusion (of course played by a real actor in the theatre), it is brand-new, but there are already cheap fakes on the market destroying the business. Alex's relationship with his wife is also foundering, and he moves in with a young actress, only for that relationship to break up as well, founded as it was on little more than sex and boredom. His best friend and business partner has also walked out on him and at the end he has nothing. This is the fifty-sixth play in the official canon, and it is unlike anything he has written before but it is also about the subject of just about all his plays – farces, comedies, dramas, thrillers and fantasies – which is the way relationships are never, can never be, everything that we hope for when they start. It continues, I think, the small trend started in *Things We Do For Love*, a direct engagement with the terrifying irrationality of sexual attraction and the vacuum when personal communication fails. People had sex in Alan's plays almost from the beginning: the climax, in every sense, of *Mr Whatnot*; the young lovers in *Relatively Speaking*; even husband and wife in *The Norman Conquests*, though that particular husband will have it with anybody. But these plays deal with the start of a sexual relationship which is serious and breaks social rules and existing bonds; it is hard for us to laugh unrestrainedly at it or even feel simple indulgence towards it though, like all sex, it is often funny too. Was the story of an older, creative man and a young actress autobiographical? There is no evidence for that, only a sense that the sex is getting more central and raw. But, from the computer of this lover of gizmos, gadgets and technological advance, this play is also a passionate plea for us to keep our live human relationships in good order, and that means theatre. The more electronic our other dialogues become, the more we shall need it.

The play was written for the McCarthy auditorium, on to whose cramped stage two 'revolves' had to be fitted to allow us to see Mr MacGregor's garden as well as a number of interiors. Designer Roger Glossop knew Mr MacGregor well from his own Beatrix Potter visitor centre in the Lake District. *Virtual Reality* toured happily enough and returned to Scarborough but seems unlikely to be picked up by a commercial producer. It kept the 'Mac' open for another season in spite of the economic logic of closing your smaller auditorium and putting your best-selling author into the bigger one. Alan remains as stubbornly determined to make things work as ever.

At Christmas 2000 he unveiled *Whenever*, a 'family' play which was also a musical, written with the accomplished Denis King who had also contributed to *Cheap and Cheerful*. The story deals with time-travel but the heroine is another unhappy orphan and at the otherwise happy ending the friend she has made on her journeying announces he is going off to a war which will put a stop to all wars. His destination is 1914. The melancholy, then, is still edging the rosiest of stories with black.

Does he write too much? He concedes that there may have been times when he has done but argues that other playwrights are busy with film scripts, newspaper articles, even novels – none of which he does. Less internally driven than he was, he is under more external pressure than ever to provide material for a theatre he refuses to refer to as his, though everybody else does. While that material still 'comes up fresh' he will carry on. If he had five years of thin responses, he guesses, he would take his bat home. He shows no sign of any interest in posterity, which rather shocked Ian Watson, but merely reflects the here-and-now preoccupation of theatre-making. What will happen to the Stephen Joseph Theatre without him? Robin Herford proved that it could still do the business in Alan's absence and there is now a much stronger managerial infrastructure than there used to be. It is possible to imagine a post-Ayckbourn theatre, but not to say whose image it would be made in. Stephen Joseph himself, of course, thought theatre companies should implode anyway after seven years. He would never have secured lottery funding.

The statistics of Alan's career are impressive: 35 plays (counting *House* and *Garden* as one) presented in the West End or by the national companies; translations into over 30 languages and into vastly different cultures. Nobody alive today can match this, and precious few who are dead. When he is described, as he sometimes is by me, as undervalued, this is only in the sense that critics and theatre historians often leave him out of their assessments of major developments in dramatic theory and practice, sometimes adding him as an afterthought, usually in a category all his own, if you point it out. He is valued above all by people who part with their own money in the keen anticipation of a life-enhancing, however pessimistic, night in the theatre.

But in *Joking Apart*, not the play but the belated sixtieth birthday tribute on Radio 4 on Christmas Eve 1999, Ayckbourn told Susannah Clapp of his long-held belief that if you put three Englishmen on a desert island they would immediately formulate a class system, and that the modern British theatre has connived at that, creating a society in which large numbers of the population genuinely believe that the theatre is 'not for me'. He had worked all his life, he said, to tear down these fences but felt he had managed to uproot 'about one stick'. If pressed to philosophise further he wants us to put something – love, even though his life's work has chronicled its disappointments – ahead of material wants, or power. It is the dramatic study of this last, often meticulous in its domestic detail but sometimes on a much wider canvas, which makes us think in terms of morality, of good and bad people rather than just good and bad behaviour. This is unfashionable of course, but it is an eternal preoccupation.

It is dangerous to develop a thesis about a life's work that is unfinished. What there is, in this book, picks up on Alan Ayckbourn's own acceptance that his essential view of the world was formed when he was still a relatively small child. Whatever else may be laid at his mother's door, he bears out the conclusion drawn by Shere Hite, that the male children of single mothers are more likely to be able to relate properly to women in later life. Adults, the child sees, behave in ridiculous ways, and the male adult on the whole is more cruelly insensitive than the female but capable therefore of turning the female into a monster too; best deal with it all by making a joke of it, best create your own world of play, or plays, in which the monsters can be confronted and understood and, on occasion, wrongs righted and villains despatched with a well-placed can of baked beans. But even in the world of play, or plays, you do not always get your own way, and many people have testified to the fact that he 'looks like a child whose toy has been taken away' when things even threaten to go wrong, such as the 'bodies' for the revival of *Body Language* not being available in time for the 1999 company to rehearse in before they went in front of the audience: in fact they did turn up – it was just that the supplier's telephone was out of order. The world of play and plays does not equip you for negotiating with officialdom and politicians. Nor does it make you good at taking care of your company and staff if they are in trouble; best have somebody else to attend to those things that you can't simply buy in, best let Heather Stoney visit the sick, watch the bills, answer the letters.

He has the gift for self-protection of children and animals, and sometimes he will do things that hurt other people without really understanding why, withdrawing from them rather than confront the hurt. He cannot always ask Heather to see to this. There must be times when she is the one who is hurt. But to identify the child in Alan Ayckbourn is at most only half the story. Few other employers are mature enough to give the professional trust he does to the people who work for and with him, even though he can do all their jobs. Few other adults have as conscientiously worked at improving the areas of themselves that they need to in order to pursue their chosen paths – making himself into a good interviewee, making himself available to the public in defiance of his own diffidence, recognising the need to protect your own employees from exploitation even though you yourself cannot imagine anything more absorbing than continuing to work round the clock at your favourite activity. 'He pushes you hard but he is realistic when something really cannot be done,' says a senior member of his staff; children are not. It was Caroline Smith, who has known him as long as anyone except Elizabeth Bell, Christine and Heather, who likened him to an animal, with Scarborough as the lair in which he can take care of himself and lick his wounds, if any. Two other long-time associates likened him specifically to a cat. There is something in all this, but it was also Smith who finished off by telling me simply: 'He is a good man.'

5 : National Hero

Let us end with a millennial triumph. Trevor Nunn, who succeeded Richard Eyre as director of the National Theatre, has reinterpreted the word 'national' by increasing his own company's touring and by bringing the best of regional theatre to the South Bank. His first attempt to get Alan back into the theatre – with the adaptation of *The Forest* – had lukewarm results. Now, after seeing the last two performances in Scarborough, he immediately offered his two big auditoria, the Lyttelton and the Olivier, for six weeks in the summer of 2000 for *House* and *Garden*. I confess I was among those who thought the idea of the National Theatre foyer hosting a village fête after the shows was exposing a jolly community idea from a small town to metropolitan ridicule. Further, the back-stage connections between the two theatres are much more complicated than in Scarborough. Not only would it take actors longer to get from one to the other, there were myths of actors disappearing down the Olivier 'voms' and getting lost for days. Would it work?

Alan wrote some new material – what he called 'gusset' speeches that could be let out in an emergency – to cover any gaps if actors were late getting from one stage to the other. But according to Jane Asher even he seemed nervous in rehearsals and picked up hints of actors' nervousness too. Rehearsing in two adjacent rooms, actors were sent off on a journey around the bowels of the building – marked out with tape – equivalent to the distance they would have to travel in performance. When they started to work on stage, new taped routes were laid to make sure that nobody got completely lost. As he would in Scarborough, Alan made himself available to the workshops, who rarely see directors in the flesh. The atmosphere at the National, as it always has done when he has been in the building, became infectiously enthusiastic. The *House* gang even talked to the *Garden* gang. He wished he'd walked the territory more when *Way Upstream* was in rehearsal.

What was at stake was the ghost of *The Revengers' Comedies*, and Alan's place at the heart of British – and world – theatre. Would *House* and *Garden* transfer from his guerrilla outpost on the Yorkshire coast to what is arguably the most important theatre institution in the world? Would it sustain his belief that a major event can put theatre itself, however momentarily, at the heart of the community? Half-way through rehearsals, the production's experienced press officer Mary Parker saw that ticket sales had stuck at around 20 per cent of capacity. Alan threw himself into her publicity campaign, giving interviews in his lunch breaks and at the end of the day. He was also dieting and exercising on a bike; he not only lost a lot of weight but got himself through a punishing schedule. When it came to the technical rehearsals, he finished well within the allotted time, only to find the first two previews relatively empty. It turned out the audience was so used to the National cancelling its initial previews that it played safe and waited for a performance that was more likely to happen.

The two plays eventually filled 89 per cent of the available seats, or just over 92,000 people, and took around £1.5 million. Since the Lyttelton is smaller than the Olivier the capacity for the two shows together was effectively a little reduced and this figure reflects what was virtually a sell-out. It was now *House* that commanded the rapturous response which *Garden* had enjoyed in Scarborough and the general view of the critics and many of the cast was that it was the better play, with Malcolm Sinclair adding a cold and steely power (just a hint of Michael Codron in there perhaps?) to the seductive amorality of Ryng-Mayne, and David Haig cranking up the mad virility of Teddy Platt. More of *Garden* was intelligible if you saw *House* first, but the difference in the effectiveness of the two had more to do with the difficulty of playing light, naturalistic comedy in the vast and unfocused Olivier. A woman goes mad in *Garden* – it is almost Ayckbourn's signature – and perhaps this also made it slightly more uncomfortable. Already in despair in a very early scene, Joanna (Janie Dee in Scarborough, Sian Thomas in London) tries to work out how to commit suicide, and in Scarborough contemplated throwing herself under a small lawn-mower, a gag which was both intrinsically funny and unrealistic enough to take some of the darkness off the scene. With a much bigger set at his disposal Ayckbourn now made her throw herself off a balustrade at the back, which was more truthful but served the play less well (two critics claimed he had 'cut the best scene' rather than a single gag). It also led to Sian Thomas injuring herself as she twisted and fell on to the mattress provided. Eventually Alan put the lawn-mower gag back, to the satisfaction of everyone else. But Joanna also has to run off into the bushes and by now Thomas was injuring herself on these too, turning up for work slightly more damaged every day: how like an Ayckbourn play, people said. The character's madness, however, takes the form of believing people close to her have been stolen away and replaced by aliens. Improbable as it may seem, this is a scientifically identified syndrome; Ayckbourn never researches, but Jane Asher takes the *New Scientist*. She thinks Alan has some sort of information-recording device implanted in his big forehead and she swears a light went on when she mentioned the syndrome in conversation. Now she was in a play in which it came back to her.

And the fête? The actors didn't like having to turn up at it, but it was in their contracts. They made sure the cold beers and glasses of Chardonnay were conveniently placed, to help them through it. Genuine celebrities turned up to open it: Mary Soames, a Churchill by birth and chairman of the National Theatre board, on the press night; Tamzin Outhwaite, star of TV's *EastEnders*, who had moved from being a singer-dancer into straight acting through being cast by Alan in a revival of *Absent Friends*, repaid the favour on a subsequent night. The audience, sophisticated London theatregoers or not, seemed delighted. And for the Platform – the National's series of events in which public interviews are given about the plays on stage – both theatres were again used simultaneously. Michael Billington acted as chairman in one and I was in the other, while Ayckbourn himself, Jane Asher, Malcolm Sinclair and Zabou Breitman gamely commuted between the two. And it still worked. The plays always felt like lighter Ayckbourn to me, despite the madness, and the sadness of everyone's loneliness at the end. But there is one extraordinarily innovative scene. The French actress and Teddy sit opposite each other on the parapet of the small pond surrounding a blocked fountain and spell out their troubles. Neither understands the other but, almost miraculously, we understand both. Zabou Breitman was understandably nervous about a long speech in French which, given the thin reputation of the English as linguists, she thought must serve only for Teddy to react to. In rehearsal she raced through it until gently stopped by Alan. She had to *feel* her tale of missed opportunities (playing Cleopatra), brutish husbands, addiction and loss. If she felt it, the audience would too. Alan doesn't speak enough French to have written this scene in the language; he wrote it in English and had it translated by a Scarborough French teacher. But he was right. And when Teddy sounds Alan's own plaint: 'Where's the fun gone?' we are feeling very much the same through the gnawing melancholy of a speech in a foreign language – without realising, I suggest, the enormity of what was taking place.

While Ayckbourn lives, any biographer will be left chasing his coat-tails. This is frustrating but also part of the fun. If Ayckbourn were really as self-absorbed as Jerome in *Henceforward* . . . this would be reflected in his art. There is a difference between playing, as someone who remains only an overgrown child might do, and plays. The first is satisfying to the player but excludes the rest of the world. Plays, on the other hand, draw us in.

Index

NOTE: Works by Alan Ayckbourn appear directly under title; works by others under author's name

GIELGUD
A THEATRICAL LIFE

Jonathan Croall

'Elegant, compendious and hugely enjoyable . . .
A biographical tribute of a quality few artists ever receive'
Joyce McMillan, *Scotsman*

John Gielgud was the last of a generation of theatrical giants. He
stood alone as the finest interpreter of Shakespearean verse the stage
had seen. This hugely praised, authoritative and entertaining
biography covers in full an astonishing career, spanning nearly
eighty years in film, radio, television and the theatre.

'Scrupulously researched, free of hagiography, and vastly entertaining
. . . Croall's portrait of the man behind the performer is unlikely
to be surpassed'
Charles Osborne, *Sunday Telegraph*

Selected biography and autobiography titles available from Methuen

ISBN	TITLE	AUTHOR	PRICE
☐ 0413 70600 1	David Garrick	*Jean Benedetti*	£20.00
☐ 0413 73300 9	Threads of Time: A Memoir	*Peter Brook*	£12.99
☐ 0413 72800 5	Peggy: The Life of Margaret Ramsay	*Colin Chambers*	£19.99
☐ 0413 72390 9	Dear Writer, Dear Actress: The Love Letters of Anton Chekhov and Olga Knipper		£10.99
☐ 0413 73380 7	The Autobiography of Noël Coward		£12.99
☐ 0413 77129 6	Gielgud: A Theatrical Life	*Jonathan Croall*	£8.99
☐ 0413 70910 8	Dario Fo and Franca Rame: Harlequins of the Revolution	*Joe Farrell*	£19.99
☐ 0413 77340 X	Timebends: A Life	*Arthur Miller*	£9.99
☐ 0413 74000 5	Ralph Richardson: An Actor's Life	*Garry O'Connor*	£9.99
☐ 0413 73650 4	The Orton Diaries	*Joe Orton*	£9.99
☐ 0413 76710 8	Shakespeare: the Poet and his Plays	*Stanley Wells*	£10.99

• All Methuen books are available through mail order or from your local bookshop. Please send cheque/eurocheque/postal order (sterling only) Acess, Visa, Mastercard, Diners Card, Switch or Amex.

☐☐☐☐☐☐☐☐☐☐☐☐☐☐☐☐

Expiry Date: _____ Signature: _____

UK customers please allow £1 for the first book and 50p thereafter up to a maximum of £3 for post and packing.

Overseas customers please allow £1.50 for the first book and 75p thereafter up to a maximum of £5 for post and packing.

ALL ORDERS TO:

Methuen Books, Books by Post, TBS Limited, The Book Service, Colchester Road, Frating Green, Colchester, Essex CO7 7DW.

NAME: _____

ADRESS: _____

_____

_____

Please allow 28 days for delivery. Please tick box if you do not wish to receive any additional information ☐

Prices and availability subject to change without notice.